SOCRATES

The Arguments of
the Philosophers

EDITOR: TED HONDERICH

Reader in Philosophy, University College London

The group of books of which this is one will include an
essential analytic and critical account of each of the
considerable number of the great and the influential
philosophers. Each book will provide an ordered
exposition and an examination of the contentions and
doctrines of the philosopher in question. The group of
books taken together will comprise a contemporary
assessment and history of the entire course of
philosophical thought.

Already published in the series

Plato	J. C. B. Gosling
Meinong	Reinhart Grossman
Santayana	Timothy L. S. Sprigge
Wittgenstein	R. J. Fogelin
Hume	B. Stroud
Descartes	Margaret Dauler Wilson
Berkeley	George Pitcher
Kant	Ralph Walker
The Presocratic Philosophers (2 vols)	Jonathan Barnes
Russell	Mark Sainsbury

SOCRATES

Philosophy in Plato's Early Dialogues

Gerasimos Xenophon Santas

Professor of Philosophy
University of California, Irvine

Routledge & Kegan Paul
London, Boston and Henley

First published in 1979
by Routledge & Kegan Paul Ltd
39 Store Street,
London WC1E 7DD,
Broadway House,
Newtown Road,
Henley-on-Thames,
Oxon RG9 1EN and
9 Park Street,
Boston, Mass. 02108, USA
Set in Journal Roman
by Hope Services, Wantage
and printed in Great Britain by
Lowe & Brydone Ltd
Thetford, Norfolk

British Library Cataloguing in Publication Data

Santas, Gerasimos Xenophon

Socrates. — (The arguments of the philosophers).
1. Socrates
I. Series
813'.2   B317   78–40735

ISBN 0 7100 8999 6

To Mac

Contents

CONTENTS

CONTENTS

Preface

This is a philosophical study of Plato's Socrates — the man and his talks, his philosophical method, his questions, his arguments, and his beliefs about what is good and right. Xenophon's Socrates and the Socrates of Aristophanes are very much of secondary importance in this study. I make use of Xenophon and Aristophanes only in the first chapter and only in order to bring into sharper relief Plato's Socrates, and the man and the philosopher. This virtual exclusion of Xenophon and Aristophanes is not based and does not depend on a historian's judgment that only Plato's account of Socrates is historically accurate, or that it is more accurate and trustworthy than those of Xenophon or Aristophanes. The latter view is in my personal opinion correct, but nothing in this book hangs on it (cf. Vlastos, 1971). So far as the famous historical problem of Socrates is concerned, I offer only the amateur opinion that not much progress is likely to be made unless new evidence is discovered; and that the whole historical problem should be kept in perspective by considering what questions new evidence — say, some writings about Socrates by another contemporary — is likely to settle and how far it might settle them.

The concentration on Plato's Socrates, exclusively so after the first chapter, is rather based on the far less controversial judgment that it is only Plato's Socrates that is of major interest to the contemporary philosopher. (In any case there have been recent studies of Socrates based on wider sources — e.g., Gulley and Guthrie.) There is no doubt that the Platonic Socrates is a character of great philosophical originality and depth, a philosopher whose views and arguments it is still profitable to discuss and analyze today. The prevalence of Socratic technique in teaching and philosophizing, the dominance of Socratic questions in contemporary philosophy

(What is a work of art? What is knowledge?), the attacks on essentialism, the recent work on moral weakness — all these testify, if testimony is needed, to the fruitfulness and staying power of Socrates' ideas. In this study I wish to discuss these ideas in the spirit of contemporary philosophizing. My aim is clear exposition and development of Socrates' ideas as we find them in Plato's writings, and criticism of his ideas and arguments in the setting of contemporary philosophy.

Though my concern is with Plato's Socrates, I do not of course discuss all the Dialogues in which Socrates is the protagonist. I take as a starting point the accepted division of Plato's Dialogues into early, middle, and late, and I deal almost exclusively with the first third, appropriately called the Socratic Dialogues. The organization of the book, however, is by topics and problems, not Dialogues. Part One is a brief study of Plato's Socrates, the man, the philosopher, and the citizen. Chapter I is a sketchy portrait of Socrates, the man, the philosopher, the gadfly of the Athenians, the master of Plato. Chapter II is a detailed study of Socrates' arguments about the obligation to obey the laws and about civil disobedience in the *Apology* and the *Crito*; here an attempt is made to resolve apparent inconsistencies in Socrates' stand on these matters in the two works. Parts Two and Three are detailed studies of the two major contributions of the Platonic Socrates: philosophical method — the so-called 'Socratic method' — and Socratic ethics. The Socratic method consists essentially in raising certain kinds of questions, in seeking definitions as the first step in the quest for knowledge, and in constructing arguments by which definitions and other answers are tested. Accordingly, Part Two consists of three chapters, one on Socratic questions, one on Socratic definitions, and one on Socratic arguments. Socratic ethics consists primarily in two main, related views: the view that virtue is knowledge, or the so-called 'Socratic paradoxes,' and the view that virtue brings happiness and vice unhappiness. Accordingly Part Three consists of three related chapters: one on the Socratic paradoxes, one on the related attack on non-Socratic explanations of weakness, and the final chapter, a detailed study of Socrates' arguments in the *Gorgias* to the conclusion that virtue brings happiness and vice misery.

Needless to say, the present work does not examine all the topics that Socrates discusses in the early Dialogues; such an examination would involve a study several times the length of this book. Rather, I have selected for study what I consider to be Socrates' greatest contributions to philosophy. And even here I have concentrated on the topics in which I thought that I could make some progress, using contemporary techniques of analysis and scholarship, in understanding and assessing Socrates' contributions. For other contributions to understanding and assessing the Socratic philosophy, by the author and others, the reader is referred to the Bibliography.

All the work in this book is new and previously unpublished, except for chapters VI and VII. Chapter VI is reprinted with minor revisions from the *Philosophical Review* (1964); it also appeared in A. Sesonske and I. Fleming, *Plato's Meno* (1965), and in *Philosophy and Religion*, The Library of Liberal Arts Reprints of Scholarly Articles (1969—70). Chapter VII is reprinted with minor revisions from the *Philosophical Review* (1966); it also appeared in G. Vlastos, *The Philosophy of Socrates* (1971) and in G. W. Mortimer, *Weakness of Will* (1971).

Some of the work for the book was supported by a fellowship from the American Council of Learned Societies, a faculty grant from the Johns Hopkins University, and a grant from the Humanities Institute of the University of California. I wish to express my gratitude to these institutions. I wish also to acknowledge my great debt to Professors David Sachs, Gregory Vlastos, and Benson Mates: their friendly encouragement and careful criticisms of various parts of this work has sustained my ability to philosophize for many years now; I can only hope that I have succeeded somewhat in approaching their standard of work. I am also indebted to Mr M. F. Burnyeat, who read the whole manuscript and saved me from several mistakes, and to Dr Ted Honderich for much help and advice. I wish also to thank my former wife, Dr Marianne McDonald, who was writing on Euripides while I was writing on Socrates; she read and helped me with most of this work, and she sustained me with her discipline, her energy, and her dedication to classical studies.

Abbreviations

Assoc.	Association
Charm.	*Charmides*
DN	double neagative
equiv.	material equivalence
Eud. Eth.	*Eudemian Ethics*
exp.	exportation
Gorg.	*Gorgias*
Hip. Maj.	*Hippias Major*
Hip. Min.	*Hippias Minor*
HS	hypothetical syllogism
impl.	Material implication
Nic. Ethics	*Nicomachean Ethics*
Prot.	*Protagoras*
Rep.	*Republic*
simp.	simplification
Symp.	*Symposium*
taut	tautology
UG	Universal Generalization
UI	Universal Instantiation

PART ONE

The Philosopher and the Citizen

I

Introduction to Plato's Socrates

Socrates was sentenced to death by a jury of some 500 fellow Athenians and died by taking hemlock in a jail in Athens in 399 BC. He was born in Athens ten years after the final defeat of the Persians, and spent all his seventy years in that city. During his life he was part of the rise of Athens to her glory, but during the devastating Peloponnesian War he also saw the rapid decline of Athens. During his years Greece was the centre of the world, and Athens was the centre of Greece. He met, mixed, and talked with all manner of men: great statesmen like Pericles, brilliant dialecticians like Zeno, clever and dazzling sophists like Protagoras, eminent generals like Nicias and Laches, and the greatest sculptors, architects, poets, and playwrights of Greece; he also cross-examined lesser know-it-alls like Euthyphro and Meno, silly jacks-of-all-trades like Dionysodorus and Ctesippus, corrupt politicians like Critias, and dozens of ordinary citizens, clever and dull, honest and dishonest. He tried to teach philosophizing to beautiful and willing youths, like Charmides and Lysis, wild and brilliant Greeks like Alcibiades, devoted friends and pupils like Crito and Phaedo; and he succeeded beyond any teacher's expectation in what has to be the most brilliant pupil of all time, Plato himself. In the midst of the terrible upheavals around him and the variety of his experiences with people Socrates displayed an awesome presence, maintained a vast philosophic calm, and must have been the only stable thing in Athens in the last half of the fifth century. Day in and day out he went to the same places, talked to the same people, raised the same questions, discussed them in the same way, and ended up with the same mixture of success and failure. In this way, having the fortune of many brilliant pupils and at least one great one, Socrates created a revolution in Greek philosophy.

This revolution is brilliantly portrayed by Plato in his early Dialogues; it is caricatured beyond recognition by Aristophanes, and it is entirely missed by Xenophon. It is perhaps not surprising that men of such different and unequal talents as Xenophon, Aristophanes, and Plato would produce such different portraits. To begin with, Socrates was not easy to understand. He was a man of modest means, and equally moderate desires, but he was not a simple man. His habits were strange, his questions unfamiliar, the points of his arguments difficult to grasp, and the most characteristic result be brought about was bafflement — certainly it was not easy to see what he was about. Without the benefit of subsequent philosophy it would take a philosophic genius to understand and appreciate the originality, depth, and sweep of Socrates' philosophizing. Aristophanes was not a philosophic genius, and Xenophon was not a genius at all. Aristophanes did not pretend to understand Socrates, but in his business he could not afford to be baffled either. The Socrates of *The Clouds* is a petty buffoon, a mighty babbler, a trivializer of trivia, not recognizable as a philosopher at all; if one has read Plato's Dialogues, he is entirely unrecognizable. Even on its own terms *The Clouds* is not a great success. The subject, if it can be treated at all by Aristophanes, calls for intellectual comedy. Aristophanes gives us silly and not very clever burlesque. *The Clouds* misses the mark, for Socrates without his thoughts is not Socrates at all. Plato's *Euthydemus*, a comedy of fallacies, is a lot funnier and has to be put down as a greater success.[1]

Xenophon's Socrates is strikingly different. Xenophon clearly thought he understood Socrates, but the Socrates he understood is no more than a conventionally wise old man mistakenly judged by the jurors to be unconventional. Not a buffoon, but more like Jesus Christ. Xenophon revered Socrates, and introduces him a little like the evangelists introduce the Lord. He begins chapters in *Memorabilia* with 'He said' and 'At another time he said.' His Socrates is preachy, not philosophic. A comparison between the Platonic Socrates and Xenophon's hero is a study in difference and contrast. There is nothing baffling about Xenophon's Socrates, nothing ironic either. Where the Platonic Socrates seizes the occasion of advice-seeking about practical matters to disclaim any expertise and to raise penetrating and original questions about the subject matter, Xenophon's Socrates is ready to give advice on anything without philosophic qualms: simple and even embarrassingly obvious pointers on how to make friends, how to prosper, how to treat friends and enemies, how to become a good general, really anything at all. Just come to Socrates, O youth! And he will

tell you how to fare well. No problem. Nor is his talk 'wiry argument' (Vlastos), as in Plato. Instead of universal definitions,
arresting analogies, suggestive inductions, deadly reductios, and
streamlined deductions, we find stories and anecdotes of dubious
relevance and simple moralistic messages too obvious to miss.
There are, of course, points of similarity, especially in the frequent
use of analogies between morals, politics and the arts and crafts.
But all the same, Xenophon's Socrates is dull, and not much of a
philosopher — certainly not a great one. Xenophon really makes
it impossible for us to see either why the Athenians were upset or
why Plato was inspired. Plato's portrait makes it possible for us to
see both of these things.[2]

What upset the Athenians was the central thing that Socrates
did day in and day out: the *elenchus*, the destructive cross-
examination of the concepts and principles that the Athenians
lived by and Pericles boasted of. It is not only that he refuted
prominent and lesser Athenians on the very things they were
supposed to know, and famous foreigners on the very things they
professed to teach; and that he did it in a humiliating manner, in
front of company, with plenty of irony and sarcasm thrown in.
The thing that really hurt was the fact that he attacked the most
fundamental principles of Athenian life, the Greek ideals of moderation, courage, justice, piety, wisdom, and versatility — he cut to
pieces the intellectual foundation of the body politic and never
even tried to sew it back together. Did not Socrates show in the
Charmides that Critias and Charmides, who represented two
generations of the flower of Athenian aristocracy, did not know
what temperance or moderation, the most pervasive of the Greek
virtues, was? Did not Charmides and Critias produce seven different
definitions of temperance all of which Socrates refuted? Did not
Socrates confuse them about temperance and bring them to the
end of their wits? And is not this intellectual confusion a perfect
Socratic explanation of Charmides' and Critias' later intemperance? Did not Socrates similarly show in the *Laches* that the
generals of the day, Laches and Nicias, did not know what courage
is? Did he not show in the *Euthyphro* and the *Meno* that lesser
Athenians and foreigners did not know what piety and virtue is?
Did he not show in the beginning of the *Republic* that none of the
interlocutors, including Plato's aristocratic siblings, knew what
justice is? Did he now show in the *Gorgias* and the *Protagoras* that
the two great sophists, whom the Athenians took into their homes
and gladly paid for instruction in the fundamental excellences of
life, did not really know what they were talking about? And did
he not undermine an essential principle of Athenian democracy

when he argued that public officials should not be selected by beans, and decisions not made by vote but by experts on the basis of knowledge of the subject at hand?

Nor did the irritating manners that Socrates displayed while conducting these investigations endear him to the Athenians. Here is an accurate and terse summary by Vlastos of the tiresome side of Socrates in the *Protagoras*:[3]

> He is not a wholly attractive figure in this dialogue [*Protagoras*].
> His irony, so impish in the *Hippias Major*, breath-taking in its
> effrontery in the *Hippias Minor*, somber, even bitter, yet under
> perfect control, in the *Euthyphro*, seems clumsy, heavy-handed
> here. His fulsome compliments to Protagoras, continued after
> they have lost all semblance of plausibility, become a bore. In
> his exegesis of the poet he turns into a practical joker, almost a
> clown. He is entitled to his opinion that looking to poets for
> moral instruction is like getting your music from the clever
> harlots who dance and play the flute for the stupid bourgeois.
> But why act out this dubious metaphor in a labored one-man
> charade, throwing in some philosophic edification on the side,
> as when he drags in (by a misplaced comma) his doctrine that
> no man sins voluntarily?

There are many passages in the Dialogues where the disturbing effects, the exasperation, the anger, the resentment, even the fear caused by the substance of Socrates' refutations and the mannerisms of his attacks, are brought out by Plato far more effectively than by any of Socrates' detractors. It is plain that Socrates, besides being an original and powerful mind, was also something of an intellectual clown, a reveler in circus debate, a diabolical needler of his contemporaries. He is constantly on stage, in the agora, gymnasia and wrestling schools, festivals, dinner parties, the courtyards of great houses. He chooses his antagonists, fixes the subject, makes sure he has the attention of the audience, invites his opponent to speak his mind freely and without fear, elicits from him an opinion, a speech, a dogma, and then proceeds to counterpunch the poor man and his opinion to death, mixing in his blows not only philosophical points and arguments but also sarcasm, irony that borders on insincerity, and personal insults; and he does not rest until he has extracted from his victim a public confession of utter helplessness. At the end, when it is painfully obvious that his opponent will never recover, he proposes that they all go home and start all over again another time. It is no wonder that he never has a second dialogue with the same man. All this calmly and coolly. No excitement please. This is not

6

the law courts or the assembly. Matters here are not decided by mobs and votes. The subject calls for reasoned examination by men of knowledge on the basis of their knowledge. How could Socrates not have baffled and upset the Athenians? He was unreal, a unique phenomenon, a Greek upside-down, an Athenian with a Dionysian mind, Apollonian emotions, and Orphic habits. And his philosophy too, a perfect extension of the man and his life if ever there was one, turned life upside-down, as Callicles helplessly complains.

All this Plato saw and drew with superb artistry. But he also saw more than this, much more than the Athenians were able to see and appreciate. He saw the immense strength of Socrates' life in the midst of folly, corruption, weakness, and cowardice. He saw Socrates as the star example of the virtues of wisdom, moderation, courage, and justice, the nearest possible approximation on earth of the perfection of Platonic forms. He has Phaedo say that Socrates, 'of all those of his time whom we have known, was the best, and wisest and most just.' And he says himself that Socrates was 'the most just of men then living.' From a man of Plato's understanding of excellence and wisdom and justice, these simple words are an immense tribute. Plato also saw, understood, and built on Socrates' greatest intellectual achievements. He saw that, where all the Greeks praised the virtues to the skies, Socrates raised the simplest and yet more startling question, a question that apparently nobody had thought of before, and certainly nobody understood or pursued in a Socratic way: What *is* virtue? That is, what is it that is common to all the things we count as virtue and by reason of which they are virtue? And similarly with each of the several virtues, in the same spirit. We have repeated testimony of the startling originality of Socrates' question in the fact that again and again the interlocutors do not understand what Socrates is asking; he has to amplify and illustrate in order to make them understand his sort of question, and he has to set them straight about what *sort* of answer he is seeking. And we have mountains of testimony to the complexity and fruitfulness and depth of this question in the philosophical discussions which to this day raise or examine Socratic questions and debate the validity of the presuppositions of such questions.

Plato also saw that, where the great poets and dramatists took their perceptions of human experience at face value and proceeded to portray superbly the conflict between reason and passion and the frequent overthrow of reason by passion, Socrates sought to understand this conflict and wondered how such overthrow was possible. Where the dramatists and the poets worked on the level

7

of perception and intuition, Socrates sought an understanding of the concepts that are unreflectively formed by such perceptions and intuitions and are built imperceptibly into the fabric of language. For the first time in the history of thought Socrates began to feel his way toward what we have come to call moral psychology: what, from the point of view of motivation and conceptual reconstruction — description and explanation — goes into men's acting rightly or wrongly, into the understanding of good and evil deeds. Again, Plato saw that, where the Greeks did not think about or took for granted the teaching of virtue, Socrates tried to understand what such teaching could be. Could virtue really be taught? Plato saw that, where the Greeks enjoyed great success in the arts and crafts, Socrates perceived an opportunity in this success to try to conceive of a parallel success in the art of living and ruling: he sought to explore the parallels in the roles of knowledge, motivation, and performance, in the two areas of art–crafts and conduct. Plato saw that, where the Greeks prized the maxim 'Nothing in excess' but took it for granted that they understood what it meant, Socrates not only prized it but also tried to understand what excess and moderation were and what their measure could be. Plato saw that, where the Greeks prized and again took for granted the meaning of another maxim, 'A sound mind in a sound body,' Socrates sought to examine the meaning of this maxim, and tried to construct a strict parallel in which virtue in the soul corresponds to health in the body and the arts that tend the soul correspond to the arts that tend the body; a parallel with revolutionary implications for our conceptions of wrongdoing and punishment. In every Socratic enterprise Plato saw Socrates beginning with the ordinary conceptions of Greek life, but digging deep to unearth underlying assumptions, to overthrow some, to try to understand the implications of others, to build theoretical foundations for yet others. In the Socratic enterprise Plato saw a new world, supremely worth exploring, the world of philosophy. In Socrates himself Plato saw a man with an endless passion for reason, a man who had achieved a complete harmony between reason and passion, and between word and deed — a fantastic integration of life and thought. Only by stretching our imagination to catch this integration can we make believable to ourselves the Socrates of the *Apology*, the *Crito*, and the *Phaedo*, the Socrates who inspired Plato. To my mind, it is Russell, a man of a very different type, who comes nearest to capturing this Socrates in a simple sentence:[4]

The *Apology* gives a clear picture of a man of a certain type: a man very sure of himself, high-minded, indifferent to worldly

8

success, believing that he is guided by a divine voice, and persuaded that clear thinking is the most important requisite for right living.

Few subsequent philosophers have achieved this integration between philosophic thought and philosophic life. One thinks of Spinoza. Perhaps even fewer philosophers have considered such integration necessary. And we certainly have many instances of great philosophic achievements, whether systematic or analytic, that have not been accompanied by equally great lives. Great as these achievements are, they are not always as convincing. And they are never as inspiring. It is certainly a stroke of good fortune that the first great philosopher could inspire and teach as well as he could philosophize.

II

Socrates and the Laws of Athens

Introduction

Plato's *Apology* and *Crito* afford us an opportunity to understand Socrates the citizen: his attitude and his reasoned views about his native city, his fellow citizens, and the laws of the city. The dramatic dates of these two works are no more than a few days apart, and the dates of composition no more than two or three years apart and very close to Socrates' death. Probably Plato's first two compositions, they form a natural unit, and they contain discussions by Socrates of some of the most important issues a citizen has to face in his relations to his city or country and its laws. In the *Apology* Socrates rejects the charges against him, and defends the way of life for which he is on trial, the way he philosophized, by examining himself and others about the conduct of life and about human wisdom. He argues that doing this he is not doing anything unjust, as the charges state; rather, he is following the command of god, and carrying out this divine mission is the greatest good that can come to the city of Athens. Further, he gives proofs that he is not afraid of death, and says that his philosophizing is worth dying for. He declares that if the court were to acquit him but order him to cease philosophizing on pain of death, he would disobey the court; he is absolutely convinced that it is better to continue philosophizing at the risk of death rather than to cease philosophizing and live. In the *Crito*, urged by Crito to escape from jail and avoid what they both consider to be the unjust sentence of death, Socrates refuses on the ground that it would not be right to do so. He argues that if he were to escape he would be doing harm and injustice, which one must never do, he says, even in retaliation for injustice and harm done to one. He also

argues that if he were to escape he would be breaking his agreements to obey the laws of his city; and this too one must never do,
provided that certain conditions are satisfied, which, he proceeds
to state, are very much satisfied in his case. Therefore, he ought
not to escape.

Even from this brief review it is clear that Socrates is discussing
the most difficult questions that a citizen sometimes has to face in
his relations to his city and its laws: specifically, the question of
the grounds for the obligation to obey the laws of one's country,
including laws one might think unjust; the question of the priority
of this obligation relative to other obligations one has; and the
question of the justification of civil disobedience or conscientious
refusal. Despite the difficulty and importance of the issues Socrates
is discussing, his arguments have not been closely analyzed. Discussions have tended to be unsystematic and to treat the texts
casually. In this chapter we try to analyze closely Socrates' views
and arguments by paying close attention to exactly what he says,
the context in which he says it, and the clear implications of what
he says. Specifically, we shall take up the following questions in
order: (1) What exactly are Socrates' arguments in the *Crito* to the
conclusion that he ought not to escape from jail? (2) How does
Socrates, in the *Apology,* view himself and his work in relation to
his city and its laws? (3) Is Socrates' conclusion in the *Crito*, that
he ought not to escape, and all his arguments to that conclusion
(including the arguments to the conclusion that one ought to
obey the laws of one's city), consistent with his readiness, in the
Apology, to engage in civil disobedience or conscientious refusal,
and with his reasons for that readiness?

1 Socrates' arguments in the Crito that he ought not to escape from jail

Crito brings up a number of considerations on the basis of which
he urges Socrates to escape: Crito will lose a friend he can never
replace; people will say Crito was not willing to spend money to
save his friend, and this is disagraceful; Socrates need not hesitate
either because of the money involved or the risk to his friends — it
has all been arranged safely. Further, Socrates is not doing the
right (just) thing in submitting to the sentence: he is betraying
himself, he is doing just what his enemies want him to do, and he
is abandoning his children; people will think that the whole affair
'has been conducted with a sort of cowardice on our part' — the
case coming to trial at all, the way the trial was carried on, and
now not escaping when the opportunity presents itself (44B–46B).

11

In response, Socrates explains to Crito two preliminary matters: (1) how the issue Crito has brought up is to be decided, and (2) what the issue exactly is (46B–48D). These preliminaries out of the way, Socrates advances the arguments that settle the issue (49–53).

Socrates begins by saying that he is going to decide whether what Crito proposed is to be done in the same way as he has always decided matters: by following nothing else than the reasoning (or argument) that upon consideration seems best to him. He is not going to abandon now, just because of what has happened to him, the principles he has maintained all his life (46B). One of the things he has always maintained is that on any given matter it is not the opinions of most people that one must follow but rather the opinions of those who have knowledge of the matter at hand. Thus, in the present case, it is not what most people think that matters, as Crito seems to suppose, but rather those who have knowledge of the subject of their present deliberations: the subject of just and unjust things, noble and disgraceful things, and good and bad things (47CD). Further, Socrates continues, even though most people have the power to put him to death, he still maintains what he has always maintained, that it is not living but rather living well that must be made most important. Finally, he still holds that living well and living justly (rightly) are one and the same thing (48B).

Crito agrees, and Socrates proceeds to state, on the basis of what has just been admitted, what exactly they must deliberate about (48CD):

> Given these admissions, then, this is what must be considered, whether it is just (right) for me to try to leave this place without the permission of the Athenians or not just. And if it seems just, let us attempt it, if not, let us give it up. But the thoughts that you bring up, about spending money, and about reputation, and bringing up my children, these are really, Crito, the reflections of those who lightly put men to death, and would bring them to life again, if they could, without any sense, these [are the reflections] of the multitude. But we, since our argument so constrains us, must consider nothing else than what we just said, whether we shall be doing just things in giving money and thanks to these men who will help me to escape, and in escaping or aiding the escape ourselves, or in truth shall be doing injustice in doing all these things.

Socrates makes it clear, then, that his decision about whether he is to escape depends *entirely* on whether it is just to do so: if it is just to escape he will try to escape, and if it is unjust he will not. Thus the only question to be investigated is: Is it just to escape?

Having secured Crito's agreement on the manner and the subject of the investigation, Socrates asks Crito whether he agrees with him on what to take as the starting point of the investigation (48E). This starting point consists of certain general principles which are later used as premises in the arguments Socrates advances to the conclusion that he must not escape. We state these principles in the order in which Socrates advances them, putting in brackets connecting remarks that indicate some of the relations among these principles.

P1   To do injustice in any way is neither good nor praiseworthy (as we have admitted on many occasions before now). (49A)

P2   To do injustice in any way is bad and disgraceful to the wrongdoer. (49B)

P3   (Then) One must not do injustice in any way (or, in any circumstance). (49B)

P4   One must not do injustice in return for injustice done to one (as the many think, since one must not do injustice in any way). (49B)

P5   One must not do harm (or evil). (49C)

P6   To return harm for harm (evil for evil) is not just (as the many say). (49C)

P7   (For doing harm (evil) to people does not differ at all from doing injustice.) (49C)

P8   (Then) One must not return injustice for injustice nor do harm (evil) to any men, no matter what one has suffered from them. (49C)

Socrates urges Crito to consider these principles carefully and make sure he agrees to them; very few people, he says, hold these principles, and between those who hold these principles and those who do not, there is no common (shared) deliberation. He adds: 'Do you therefore consider very carefully whether you agree and share in this opinion, and let us take as the starting point of our discussion that it is never correct to do injustice or to return injustice for injustice or having suffered harm (or evil) to defend oneself by returning harm (or evil)' (49DE). From this summary, and from the connecting remarks we place in brackets, it is clear that Socrates is going to use principles P3, P4, P5 and P8, and that the other principles were used as premises for deriving these (thus, he seems to derive P3 from P1 and P2, P4 from P3, P7 from P6 and P3, and P8 from P6 and P3).

13

Finally, Socrates secures agreement to one more principle:

P9   One must do what one has agreed to do, provided it is just.
(49E)

We may call this a secondary principle, to mark the fact that
unlike the other principles it is qualified or conditional. Moreover,
the condition 'provided that it is just' shows that principles P3 and
P4 are prior to it in this sense: if one has agreed to do something,
and that thing is just or at least not unjust, then one must do that
thing; but if one has agreed to do something and that thing is not
just, then not only one need not do it, one must not do it.

Having secured agreement to all these principles, Socrates next
raises the question that clearly shows how he proposes to argue
that he must not escape (50A):

Consider then whether if we go away from here without the
consent of the city, we are doing harm to those we must least
harm, and we are abiding by those things we agreed to provided
they are just.

He then proceeds to argue: (A) that if he were to escape he would
be doing harm, and this, by the principles admitted (P5), one must
not do; and (B) that if he were to escape he would be breaking his
agreements which are just, and this by the principles admitted (P9)
one must not do. Therefore, he must not escape.

That these are his arguments is also shown by the summary of
these arguments Socrates gives near the end of the dialogue (54C)
on behalf of the laws:

Now, however, you will go away (die) wronged, if you go away,
not by us, the laws, but by men; but if you escape, having so
disgracefully returned injustice for injustice and harm (evil) for
harm (evil), and having broken your agreements and compacts
with us, and having worked harm (evil) on those whom one
must least harm — yourself, your friends, your country, and us —
we shall be angry with you while you live, and there our brothers,
the laws in Hades' realm, will not receive you graciously; for
they will know that you tried to destroy us, in so far as this is in
your power. Do not let Crito persuade you to do what he says,
but take our advice.

Clearly, then, Socrates is arguing, on behalf of the laws of his
city, that if he were to escape he would be returning injustice for
injustice, harm for harm; he would be breaking just agreements,
and he would be harming himself, his friends, his country, and the
laws of his country; and all these things are clearly forbidden by

the principles he has advanced and to which, he says, he has sub-scribed all his life. Though this much is clear, the details of Socrates' arguments are obscure and contain many ambiguities. The style and the various devices used by Plato do not contribute to clarity. Socrates puts his arguments in the mouth of the laws of the city, and in the form of questions; he asks far too many questions, and the transitions from argument to argument are unclear. At times both the *Apology* and the *Crito* read more like scornful and emotional defences or high-minded and impassioned argumenta-tions rather than works of the cool reasoning that characterizes the typical Socratic Dialogues. For these reasons both works are difficult to interpret confidently when it comes to matters of detail. In attempting to reconstruct Socrates' arguments in detail we shall stay very close to the text, to insure accuracy, and we shall also be guided by the undisputed fact, demonstrated above, that his arguments consist in applying general principles to his particular circumstances.

Argument A: the argument from harm (50AB)

A1 If Socrates were to leave the jail without the consent of the Athenians, we would be rendering the decision of the court of no force, making it invalid and annulling it as a private person.

A2 If the decisions reached by the courts of the city have no force and are made invalid and are annulled by private persons, the laws of the city are destroyed and the whole city overtuned.

A3 Hence, if Socrates were to leave the jail without the consent of the Athenians, he would be destroying the laws and the whole city in so far as it is in his power.

A4 If Socrates were to destroy the laws and the whole city in so far as it is in his power, he would be doing harm. (supplied)

A5 Hence, if Socrates were to leave jail without the consent of the Athenians he would be doing harm (to the laws, and presumably to the citizens).

A6 One must not do harm. (P5)

A7 Hence, Socrates must not leave the jail without the consent of the Athenians.

Several points need to be noticed about this argument in order that our reconstruction be understood and the use that Socrates makes of this argument be understood. First, premise A2 is explicit

15

in the text, and premise A1 is stated indirectly; conclusion A3 can be derived from A1 and A2 by hypothetical syllogism; premise A4 is supplied in order to make principle P5 operative, the only admitted principle that can be applied to in this argument, and this premise is clearly very plausible; and A7 can be derived from A5 and A6 by *modus tollens*.

Second, there is a problem with the first derivation: the antecedent of A2 is not the same as the consequent of A1; specifically, the former is a general statement, the latter is a singular statement. This gap can be filled in two different ways, depending on whether we conceive Socrates' argument as an act or rule utilitarian argument. Taking it as an act utilitarian argument, we interpret A2 as follows:

A2.1   If *anyone* were to render a decision reached by the courts of his city of no force and to make it invalid and annul it as a private person, he would destroy the laws of his city and would overturn the whole city in so far as in him lies.

From A2.1 by instantiation we obtain:

A2.2   If Socrates were to render the decision of the court of his city of no force and to make it invalid and to annul it as a private person, he would destroy the laws of his city and would overturn the whole city in so far as in him lies.

A2.2 would then take the place of A2 in the argument, and the rest of the argument would remain unchanged; this would enable us to obtain A3 from A1 and A2.2 by hypothetical syllogism, and the gap from the consequent of A1 to the antecedent of A2 would be closed. The chief disadvantage of this interpretation is that both A2.1 and A2.2 appear to be false. However, the phrase 'in so far as it is in his power' (the Greek equivalent of which we have in the text) perhaps mitigates this difficulty: for the phrase suggests that the idea behind A2.1 and A2.2 is not that one does, in fact, succeed in destroying the laws and overturning the whole city by rendering a decision of the court of no force, and so on, which one does in turn by disobeying; but rather that by doing so (rendering a decision of the court of no force, and so on, by disobeying it) one *intends to* destroy the laws and the city, or that by doing so one does something that *tends to* destroy the laws and the city, or both. This interpretation is supported not only by the phrase 'in so far as it is in your power,' but also by the questions, 'What do you have in mind to do?' and 'What are you intending to do other than destroy the law . . .?' (50AB).

The second way of interpreting the argument is as a version of a rule utilitarian argument or some sort of generalization argument. This interpretation is obtained by interpreting A2 as follows:

A2.11   If *everyone* were to render decisions reached by the courts of his city of no force and make them invalid and annul them as a private person, the laws of the city would be destroyed and the whole city overturned.

The argument then would follow a different course as follows:

A2.11   If everyone were to render decisions reached by the courts of his city of no force and make them invalid and annul them as a private person, the laws of the city would be destroyed and the whole city overturned.

A2.21   If the laws of a city were destroyed and the city overturned, the laws and that city (and the citizens?) would be harmed. (supplied)

A2.3   Hence, if everyone were to render decisions reached by the courts of his city of no force and make them invalid and annul them as a private person, the laws and the city (and the citizens?) would he harmed. (from A2.11 and A2.21 by hypothetical syllogism)

A2.4   If everyone's doing something resulted in harm then no one must do that thing. (a version of the generalization principle)

A2.5   Hence, no one must render decisions reached by the courts of his city of no force and make them invalid and annul them as a private person. (from A2.3 and A2.4)

A2.6   If Socrates were to leave jail without the consent of the Athenians, he would be rendering the decision of the court of his city of no force and invalid and would annul it as a private person.

A2.7   Hence, Socrates must not leave the jail without the consent of the Athenians. (from A2.5 and A2.6 by *modus tollens*)

The advantage of this interpretation is that the first two premises of this argument are very probably true, whereas the first two premises of the first argument are very dubious, to say the least. Clearly, if Socrates were to escape he would not thereby be destroying the laws and the city; though it might be said that he would be doing *some* harm, and this might be enough for the argument since principle P5 is very strong and seems to forbid all harm

17

whatsoever. Equally clearly, if *everyone* were to escape or evade court sentences, the laws would be of no force and the city would be harmed. This much favors the last interpretation. On the other hand, the generalization argument interpretation has several disadvantages: first, there is nothing resembling the generalization principle (premise A2.4) in the text; second, this principle seems dubious in that it appears to be too strong, at least in the form stated (consider this application of it: if everyone moved to California the results would be disastrously harmful; therefore, no one ought to move to California); and third, the generalization principle, which seems to take the place of P5 in the argument, is not implied by P5, since it is perfectly possible that *everyone's* doing some particular thing is harmful while *someone's* doing that same thing is not harmful. All things considered, the first argument seems closer to the text, but we see no way of absolutely excluding the generalization argument as a possible interpretation.

Finally, the last comment Socrates makes about this argument and his transition to the next argument are worth noting (50C):

> What shall we say, Crito, in reply to this question and others of the same kind? For one might say many things, especially if he is an orator, in defence of the destroyed law which commands that the judgments [verdicts? punishments? both?] reached by the courts be supreme? Or shall we say to them that the city did me injustice and did not judge the case correctly?

In the first half of the comment Socrates refers us to the law he would be breaking if he were to escape, the law that commands that the judgments of the jury courts shall be supreme. In the *Athenian Constitution* (XLV) Aristotle tells us that the people passed a law saying that verdicts of guilty and penalties, in cases involving fines, imprisonment, and death, by the Council were not final; he also says that appeal could be made to the jury courts and that their judgments *were* final or supreme (κύριον — the same word Socrates uses in his statement of the law).[1] Clearly then, Socrates was tried by a court that had final judgment in such cases, and disobeying the judgment of the court by escaping would be disobeying the law that states that judgments by the jury courts are supreme. Socrates' argument, in all its versions, is an argument to the conclusion that he must not escape, on the grounds that he would be disobeying *this* law, that disobeying *this* law would be rendering it of no force, rendering it not supreme, and annulling it; and that this in turn would be destroying the city and the laws. We do not know whether Socrates would make the same argument against disobeying *any* law. The law he would be dis-

18

obeying is a very important one since it sets the jury courts as the courts of final appeal and final judicial judgment; and it may be that disobeying this law, whether by Socrates or generally, would have the severe-sounding effects (destroying the laws and the city) Socrates cites, whereas disobeying other laws may not. In any case, his argument would apply to any similar disobedience of this law, but not necessarily to the disobedience of any law.

The last question Socrates asks in the quote above is important on its own account and also provides a transition to his next argument: 'Or shall we say to them that the city did me injustice and did not judge the case correctly?' Socrates and Crito agree that the verdict of guilty was mistaken and that consequently the sentence of death was unjust. As we shall see, in the *Apology* Socrates is charged with doing certain unjust things and he denies explicitly that he did any injustice. Later in the *Crito* (54C) Socrates has the laws say that Socrates was wronged, done injustice to, not by the laws but by men. Socrates' view of his own case, then, is not that he was judged and tried under unjust laws, but that men mistakenly found him to be guilty during his trial, and that his sentence was undeserved and unjust. This belief clearly does not give him any grounds for doing anything that he considers unjust, since principle P4 which he has advanced forbids returning injustice for injustice. So, he cannot argue that escaping, though indeed unjust, is in this case justified because the sentence is itself unjust; or that escaping would indeed harm the laws and the city (and the citizens?) but is nevertheless justified because it is returning the harm that was done to him, since he has also advanced principle P8 which forbids returning harm for harm. However, the point of the question may be that, given that the verdict was mistaken and the sentence of death unjust, perhaps to escape would not be to do anything unjust. It is by no means clear that escaping an unjust sentence of death illegally is doing something unjust. At any rate, given the principles Socrates has advanced, the only point that his question can have is that escaping, under the circumstances, may not be unjust.

Argument B: the argument from just agreements

The second main argument begins with a question that suggests an answer to the last question and also introduces the second main argument (50C):

> What then if the laws should say: Socrates, is this what you agreed with us, or did you agree to abide by the judgments

[verdicts? sentences? both?] which the city [through its courts] judges?

The reference in the first alternative is clearly to the content of the previous question, so that the two alternatives presented by the question are:

> Q1 Socrates agreed to abide by the judgments rendered by (the courts of) the city unless he thought (or perhaps even knew) a judgment to be incorrect and to do him injustice;

or

> Q2 Socrates agreed to abide by the judgments reached by (the courts of) the city (or Socrates agreed to abide by the law that commands that the judgments of the jury courts shall be supreme) even if he thinks (or even knows) that a judgment is incorrect and does him injustice.

Parts of the long argument from 50C to 52A are in support of alternative Q2. But to understand them we need to consider several preliminary points. First, alternative Q2 clearly brings principle P9 into play:

> P9 One must do what one has agreed to do provided it is just.

Second, P9 has two parts: one must do something if one has agreed to do it *and* if what he has agreed to do is just. Finally, Q2 and P9 are not sufficient to yield the conclusion that Socrates must abide by the judgment of the court. If principle P9 is to be the principle appealed to in the argument, as it clearly is, another proposition besides Q2 is needed as a premise, namely: what Socrates has agreed to do, to abide by judgments reached by the courts of the city even if he thinks or knows that a judgment is incorrect and does him injustice, is just. From this proposition and Q2 and P9 we can, with suitable additional premises not in dispute, derive the conclusion that Socrates must abide by the judgment of the court, that he must be put to death, and hence that he must not escape. This is how I construe the long and somewhat confusing argument between 50C and 53B. I will state this argument and then I will consider various sub-arguments in support of its premises.

Argument B

> B1 Socrates has agreed to abide by the judgments reached by the courts of his city (or, Socrates has agreed to abide by the law that commands that the judgments reached by the

jury courts of his city shall be supreme), even if he thinks or knows that a given judgment is incorrect and does him injustice. (Q2) (50C, 51E, 52D, 52E)

B2   What Socrates has agreed to do, namely abide by the judgments reached by the courts of his city even if he thinks or knows a judgment to be incorrect and do him injustice, is just. (50D—51C)

B3   One must do what he has agreed to provided it is just. (P9)

B4   Hence, Socrates must abide by the judgments reached by the courts of his city, even if he thinks or knows that a judgment is incorrect and does injustice to him. (from B1, B2, and B3)

B5   The courts of Socrates' city have reached the judgment that Socrates is to be put to death. (known truth)

B6   Hence, Socrates must abide by the judgment reached by the court of his city that he is to be put to death, though he thinks it unjust. (from B4 and B5)

B7   If Socrates must abide by the judgment reached by the court of his city that he is to be put to death, he must not escape (undisputed assumption).

B8   Hence, Socrates must not escape. (from B6 and B7)

Having raised the question we have analyzed, at 50C Socrates proceeds to argue in support of premises B1 and B2. In 50D—51C he argues in support of premises B2; in 51C—52A he argues in support of premise B1, and in 52A—53A he further reinforces the argument in support of premise B1. We shall take up these sub-arguments in the order given in the text.

Sub-argument for B2. Here Socrates argues for some general propositions that are actually logically stronger than B2 and that imply B2. Specifically he argues that the relation between a citizen of Athens *and* Athens and its laws is such that: (i) it is not just for a citizen to do to his city and its laws what the city and its laws try to do to him, and hence, if the laws try to destroy Socrates thinking it just to do so, it would not be just for Socrates to try to destroy them in return (51A); (ii) justice, in the relations of citizen to his city and its laws, consists in the citizen either doing what the city and the laws command (in whatever station the citizen is placed, whether in war or in court) or else convincing the city and the laws where the right (justice) lies (51B). These two propositions are supported, in turn, by an analogy between parents and children on the one hand and laws and citizens on the other, an analogy that is supposed to show that the relation between laws and

21

citizens is one of inequality, and inequality such that justice between laws and citizen is what (i) and (ii) specify. The paragraph in which all this is done is not neat argumentation: it is full of questions, reasons, hints, with hardly any semblance of order; one sentence in it, for example, takes up eighteen lines and ends with a question mark. To distinguish the many different assertions made through questions, to see what is reason for what, to reconstruct the analogies, and to put it all in what looks like an argument in the grossest possible form, requires at a minimum very close reading of the text and constant attention to narrow and wider context. With these warnings about the difficulties, we reconstruct the argument as follows.

Argument for (i)

1 Socrates, like other citizens, was born, nurtured, and educated, through the laws of marriage and education. (50D)
2 Hence, Socrates (and his ancestors), like other citizens, is the offspring and even the slave of the laws. (50E; from 1)
3 Justice between parents and offspring (and masters and slaves) does not consist in equality: it is not just that children do back to parents what parents do to children (whether it is talking back or hitting back and other such things). (50E)
4 Hence, justice between Socrates, as with any other citizen, and the laws does not consist of equality: it is not just that Socrates, or any other citizen, does back to the laws what the laws do to him. (50E; from 2 and 3)
5 Hence, it is not just that Socrates try to destroy the laws (by escaping) if the laws try to destroy him (by putting him to death). (51A; from 4)

Three main points need to be noted. First, this argument is not necessary (or sufficient) to support premise B2; the subsequent argument in support of (ii) is sufficient for support of B2. However, the argument is clearly a direct answer to the question raised just before the argument is given, at 50C: 'Or shall we say that the city did me injustice and did not render a correct judgment?' The argument provides the answer that it is not just for a citizen to do back to the city and its laws what they do to him; in this case, it is not just that Socrates try to destroy, in so far as he can, the laws (by escaping) in return for the laws destroying him (by putting him to death). Given this conclusion, both principles P3 and P4 come into play, and it can be directly inferred that Socrates must not escape (given the first main argument to the effect that escaping would destroy or tend to destroy the law). Second, though the argument is not needed and does not suffice for B2, nevertheless it prepares the ground for the next argument that does suffice for B2: it establishes, through the analogy of parents: offspring:: laws: citizens, that certain *equality* of treatment between citizens and laws is *not* just. And the subsequent argument, presumably relying on the same analogy, establishes that certain *in*equality between laws and citizens *is* just.

Finally, even though premise 2 states accurately what the text says, it can hardly be supposed that Socrates means to say that the citizens are literally the offspring of the laws. If offspring is biologically defined, it must be an analogy that we have here, since citizens are not biological offspring of the laws; if, on the other hand, offspring is not biologically defined, a definition must be produced before we can know what inference can be drawn from saying that citizens are offspring of the laws.[2] No definition is given in the text, and an analogy that fits the text can be reconstructed as follows.

Revised argument for (i)

- a1 Offspring are born or come into existence and are nurtured and are educated through and/or by their parents, and not conversely. (assumption)
- a2 Similarly, citizens come into existence and are nurtured and educated through and/or by the laws of marriage and education of their city. (assumption)
- a3 It is not just that offspring do back to their parents what parents do to their offspring. (assumption, and/or inference, from a1)
- a4 Similarly, therefore, it is not just that citizens do back to the laws of their city what the laws of their city do to them. (inference from a1, a2, a3)

From a4 we can obtain 4 of the previous argument by simply adding the undisputed premise that Socrates is a citizen; or we can continue the present argument, and regard *it* as the argument given in 50D—51A, as follows:

- a5 Socrates is a citizen (of Athens). (assumption)
- a6 Therefore, justice between Socrates and the laws of Athens does not consist in equality: it is not just that Socrates do back to the laws what the laws do to him. (from a4 and a5)
- a7 Therefore, it is not just that Socrates try to destroy the

laws (by escaping) if the laws try to destroy him (by putting him to death). (from a6)

The reasoning by analogy to a4 seems quite weak. First, it is not clear that the relations signified by the ambiguous prepositions 'through' and 'by' are the same in a1 and a2. Even if they are, it is not easy to see why one should grant a3. If a3 is an inference from a1, the inference to a4 is thereby strengthened, but it is difficult to see why the inequalities described in a1 are a basis for the inequalities described in a3. The benefits that parents bestow on children might possibly give rise to duties of gratitude, but this does not seem to be a matter of justice, and the benefits are not received as a result of voluntary acts by the children. Aside from all this, it is difficult to see, to say the least, how it is supposed to follow, from the fact that children receive these benefits from their parents, that it is unjust for the children, e.g., to strike back at their parents, or to revile their parents in return for being reviled, or to destroy their parents if their parents try to destroy them. It may be, of course, that in the Greek culture a3 would be readily granted, and that a1 would be regarded as the chief reason for a3. Even so, the similarities in a1 and a2 would have to be closely looked at before the inference by analogy to a4 could become convincing; for example, children can come into existence and be nurtured, and possibly be educated, without laws, but they cannot come into existence without parents. This is, of course, not to say that there are no similarities at all: clearly benefits are derived from being under laws, benefits in many ways similar to the benefits derived in childhood from parents.

Argument for (ii). This argument is contained in a long question which comes right after the last argument, and which takes up some eighteen lines of the text. We quote it in full since it has to be seen to be believed (51BC):

Or are you so wise that you do not see that your country is a more valuable thing and more to be revered and a holier thing and is held in higher esteem among gods and men of understanding than your father and mother and your other ancestors, and you must show her more reverence and obedience and humility when she is angry than to your father, and you must either persuade her or do what she commands, and [you must] suffer in silence if she commands you to suffer, and if she orders you to be scourged or imprisoned, and if she leads you to war to be wounded or slain, these things must be done, and thus justice has it, and you must not give way or draw back or leave

24

your post, but in war and in court and everywhere you must do what your city and country commands or you must convince her where justice lies, but to use violence against your father and mother is not pious, and it is much less so against your country? What shall we reply to this, Crito? That the laws speak the truth or not?

It is not clear whether the analogy to parents is the basis for the main assertion contained in the question, that one must either persuade one's city where justice lies or (failing that) do whatever the city commands in war, in court, or anywhere else. Several references are made to parents, but it is not stated that justice as between parents and children consists in children persuading their parents where justice lies or doing what they command, and without this statement the inference by analogy to the parallel main assertion cannot be drawn; perhaps, however, this proposition is regarded as obvious and could be supplied. If so, the argument from analogy would run as follows:

b1　Offspring come into existence and are nurtured and educated through or by their parents. (50D; assumption)

b2　Similarly, citizens come into existence and are nurtured and educated through or by the laws of their city. (50E; assumption)

b3　It is just that offspring either persuade their parents where justice lies or (failing that) do whatever the parents command. (supplied)

b4　One's city and country are more valuable things and holier things and more to be revered, and held in higher esteem among gods and men of understanding than one's mother and father and other ancestors. (51B)

b5　Hence, it is just that citizens either persuade their country where justice lies, or (failing that) do whatever their country commands whether in war, or in court, or anywhere else, including being scourged, imprisoned, wounded, or slain, or enduring any other suffering. (51BC; inference by analogy)

The problems that we found in connection with the argument for (i) are also to be found here. If anything, the problems are worse here, since the same analogy is supposed to support b5, which seems to be a stronger proposition than the conclusion of the previous argument, a4.

The two arguments, in support of (i) and (ii), constitute the support for premise 2 of argument B. It must be noted, however,

25

that the conclusions of these are far stronger than premise 2 of argument B. Premise B2 says that it is just that a citizen abide by the judgments reached by the jury courts of his city even if the citizen thinks or knows that a judgment is incorrect and does him injustice (or, it is just to obey the law that judgments reached by the jury courts shall be valid or supreme even if such judgments are thought or known to be incorrect and to do injustice against a citizen). Thus B2 is about the justice of obedience to a particular law about the decisions reached by the jury courts; whereas (i) states that it is not just for a citizen to do back to the laws, *any* of the laws, what the laws may do to him, no matter what the laws may do to him. Thus (i) expands the scope of the injustice of disobedience to all laws. And (ii) goes even further: for it says that it is just that the citizen either persuade the city and the laws in a given case where justice lies, or, failing that, obey whatever the city and the laws command in whatever station and in whatever circumstances. Thus (ii) expands the scope of the justice of obedience not only to all laws but, it seems, to all commands whatsoever given by public authorities. It seems, then, that Socrates, in trying to establish that it is just to obey judgments reached by the courts even if such judgments are incorrect and do injustice to one, gives arguments which if successful would establish much more than that: that it is just to obey all laws and all commands given by public authorities even if such laws or commands are incorrect and do injustice to one. This over-arguing is puzzling, and we are unable to resolve the puzzle. In addition, Socrates seems to place no limit on the injustices that may be done to one as possible grounds for disobeying a law or a judgment reached by a court or a command given by a public authority. That is, Socrates' arguments seem to imply that, no matter what injustice is done to a citizen, by laws, court judgments, or commands, such injustice is never a ground for that citizen disobeying the law, judgment, or command. Since injustices may vary, from trivial, technical, and occasional, to monstrous and persistent, this lack of limit is also puzzling. It is perhaps partly because of these features of Socrates' arguments, in support of B2, that it has sometimes been thought that Socrates' position in the *Crito* is inconsistent with his position in the *Apology*. We shall return to these matters in later sections of this chapter.

The argument for premise B1 of argument B. In 51C–53A Socrates puts in the mouth of the law the argument that is supposed to show that Socrates, more than any other Athenian, has agreed to obey the laws of the city unless he succeeds in a given case in persuading the laws (or rather their representatives) where justice lies. In the first paragraph of this passage (51DE–52A) the laws set out the conditions under which an agreement between them and a citizen is said to exist, and in the next two paragraphs they argue that these conditions are very much satisfied in Socrates' case. We reconstruct the argument for premise B1 of argument B as follows:

B1.1   If a person (1) is a citizen of Athens, (2) has been born and nurtured and educated through the laws of Athens, (3) has come of age, (4) has seen how judgments are given in courts and how the city is governed, (5) has had the choice of leaving the city with his goods and settling somewhere else if he does not like the affairs of the city and the laws, and (6) has not left the city but has continued to live in it, then such a person has thereby (i.e. by these things being the case and by having seen and chosen these things) agreed either to persuade the laws where justice lies if he thinks the laws are not doing well or (failing that) to do whatever the laws command.

B1.2   Socrates (1) is a citizen of Athens, (2) has been born and nurtured and educated through the laws of Athens, (3) has come of age long ago, (4) has seen for many years how judgments are reached by the courts and how the city is governed and has never complained against the laws, (5) has had the choice for many years and even as late as during his trial of leaving the city with his goods if he did not like its laws and the way the city is governed, and (6) has never chosen to leave the city in all his seventy years but has continued to live in the city and has had children in the city.

B1.3   Therefore, Socrates has thereby (by his action described in (4), (5) and (6)) agreed either to persuade the laws where justice lies if he thinks the laws are not doing well or to do whatever the laws command.

B1.3 differs from B1 (p. 20) in two respects: B1.3 states that Socrates has agreed to obey what the laws, presumably *all* the laws, command, while B1 states that Socrates has agreed to obey one particular law, the law that states that jury court judgments are supreme, and in this respect B1.3 is stronger than B2; and B1.3 is disjunctive whereas B1 has only one of the disjuncts, and in this respect B1 is stronger than B1.3. However, given that one of the laws Socrates agreed to obey by B1.3 is the one referred to in B1, and given that Socrates tried and failed to persuade the jury court that their judgment was incorrect and unjust, B2 follows from

B1.3. But it is noteworthy that, once more, Socrates gives an argument which if successful establishes more than the proposition he set out to establish.

Socrates has the laws make some comments that strengthen the argument. For example, at 52E the laws say to him:

> you were not led into them [your compacts and agreements
> with the laws] by compulsion or fraud, and were not forced to
> make up your mind in a short time but had seventy years in
> which you could have gone away, if we did not please you and
> if you thought the agreements unjust.

So the agreements were not entered under compulsion or fraud, conditions that would have invalidated them; nor did Socrates ever give evidence that he thought these agreements were unjust, which presumably puts him in a very poor position to do that now.

Having presented the arguments we have analyzed, Socrates finishes with an argument that answers directly some of the points Crito brought up at the beginning of the dialogue. If Socrates were to escape, he has the laws say, he would be harming his friends and himself, and his children, and this is forbidden by principles P3 and P5. Some of the passage is worth quoting (53B—D):

> For it is pretty clear that your friends also will be exposed to
> the risk of banishment and the loss of their homes in the city or
> of their property. And you yourself, if you go to one of the
> nearest cities, to Thebes or Megara — for both are well and law-
> fully governed — will go as an enemy, Socrates, to their govern-
> ment, and all who care for their own cities will look askance at
> you, and will consider you a destroyer of the laws, and you will
> confirm the judges in their opinion, so that they will think they
> judged the case correctly. For he who is a destroyer of the laws
> might certainly be regarded as a destroyer of young and thought-
> less men. Will you then avoid the well and lawfully governed
> cities and the most civilized men? And if you do this will your
> life be worth living? Or will you go to them and have the face to
> carry on — what kind of conversation, Socrates? The same kind
> you carried on here, saying that virtue and justice and lawful
> things and the laws are the most precious things to men?

Finally, Socrates summarizes his arguments by stating his alternatives and the consequences of each alternative as brought out by
his arguments: if he choses to obey the court, he will go away
(die) wronged (having suffered injustice) not by the laws but by
men; but if he escapes, he will be discracefully returning injustice
for injustice and harm for harm, he will be breaking the compacts

and agreements he made with the laws, and he will be doing harm to those he must least harm, himself, his friends, his country, and the laws. Thus, he thinks that if he obeys the court he will be *suffering* but not doing injustice, whereas if he escapes he will be *doing* injustice and harm. It is noteworthy that the choice Socrates makes in the *Crito* is identical with the choice (as between suffering and doing injustice) Socrates recommends to Polus in the *Gorgias*.

2 Socrates' views in the Apology about the citizen, his city, and its laws

Socrates' principles, arguments, and views in the *Apology* are markedly similar to those he expounds in the *Crito*. This is not surprising, since Plato's Socrates is a character and philosopher of remarkable consistency, and since he says in the *Crito* (46B), as we noted, that he is not going to change his principles and arguments but is going to proceed as he always did. These similarities will be brought out in our exposition of the relevant passages of the *Apology*. Our concern is not with the whole of the *Apology* but only with those portions that reveal his views on the relations of the citizen to his city and its laws. As we did in the case of the *Crito*, we shall try to state Socrates' views and reconstruct his arguments as accurately as we can, paying close attention to exactly what he says and the context in which he says it.

After certain preliminaries, Socrates states at 18A that he will defend himself against two accusations or charges: an old charge, at least twenty years old since Socrates cites Aristophanes (*The Clouds*) as having made it, and the new charge for which he is on trial. (Socrates considers both charges because he thinks that the two charges are so connected that unless he can convince jurors that the old charge, which they heard when they were young and impressionable, is false, he has little chance to convince them that the new charge is false.) Socrates states and defends himself against each of these charges in turn. Then, at 28B, he uses the device of raising and answering a hypothetical question in order to justify further his conduct, in his relations to the city and its laws, during his life and during the trial. It is chiefly in this passage (28B–35D) that we find his reasoned views concerning his city, its laws, and its citizens. We shall discuss these matters in turn.

Socrates states the old charge twice. First at 18BC:

There is a certain Socrates, a wise man, a ponderer over the things of the air and one who has investigated all the things beneath the earth and who makes the weaker argument stronger.

29

> These, men of Athens, who have spread abroad this report, are
> my dangerous enemies. For those who hear them think that
> men who investigate these matters do not even believe in gods.

Then he repeats the charge, somewhat differently at 19B:

> Socrates does injustice and is a busybody, investigating the
> things beneath the earth and in the heavens and making the
> weaker argument stronger and teaching others these same
> things.

The second statement is more in a legal vein: it says that Socrates
does injustice and meddles, which presumably is illegal, and then
goes on to list the actions that constitute such injustice and
meddling. Socrates defends himself against this old charge not by
arguing that these actions do not constitute injustice and meddling,
but rather by denying that he ever did any of these things listed in
the charge: he does not have any knowledge of things above and
below the earth, he never concerned himself with them, and he
has never taught for a fee like the sophists. He then proceeds to
explain how these false accusations and prejudices have arisen
against him (21–24B). His impulsive friend Chaerophon went to
Delphi and asked the oracle if anyone was wiser than Socrates.
Pythia answered that no one was wiser, and Socrates was puzzled
by this since he considered himself as having little or no wisdom.
To resolve the puzzle, he went around the city and questioned
men who had a reputation for wisdom in a variety of things, such
as public affairs, poetry, the arts and crafts. To his surprise, he says,
he found that these people thought they knew many things but
really didn't, since they were not able to stand up to his questions
about their areas of expertise; and he concluded that he was
indeed wiser than they, for they thought they knew a number of
things but in reality did not, whereas he neither had such knowledge nor did he think he had. However, during these inquiries in
public encounters with a number of prominent and lesser mortals,
he began to be hated by the men he exposed. To make matters
worse, bright young men from wealthy families followed Socrates
around, enjoyed the performances, and began imitating him. The
people *they* exposed became angry at *him*, and began saying that
he was corrupting the youth. And if one asks them how he did
this, they are at a loss and find it convenient to say the usual
things people say against all philosophers: they study the things
above and below the earth, they don't believe in gods, and they
make the weaker argument stronger. But despite the hate he
caused, Socrates persisted. Why? He tells us several times in no

unclear terms: 'it seems [to me] necessary to do above all the god's business' (21E). Seven lines later he tells us that he was carrying on the investigation 'at the god's behest.' And at 23B, near the end of this long explanation of his bad reputation, he says:

> For this reason, I am still even now going about and searching and investigating at the god's behest anyone, whether a citizen or foreigner, who I think is wise; and when he does seem so to me, I give aid to the god and show that he is not wise. And by reason of this occupation I have no leisure to attend to any of the affairs of the state worth mentioning, or of my own, but I am in vast poverty on account of my service to the god.

In sum, Socrates' defence against the old accusation is that he never did the things listed in the accusation, that the prejudice against him arose when he started examining people about their wisdom and exposing their ignorance, and that he did this at the god's behest and persisted because it seemed to him necessary to place the god's business above everything else.

Socrates now proceeds to defend himself against the new charge, the charge for which he is now before the court (24B):

> It [the accusation] is about as follows: it states that Socrates does injustice, corrupting the youth, and not believing in the gods in which the city believes but in other new spiritual beings.

It is noteworthy that this second accusation, like the first one (second version), begins by stating that Socrates does injustice; and then proceeds to list various actions which, according to the accusation, constitute injustice. Thus Socrates clearly conceives the issue before the court to be whether or not he has done injustice, and he conceives a successful defence as one in which he shows that he has not done injustice. This is a fundamental similarity to the way in which he conceives the central issue in the *Crito*: for there, too, we saw the fundamental issue for him is whether by escaping he would be doing injustice. In both Dialogues, the central issue is conceived to be the justice or injustice of certain actions. And as in the case of the old charge, Socrates proceeds to defend himself against the present one by trying to show that he did not do the things which according to the charge constitute injustice — corrupting the youth, and not believing in the gods the city believes but in new spiritual beings. On the first point, he argues *ad hominem* against one of his accusers, Meletus: he is ignorant of what is good for the youth and has never cared for their welfare. (He also uses a number of other arguments not of interest to us here.) Finally, he tries to knock out both parts of the accusation at once as follows: first, he extracts from Meletus the interpretation that it is by teaching the youth not to believe in the gods the city believes in but in new spiritual beings that he corrupts them; and second, he tries to show that the second part of the charge is self-contradictory, for since spiritual beings are either gods or children of gods it follows that anyone who believes in spiritual beings believes in gods. Aside from whether this follows or not (since 'believes' is not transparent, or introduces indirect discourse, it does not in fact follow), this argument is not successful: for the accusation does not say or imply that Socrates does not believe in gods, but only that he does not believe in the gods the city believes in; therefore, even if believing in spiritual beings entails believing in gods, it remains possible that these gods are not the gods the city believes in.

Whether or not Socrates' defence is successful, how he conceives the issue and the outline of his defence are clear. He conceives that he is accused of injustice, and he denies that he ever did any injustice (unless unknowingly). This denial takes the form of denying that he did any of the actions that according to the two accusations constitute injustice. What he was doing was not what the accusations state but something different: he was examining various Athenians and foreigners with a reputation for wisdom in order to find out what their wisdom consisted in, and whether they were wiser than Socrates, as the oracle said. Because these people were exposed for their ignorance they became resentful and began to hate Socrates, and his bad reputation and the present accusations are a result of this resentment and hate. Though Socrates was aware of this resentment and hate he continued in his examinations because this was the god's business and he considered the god's business to be of the highest importance.

We come now to the hypothetical question and Socrates' long reply (28B):

> But perhaps someone might say: Are you then not ashamed, Socrates, of having followed such a pursuit, that you are now in danger of being put to death as a result?

The main elements of Socrates' reply to this question are as follows (28B):

> I should make him a just reply: You do not speak well, Sir, if you think a man in whom there is even a little merit ought to consider danger of life or death, and not rather consider this only, when he does things, whether the things he does are just or unjust and the works of a good or bad man.

Socrates seems to be advancing in this passage what we might call a principle of choice, or at any rate a principle that tells us what sorts of things to consider when making a choice:

A1 When one acts one ought to consider only this, whether what he does is just or unjust and the work of a good or bad man.

After describing Achilles making the choice of punishing the wrongdoer (Hector) and dying rather than living as a ridiculous coward, Socrates advances another general principle (28D):

For thus it is, men of Athens, in truth:

A2 Wherever a man stations himself, thinking it best to be there, or is stationed by [his] ruler, there he must stay, it seems to me, and run his risks, considering neither death nor anything else more than disgrace.

He continues with a comparison between his behavior during campaigns and his philosophizing (28E—29A):

So I should have done a terrible thing, if, when the commanders whom you chose to command me stationed me, both at Potidaea and at Amphipolis and at Delium, I remained like anyone else where they stationed me and ran the risk of death, but when the god gave me a station, as I believed and understood, with orders to spend my life philosophizing and examining myself and others, I were to desert my station through fear of death or anything else whatsoever. [Three lines later it becomes clear that Socrates is referring to the oracle and his interpretation of it when he speaks of god giving him a station with orders to philosophize.]

It is clear from this passage that Socrates conceives of himself as being commanded by god, or as having been stationed by god, with orders to philosophize. This case, however, unlike the case of the campaigns, does not seem to come under principle A2 since A2 says nothing about god. However, the passage certainly suggests that Socrates thinks that if one must stay where one is stationed by his ruler even at the risk of death, one must certainly also do so when one is commanded or stationed by god. And Socrates goes on to advance another principle which does explicitly refer to god (29B):

But I know that

A3 It is evil and disgraceful to do injustice to and [or?] to disobey him who is better whether he be a god or man.

33

Just before this he has said that no one knows that death is evil, and it could be the greatest of blessings. And just after he advanced A3 he says that he shall never fear or avoid those things that he does not know to be good or bad (e.g. death) more than those things he knows to be bad (e.g. doing injustice and disobeying one who is better). And from these particular statements and A3 he seems to conclude as to how he would act if the court were to order him to stop philosophizing (29CD):

> And therefore, even if you acquit me now and are not con-
> vinced by Anytus, who says that either I ought not to have been
> brought to trial at all, or since I was brought to trial, I must
> certainly be put to death, adding that if I were acquitted your
> sons would all be utterly ruined by practicing what I teach — if
> you should say to me in reply to this: Socrates, this time we
> will not do as Anytus says, but we will let you go, on this con-
> dition, however, that you no longer spend you time in this
> investigation or in philosophy, and if you are caught doing so
> again you shall die; if you should let me go on this condition
> which I have mentioned, I should say to you, 'Men of Athens,
> I respect and love you, but I shall obey the god rather than you,
> and while I live and I am able to continue, I shall never give up
> philosophy or stop exhorting you and pointing out the truth to
> anyone of you whom I may meet.'

He goes on to describe how he would try to shame the Athenians into caring more for wisdom and truth and the soul than for wealth and reputation and honor, and then continues (30AB):

> This I shall do to whomever I meet, young and old, foreigner
> and citizen, but most to the citizens, inasmuch as you are more
> nearly related to me. For, listen, god commands me to do these
> things, and I believe that no greater good ever came to pass in
> the city than my service to the god. . . . Therefore, I say to you,
> men of Athens, either do as Anytus tells you, or not, and either
> acquit me, or not, knowing that I shall not change my conduct
> even if I am to die many times over.

Socrates completes his defence by recounting to the jurors two cases in which his actions constitute 'great proofs' that 'I would never yield to anyone, if that was unjust, through fear of death but would rather die than yield' (32A). The first case was when the senate wanted to try the ten generals collectively and not individually, which was contrary to law. Socrates opposed this at the risk of death because it was contrary to justice and law (32BC):

At that time I was the only one of the *prytanes* who opposed doing anything contrary to the laws, and although the orators were ready to impeach and arrest me, and though you urged them with shouts to do so, I thought I must run the risk to the end with law and justice on my side, rather than join you though your wishes were unjust, through fear of imprisonment or death. That was when the democracy still existed.

Socrates continues right away with the second case (32DC):

And after the oligarchy was established, the Thirty sent for me with four others to come to the rotunda and ordered me to bring Leon the Salaminian from Salamis to be put to death. They gave many such orders to others also, because they wished to implicate as many in their crimes as they could. Then I, however, showed again, by action, not in word only, that I did not care a whit for death if that not be too crude an expression, but that I did care with all my might be not do anything unjust or unholy. For that government, with all its power, did not frighten me into doing anything unjust, but when we came out of the rotunda, the other four went to Salamis and arrested Leon, but I simply went home; and perhaps I should have been put to death for it, if the government had not been quickly put down.

In this long passage Socrates presents us with six cases and three principles: how he acted in the campaigns of Potidaea, Amphipolis, and Delium, how he was prepared to act if the court ordered him to stop philosophizing on point of death, how he acted in the case of the trial of the ten generals, and the case of Leon of Salamis; and principles A1, A2, and A3. Though it is not entirely clear which cases are supposed to be subsumed under principles, it is clear that Socrates believes that in all these cases he was acting on the basis of some or all of these principles, and that he believes that he was acting consistently throughout all his life. Thus, the arguments that lead to the decision to perform these actions or the arguments that are meant to justify these actions, will be of the same kind as the arguments in the *Crito*: they consist in showing that a given action is subsumed under some general principle, and that, consequently, the action is required, forbidden, or permitted, depending on whether the general principle requires, forbids, or permits. We shall be able to reconstruct Socrates' arguments (reasons) for his decisions and actions clearly in so far as we can get clear about his principles (their content and priorities among them, if any) and the particular circumstances of his actions. We shall not try to resolve all the unclarities (even if we could), how-

35

ever, but only those that we need to resolve to interpret the passage accurately. We shall start with things that are clear and proceed to the more difficult.

The least problematic and clearest cases are Socrates' actions at Potidaea, Amphipolis, and Delium. At 28D—29A, in the passages already quoted, it is clear that Socrates conceives these cases as being subsumed under principle A2. In these three cases we shall forgo particular descriptions of his actions, and shall use the general description that he uses and which is true of all three cases: Socrates 'remained like anyone else where they [rulers or commanders] stationed [him] and ran the risk of death' (28E). Clearly then, the argument that leads to his decision to act as he did in these three cases, or the argument that justifies his action in these three cases, is as follows.

1 Wherever a man stations himself, thinking it best to be there, or is stationed by his ruler or commander, there he must stay or remain and run his risks considering neither death nor anything else more than disgrace. (A2)
2 Socrates was stationed by his rulers or commanders at Potidaea, Amphipolis, and Delium (with orders) to remain (at his post) and run the risk of death.
3 Therefore, Socrates must remain (at his post) and run the risk of death at Potidaea, Amphipolis, and Delium.

In the case of the ten generals Socrates characterizes what the senators and the other *prytanes* wanted to do — to try the generals collectively — as both illegal and unjust, and it is because of this that Socrates opposed their wishes. His action could conceivably be subsumed under all three principles, A1, A2, and A3. Thus it could be subsumed under A2 as follows:

1 A2.
2 Socrates was stationed as a *prytanis* with orders to uphold the laws.
3 To uphold the laws Socrates must oppose those who wish to try the ten generals collectively.
4 Therefore, Socrates must oppose those who wished to try the ten generals collectively.

Socrates' action can also be subsumed under A1, or rather under a principle that Socrates clearly means to advance in advancing A1, namely:

A1.1 One must never do injustice and/or the work of a bad man.

Since Socrates believes that if he allowed the ten generals to be tried collectively he would be doing something unjust, it follows from this belief and A1.1 that Socrates must not allow the ten generals to be tried collectively. Finally, Socrates' action can also be subsumed under A3, or rather under a principle that Socrates clearly means to advance in advancing A3, namely:

A3.1   One must never do injustice to and/or disobey him who is better whether he be a god or a man.

From this principle and the characterization of the action as unjust, it follows once more that Socrates must not try (or allow to be tried) the ten generals collectively.

Socrates' action in the case of Leon of Salamis, namely his refusal and disobedience of the order to go arrest Leon of Salamis, can be subsumed under A1.1 or A3.1 since arresting Leon of Salamis with the intent of putting him to death is characterized by Socrates as unjust (and also unholy). The big difference between this case and the previous one is that in this case Socrates is disobeying an order given by the government, whereas in the previous case he is upholding the law; further, he himself points out that the case of the ten generals occurred during the democracy, whereas the case of Leon of Salamis was during the oligarchy of the Thirty Tyrants. However, though Socrates points out this last fact, he does not argue that the order of the Thirty was illegal since they were not a properly constituted (democratic?) authority. Rather he argues that their order was unjust. The proper conclusion from these points is that in both cases Socrates is concerned not to do anything unjust, and his actions in both cases can be subsumed under principles A1.1 and A3.1. But in the case of his action under the democracy, he is also concerned not to do anything illegal (and he makes the action's being illegal a reason for refusing to participate in it); whereas in the case of the action under the Thirty Tyrants *his own* action is illegal (since it is disobedience of an order by the Thirty who constituted the government), but Socrates is not concerned about that. It would seem then that for Socrates something being illegal (contrary to laws or orders) in a democracy constitutes a reason for not doing it; whereas something being illegal under the Thirty (or presumably a similar regime) does not constitute a reason for not doing it.[3]

If now we look at principle A2 with the above considerations in mind, we see that we must suppose either that 'ruler' in that principle means 'some properly constituted authority in a democratic regime', or that when this principle conflicts with either of the other two principles it is overridden. We must suppose this because Socrates' action of disobeying the order of the Thirty can be justly interpreted as violating principle A2. We can easily construct the argument that shows that Socrates must obey the order:

1 A2.
2 The Thirty are Socrates' ruler.
3 The Thirty stationed Socrates with orders to arrest Leon of Salamis.
4 Therefore, Socrates must arrest Leon of Salamis.

Thus A1.1 and A3.1 require Socrates to disobey the order and A2 requires him to obey it. Since Socrates decided to disobey the order on the ground that it was unjust, either he holds that principles A1.1 and A3.1 are prior to A2, or he holds that A2 is valid only under a democratic regime (which is equivalent to interpreting 'ruler' to mean 'properly constituted authority in a democratic regime'). These alternatives of course are not incompatible and Socrates may hold both. Since he mentions that the case of Leon of Salamis took place under the Thirty, whereas the case of the ten generals was tried during the democracy, we are inclined to think that he has the second alternative in mind; but the first is not thereby excluded.

We come now to the case where Socrates declares that he would disobey an order from the court to cease philosophizing. We note that this case comes after Socrates has advanced all three, or rather five, principles; that Socrates conceives his choice in this hypothetical case to be between obeying a court order to cease philosophizing, which (obedience) would allow him to live, and continuing to philosophize, which would result in his death; that he characterizes his decision as 'I shall obey god rather than you'; that he believes that he does not know that death is the greatest evil or even an evil at all; and that he believes that 'no greater good ever came to pass in the city than my service to the god,' i.e., that no greater good ever came to the city than his philosophizing.

It is clear that this case, unlike the first four, involves conflict of orders, possibly also what we should now call conflict of duties or obligations, and possibly also conflict of goods. Let us begin with the conflict of orders. The hypothesis under which everything is considered in the present case is that the court acquits Socrates but orders him to cease philosophizing with the penalty for disobedience being death. Now clearly principle A2 cannot be used to justify Socrates' decision to disobey the court. On the contrary, it follows from the principle, and the fact that the court, which was a properly constituted authority in democratic Athens, ordered Socrates to cease philosophizing, that Socrates must cease philosophizing.

A:1 Wherever a man stations himelf, thinking it best to be there, or is stationed by his ruler, there he must stay . . . . (A2)

A:2 Socrates is stationed by the court (his ruler) with orders to cease philosophizing.

A:3 Therefore, Socrates must cease philosophizing.

Equally clearly, Socrates believes himself to have been stationed by god with orders to philosophize, which he interprets as spending his whole life philosophizing until his death. But to what principle can we join this particular fact to obtain his decision that he shall obey god rather than the court and continue philosophizing? Passage 28E–29A, which comes right after principle A2 is advanced, implies that Socrates holds a principle parallel to A2, which can be obtained by simply substituting 'god' for 'ruler' in A2. Using *that* principle we can construct a parallel argument in which the opposite conclusion (to the conclusion of the last argument) can be obtained:

B:1 Wherever a man stations himself, thinking it best to be there, or is stationed there by god, there he must stay . . . . (A2.1)

B:2 Socrates was stationed by god with orders to philosophize the rest of his life.

B:3 Therefore, Socrates must continue to philosophize.

We have not, of course, arrived at Socrates' decision; we have only constructed the arguments that show that, given that Socrates has conflicting orders and that he subscribes to principles A2 and A2.1, he has conflicting duties or obligations. To obtain Socrates' decision we clearly need some general statement or principle that assigns priorities in case of conflicts of orders between god and man or conflicting duties to god and man. Socrates does not make an explicit statement to this effect. The closest he comes is principle A3: this principle is advanced just before he declares he would obey god rather than the court, it contains a reference to god, and it is suitably comparative. If we are allowed to construct the comparison in a certain way we can obtain the required result, i.e. Socrates' decision. The principle, it will be remembered, is as follows:

A3 It is bad and disgraceful to do injustice to and disobey him who is better whether he is a god or a man.

39

Better than whom? The usual translation (Fowler in Loeb and Croiset in the Bude edition) says 'better than I' (Socrates speaking in the first person). But this translation makes the principle too weak to support Socrates' decision, since we have two orderers here, god and the court, and both might be better than Socrates.[4] And in any case the text does not say 'better than I' but rather has the more abstract 'the better, whether a god or man.' This allows the sense to be 'the one who is better than any other, whether a god or man,' i.e. better than the agent (the one who is ordered) and better than any other orderer. So interpreted, principle A3, together with beliefs we may plausibly attribute to Socrates, that god is better than he and better than the court, enable us to obtain the decision Socrates actually reached, to obey god rather than the court, as follows:

C:1   It is bad and disgraceful to do injustice to and disobey the better, i.e. the one who is better than the agent and better than any other orderer, whether he is a god or man. (A3)

C:2   Socrates is ordered by the court to cease philosophizing. (hypothesis)

C:3   Socrates is ordered by god to continue philosophizing. (believed by Socrates)

C:4   Socrates must either cease philosophizing or continue philosophizing, but not both. (assumption)

C:5   Therefore, Socrates must either disobey god and obey the court, or obey god and disobey the court, but not both. (inference from 2, 3, and 4)

C:6   God is the better, i.e. he is better than Socrates and better than the court. (belief attributed to Socrates)

C:7   Therefore, to disobey god and obey the court is to disobey the better. (inference from 6)

C:8   Therefore, it is bad and disgraceful to disobey god and obey the court. (inference from 1 and 7)

C:9   Therefore, Socrates must not disobey god and obey the court. (inference from 8 and assumption that one must not do what is bad and disgraceful; for this assumption and the inference see *Crito* 49B)

C:10   Therefore, Socrates must obey god and disobey the court. (inference from 5 and 9)

This argument may seem unnecessarily complex, but this need not disturb us; it does not contain anything not in the text or not very plausibly attributed to Socrates, and it has the merit of bringing out all the relevant points in Socrates' decision and setting out the steps of the reasoning. Once all the steps are understood one can easily abbreviate the argument as follows:

1   A3 (p. 33).
2   Socrates must either disobey god and obey the court or obey god and disobey the court, but not both.
3   To disobey god and obey the court is to disobey the better.
4   Therefore, Socrates must not disobey god and obey the court, but rather obey god and disobey the court.[5]

Socrates seems also to have another argument for his choice of obeying god rather than the court; for in addition to comparing his alternatives with respect to obeying or disobeying god or man, he also compares them, as we saw, with respect to the goodness or badness they contain. His alternatives are: to cease philosophizing and live (also: obey the court and disobey god); or to continue philosophizing at the (almost certain) risk of death (also: obey god and disobey the court). Now in the passage, just before he declares he would obey god rather than the court, he says, as we saw, that men fear death as if it were the greatest evil (i.e. they fear it most), and yet for all anyone knows, death is the greatest of blessings: to fear death, he says, is to think that one knows those things one does not know (i.e., to think that one knows that death is evil, which no one knows). He goes on to say that he knows that doing injustice and disobeying the better is evil and disgraceful; and that he shall not fear and avoid those things he does not know to be good or evil (death) rather than those things he knows to be evil (doing injustice and disobeying the better).

It seems that from these remarks we can reconstruct the following argument:

D:1   One must fear and avoid those things one knows to be bad more than those things one does not know to be bad.
D:2   Socrates knows that doing injustice to and/or disobeying the better is bad.
D:3   Socrates does not know that death is bad.
D:4   Therefore, Socrates must fear and avoid doing injustice and/or disobeying the better more than he fears and avoids death. (from 1, 2, and 3)
D:5   If Socrates disobeys god and obeys the court he disobeys the better.
D:6   If Socrates obeys god and disobeys the court he meets death.
D:7   Therefore, Socrates must fear and avoid disobeying god and obeying the court more than he must fear and avoid

41

obeying god and disobeying the court. (inference from 4, 5, and 6)

D:8   Socrates must either disobey god and obey the court or disobey the court and obey god but not both.

D:9   Therefore, Socrates must obey god and disobey the court. (inference from 7 and 8)

This argument presents Socrates' choice as one between bad things or rather between a known bad thing and a thing regarded by some as bad but not known to be bad; and it is based on a plausible principle of rational choice (the idea behind premise 1), that when one is faced with a choice between a thing known to be bad and one not known to be bad one must avoid the known bad or must choose the thing not known to be bad.

Finally, we must consider Socrates' remark, made after he declares that he would obey god rather than the court and right after he describes briefly how he would continue philosophizing in his accustomed manner (30A):

> This I shall do to whomever I meet, young and old, foreigner and citizen, but most to the citizens, inasmuch as you are more nearly related to me. For know that the god commands me to do this, and I believe that no greater good ever came to pass in the city than my service to the god.

That no greater good came to pass in the city than his service to the god, i.e. his philosophizing, appears to be given by Socrates as a further reason for his decision to continue philosophizing even if the court orders him to stop with the penalty of death for disobedience. Conceivably this reason refers us back to principle A1: for it is plausible to think that Socrates would hold that ceasing to do the greatest good that ever came to pass in one's city, in order to avoid death, which is not known to be a bad thing, is not the work of a good man, but of a bad one.

We may summarize how Socrates conceives his alternatives and the reasons for his choice, on the hypothesis that the court acquitted him but ordered him to stop philosophizing with the penalty of death for disobedience, as follows. Socrates is faced with the choice of obeying the court or not obeying the court. If he obeys the court, (1) he disobeys god, (2) he ceases to do the greatest good that ever came to pass in the city, and (3) he avoids death. If he disobeys the court, (1) he obeys god, (2) he continues to do the greatest good that ever came to pass in the city (or at least he affirms by his choice that this is the best thing to do), and (3) receives the penalty of death. Disobeying god is disobeying the better, which he knows to be bad and disgraceful; ceasing to do the greatest good in the city is not the work of a good man but of a bad one; and avoiding death is not avoiding a known evil. On the other hand, obeying god is presumably a good thing since it is obeying the better; continuing to do the greatest good in the city is the work of a good man; and receiving the death penalty is not receiving a known evil. Therefore, all things considered, Socrates decides to obey god and disobey the court.

Before we end this section we might note an important point that emerges from our discussion of the hypothetical case and our summary of it. Though Socrates conceives the case as involving a conflict of orders, and possibly a conflict of duties, and a conflict of goods (or evils), he does not cite all the arguments he could have cited against disobeying a court order; in particular, he does not cite the argument he gives in the *Crito* against disobeying laws including the law that court judgments (verdicts and sentences) shall be supreme. But surely these arguments have some application against disobeying the (hypothetical) court order in the *Apology*?

3 Is there any inconsistency between the Apology and the Crito?

Many writers, from George Grote in the last century to A. D. Woozley in 1971, have thought that there is a real or apparent contradiction between Socrates' views in the *Crito* and his decision not to escape, on the one hand, and his views in the *Apology* and his decision to disobey the court order, on the other.[6] A charge of inconsistency is the strongest criticism one could make of Socrates' views, according to his own lights. His chief weapon against others' views is the *reductio*, which is an instrument designed to bring out inconsistencies. Moreover, in the *Apology* and the *Crito* Socrates' whole life and work is on public trial, and in these works Socrates' is making some of the most important decisions of his life. It would be a supreme and bitter irony for Socrates to be inconsistent when everything is on the line. For these reasons any serious criticism of inconsistency must be carefully examined. But aside from this, an examination of such criticism is likely to prove illuminating in understanding the views we have examined separately in each of the two works.

On the contradiction Woozley writes as follows:[7]

there appears to be a flat contradiction between the two works. In the *Apology* Socrates says (29D) that if the court were to discharge him conditionally on his giving up engaging in philosophical inquiry and debate, he would unhesitatingly disobey the order. In the *Crito* he suggests (50B) that a city cannot survive if its courts' verdicts and orders do not prevail; furthermore, if it is his general principle that any law must be obeyed, that, taken together with the statement (50C) that there is a law of Athens laying down that the judgment of a court is legally binding, entails the conclusion that one must not try to evade the court's judgment, including the prescribed sentence. The *Crito* proceeds to develop arguments, not merely for obeying the laws in general, but also for abiding by court decisions in particular, even if, in a particular case, the decision was unjust or wrongly given (50C).

After rejecting Grote's solution, Woozley prepares the way for a resolution of the apparent contradiction as follows:[8]

> In default of other evidence we have, then, to take it that as presented by Plato, Socrates was speaking sincerely both in the *Apology* and the *Crito*; which rules out *knowing* inconsistency. Similarly, we can rule out a change of mind within the last month of his life, for in the *Crito* he insists that there has been none; he cannot abandon his old principles unless confronted by arguments better than anything so far produced (46B–C). We are left, then, with two alternatives: (a) that there was an inconsistency, but he was unaware of it; (b) that there is an interpretation of the passages involved which does not render them incompatible. (a) is so implausible that it is very hard to accept. How could a man with any pretentions of being reasonable and high principled, let alone a Socrates, declare at his trial that he would not obey a particular court order, and then less than a month later refuse to disobey a court order because such orders must always be obeyed — and *not* notice the contradiction? Such an inconsistency cannot be rationally explained; it will have just to be accepted, but only if no alternative under (b) can be found.

Woozley proceeds to discuss five different possibilities under alternative (b), rejects the first four and accepts the fifth as a solution to the problem. I find his solution faulty.[9] In searching for a solution we must begin by getting clear about the logic of the problem.

To begin with, we must get clear about the logic of the alleged contradiction. There is clearly no contradiction between Socrates' decision to disobey the court order in the hypothetical case of the

Apology and his decision to obey a different court order that he be put to death in the *Crito*. If there is a contradiction it might be either one of the following.

(A) The principles he uses in the *Crito* as premises in his arguments, the arguments to the conclusion that he must not escape, might, together with the particular facts of the hypothetical case in the *Apology*, entail that Socrates must obey the order of the court in the hypothetical case; and this conclusion of course would conflict with the actual conclusion he reached that he must disobey the court order, since he cannot both obey and disobey it.

(B) The principles he uses in the *Apology* to reach the conclusion that he must disobey the court order in the hypothetical case might, together with the particular facts of his situation in the *Crito*, entail that he disobey the court order that he be put to death; and this conclusion would of course conflict with the actual conclusion he reached in the *Crito* that he must obey the court order, since he cannot both obey and disobey the same order.

All this is not incompatible with the way Woozley presents the matter in the two quotes just given; though he does not state it in exactly this way, and does not mention (B) at all, nevertheless this seems to be the way he is thinking of the alleged contradiction.

In the second place, if what we have said in the last paragraph is correct, the way to determine whether there is in fact such a contradiction is clear: we must discover whether the principles used in Socrates' arguments in the *Crito* entail that Socrates obey the order of the court in the hypothetical case in the *Apology*; or whether the principles he uses in his arguments in that hypothetical case entail that he disobey the actual court order to be put to death in the circumstances described in the *Crito*. Having reconstructed the arguments in detail in each dialogue, we are in a position to do this, which Woozley does not do.

Finally, even if we discovered that contradictions (A) or (B) obtain, this would not be sufficient to show that Socrates was inconsistent. The reason for this is that, as we saw, Socrates conceives the hypothetical case in the *Apology* as involving a conflict of orders, and, given principles A2 and A2.1, a conflict of duties (at any rate a conflict of 'musts'), and even a conflict of goods or evils. In order to understand such cases properly we need the distinction between what one must do, *other things equal* (or, a *prima facie* duty), and what one must do, *all things considered* (or, actual duty). It will be useful to quote Rawls's recent statement of this distinction, since it is clearer that Ross's older statement of a similar distinction:[10]

45

the phrases 'other things equal' and 'all things considered' (and other related expressions) indicate the extent to which a judgment is based upon the whole system of principles. A principle taken alone does not express a universal statement which always suffices to establish how we should act when the conditions of the antecedent are fulfilled. Rather, first principles single out relevant features of moral situations such that the exemplification of these features lends support to, provides a reason for making, a certain ethical judgment. The correct judgment depends upon all the relevant features as these are identified and tallied up by the complete conception of right. We claim to have surveyed each of these aspects of the case when we say that something is our duty all things considered; or else we imply that we know (or have reason for believing) how this broader inquiry would turn out. By contrast, in speaking of some requirement as a duty other things equal (a so-called prima facie duty), we are indicating that we have so far only taken certain principles into account, that we are making a judgment based on only a subpart of the larger schemes of reasons. I shall not usually signal the distinction between something's being a person's duty (or obligation) other things equal, and its being his duty all things considered. Ordinarily the context can be relied upon to gather what is meant.

Plato nowhere makes this distinction, so far as I know. Yet clearly this distinction or a very similar one needs to be used to understand the hypothetical case of the *Apology*. For, it will be remembered, we ourselves constructed two arguments to opposite conclusions based on principles Socrates states or implies *within* the *Apology*:

A:1 Wherever a man stations himself, thinking it best to be there, or stationed by his ruler; there he must stay . . . . (principle A2)

A:2 Socrates is stationed by the court (which is his ruler) with orders to cease philosophizing.

A:3 Therefore, Socrates must cease philosophizing.

B:1 Wherever a man stations himself, thinking it best to be there, or is stationed there by god, there he must stay . . . . (A2.1)

B:2 Socrates was stationed by god with orders to philosophize the rest of his life.

B:3 Therefore, Socrates must continue to philosophize.

We saw that Socrates explicitly states A2, and that 28E—29A

46

clearly suggests A2.1. And clearly A3 and B3 express conflicting requirements since Socrates cannot both cease and also continue to philosophize. Was Socrates then contradicting himself in making these two arguments, or are we attributing to him a contradiction in attributing to him these arguments? The answer is no, and the reason is that, in the context, judgments A3 and B3 can only be plausibly interpreted as judgments other things equal, not as judgments all things considered. Conclusion A3 should be taken in the sense that Socrates must cease philosophizing other things equal; that is, the judgment that he must cease philosophizing is reached on the basis of some but not necessarily all relevant principles: and similarly with B3. Moreover, since the principle relative to which A3 is reached is different from the principle relative to which B3 is reached, A3 and B3 so interpreted can both be correct. It should be noticed at once, however, that if Socrates were, alternatively, interpreted as meaning by A3 and B3 that he must cease philosophizing all things considered, and also that he must continue (not cease) philosophizing all things considered, he would indeed be contradicting himself. For in that case Socrates would be interpreted as concluding and deciding that he must cease philosophizing and also concluding and deciding that he must continue philosophizing, relative to the very same principles and facts: for all the things considered would be the same in the two cases. (A judgment that one must do so and so, other things equal, and a judgment that one must not do so and so, other things equal, can also contradict each other provided that the other things that are equal are exactly the same in the two cases.) Now in context, it is more than plausible to take Socrates' judgments A3 and B3 to be judgments other things equal, and to take his judgment that he shall obey god rather than the court to be a judgment all things considered. And the conclusions of arguments C and D (pp. 40 and 41–2 above) should be taken as representing Socrates concluding and deciding to obey god and disobey the court all things considered: for both arguments allow that there are reasons that favor each of the two alternatives facing Socrates, and the operative principle in each argument is comparative and assigns relative weight or priorities to the reasons supporting each alternative. Thus argument C allows that one must obey one's ruler and that one must also obey god. It also assigns priorities in case of conflicts of orders or laws whether between men or between men and gods: one must obey the better. In this case, Socrates is ordered by the court to cease philosophizing, and other things equal, Socrates must do that; he is also ordered by god to continue philosophizing, and other things equal, he must do *that*. But the two orders conflict, and in such cases one must obey the better. God is clearly better than the court. Moreover, if he ceases to philosophize he will cease doing the greatest good that ever came to pass in the city, and this would not be the work of a good man. Finally, he knows that disobeying the better is bad, whereas he does not know that death is bad. Therefore, all things considered, Socrates must obey god rather than the court.

We are not in a position to determine whether there is an inconsistency between Socrates' treatment of the hypothetical case in the *Apology* and his treatment of the actual situation he finds himself in in the *Crito*. Specifically, and in accordance with the preceding remarks, we shall first consider two questions:

(A) Do the principles Socrates uses in the *Crito* as premises in the arguments to the conclusion that he must not escape, together with the facts of the hypothetical case of the *Apology*, entail that Socrates obey the court order that he cease to philosophize?

(B) Do the principles Socrates uses in the hypothetical case of the *Apology* as premises in the arguments to the conclusion that he must disobey the court, together with the facts of his actual situation in the *Crito*, entail that Socrates disobey the court order that he be put to death?

Finally,

(C) Does an affirmative answer to questions (A) or (B) or both imply that Socrates was inconsistent in his treatment of the two cases?

(A) If we look back at the two main arguments we reconstructed from the *Crito* (pp. 15 and 19 above), it is clear enough that these two arguments (argument A and argument B) do indeed apply to the hypothetical case of the *Apology* and lead to conclusions opposite to what Socrates decided to do in that case. Here are the two arguments applied to the hypothetical case of the *Apology*.

The argument from harm applied to the Apology *case: AC*

1   If Socrates were to continue philosophizing without the consent of the Athenians, he would be rendering the court order that he cease philosophizing of no force and making it invalid and annulling it as a private person.

2   If the decisions (or orders) reached by the courts or the city have no force and are made invalid and are annulled by private persons, the laws of the city are destroyed and the whole city overturned.

3   Hence, if Socrates were to continue philosophizing without the consent of the Athenians, he would be destroying the laws and the whole city in so far as in him lies.

4   If Socrates were to destroy the laws and the whole city in so far as in him lies, he would be doing harm.
5   Hence, if Socrates were to continue philosophizing without the consent of the Athenians, he would be doing harm (to the laws, the city, and presumably to the citizens).
6   One must not do harm.
7   Hence, Socrates must not continue philosophizing without the consent of the Athenians (i.e., he must not disobey the court order that he cease philosophizing).

The argument from just agreements applied to the Apology *case:*
BC

1   Socrates has agreed to abide by the judgments reached by the courts of his city (or, Socrates has agreed to abide by the law that commands that the judgments reached by the jury courts of his city shall be supreme), even if he thinks or knows that a given judgment is incorrect and does him injustice.
2   What Socrates has agreed to do, namely abide by the judgments reached by the courts of his city even if he thinks or knows a judgment to be incorrect and to do him injustice, is just.
3   One must do what he has agreed to do provided that it is just.
4   Hence, Socrates must abide by the judgment reached by the courts of his city, even if he thinks or knows that a judgment is incorrect and does him injustice.
5   The courts of Socrates' city have reached the judgment that Socrates must cease philosophizing.
6   Hence, Socrates must abide by the judgment of the court that he cease philosophizing (or, Socrates must obey the order of the court that he cease philosophizing).

We see then that both the main arguments of the *Crito*, when applied to the hypothetical case of the *Apology*, yield the conclusion that Socrates must obey the court order to cease philosophizing. So far as I can see, the second argument remains completely intact and has the same power as applied to the *Apology* as it has in the *Crito*; and the sub-arguments in support of its first two premises also remain completely intact. The first argument, however, is a different story. Its application to the hypothetical case of the *Apology* is crippled by two fundamental differences between the two cases. The first difference is that in the *Crito* his escaping from jail is construed as being contrary to the whole judgment of the court, that is, the verdict of guilty of the charges brought against him and the sentence of death; and the first premise of argument A, therefore, has considerable force. In escaping, Socrates would be showing disrespect for the law, and he would be, in intent and in so far as it is in his power, rendering the decision of the court of no force and invalid and annulling it as a private person. But his disobedience in the *Apology* has a very great redeeming feature: for it is perfectly clear that Socrates, while prepared to disobey a court order to cease philosophizing, is also perfectly prepared to accept the penalty of death for such disobedience; and this makes a huge difference in the case, since his being willing to accept the penalty and not trying to evade it by escaping it shows that by deciding to disobey the order he does not intend to subvert and destroy the laws of his city, but rather has respect for the laws and recognizes that he must, in general, obey the laws. Moreover, his disobedience in the *Apology* is open and public, whereas his disobedience in the *Crito* would be secret and evasive. Disobedience that is openly declared and publicly carried out, and, at the same time willingness to take the penalty for such disobedience, are some of the essential marks that distinguish the civil disobedient and the conscientious objector from the criminal and the destroyer of laws.[11] The result of all this is that premise 1 of argument AC would have to be substantially qualified. The second main difference between the two cases stares us in the face when we look at premise 5 of argument AC and compare it with premise 5 of argument A: Socrates agrees with the latter but absolutely disagrees with the former. He agrees that by escaping he would be harming the city, the laws, and the citizens; for he would be rendering the decisions of the courts invalid, etc., and there would be no redeeming features. But he certainly disagrees that by continuing to philosophize he would be harming the city, the laws, and the citizens: for we saw that he claims in the *Apology* that by philosophizing he is doing the greatest good that ever came to pass in the city. At most, Socrates might consistently agree that, by continuing to philosophize contrary to a court order, he is doing some harm since he is disobeying the laws; but that harm is countered by his willingness to accept the penalty, and in addition his philosophizing is the greatest good that ever came to pass in the city. Whereas, in the case of escaping in the *Crito*, there is the harm but neither of these two corresponding redeeming features.

(C) It is clear from this discussion that, when the arguments of the *Crito* are applied to the hypothetical case of the *Apology*, the results do *not* show that Socrates by the arguments of the *Crito* should have decided, in consistency, to obey the court order (had it been given to him). For, first, we saw that though the second main argument remains intact, the first argument's application and power is considerably reduced by two fundamental differences in the two cases. And, second, it is perfectly clear that the two arguments present considerations only on one side of the case, and that they do not include all the principles that Socrates clearly thinks relevant and all the features of the case Socrates thinks must be taken into account, in particular, the principle that one must obey the better, the fact that Socrates was ordered by god to continue philosophizing, and the fact that (as Socrates believes) Socrates' philosophizing is the greatest good that can ever come to pass in the city. Clearly, therefore, when we apply the arguments of the *Crito* to the *Apology*, the conclusions that *they* yield are judgments as to what Socrates must do other things equal, not judgments as to what Socrates must do all things considered. Given that Socrates' decision that he must obey god rather than the court is a decision or a judgment all things considered, the judgments reached by these two arguments do not contradict it. It should be noted at once that we have reached this result not only by means of the distinction between judgments made other things equal and judgments made all things considered, but also by means of several fundamental differences noticed between the case of refusing to disobey the court in the *Crito* and the case of willingness to disobey the court order in the *Apology*.

Let us now see (B) what results we obtain when we apply the arguments used by Socrates (as we reconstructed them) in the hypothetical case of the *Apology* to the case of the *Crito*. The first argument, or argument A, clearly supports Socrates' decision to remain in jail and die:

1 Wherever a man stations himself, thinking it best to be there, or is stationed by his rulers, there he must stay . . . . (principle A2)
2 Socrates was stationed by the court (his ruler) with orders to die.
3 Therefore, Socrates must die (rather than escape).

The second argument, or argument B, also p. 39 above, seems at first inapplicable to the case of the *Crito*, and so do the remaining arguments of the *Apology* case, arguments C and D (pp. 40 and 41–2 above); for in all these arguments in the *Apology* it is a crucial premise that Socrates is commanded by god to philosophize, which is contrary to what the court (by hypothesis) ordered him to do; whereas in the *Crito* it is not the case that Socrates

believes that he is commanded by god to do something contrary
to what the court has ordered to be done, namely that he be put
to death. Therefore, all three arguments are inapplicable to the
case of the *Crito*. One might raise the objection, however, that,
though indeed it is true that Socrates in the *Crito* does not consider
that he is commanded by god to do something contrary to the
order of the court, perhaps he *should* have given the principles
and arguments of the *Apology*; for, the objection continues, the
command of god to philosophize is a command that is conceived
by Socrates to apply to his whole life, and hence to his situation
in the *Crito* and not just to his situation in the *Apology*; and,
further, surely the command to philosophize is incompatible
not only with the hypothetical order in the *Apology* that he
cease to philosophize but also with the actual order that he be
put to death, since if he is put to death he cannot philosophize.
Therefore, all three arguments of the hypothetical case of the
Apology do apply to the case of the *Crito* and all three lead to the
conclusion that Socrates must not die, or that Socrates must
escape. This objection has some power, but it is not valid, I believe,
for two main reasons. First, in the *Apology* itself Socrates does
not consider submitting to the penalty of death incompatible with
the command of god to philosophize. It will be remembered that
on the hypothesis that the court would acquit him but order
him to cease to philosophize with the penalty of death for disobedience of that order, Socrates chooses to continue to philosophize
and take the death penalty on the ground that god commands him
to philosophize. So, in not considering submitting to the death
penalty in the *Crito* incompatible with god's command to philosophize, he is not contradicting the view he took of the same matter
in the *Apology*. Second, toward the end of the *Crito* (53B—54A)
Socrates considers what his life would be like in other cities if he
were to escape: he believes that if he were to escape and go to
other cities, he would be justly thought of as a destroyer of the
laws, a corrupter of the youth, and a man who does not live by his
views, but on the contrary one who shows by escaping that he
prizes his life more than virtue and justice and lawful things and
the laws. Under these conditions his philosophizing would be
totally destroyed. Given that Socrates takes this view of the consequences of escaping, clearly he cannot have argued that he must
escape in order to obey god's command to philosophize. And for
the very same reason, the last argument he brings up in the
hypothetical case of the *Apology* has no valid application to his
situation in the *Crito*: he says that his philosophizing is the greatest
good that ever came to pass in the city; immodest as this may

seem, it cannot be invoked in favor of escaping in the *Crito*, since escaping would not enable him to continue philosophizing either in Athens or anywhere else. It is noteworthy that Socrates himself in the *Crito*, far from thinking that his decision not to escape contradicts his stand in the *Apology*, seems to think that escaping would be inconsistent with the stand he took in that work (52C):

> And moreover even at your trial you might have offered exile as your penalty, if you wished, and might have done with the city's consent what you are now undertaking to do without it. But you then put on airs and said that you were not disturbed if you must die, and you preferred, as you said, death to exile. And now you are not ashamed to think of those words and you do not respect us, the laws, since you are trying to bring us to naught . . . .

In sum, the very first argument in the hypothetical case of the *Apology* supports the *Crito* decision not to escape, and the remaining arguments do not contradict it. Relative to the arguments of the hypothetical case of the *Apology*, therefore, Socrates is not being inconsistent in deciding not to escape in the *Crito*.

Summarizing our results in this section, we can say that Socrates was certainly not inconsistent in his treatment of the hypothetical case of the *Apology* and the actual case in the *Crito*, because the two cases are fundamentally different and because it is not the same body of principles that apply to both of them. Socrates' stand in the hypothetical case of the *Apology* is an instance of civil disobedience or conscientious refusal: it is a public declaration in court that he would disobey a certain order of the court and that he would accept the maximum penalty for such disobedience — death — not out of disrespect for the laws or the court or the city, but because obeying such an order would entail disobeying god, who is the better, and because obeying such an order would also entail ceasing to do the greatest good in the city; and these things are to be feared and avoided more than death, and more than the harm done by disobeying the laws and breaking one's agreements to obey the laws, harm that is mitigated by willingness to take the penalty for such disobedience. On the other hand, escaping from jail is a secret and evasive act of disobeying the laws, an act that shows disrespect for the laws, an act that harms the laws, the city, and its citizens, an act that breaks one's agreements to obey laws that one admits to be just, an act without the redeeming features of countering the harm done thereby or doing greater good, and an act without divine sanction. The act of disobedience in the *Apology* is seen by Socrates as involving a conflict of orders and, given his principles, a conflict of obligations or 'musts', and also a conflict of goods or evils; whereas the act of escaping in the *Crito* is not seen by him as involving a conflict of orders or a conflict of 'musts', but at most a conflict of goods or evils which in his eyes is easily won by the alternative of not escaping. Because of all these differences, it is not the same body of principles, out of all of Socrates' principles in the *Apology* and the *Crito*, that is applicable or applied by Socrates to the two cases. The decision in the *Apology* is reachable or is reached by applying to the facts all the principles of the *Apology* and all the principles of the *Crito*; whereas some of the principles of the hypothetical case of the *Apology* are not applied and are not applicable to the case of the *Crito*, in particular the principle that one must obey god, and the principle that one must obey the better (in conjunction with Socrates' belief that god is the better). Given all of Socrates' principles that apply to the hypothetical case of the *Apology*, the decision is correctly reached that Socrates must disobey that order. And given all of Socrates' principles that apply to the *Crito* case, the decision is correctly reached that Socrates must not escape. The two sets of principles are not identical. There is no inconsistency. Socrates might of course have been mistaken in his beliefs as to the particular features of the two cases, but that is quite another matter, and in any case it is doubtful that we are in a better position to judge this matter than he was.

Some uneasiness is likely to remain over our results. There are good reasons for this, but they have to do not with inconsistency between the *Apology* and the *Crito*. Rather, they have to do with the fact that there are great differences in emphasis between the two works; with the fact that there is passionate pleading and emotional overwriting, overstating, and over-arguing in each of them; with the fact that the arguments in each work are not applied to the other even though they are clearly relevant; with the fact that Socrates is scornful and defiant of the court in the *Apology* and over-reverent of laws and orders in the *Crito*; with the fact that his appeals to god in the *Apology*, besides seeming arrogant and immodest, appear to be *ad hoc*, all too convenient, far too absent in the *Crito*, and not entirely in accord with his attitude toward gods in other Socratic Dialogues. These are undeniable facts, but they do not show inconsistency, and they must be kept in perspective.

It must be remembered first of all that the dramatic occasions of the two works are very different. In the *Apology* Socrates is on public trial for his work which was his whole life. This is the right time, and perhaps the last time, for him to defend himself against all the charges that were brought against him for many years, to explain to his fellow citizens what he was doing, which they appeared to misunderstand, to put a value on what he was doing, to say what his work was worth to him, and to prove its worth with his life. This was the time for him to prove, if he could, that his work was right and good and that it was worth more to him than anything else in the world. But in the *Crito* all this is past. The time for convincing the Athenians that his work is right and good is gone. It only remains now to abide by the principles on which his work and his life was based and by the choices he made all his life and in court.

Further, there is some truth in Grote's view. Even though there is no inconsistency, each work is very one-sided. Having written the *Apology* first, in which Socrates appears scornful and defiant of the court, perhaps Plato, in part seeking to correct this impression, over-argued and overstated Socrates' loyalty to the city and the laws in the *Crito*. But if we make allowance for this, the two works can be seen as balancing each other rather well. Socrates was a pitiless critic of his fellow citizens but he also loved Athens and was devoted to the democracy. In the *Apology* he is shown to be the pitiless critic of the men of Athens. But he has never had any quarrel with the laws of Athens, and the city has been his favorite and only home. And all this is certainly brought out in the *Crito*. Each work has a very different focus, and each corrects possible misunderstandings of the other. In addition much of the emotional writing and overwriting and the very different emphasis of the two works is perhaps partly due to the fact that at the time of writing Plato was a young man; he was still very close to Socrates' trial and death, and he was still attached to Athens. Though the principles and the arguments are Socrates', the emotion, the adoration, and the passion may be Plato's.

Finally, it is true enough that Socrates overdoes the appeals to god in the *Apology*. There are no fewer than thirteen passages in which Socrates says or clearly implies that his philosophizing was ordered or sanctioned by god (21E, 22A, 23B, 23C, 28E, 29D, 30A, 30D, 30E, 31A, 33C, 35D, 37E). The evidence is unambiguous, unmistakable, and overwhelming: there is no doubt whatsoever that Socrates believes in the *Apology* that he was commanded by god to philosophize. He was commanded to do this by god, he says, 'through oracles and dreams and in every way man was ever commanded by divine power to do anything whatsoever' (33C). Not only this, but apparently he considers himself no less than 'the gift of god to you' (30D). It is difficult to know what to make of all this. One would like to have the Socrates of the *Euthyphro* or the Socrates of the *Hippias Major* ask the Socrates who says all this a few questions. But the evidence is unshakable. In the *Apology* Socrates is portrayed as religious and even superstitious. And he may appear to us not only arrogant but even deluded. But once more, there is a very great redeeming feature: god commands, it appears, what Socrates believes is good and right on grounds quite independent of the alleged fact that god commands it. And this is not inconsistent with Socrates' view in the *Euthyphro* that the god's commanding or loving or approving of something is not the reason for that thing being right or good. Some people, it would seem, rationalize their gods, their religion, and their superstitions; that is, their reason adjusts to beliefs, previously formed by teaching, habit, and conditioning, as to what the gods are, what they do, and what they command. But Socrates, it appears, has managed to have his religion and his superstitions follow his reason. His god commands what Socrates has already concluded, on the basis of his usual principles and arguments, is good and right.

PART TWO

Socratic Method

III

Socratic Questions and Assumptions

Introduction

Nothing is more characteristic of Socrates than talking, and nothing is more characteristic of his talks than asking questions. Socrates is asking questions all the time. He greets people with questions, he teaches and refutes them with questions, he leaves them with questions — he actually *talks* to them with questions. The center of every Socratic session consists of Socrates asking questions and demanding answers that are short and to the point. If the interlocutor declines to answer, Socrates *imagines* an interlocutor — *hoi polloi* in the *Protagoras*, his rude house-guest (his alter ego) in the *Hippias Major* — and holds a question-and-answer session with *him*. When Socrates is not talking, he is probably holding a *silent* question-and-answer session with himself (*Apology*, 21B). Hence, Plato's definition of thinking: 'dialogue without voice of the soul with itself' (*Sophist*, 263E). In a large measure we know Socrates from his questions, and so it makes good sense to study and examine his questions in some detail. We shall proceed by collecting a sample of Socrates' questions from Plato's early dialogues, by sorting out the questions that can be raised about Socrates' questions, and by discussing the pragmatics, syntactics, and semantics of Socrates' questions.

1 A sample of Socrates' questions

(1) 'Callias,' said I, 'if your two sons had happened to be two colts or two calves, we should be able to get and hire for them an overseer who would make them excellent in the kind of excellence proper to them . . . a horse trainer or a

husbandman; but now since they are two human beings, whom do you have in mind go get as overseer? Who has knowledge of that kind of excellence, that of a man and a citizen?'   [*Apology*, 20B]

(2) For when I heard this I thought to myself: 'What in the world does the god mean, and what riddle is he propounding? For I am conscious that I am not wise either much or little. What then does he mean by declaring that I am the wisest?'   [*ibid.*, 20B]

(3) And is not this the most reprehensible form of ignorance, that of thinking one knows what one does not know?
[*ibid.*, 29B]

(4) Men of Athens . . . I shall never give up philosophy or stop exhorting you, saying in my accustomed way: 'Most excellent man, are you who are a citizen of Athens, the greatest of cities and the most famous for wisdom and power, not ashamed to care for the acquisition of wealth and for reputation and honour, when you neither care nor take thought for wisdom and truth and the perfection of your soul?'   [*ibid.*, 29B]

(5) If a man is an athlete and makes that his business, does he pay attention to every man's praise and blame and opinion or to those of one man only who is a physician or a trainer?   [*Crito*, 47B]

(6) Do we say that one must never willingly do wrong, or does it depend upon circumstances? Is it true, as we have often agreed before, that there is no sense in which wrong-doing is good or honorable?   [*ibid.*, 49A]

(7) Tell me then, what do you say holiness is, and what un-holiness?   [*Euthyphro*, 5D]

(8) What do you say is the nature of piety and impiety, in reference to murder and other things? Is not the holy always one and the same thing in every action . . . ?
[*ibid.*, 5D]

(9) Now call to mind that this is not what I asked you, to tell me one or two of the many holy acts, but to tell me that kind itself by which all holy things are holy.
[*ibid.*, 6D]

(10) Is that which is holy loved by the gods because it is holy, or is it holy because it is loved by the gods?
[*ibid.*, 10A]

(11) Just see whether you do not think that everything that is holy is right. . . . But is everything that is right also holy? Or is all which is holy right, and not all which is right

holy, but part of it holy and part something else?
[*ibid.*, 12A]

(12) Now, it is clear that, if you have temperance with you,
you can hold an opinion about it. For being in you, I
presume it must, in that case, afford some perception
from which you can form some opinion of what temperance is, and what kind of thing it is: do you not think so?
[*Charmides*, 159A]

(13) Well, which is most honorable at the writing-master's, to
write the same sort of letters quickly or quietly?
[*ibid.*, 159C]

(14) Then it would seem that in doing what is helpful he may
sometimes do temperately and be temperate, but be
ignorant of his own temperance?   [*ibid.*, 164D]

(15) For if temperance is knowing anything, obviously it must
be a kind of science, and a science of something, must it
not?   [*ibid.*, 165C]

(16) Now tell me: when one person loves another, which of
the two becomes friend of the other — the loving of the
loved, or the loved of the loving? Or is there no difference?   [*Lysis*, 212B]

(17) Then are we to say that the opposite is most friendly to
its opposite?   [*ibid.*, 216A]

(18) For I declare that the good is beautiful: do you not
agree?   [*ibid.*, 216D]

(19) When a man is a friend, is he friend to some one or not?
[*ibid.*, 218D]

(20) Is health a friend or not? . . . And disease is a foe?
[*ibid.*, 219A]

(21) But tell me this: at which of the cities that you go to did
you make the most money?   [*Hippias Major*, 283B]

(22) And say now: is not your wisdom such as to make those
who are in contact with it and learn it, better men in respect of virtue?   [*ibid.*, 283C]

(23) Stranger from Elis, is it not by justice that the just are
just?
. . .
Then this, justice, is something?
Then, too, by wisdom the wise are wise and by the good
that all good things are good, are they not? [*ibid.*, 287C]

(24) . . . but still, my good friend, consider: for he asked you,
not what is beautiful, but what the beautiful is.
[*ibid.*, 287DE]

(25) Then, he will say, when you were asked for the beautiful

do you give as your reply what is, as you yourself say, no more beautiful than ugly?   [*ibid.*, 289C]

(26) But do you still think that the beautiful itself, by the addition of which all other things are adorned and made to appear beautiful, when its form is added to any of them — you still think that is a maiden or a mare or a lyre?   [*ibid.*, 289D]

(27) ... are you not able to remember that I asked for the beautiful itself, by which everything to which it is added is beautiful by it, both stone and stick and man and god and every act and every learning?   [*ibid.*, 292D]

(28) For the beautiful is always beautiful, is it not?   [*ibid.*, 292E]

(29) It is impossible, then, for things which are really beautiful not to appear to be beautiful, at any rate when that is present which makes them appear so?   [*ibid.*, 294C]

(30) And how are you to know who produced a speech or anything else beautifully when you are ignorant of the beautiful? And when you are in such a condition, do you think it is better for you to be alive than dead?   [*ibid.*, 304E]

(31) Then our first requisite is to know what virtue is?   [*Laches*, 190B]

(32) Come, try and tell me, as I suggest, what is courage.   [*ibid.*, 190E]

(33) Then we say, Laches, that we know it is .... And of that which we know, I presume, we can also say what it is?   [*ibid.*, 190C]

(34) What each of them [courage and cowardice] is — that is what I wanted to know. So try again, and tell me first what is this thing, courage, which is the same in all these things; or do you still not understand my meaning?   [*ibid.*, 191E]

(35) Well then, suppose someone asked me: Socrates, what do you say is this thing, which in all these activities you call quickness?   [*ibid.*, 192B]

(36) What power is it, the same whether in pleasure or in pain or in any of the things in which we said just now it was to be found which is called courage?   [*ibid.*, 192B]

(37) Now do you think my excellent friend, there could be anything wanting to the virtue of a man who knew all good things and all about their production in the present, the future, and the past, and all about evils, likewise?   [*ibid.*, 199D]

(38) That by which they [bees] do not differ but are all the same, what do you say that is? [*Meno*, 72C]

(39) And likewise also with the virtues; though they are many and various, they have one kind (character, nature), the same in all, by which they are virtues, and on which one would be wise to keep an eye when one is answering the question about the nature of virtue; you see what I mean, don't you? [*ibid*., 72C]

(40) Do you consider that there is one health for a man, and another for a woman? Or, wherever we find health, it is the same nature (or kind) in all cases, whether in a man or anyone else? . . . Is it not so with size and strength also? [*ibid*., 72D]

(41) . . . [for justice, Socrates, is virtue]. Virtue, Meno, or a virtue? [*ibid*., 73E]

(42) Now suppose that, like me, he pursued the argument and said: You are always arriving at a variety of things, but let me have no more of that: since you call these many things by one single name, and you say that none of them is not figure, even when they are opposed to one another, tell me what is that which comprises round and straight alike, and which you call figure, counting straight no less than round as being figure. Or don't you say so? [*ibid*., 74DE]

(43) Don't you see that I am looking for that which is the same in all such things? [*ibid*., 75A]

(44) What do you say desiring something is? [Desiring it] to become one's own? [*ibid*., 77C]

(45) For what is being miserable but desiring evil things and possessing them? [*ibid*., 78A]

(46) Do you suppose that anyone can know that something is an element (part) of virtue when he does not know virtue? [*ibid*., 79C]

(47) Do you see what a contentious argument you are introducing, that a man cannot inquire either about what he knows or about what he does not know? [*ibid*., 80E]

(48) Now, by causing him to doubt and giving him the torpedo's shock, have we done him any harm? [*ibid*., 84B]

(49) So that he who does not know about any matters, whatever they be, may have true opinions on such matters, about which he knows nothing? [*ibid*., 85C]

(50) Or is not this evident to everyone, that nothing else can be taught to me than knowledge? . . . Then if virtue is

some sort of knowledge, clearly it can be taught?

[*ibid.*, 87C]

(51) The next question is whether virtue is knowledge, or something other than knowledge. [*ibid.*, 87D]

(52) Now is it by virtue that we are good? . . . And if good, beneficial (or useful)? [*ibid.*, 87DE]

(53) If anything at all, not merely virtue, is teachable, must there not be teachers and learners of it? [*ibid.*, 89D]

(54) Since then rhetoric is not the only art that achieves this effect (persuasion) . . . what kind of persuasion, and of persuasion dealing with what, is rhetoric the art?

[*Gorgias*, 454AB]

(55) If someone asked you — Is there, Gorgias, a false and a true belief? — you would say yes, I imagine?

. . .

And now, is there a false and a true knowledge?

[*ibid.*, 454D]

(56) Then would you have us assume two kinds of persuasion, one providing belief without knowledge, the other knowledge? [*ibid.*, 454E]

(57) So he who does not know will be more convincing to those who do not know than he who knows, supposing the orator to be more convincing than the doctor. Is that the consequence or something else? [*ibid.*, 459B]

(58) Well now, a man who has learnt building is a builder, is he not?

. . .

And he who has learnt music, a musician?

. . .

And he who has learnt medicine, a medical man?

. . .

And, according to the same principle, he who has learnt what is just a just man? [*ibid.*, 460B]

(59) And the just man does what is just? [*ibid.*, 460B]

(60) There are things, I suppose, that you call body and soul?

[*ibid.*, 463E]

(61) Now is it your view that people wish merely that which they do each time, or that for the sake of which they do what they do? [*ibid.*, 467C]

(62) Now is there any existent thing that is not either good or bad or between these — neither good nor bad?

[*ibid.*, 467E]

(63) You consider it possible for a man to be happy wrong-doing and being a wrongdoer, is not that your opinion?

[*ibid.*, 472D]

(64) Which of the two seems to you, Polus, to be worse, doing wrong or suffering it? [*ibid.*, 474B]

(65) Or is the definition of the better and the superior the same? [*ibid.*, 488D]

(66) First of all, tell me whether a man who has an itch and wants to scratch, and may scratch in all freedom, can pass his life happily in continual scratching. [*ibid.*, 494C]

(67) But come, try again now and tell me whether you say that pleasant and good are the same, or that there is some pleasure that is not good. [*ibid.*, 495A]

(68) Are pleasure and knowledge the same thing or different? [*ibid.*, 495D]

(69) But answer me, Callicles, which do you think, that Polus and I were right, or not, when we were forced to admit in our previous discussion that no one does wrong willingly but all those who do wrong do so involuntarily? [*ibid.*, 509E]

(70) They call Pheidias a sculptor and Homer a poet: what do they call Protagoras? [*Protagoras*, 311E–312A]

(71) Tell me more precisely whether virtue is one thing, and justice and temperance and holiness are elements (parts) of it, or whether all these things I just mentioned are names of one and the same thing. [*ibid.*, 329CD]

(72) Do you mean parts in the sense of the parts of the face, as mouth, nose, eyes, and ears, or as in the parts of gold, is there no difference among the pieces, whether between the parts or between a part and a whole, except in greatness or smallness? [*ibid.*, 329D]

(73) . . . the thing you named just now, justice, is that itself just or unjust? [*ibid.*, 330C]

(74) It is hard to see how anything could be holy, if holiness itself is not to be holy — how about you, wouldn't you make the same reply? [*ibid.*, 330E]

(75) 'Now', I went on, 'each single opposite has but one opposite, not many?' [*ibid.*, 332C]

(76) Tell me, does a man who acts unjustly seem to you to be temperate in so doing? [*ibid.*, 333B]

(77) Are not things good in so far as they are pleasant, putting aside any other result they may have? [*ibid.*, 351C]

(78) Now do you agree with this view of it, or do you consider that knowledge is something noble and able to govern man, and whoever learns what is good and what is bad will never be swayed by anything to act otherwise than as knowledge bids, and that intelligence is a sufficient succor for mankind? [*ibid.*, 352C]

I have selected the questions of this sample with a view to representing some of the range and variety of Socratic questions, in terms of subject matter, form of the questions, the use that Socrates makes of his questions, and also something of the 'Socratic humor,' the so-called sarcasm and irony. The sample includes probably no more than one per cent of all the questions that Socrates asks in the dialogues covered.

2 *Questions about Socratic questions*

What questions should we ask about Socrates' questions? We can gain some understanding of the Socratic enterprise by raising questions about his questions in, roughly speaking, three categories. First, we can ask about Socrates' respondents (who and what they are), about the situations in which Socrates asks them questions, about Socrates as a questioner, and about the presuppositions of his *asking* the questions he asks (as distinct from the presuppositions of his questions); all these questions pertain, roughly speaking, to the *pragmatics* of Socrates' questions. Second, we may ask about the (syntactic or logical) form of Socrates' questions, and about the form the answers must have given the form of the questions; these issues pertain, roughly speaking, to the *syntactics* of Socrates' questions. Third, we may ask what Socrates' questions are about, what are the presuppositions of his questions, and whether his questions are 'valid,' at least with respect to the truth-value of their presuppositions; these issues pertain, roughly speaking, to the *semantics* of Socrates' questions.

3 *The pragmatics of Socrates' questionings*

Who are the people whom Socrates questions?

Meletos was a 'youthful and unknown' tragic poet, Anytos a leader in the restored democracy, both hostile to Socrates. Callias was a wealthy Athenian who played host to Protagoras. Crito was a friend and associate who tried to convince Socrates to escape. Euthyphro was a minor know-it-all, and so was Meno, a Thessalian and a pupil of Gorgias. Lysis and Charmides were beautiful and bright Athenian youths, second only to Alcibiades in beauty, brains and aristocracy. Critias, another aristocratic Athenian, mentor of Charmides and uncle to Plato, was a poet and politician. Hippias was a prominent sophist, Gorgias an even more famous one, Polus one of his brash young followers, Callicles another one though further along. Protagoras was probably the greatest of the Greek sophists both in originality and brilliance; Prodicus one of the ablest grammarians and a fine semanticist. Lysimachus and Melesias were two elder Athenians from great families, Laches and Nicias two prominent generals of the Peloponnesian War. Elsewhere, we have others of Socrates' circle, including Socrates' favorite young man, Alcibiades, a brilliant and wild Greek, a cross between General MacArthur and a playboy.[1]

The list of people Socrates questioned includes hostile prosecutors, friendly associates, receptive youths, slave boys, poets and men of letters, democratic and aristocratic politicians, great and lesser sophists, eminent generals, ordinary Athenians and foreigners. Craftsmen and philosophers are significant omissions. The more significant, perhaps, is philosophers: none of Socrates' respondents in the early Socratic Dialogues is a philosopher, either by profession or by actual performance, either of the pre-Socratic natural philosopher variety or the Socratic dialectical variety. This is one common feature of all Socrates' respondents. In all these Dialogues Socrates is talking philosophy with non-philosophers (which of course is not true of all Dialogues, say, the *Parmenides* or the *Sophist*, where the Stranger is introduced as very much a philosopher). These talks consequently should be viewed as more akin to teaching philosophy than to debates among philosophers. They are dramatic introductions to philosophic subjects and philosophic techniques, not shop talks among professionals. It is this teaching context that explains why Socrates asks a great variety of questions and uses questions for many more purposes than finding out the truth or obtaining information he does not have: he questions to puncture bloated self-images, to arouse curiosity, to remind, to correct ('Virtue, Meno, or a virtue?'), to make one think, to get one to see the consequences of one's beliefs, and so on.

What are the situations in which Socrates questions people? We may take 'situations' here to include physical and social setting and the occasion for Socrates raising his questions. In physical and social setting we see great variety again: the court, the jail, wrestling schools and gymnasia, public meetings in private houses, the public streets and the agora during festivals and ordinary days. The significant things that all these places have in common are that they are all in Athens (including Piraeus), and none of them is Socrates' own place. Socrates has no place, other than Athens at large, in which to talk and philosophize. He questions in public, his questions are public, and so is he. Perhaps we know so little of his 'private life' because he had so little a private life. And perhaps, in view of this, his conversations with 'the laws of Athens' in the *Crito* become more understandable. The occasions, too, that he takes to raise his philosophical questions are public; they have been characterized by commentators as 'practical,' but they are more occasions of common concern than practical; they are natural for raising large questions of interest to all. This is true of all the occasions: a great public trial; the death or escape of the convicted man; bringing suit against one's father for murder; the beauty, bearing, and friendship of aristocratic youths who are the next leaders of the city; the training of these youths to fight in the midst of a great war; dazzling displays by the great sophists, the self-proclaimed educators of the Athenian youths. Socrates frequently changes the subject from that of the original occasion; but the new subject has even greater common concern, though it is not perhaps as temporally immediate as the original occasion: and it has implications for the original occasion. Here is a display of a new military exercise, fighting in armour; wouldn't this be a good thing for our boys to learn? In the middle of war, this is an occasion of common interest and a question of common and immediate concern. If the exercise, and others like it, is intended to develop courage, Socrates says, we should decide the original question by considering what courage is. Given the connection, the interest of the first question carries over to the new one, in addition to the interest that the new question carries on it own.

What are the pragmatic presuppositions of Socrates' questionings, and what role does Socrates assume in his questioning?

We must at once distinguish between the presuppositions of a question and the presuppositions of asking a question; it is with the latter that we are concerned at the moment and it is these that we call pragmatic presuppositions.[2] The pragmatic presuppositions of asking a question depend on who the questioner is and what his purpose is in asking the question, as well as who the respondent is, and what is the actual empirical context in which the question is raised. The asking of the same question may have different pragmatic presuppositions in different contexts while the non-pragmatic presuppositions of the question itself remain the same. Pragmatic presuppositions are empirical-context bound (where 'context' includes all the factors we mentioned two sentences back), whereas other presuppositions are not. Consider, for example, the case of a traveller who just rented a car from a travel agent in order to go to Larissa, and while trying to find Larissa on a map asks the agent, 'Which way is Larissa relative to Athens, north or south?' From the context and the traveller's asking of the question we can reasonably infer that the traveller does not know the answer to his question and that the purpose of his question is to find out the answer. These two items are the pragmatic presuppositions of asking this question in this context; we might call this context 'the information-seeking' context. But suppose now we find the very same question, 'Which way is Larissa relative to Athens, north or south?' in an examination made by a geography teacher and given to his geography class. Very likely we would go wrong if we supposed that the teacher did not know the answer and asked the question in order to find out what the answer is. It is much more likely from the context he does know the answer and puts the question in the examination in order to find out not what the answer is but whether his pupils know the answer. We might call this, broadly, 'the teaching' context. There are two interesting sub-species of the teaching context. One is the case where the respondent gives an incorrect answer, but is very confident, perhaps even bombastic, about his 'knowledge' of the subject: here the teacher may ask questions with the purpose of making the respondent aware that he does not know the answer, perhaps even with the aim of 'taking him down a peg or two.' We might call this 'the know-it respondent' context or even 'the know-it-all respondent' context (this is the reverse of what we might call 'the interrogation of the suspect' context in which the interrogator, say an FBI agent, suspects that the suspect knows the answer but refuses to tell, rather than telling without knowing as in the previous context). The other sub-species of the teaching context is that in which the respondent in some sense knows the answer (virtually knows, implicitly knows, potentially knows) but doesn't know that he knows it: here the teacher may ask questions the answers to which the respondent knows, and which are a basis for answering the original question. We might call this 'the don't-know respondent' context.

It is not difficult to see that we find all these contexts, and yet others, in Socrates' conversations, and that the pragmatic presuppositions of his questionings vary with these contexts. Some of the main questions he asks — say 'What is virtue?,' 'What is temperance?,' 'Is virtue teachable?' — he asks in an 'answer-seeking' context. Socrates repeatedly says that he does not know the answers to these questions, and there is no reason to doubt this, especially when we remember that he distinguishes between knowledge and true opinion or belief, so that his 'I don't know' does not exclude 'I have a belief or opinion or hypothesis.' The teaching context, however, is the more common context, and the 'know-it' or 'know-it-all' variety the more frequent: his asking questions of Laches and Nicias is mostly in the 'know-it respondent' species, most of his questions to Euthyphro, Meno, and Hippias within the 'know-it-all respondent' context. The slave-boy passage in the *Meno* begins with Socrates asking questions in the 'know-it respondent' context and converts to the 'don't-know respondent' context, perhaps indicating that this is the fruitful teaching sequence with 'know-it' respondents, and possibly an essential teaching sequence with 'know-it-all' respondents. There are very few examples of 'don't know respondent' context, mostly with Socrates as the respondent or both the questioner and the respondent, and no examples at all of the 'interrogation of the suspect' context. The Athenians were not modest, and they had no police force.

These distinctions are worth making not only for understanding the richness and variety of the Socratic enterprise, but also because they correct somewhat the rather exaggerated importance attached to the information- and answer-seeking contexts and the pragmatic presuppositions of these contexts. Richard Robinson's overdrawn charges of insincerity on the part of Socrates are, I think, partly due to this. Consider Robinson's charges:[3]

> This denial that he is conducting an elenchus is insincere, and constitutes what is known as the Socratic slyness or irony . . . .
>
> The statements that he is 'seeing whether the answer is true' are insincere. So are the earnest requests for instructions by which he obtains the primary answer. So are his occasional invitations to reciprocity in elenchus (e.g., *Gorg.* 462A); he makes them only to persuade the other man to submit to questioning; and when he is taken at his word and made the answerer, his answers soon become speeches. Insincere is also the pose of suffering from bad memory.
>
> In the *Meno* (71C) it is the way to entrap Meno into pontificating, so that he can be refuted. In the *Protagoras* (334CD) it is a way of forcing Protagoras to answer questions; and Plato makes an imprudent admirer of Socrates point out the inaccuracy (336D). Socrates seems prepared to employ any kind of deception in order to get people into this elenchus . . . .
>
> 'You treat me', he says in the *Charmides* (165D), 'as if I professed to know the matters I ask about, and as if I might agree with you if I wished to. But that is not so. On the contrary, I inquire into the proposition along with you because I do not know. I will tell you whether I agree or not after I have examined it.' (Cf. *Apology*, 23A) That is always his attitude; and in harmony therewith he always puts the primary question as a request for information and not as if he were examining a candidate . . . .

There is no evidence in the *Charmides* that Socrates knew what temperance was, that is, had knowledge of the definition of temperance — which is what he understands by 'knowing what temperance is' — and therefore that he was being insincere in telling Critias that he did not know the answers to the main questions he asked.[4] The notion of 'request for information' can be misleading. Socrates requests answers to his main questions; the answers would be more in the nature of discoveries than of information, unless the respondent simply reports what, say, the Thessalians think on the subject. Socrates' self-deprecating remarks are perfectly in line with the importance he attaches to self-knowledge, which includes knowing what one knows and what one does not know (*Charmides*, 167A). His motive, he says when Critias accuses him of trying to refute Critias, is not to refute Critias, but 'to investigate the meaning of my own words — from a fear of carelessly supposing, at any moment, that I knew something while I knew it not' (166C).

Speaking of the same passage (*Charmides*, 165D) that Robinson quoted, Vlastos points out that Socrates can really mean what he says:[5]

> if in such passages he is using 'knowledge' in a sense in which the claim to know something implies the conviction that any further investigation of its truth would be superfluous . . . . This, I suggest, is the conception of wisdom and knowledge Socrates has in mind in those contexts where he disclaims it. When he renounces 'knowledge' he is telling us that the question of the truth of anything he believes can always be sensibly reopened; that any conviction he has stands ready to be re-examined in the company of any sincere person who will raise the question and join him in the investigation.

Robinson seems to suppose that Socrates is operating in one pragmatic context, the examining-of-candidate or teaching context, while pretending to operate in another, the information-seeking context. In Robinson's view, Socrates would be cleared of the charges of insincerity and deception if he proclaimed openly that he is asking questions in the 'examining-a-candidate' context, and with the intention to refute any answers one might give, at that! But this is not so. Socrates is operating, asking questions, both in the 'seek-an-answer' context and in the 'teaching context' (of which 'examining the respondent's answer' is a sub-species). Socrates is doing several things at once, rarely any single one of them. He is trying to discover answers to some very difficult questions, raised by him for the first time in the history of man; and his main way of discovering true answers is by examining answers that others give; thus he has to deal with many of the confidently held beliefs of his time. The pragmatic presuppositions of his questions therefore shift back and forth quite often and sometimes in a confusing fashion: sometimes he does not know the answer to his question, sometimes he does. Sometimes he needs to take a bombastic respondent down a peg or two and uses sarcasm to accomplish this end, or perhaps a debater's fall as well. Sometimes he needs to bring out a shy or over-cautious respondent, so he resorts to a bit of self-deprecation, though this is in obvious contrast to his reputation and thus ironic. The reason he refutes all the answers he gets — which Robinson thinks can be explained only by the intention to refute — is probably that all the answers he gets are inadequate: some are the wrong sort of answer, some too narrow, some too wide, others false, or at least contrary to what Socrates believes, or have difficulties in them. But all this is in perfect line with his main way of finding out an answer to one of his own difficult questions: by examining an actual answer to that question that others or himself have given. Burnet's remark, apropos of Socrates' irony, sarcasm, slyness, or cannyness, catches well the integration between Socrates' pragmatic tactics and his philosophical method:[6]

> He did not like to commit himself further than he could see, and he was apt to deprecate both his own powers and other people's.

Socrates' main way of testing a belief or an answer was by seeing what the belief committed the believer to, and one's powers to see such commitments are always limited, Socrates' powers only a bit less so than most people's. All this is also in line with Socrates' overwhelming emphasis on knowing what one knows and what one does not know. A man who makes such a great virtue of this had better be careful, especially in debate, about what he claims to know.

4 *The syntactics of Socrates' questions*

Nuel D. Belnap, Jr has made a useful beginning in the investigation of the logic of questions. We shall use some of his basic notions in order to sort out in terms of syntax or logical form the different kinds of questions Socrates raises, and in order to identify some of the more significant presuppositions that his questions have in virtue of their form.

On Belnap's analysis, 'every question is completely determined by specifying, first, the alternatives it presents, and second, the request it makes of the respondent concerning these alternatives.'[7]

Let us illustrate these two concepts, of presented alternatives and of different kinds of requests concerning these alternatives, from our sample of Socratic questions. Very frequently, Socrates raises a question by stating explicitly or presenting a number of alternatives and by making some request of the respondent concerning these alternatives. Thus question

(10)   Is that which is holy loved by the gods because it is holy, or is it holy because it is loved by the gods?

clearly presents two alternatives:

(10a)   That which is holy is loved by the gods because it is holy

and

(10b)   That which is holy is holy because it is loved by the gods.

Again, question (13) clearly presents the following two alternatives:

(13a)   At the writing master's it is most honorable to write letters of sort S quickly

and

(13b)   At the writing master's it is most honorable to write letters of sort S quietly.

Other questions in our sample in which Socrates presents alternatives explicitly to the respondent are (5), (6), (11), (16), (26), (30), (40), (41), (51), (56), (61), (67), (68), (71), (72), (73), (75), (78). It is worth noting that in these questions and others in which Socrates explicitly states alternatives, most frequently he presents alternatives that are exclusive of each other, though occasionally he also presents alternatives that are not exclusive of each other as if they were ((5), for instance). It is also worth noting that frequently Socrates presents a complete list of alternatives (exhaustive alternatives), always so of course where the alternative consists of a proposition and its negation; though occasionally he will leave out some alternatives which perhaps might be the least plausible for making up an answer (thus in (11), the implausible alternative, that nothing which is holy is right, is not presented at all, and similarly in (16) and (62)). We might sum up by saying that in the questions in which he presents alternatives his most frequent practice is to present exclusive and exhaustive alternatives. This no doubt serves him well in his examination and refutation of the respondent's beliefs.[8]

In addition to presenting a number of alternatives, a question makes some request concerning these alternatives. On Belnap's analysis, a question may make one of three possible requests con-

cerning the alternatives it presents: it may request of the respondent to select the uniquely true alternative, or to give a complete
list of the true alternatives, or to give any one of the true alternatives. Belnap illustrates these three requests with the following
three questions, noting that the presented alternatives are the
same in all three questions:

Which prime lies between 10 and 20?
Which primes lie between 10 and 20?
What is an example of a prime lying between 10 and 20?

It should be noted that this classification of three types of requests
relative to presented alternatives is made in terms of the syntax or
the form of the question raised; the fact that, say, there is more
than one prime lying between 10 and 20 has no bearing on the
point that the first question requests of the respondent to select
the uniquely true alternative.

In all those cases where Socrates presents in his question mutually exclusive alternatives (the great majority of his questions), he
of course is requesting of the respondent that he select the uniquely
true one, e.g., in (10) and (5). This is true of all his so-called 'yes-
or-no' questions where the presented alternatives are a proposition
and its negation. But there are also examples of requesting a complete list of the true alternatives (e.g. (11) and (16)), and also a
few that request one of a number of true alternatives.

The value of Belnap's analysis, for our purpose, is that it enables
us to understand much better the 'form' of some of Socrates'
more important questions, an issue that has exercised the commentators.[9] Belnap sorts out questions with respect to the two
factors that completely specify a question, the alternatives it
presents and the request it makes. One classification is according
to the three types of requests a given question makes. Another
more interesting classification that Belnap makes harks back to the
oldest and more common classification of questions but is significantly different and more fruitful. The older classification is
between 'dialectical' or 'whether' questions and non-dialectical or
'What is it?' questions.[10] Though this distinction is not clear, it is
usually made in terms of the number of alternatives presented,
implicitly or explicitly, by the question. 'What is it?' questions
present an infinite or at least indefinite number of alternatives,
whereas dialectical questions always, and usually explicitly,
present a finite number of alternatives. Of the dialectical variety
the 'yes-or-no' species is the most interesting: these are questions
to which 'yes' and 'no' are the appropriate answers. The alternatives presented in these questions are usually a proposition and its

contradictory. Socrates asks plenty of this sort of questions, a fact not very surprising since questions of this kind present great strategic and tactical advantages in discussions and debates: the presuppositions of such questions are usually not risky, and so they make it appear as if the respondent *has* to make a choice between the presented alternatives; the respondent's alternatives are limited; the respondent's alternatives are known ahead of time by the questioner; and, given the last two points, the questioner can easily plot his next move no matter what alternative the respondent selects. All this is true of (6), (17) through (20), (23), (28), and many others. By contrast, 'What is it?' questions leave a great latitude to the respondent; indeed, the presented alternatives are supposed to be infinite (these sometimes being called 'infinite questions', accordingly), and thereby unknown to the questioner, the response unpredictable. There are of course also a lot of questions of this kind in Socrates' repertory, indeed some of his most famous ones, the requests for definitions.

Belnap, however, makes a classification into 'which-questions' (akin to the 'what is it' or 'infinite' questions) and 'whether-questions' (akin to 'dialectical' questions), not on the basis of how many alternatives are presented but rather on[11]

> the *manner* of their presentation: they are either explicitly mentioned in the question or else they are described by reference to some condition. (A *condition* is a statement form, with variables holding the place of nouns.) For example, the alternatives 'She wore the red hat' and 'She wore the green hat' are explicitly contained in the question, 'Did she wear the red hat or the green hat?'; but the infinitely many alternatives presented by 'What is the square of 3?' are presented by reference to the condition 'x is the square of 3.' And this distinction leads to our first principle of classification: whether-questions vs. which-questions.

Our interest now is in which-questions, and Belnap explains his concept of these further:[12]

> Which-questions present their alternatives by reference to two items: (i) some condition and (ii) an appropriate set of names or terms. For example:
> (1) What is the smallest prime number greater than 45?
> presents infinitely many alternatives by reference to the condition.
> (1a) x is the smallest prime number greater than 45, together with the set of numerals; for each of the infinitely many alterna-

tives presented by (1) can be got from (1a) by substituting some numeral for 'x'.

The so-called 'What is it?,' 'Who is it?,' 'When is it?,' 'Where is it?,' and 'Why?' and 'How?' questions are all treated as species of which-questions by Belnap. For example, 'who-questions' are given the following analysis:[13]

(7a) Who is Speaker of the House
presents its alternatives by reference to the condition
(7b) x is Speaker of the House
where one obtains an alternative presented by (7a) by substituting some proper (human) name for 'x' in (7b).

And a when-question is given the analysis:

(8a) When is the rent due?
uses the condition
(8b) The rent is due on x
where alternatives are obtained by substituting a day or date-name for 'x'.

Where-questions are given similar treatment. Why- and how-questions are more difficult but these do not particularly concern us here. Finally, it should be noted that which-questions can be of the uniquely-true-alternative type or the complete-true-alternative type or the non-exclusive type, and similarly with whether-questions; so that there are six different forms of questions, this classification being based on the two factors that completely determine a question, the request it makes and the manner in which it presents alternatives.

We can now consider some of Socrates' more difficult questions, questions that have what Robinson and others call the form 'What is X?' As Robinson points out,[14] Socrates attaches great importance to this sort of question; for instance, in the opening pages of the *Meno* Socrates seems to hold that unless one knows what a thing is one cannot know any or many things about it. (See also chapter on Definitions.) But to say that this question is of the form 'What is X?' tells us very little about its form, as one can see from Belnap's analysis; Robinson and Ross do not even bother to find out for us what sort of expressions can be substituted for 'X.'

Let us first list some of the which-questions that Socrates raises:

(7)   What do you say holiness is, and what unholiness?
(8)   What do you say is the nature of piety and impiety?
(12)   What is temperance?
(21)   At which of the cities that you go to did you make the

most money?

(24) What is beautiful?

(31) What is virtue?

(32) What is courage?

(34) What is this thing, courage which is the same in all these things?

(35) What is this thing which in all these activities you call quickness?

(36) What power is it, the same whether in pleasure or in pain or in any of the things in which we said just now it was to be found which is called courage?

(70) They call Pheidias a sculptor and Homer a poet: what do they call Protagoras?

In none of these questions are the alternatives stated explicitly, and it is no doubt partly due to this that Socrates has to explain to the respondents every one of these questions before they can give an appropriate answer. It is from these explanations as well as from the questions themselves that we must gather the Belnapian elements that specify completely each which-question: first (a) the condition by which each question presents its alternatives and (b) the set of names or terms from which we can choose substituends for the free variable in the condition; and second, the sort of request the question makes concerning these alternatives.

Thus, to start with an easy case, in (70) Socrates begins his question by giving us the information we need both concerning the condition and the set of names: the condition is

(70a) They call Protagoras an x

and we can get the alternatives presented by (70) by substituting for 'x' in (70a) names of professions. Thus the alternatives are

(70b) Protagoras is a sophist

(70c) Protagoras is a rhetorician

(70d) Protagoras is a philosopher

and so on.

Socrates indicates, by examples, from what set of names or terms the alternatives are to be formed. This is, of course, necessary since the question is, we might say, wide open. Protagoras is, of course, many things — a sophist, rather than a philosopher or a cobbler; an animal, rather than a vegetable or a mineral; a man, rather than a monkey or what not, and so on — and the question is wide open in the sense that by itself it does not tell from which of these sets of alternatives the respondent is to choose a true one.

But almost invariably, given Socrates' explanatory remarks, we can specify the question he asks in a Belnapian fashion. Socrates' explanatory remarks usually consist in raising closely parallel questions (to the question he is explaining), and providing the answers himself to *those* questions (a technique that gives us at once both the Belnapian condition and the set of substituends), or in unpacking or amplifying his question, or in doing both things at once in the more difficult cases.

The difficult cases are the cases where Socrates asks his famous and familiar kind of which-questions: What is piety or holiness? (*Euthyphro*); What is friendship? (*Lysis*); What is courage? (*Laches*); What is temperance? (*Charmides*); What is virtue? (*Meno*); What is justice? (*Republic* I); What is beauty? (*Hippias Major*). Let us call these questions and similar ones *primary* Socratic questions, following Robinson for good reason, and in an Aristotelian spirit. We proceed to analyze these questions by specifying their Belnapian elements.

To begin with, in all cases except the *Charmides* and *Republic* I, Plato has the respondents exhibit certain misunderstandings in their first attempts to answer Socrates' primary question. Socrates tells them that they misunderstand his question and proceeds to explain it and correct the misunderstandings. The misunderstandings consist in the respondents not knowing the alternatives from which they are asked to make a selection or in supposing that Socrates is asking them to make one selection (non-exclusive) when in fact he is asking them to make another (uniquely true alternative). For example, Euthyphro's first answer to Socrates' question, 'What is holiness?,' is, 'Holiness is doing what I am doing now, prosecuting the wrongdoer who commits murder or steals from the temples or does any such thing, whether he be your father or your mother or anyone else, not prosecuting him is unholy' (5D). Forgetting the last clause for the moment, Euthyphro's answer consists in listing an individual action, his prosecuting his father for murder, and two types of actions, prosecuting wrongdoers who commit murder and prosecuting wrongdoers who steal from temples, and asserting that this is holiness. It is clear from this answer that Euthyphro is selecting from a set of alternatives that consist of individual actions and types of actions and that he is taking himself to be giving a few examples of actions or types of actions that are holy or possibly a complete list of actions or types of actions that are holy. Thus clearly he takes Socrates' question:

(7)   What is the holy?

to be the question:

    (7a) What is an example of a holy action?
or   (7b) What are a few examples of holy actions?
or   (7c) What are a few examples of types of holy actions?
or   (7d) Which types of actions are holy actions?

(7a) and (7b) differ only as to the selection request, (7b) and (7c) as to the set of alternatives each presents (a set of individual actions or a set of types of actions), and (7d) differs from the three others in requesting a complete list of true alternatives among the presented alternatives. Socrates does not distinguish all these questions, but he makes it quite clear that he does not intend his question (7) in any of the senses (7a) through (7d): Euthyphro does not have the correct set of alternatives from which to select an answer, and he does not even make the correct type of selection from the alternatives he has (Socrates makes it clear that he does not want an example or a few examples or even a complete list). Since Plato, as we pointed out, has respondents make mistakes of these sorts again and again in several dialogues, that is, mistaking the question Socrates is asking for some other question, we can gather that Socrates' original question, say, 'What is the holy?', is ambiguous enough or vague enough to be taken in any one of these other senses. The question, 'What is the holy?' can be answered in Euthyphro's way because it is any one of a number of different questions and some of these can be answered correctly in Euthyphro's way. This is not very surprising, because the question 'What is the holy?' gives us very little clue from which to construct alternatives, though it does not sin as much on the matter of selection request since 'the holy' is in the singular. In any case, it should be noted that Euthyphro's mistakes are mistakes relative to the question that Socrates intends to ask, not in any absolute sense, not even relative to the sentence Socrates uses to ask his question.

How does Socrates explain *his* question and how successful is he? He will meet with Belnapian success if he specifies sufficiently the condition by reference to which alternatives are to be constructed, the set of names that are substituends for the free variable in that condition, and the sort of selection request he is making. Let us look at the three things he does to help respondents to understand his question. (1) He restates or amplifies his original question; I will call this the 'long version' of the primary Socratic question as distinct from the original ('What is the holy?') short version. (2) He raises similar but easier questions and gives them what he regards as true answers. And (3) he examines what he accepts as *false* — hence formally appropriate — answers to his question.

In our sample of questions, (9) is the longer version of the first part of (7), (34) and (36) the longer versions of (32), (35) the longer version of the question 'What is quickness?,' (26) the longer version of the question 'What is the beautiful?,' (39) of the question 'What is virtue?,' (42) the longer version of the question 'What is figure?' Socrates does not always state all the elements of the long version. We form a composite long version that includes all the elements that he states at one time or another, from *Euthyphro* 6D, *Laches* 191E and 192B, and *Meno* 72C. Accordingly, the long version of

(7)   What is the holy?

is:

(7e)   What is the kind which (a) is (one and) the same in all holy things (actions and/or men), and (b) is that by reason of which all holy things are holy, and (c) is that by which all holy things do not differ but are all the same, and (d) is that which in all holy things one calls 'holiness'?

Similarly, the long version of

(32)   What is courage?

is:

(32a)   What is the power which (a) is (one and) the same in all courageous things (actions and/or men), and (b) is that by reason of which all courageous things are courageous, and (c) is that by which all courageous things do not differ but are all the same, and (d) is that which in all courageous things one calls 'courage'?

Sentence (7) can be used to ask question (7e), in addition to being used to ask questions (7a) through (7d), and it is (7e) that is the primary Socratic question, not the others. Moreover, (7e) is very different from the other four: the other four share presented alternatives, the set of actions or types of actions or both; but the presented alternatives of (7e) are neither actions nor types of actions.

In amplifying (7) into (7e) Socrates has made a tremendous advance, for (7e) tells us far more about the alternatives it presents than does (7). This can be seen from the fact that the condition by reference to which (7e) presents its alternatives is far more specific than the condition by which (7) presents its alternatives: the condition for (7) is

(7f)   X is the holy

whereas the condition for (7e) is

(7g) X is the kind which (a) is one and the same in all holy
things and (b) is that by reason of which all holy things
are holy, and (c) is that by which all holy things do not
differ but are all the same, and (d) is that which in all
holy things one calls 'holiness.'

Socrates uses subconditions (a), (b), (c), and (d) to test answers to
his questions: thus he uses (a) to reject Laches' first definition of
courage as too narrow, and (b) to reject Euthyphro's famous
definition of holiness as that which is loved by all the gods.

Our next task is to discover the set of names or terms that are
the substituends for 'X' in (7g): for then we shall be able to list
some of the alternatives in the set of alternatives presented by
question (7e); in addition, and once we have determined the
selection request that Socrates' question makes, we shall have
completely determined the form of Socrates' original question.

This matter, of the set of names or terms that are substituends
for 'X,' is more difficult to determine. It can be determined to
some extent from the answers that Socrates himself gives to some
of his primary Socratic questions, and from the answers of the
respondents which he accepts as answers to his question (long-
version), rather than to some other question, but which he rejects
as false.[15] In these answers, which are, of course, from the set of
presented alternatives of the question, we have the sentences that
are formed when a substitution is made for 'X' in the reference
condition. Thus we can try to infer from these answers the characteristics of the set of names that are substituends for 'X' in the
case of each question.

Now in the *Euthyphro* we have four such answers to the question, 'What is the holy?', 7A, 9D, 13E, 14D: 'that which is loved
by the gods' (which becomes 'the godloved' at 15C), 'that which
is loved by all the gods,' 'the tending of the gods,' and 'the science
of sacrifices and prayers.' The terms that Socrates uses that are
translated 'the holy' and 'holiness' are, respectively, the neuter
adjective in the singular, and the feminine singular formed from
the adjective by a suffix, much as 'holiness' is formed from 'holy'.
Both are abstract (though originally one supposes 'the holy' must
have been used to refer to some single holy thing (man or action)
previously mentioned). Now what we find in the four answers in
the *Euthyphro* is that, when the question is formed using 'the
holy,' in the answer we have a term that is neuter singular and
abstract; when using 'holiness' we have the feminine singular, and
also abstract. In short, the substituends for 'X' are names or terms

81

that agree in respect of number, gender, and abstractness with the name used in the question to refer to the thing the question is about. The only respect in which the terms that are substituends for 'X' disagree with the name in the question is in complexity: the name or term used to introduce the question is invariably not linguistically complex, but the terms of the answer almost invariably are (the apparent exceptions are some of the answers in *Hippias Major*). The generalizations suggested by this survey of the answers in the *Euthyphro* are completely confirmed by the four answers in the *Laches* to primary Socratic questions (192B, 192B, 192D, 195A); by the seven answers in the *Charmides* (159B, 159B, 160E, 161B, 163E, 164D, 166C); the six answers in the *Hippias Major* (293E, 295CD, 296E, 297E, 298A, 303E); and the six answers in the *Meno* (73CD, 75B, 76A, 76D, 77B, 78BC). In summary, we can say that in a given Socratic primary question, say 'What is quickness?', the alternatives can be constructed by reference to the condition 'X is quickness', where the set of names or terms that are substituends for 'X' have to agree with 'quickness' in respect of number, gender, and abstractness. This characterization does not probably completely determine the set of names or terms that are substituends for 'X,' but Socrates does not give us any more help. We can try to get some more help from the subconditions of the reference condition of the longer version of, say, 'What is courage?' From the first subcondition of the reference condition of the long version of this question (i.e., 'X is the kind (quality, power) which is common to all courageous men') we can infer that a name or term is not a substituend for 'X' in this subcondition unless it refers to something that at least *could* be common to all courageous men: thus the term 'endurance of the soul' qualifies but the term 'Alexander the Great' does not. But this is perhaps not to say much. And it still leaves us with considerable indeterminacy: would Socrates, say, have accepted the answer 'whiteness' as an appropriate though wildly false answer to his question, 'What is courage?'; or would he have rejected it as not being an appropriate answer to his question? None of the characteristics we have mentioned so far for the set of substituends for 'X' would exclude 'whiteness' as an answer, not even if we take all four sub-conditions of the reference condition into account. There remains therefore some indeterminacy in the construction of the alternatives presented by Socratic primary questions, even given the long version and all of Socrates' explanatory remarks; and to that extent his questions are unclear.

Finally, on the matter of selection request, Socrates' primary questions are a lot clearer. Invariably Socrates is requesting his respondent to select the uniquely true alternative from the alternatives presented by his question. We have already seen that he makes it clear that he is not asking for any one of a number of true alternatives (that would be by asking 'What is an example of so and so?'), and it is also clear that he is not asking for a complete list of all the true alternatives among the presented alternatives. His questions are always in the singular: he never asks, 'Which, or what, are so and sos?' but rather 'What *is* the so and so?'

In summary of this section, we can say that we have distinguished in terms of Belnapian form (i.e., selection request, alternatives presented, and manner of presentation) whether-questions and which-questions among the questions Socrates asks. In whether-questions we distinguished between yes-or-no (or true-or-false) questions and others. And within which-questions we distinguished between those that use a proper name to refer to the thing the question is about ('What is Gorgias?') and those that use an abstract singular term. We proceeded further to determine the form of a species of the last kind of question: those to which the term used to refer to the thing a question is about is a term formed from a general term by the addition of the definite article or by a suffix by which the adjective is turned into an abstract singular term. Using 'the F' and 'F-ness' as place-holders for these two kinds of terms, we represent the form of this Socratic question as 'What is the F?' and 'What is F-ness?' We called this the short version of a Socratic primary question. The long version is:

(7h)   What is the kind (characteristic, property) which (a) is the same (common) in all F things, and (b) is that by reason of which all F things are F, and (c) is that by which F things do not differ, and (d) is that which in all F things one calls 'the F'?

We then specified completely the form of this question by stating the condition by reference to which the question presents its alternatives, the set of names or terms which are the substituends for the free variable in that condition (noting that some indeterminacy remains here), and the selection request the question makes. The set of names are terms that agree with respect to number and gender and abstractness with 'the F' or 'F-ness,' though they do not agree in linguistic complexity; and the question makes a uniquely true alternative request. We shall see presently that Socratic questions of this form are identical with Socratic requests for Socratic definitions.

5 *The semantics of Socrates' questions*

What are Socrates' questions about? Are Socrates' questions 'valid' or 'legitimate'? What presuppositions or assumptions are revealed by Socrates' questions?

In response to the first question, a review of our sample tempts one to say, 'Everything under the sun!' But not quite. His primary questions usually set the main subjects of the dialogues, and the primary questions whose answers are at issue are invariably about the qualities that make for excellence in men: holiness, temperance or moderation, courage, friendship, virtue, beauty, the arts and crafts, knowledge. His secondary questions, usually of the whether-questions variety, almost invariably have a bearing, direct or indirect, immediate or remote, on the answers to his primary questions. Questions of natural science, or cosmology and cosmogony, and of mathematics, are almost entirely absent, or used only for purposes of illustration. Questions of epistemology, however, are very much present, contrary to what Gulley says (1968, p. 12); and this is no accident. Socrates was primarily interested in the powers of the individual to do well, whether in governing himself or the city, and he became very early aware of the crucial role of knowledge in such powers (probably from observation of the role of knowledge in making things in the arts and crafts). So questions such as, What knowledge is required for successful conduct? Do people who claim to have such knowledge really know? Is it possible, and if so how, to know that oneself or others have such knowledge? How it is possible to start acquiring such knowledge? – all these questions were raised by Socrates because they had a bearing on the issues of the individual's powers to do well and live well.

Let us turn now to the main subject of this section, the validity and presuppositions of Socratic questions. The question of the validity or legitimacy of a question is usually connected with the truth-value of its presuppositions. The connection is that a question is not valid or legitimate unless its presuppositions are true. To assess the validity of a question, therefore, we need to know (1) what are its presuppositions, and (2) whether these presuppositions are true. We shall not raise these two points concerning all of Socrates' questions. But it will be useful to consider the most important questions he asks: for since most of what Socrates does is to raise questions, his assumptions as a philosopher – the things he takes for granted – will be in part at least among the presuppositions of the more important and central questions he raises.

The notion of the presuppositions of a question has been discussed recently most fruitfully probably by Belnap[16] and by Henry Leonard[17] (aside from the work of such men as Collingwood and Strawson, who were concerned with the presuppositions of statements, not questions, though there are parallels between these two). We shall use a modified version of Belnap's analysis, with an assist from Leonard.

The Belnapian analysis of a question, into its presented alternatives and the selection request it makes concerning those alternatives, makes possible an attractive and simple theory of presuppositions of questions. We can say at once that every question, at the very minimum, presupposes that at least one of its presented alternatives is true. This notion of a presupposition makes sense immediately of the dependence of the legitimacy or validity of a question on the truth of its presupposition(s): for unless at least one of its presented alternatives is true, a question will not have a true answer, and a question that has no true answer is as good a candidate for an 'invalid' or 'illegitimate' question as one could wish. It should also be noted that the relation between a question and its presupposition now becomes a matter of the relation of implication between a proper answer to the question and its presupposition: that is, a proper answer to a given question, an answer that selects from the presented alternatives of the question and according to the selection request, will logically imply the presupposition of the question in the sense just defined. This is not Belnap's notion of a presupposition but a weaker one taken from it. Belnap's notion is, 'Every question presupposes that at least one of its direct answers is true.'[18] We can explain the notion of direct answer in terms of presented alternatives and selection request as follows: a direct answer to a question is an answer that selects from the presented alternatives of that question, and only from those alternatives, one or more alternatives in exact accordance with the selection request of that question, and contains nothing more. This assures that a direct answer to a given question is an answer to that question and not to some other, that it is a complete answer, and that it is just a complete answer — it contains no more information than is requested. It will be remembered that a question may make one or another of three possible selection requests: it may request of the respondent to select any one true alternative ('What is an example of so and so?'), or to select the one and only true alternative ('What is the so and so?'), or to select all the true alternatives, from the presented alternatives of the question. Thus it can be seen that Belnap's notion of presupposition is stronger than mine. Every question presupposes that at least one of its presented alternatives is true, but some questions presuppose more than that: either that exactly one or that more than one of their presented alternatives are true.

In summary, we can say that every question presupposes that at least one of its presented alternatives is true; and that some questions presuppose, in addition, that at most one of their presented alternatives is true. Let us call these the *primary* presuppositions of questions, following Leonard. We can then say, again following Leonard, that any propositions that must be true if the primary presuppositions of that question are to be true are *secondary* presuppositions of that question.

Given the concepts provided by Belnap and Leonard, we can understand each question better if we can determine the alternatives it presents and the request it makes concerning these alternatives; and we can, further, decide whether the question is legitimate if we can identify its primary and secondary presuppositions and determine whether they are all true. Let us consider an easy example of the applications of these concepts, the first question in (70) (*Protagoras*, 311E):

> They call Pheidias a sculptor and Homer a poet: what do they call Protagoras?

First we determine the presented alternatives by the reference condition and the set of substituends for the free variable in that condition. The condition is

> They call Protagoras a(n) X.

The introduction to the question that Socrates helpfully provides indicates pretty clearly that the set of substituends for 'X' is the set of names applied to persons as practitioners of professions or arts or crafts. The set of alternatives presented is then:

> They call Protagoras a sculptor.
> They call Protagoras a poet.
> They call Protagoras a sophist.
> They call Protagoras a carpenter.
> etc.

And the question appears to make a request of the respondent to select the one true alternative (but this is not entirely clear in this case). The primary presupposition of the question is that at least one of these alternatives is true, that is:

> Protagoras is at least one of the following: sculptor, poet, sophist, carpenter, etc.

86

The secondary presuppositions of the question are all the propositions that must be true if the above primary presupposition is to be true. Some of these would seem to be as follows:

Protagoras is a man or a god.
Protagoras can do reasonably well at least one of the following: make statues, compose poems, teach how to succeed by making persuasive speeches, make houses, etc.
Protagoras can teach at least one of the following: how to make statues, how to compose poetry, etc.
[etc.]

Our main interest in all these notions is their application to Socratic primary questions. Since we have described a method, if an imperfect one, for identifying the presented alternatives of Socratic primary questions, we can begin to identify with some confidence the primary and secondary presuppositions of these questions. These presuppositions probably constitute the best and most accurate account of Socrates' 'essentialism,' and, no doubt, a prelude to 'Platonism' and Plato's theory of Forms.

We shall begin by identifying the particular primary and secondary presuppositions of particular primary Socratic questions, and after doing this for one or two questions we shall consider whether Socrates commits himself to any general presuppositions.

Let us try to analyze and determine the presuppositions of the Socratic primary question about courage, following the above procedures.

Short version: What is courage?
Long version: What is the power that (a) is the same or common to all courageous persons, and (b) is that by reason of which all courageous persons are courageous, and (c) is that by which courageous persons do not differ, and (d) is that which in all courageous persons the word 'courage' names?

The reference condition (RC) is

RC: X is the power that (a) is the same in all courageous persons, and (b) is that by reason . . . .

The set of substituends is the set of names of powers that people have, including skills, knowledge, abilities, etc. Thus the set of alternatives presented by the question is

PA: Endurance of the soul is the power that (a) is the same . . . .
Wise endurance is the power that (a) is the same . . . .

Knowledge of what is to be dreaded and dared is the
power that (a) . . . .
True belief of what is to be dreaded and dared is the
power . . . .
The ability to overcome fear and act in accord with one's
beliefs is the power that . . . .
The ability to act successfully for the sake of the good in
the face of the danger is the power that . . . .
[etc.]

These being the presented alternatives to the question, the question
clearly requests of the respondent to select exactly one of these
alternatives as the true alternative. The primary presupposition of
the question, then, is that at least one, and (in this case in addition)
at most one, of these alternatives is true. That is, the primary
presupposition (PP) of the question is:

PP: There is exactly one power that (a) is the same in all
courageous persons, and (b) is that by reason of which
courageous persons are courageous, and (c) is that by
which courageous persons do not differ, and (d) is that
which in all courageous persons the word 'courage' names,
and (e) is identical with exactly one of the following:
endurance of the soul . . ., or wise endurance . . ., or
knowledge of what is to be dreaded and dared . . ., or
the ability to overcome fear for the sake of the good . . .,
etc.

The secondary presuppositions of the question are all the propositions that must be true if PP is true. Some of these would seem to
be as follows:

SP1 There is at least one power which is the same in all courageous persons.   (from (a))
SP2 There is exactly one power by reason of which all cour-
ageous persons are courageous.   (from (b))
SP3 There is at least one power by which courageous persons
do not differ.   (from (c))
SP4 There is exactly one power in all courageous persons,
which the word 'courage' names.   (from (d))
SP5 There are at least two courageous persons.
                                                     (from SP1 and SP3)
SP6 All courageous persons are courageous by reason of the
same thing.   (from SP2)
SP7 The word 'courage' names the same thing in all courageous
persons.   (from SP4)

SP8   The word 'courageous' means the same thing whenever it is applied to persons.
> (from SP7 on the assumption that 'He is courageous'
> means the same as 'He has courage')

SP9   The word 'courage' names a power.   (from SP4)

SP10 There is at least one expression other than 'courage,' in the same language in which the word 'courage' occurs, which is equivalent (names the same power as, or, is extensionally equivalent) to the word 'courage.'
> (from (d) and (e), on the assumption that 'is' in (e)
> is understood in the sense of 'is the same as' or
> 'is equivalent to')

SP11 Courage is not identical with courageous persons.

(d) and SP4 and SP7 and SP8 and SP9 and SP10 all mention the words 'courage' or 'courageous'; presumably the expression 'in the English language' is to be added to all of them, and the truth of all of them is relative to the English language.

In the case of some Socratic primary questions such as 'What is quickness?' and, possibly, 'What is virtue?' and 'What is knowledge?', the analysis would be the same as above, since quickness and virtue and knowledge are said to be powers (*Laches*, 192B; *Meno*, 78C). In the case of other Socratic primary questions, such as 'What is holiness?' or 'What is figure?', the words 'kind' or 'property' or 'characteristic' would have to be put in the place of 'power' in the above analysis. Being a kind and being a power are not of course necessarily incompatible; the point is rather that some kinds might not be powers.

We can give a generalized version of our analysis of Socratic primary questions, since we have discovered some of the properties common to all the sets of substituends for the variable in the reference condition of all such questions. It will be remembered that the set of substituends is always formed from abstract expressions (in the Greek language) in the singular, which are common nouns (masculine, feminine, or neuter, but mostly feminine), or neuter adjectives with the definite article, or (as we shall find in chapter IV) articular infinitives or relative clauses. If we use the expressions 'the F' and 'F-ness' as place-holders (or variables) whose set of substituends are the kinds of expressions in the Greek language just listed, and if in addition we use 'F' for the corresponding adjectives or nouns in predicate position, we can give a general analysis of any Socratic primary question as follows.

Short version: What is 'F-ness' (the F)?

Long version: What is the kind (property, characteristic) that

> (a) is the same or common to all F-things, and (b) is that by reason of which F-things are F-things, and (c) is that by which F-things do not differ, and (d) is that which in all F-things the word 'F-ness' (or 'the F') names?

Reference condition (where 'the G' and 'G-ness' range over the same things as 'the F' and 'F-ness', except for the limiting case where G=F):

> G-ness (the G) is the kind that (a) is the same . . . .

The set of substituends for 'G-ness' is the set of abstract singulars in the Greek language that was characterized in the last paragraph. In listing presented alternatives below, we shall use capital letters from the second half of the English alphabet, such as N, O, Q, as abbreviations for such Greek expressions.

> Presented alternatives: N is the kind that (a) is the same in all F-things, and . . . .
> O is the kind that (a) is the same in all F-things, and . . . .
> Q is the kind that . . . .
> etc.

Selection request. The question clearly requests of the respondent that he select exactly one of these alternatives as the true alternative. And the primary presupposition is that exactly one of these alternatives is true. That is, the primary presupposition of the question is:

> PP: There is exactly one kind that (a) is the same or common to all F-things, and (b) is that by reason of which F-things are F-things, and (c) is that by which F-things do not differ, and (d) is that which in all F-things the word 'F-ness' names, and (e) is identical with exactly one of the following: N or O or Q or . . . .

The secondary presuppositions of the question are all the propositions that must be true if PQ is to be true. Some of these would seem to be as follows:

> SP1 There is at least one kind that is the same in all F-things.
> SP2 There is exactly one kind by reason of which all F-things are F-things.
> SP3 There is at least one kind by which F-things do not differ.
> SP4 There is exactly one kind in all F-things, which the word 'F-ness' names (in Greek).

90

SP5   There are at least two F-things.

SP6   All F-things are F by reason of the same thing.

SP7   The word 'F-ness' names the same thing in all F-things (in Greek).

SP8   The word 'F-thing' means the same thing whenever it is applied (in Greek).

SP9   The word 'F-ness' names a kind (in Greek).

SP10 In Greek there is at least one expression, other than 'F-ness,' which is equivalent to 'F-ness.'

SP11 F-ness is not identical with F-things.

The notion of presupposition of a question that we have employed in this analysis contains the idea that a question is invalid or illegitimate (i.e. has no true answer) unless all the presuppositions (primary and secondary ones) of the question are true. Given this and our analysis, two important questions arise about Socratic primary questions: (1) Are all the presuppositions (at any rate, are all the presuppositions we have identified) of Socratic primary questions true? (2) How far was Socrates aware of the presuppositions of his questions? In the rest of the chapter we shall have brief discussions of these two questions.

(1) Though we do not have enough knowledge to determine whether these presuppositions are true, it is clear that none of them is obviously or evidently true and that most of them are controversial. Thus SP1 seems to involve the whole question of the existence of kinds or universals: abstract entities such as courage, which are not identical with their instances, courageous things; though not necessarily entities that exist separately from their instances − for nothing in Socrates' primary questions commits them to the separate existence of kinds. Again, SP2 is by no means evidently true: for it would seem that often we can give several reasons for a thing being of a certain kind. For example, we can say that a particular triangle is equiangular because it has three equal angles; or because it has three equal sides. Or, again, we can say that a number is even because it is divisible by two without a remainder; or because it is the successor of an odd number. So it would seem that SP2 presupposes a distinction between different kinds of reasons. In the next chapter we shall see that it is probable that the kind referred to by SP2 is only the kind given by a Socratic definition; though this by no means settles the matter, since it is arguable that one might have two equally correct definitions of the same kind, and indeed Socrates himself gives two definitions of figure in the *Meno* 75−6.[19] Similar remarks apply to SP6. SP3,

that there is at least one kind by reason of which F things do not differ, is ambiguous. If 'at least one kind but not necessarily F-ness' is meant, the proposition can be satisfied trivially either by finding a property that no F-things have or by finding any property that they all have. On the other hand, if 'at least one kind, namely F-ness' is meant, SP3 will be false in all cases where a substituend for 'F' is ambiguous; thus it is false (to take an example from English) that there is at least one kind, namely brotherhood, by which all brothers do not differ. Thus SP3 needs a qualification concerning ambiguity. The same remarks apply to SP4, SP7, and SP8, all of which are such that their substitution instances would mention Greek expressions and would be about expressions in the Greek language; all of them are false unless qualifications are added relating to the existence of ambiguity in the Greek language. Presumably Plato would not be averse to adding such qualifications since he uses words ambiguously often (see, for example, the different senses that ἔργον has in *Cratylus*, 383CD and 390D), and he explicitly recognizes ambiguity in the *Gorgias* (482E), where he has Callicles attack an argument by Socrates on the ground that the word καλόν was used with different senses in different premises. Just what the qualifications would be, however, is not clear. Nor is it clear how Socrates would proceed to determine that a given term is ambiguous independently of and before he has a definition of at least one of the several kinds the term may signify. SP9 and SP10 are about the Greek language, and again not evidently true. Possibly, SP9 says no more than that abstract words in the Greek language name abstract entities, where by the latter we mean such things as kinds, qualities, conditions, and by 'names' we mean 'purports to name.' Then, possibly, SP9 is true by definition or by a definitional characterization of 'abstract words.'[20] SP10 is, of course, ambiguous, depending upon what is meant by 'equivalent.' It is clear enough, however, that whether 'equivalent' is taken to mean 'synonymous' or 'intentionally equivalent' or 'extentionally equivalent,' it would take a considerable and difficult investigation to discover whether SP10 is true. Finally, in the case of SP5, that there are at least two F-things, it is not entirely clear that instances of this sentence are presupposed by Socratic primary questions. But, aside from this, SP5 presents problems. SP5 seems to be false, as it stands, since there are adjectives and common nouns in the Greek language that are not true of anything. Further, if Socrates presupposed that there are at least two instances of the kind about which he asks his primary question, that would mean that his primary question would be invalid or illegitimate whenever raised about uninstantiated kinds; and since his primary question is a request for a definition, that would imply in turn that uninstantiated kinds have no true definition. In view of these unpleasant consequences, perhaps we should interpret SP5 to mean 'there are at least two F-things, actual or possible,' where by 'possible' we mean 'imaginable' and/or 'describable.' This interpretation becomes very plausible when we see, in the next chapter, that for the discovery and testing of Socratic definitions imaginable and/or describable instances are sufficient; it is not necessary to suppose that there are actual instances.

By way of qualification, it should be said that it is not entirely clear that Socrates commits himself to the very general primary and secondary presuppositions we have attributed to him. It is clear that he commits himself to the presuppositions of the question, 'What is courage?' and of the question, 'What is piety?' and of all the other primary questions that he in fact raises. But it is not entirely clear that he commits himself to the very general view that one can raise his primary question in every case of a word (or phrase) that is applied to many things. Most of the time Socrates is interested in the particular question he is asking, and most of the time he is engaged in piecemeal analysis. It is only in the *Meno* that we have an extended general discussion of his primary questions and his definitions. And here there is at least one passage in which he seems to commit himself explicitly to the view that whenever one 'name' (word) is applied to many things his primary question is appropriate (*Meno*, 74D):

> but since you call these many things by one single name, and say of none of these that it is not figure, even though these are opposed to one another, what is it, which comprises the round no less than the straight, which you name figure, and say of the round that it is no less figure than the straight?

In sum, Socrates' primary questions presuppose a surprisingly large number of propositions of sweeping generality and importance; propositions none of which are evidently true and most of which are highly controversial. Most of these propositions are about kinds or univerals and about general terms and abstract singulars in the Greek language.

(2) When we are dealing with Socrates, a philosopher as wary as he was of what he was committing himself to, it is worth asking how far he was aware of what he was committing himself to by the primary questions he was asking, i.e., how far he was aware of the presuppositions of his questions. Needless to say, a man may ask a question without being aware of all of its presuppositions. In iden-

tifying the presuppositions of Socrates' primary questions we have not been implying that Socrates was aware of all of them. We would expect that Socrates is aware of the primary presupposition of the long version of his primary question, since the primary presupposition is 'derived' pretty directly from the long version of his question. And it would not be surprising if he were aware of some of the secondary presuppositions of his questions. And we do in fact find Socrates making certain preliminary inquiries and securing agreement on certain points before he presents his respondent with the long version of his primary question; and in these agreements we find some of the presuppositions we have stated. Thus in the *Euthyphro* we find the following preliminaries:

> What do you say is the nature of piety and impiety, both in relation to murder and other things? Is not holiness always the same with itself in every action, and, on the other hand, is not unholiness the opposite of all holiness, being the same with itself . . .? [5D]
> But, Euthyphro, you say that many other things are holy [besides prosecuting your father for murder], do you not?
> Why, so they are.
> Now call to mind that this is not what I asked you, to tell me one or two of the many holy acts, but that kind itself by which all holy things are holy; for you said that it is by one kind (characteristic) that holy things are holy and unholy things unholy. [6D]

In these passages we find SP1, SP2, SP5, and SP6, or rather instances of these general presuppositions for the case of holiness. Again in the *Laches* we find the following preliminaries (191E):

> for I take it, Laches, there are courageous people in all these cases [in addition to the case of courageous persons in battle that Laches has previously mentioned].
> tell me first what is this thing, courage, which is the same in all these cases.

Here we have explicitly SP5 and SP1. There are many preliminaries in the *Meno*; we give two passages:

> Do you say it is by being bees that they are of many and various kinds and differ from each other, or does their difference lie not in that, but in something else — for example, in their beauty or size or some other quality? Tell me, what would be your answer to this question?
> *Meno* Why, this — that they do not differ, as bees, one from the other. [72B]

Do you consider that there is one health for a man, and another for a woman? Or, wherever we find health, is it the same kind everywhere, whether in a man or anyone else?

Meno I think that health is the same, both in a man and in woman.

Soc. Then is it not so with size and strength also? If a woman is strong, she is strong by reason of the same kind and the same strength (as the kind and the strength by which a strong man is strong); by the 'same' I mean that strength does not differ as strength (relative to strength), whether in a man or in a woman. Or do you think there is any difference?

Meno I do not. [72DE]

In these passages we find presuppositions SP3 and SP2, and SP6. In the *Hippias Major* we also have some preliminaries (287CD):

> Stranger from Elis, is it not by justice that the just are just? . . .
>
> *Hipp.* I shall answer that it is by justice.
> *Soc.* Then this, I mean justice, is something?
> *Hipp.* Certainly. . . .
> *Soc.* Then are not all beautiful things beautiful by the beautiful?
> *Hipp.* Yes, by the beautiful.
> *Soc.* By the beautiful, which is something?
> *Hipp.* Yes, for what alternative is there?
> *Soc.* Tell me, then, . . . What is this, the beautiful?
> *Hipp.* Well, Socrates, does he who asks this question want to find out anything else than what is beautiful?
> *Soc.* I do not think that is what he wants to find out, but what the beautiful is.
> *Hipp.* And what difference is there between the two?

Here we find explicit the presuppositions that there are kinds and that kinds are not identical with their instances (SP11), both secondary presuppositions of Socratic primary questions.

So far as I know SP7, SP8, SP9, and SP10 are never explicitly stated in Socratic Dialogues. And though perhaps a case can be made out that, since SP7, SP8, and SP9 are directly implied by the primary presuppositions, Socrates was in some significant sense aware of them, I know of no evidence whatsoever that Socrates realized that he was committing himself to SP10.

It would seem from these preliminaries, then, that Socrates was aware of most of the presuppositions he was committing himself to when raising his primary questions. The preliminaries also show, however, that he did not seem to realize that none of his presuppositions were obviously true or that some needed qualifications and others argument or evidence: for almost all the preliminaries are given in question-and-answer sessions without argument. Plato in later dialogues argues for some of the presuppositions of Socratic primary questions: for example, he argues for the existence of kinds. But in the Socratic Dialogues, the presuppositions we have identified seem to be taken for granted.

IV

Socratic Definitions

Introduction

Several of Plato's Socratic Dialogues are quests for definitions of the various Greek virtues. Aristotle tells us that Socrates was the *first* thinker who sought definitions:[1]

> Now Socrates devoted his attention to the moral virtues, and was the first to seek universal definitions concerning these things . . .; and he did well to ask what a thing is; for he sought to reason logically, and what a thing is is the beginning of logical reasoning . . . . There are two innovations which may be justly attributed to Socrates, inductive reasoning and universal definitions. Both of these are about the beginning of scientific knowledge.

Socrates was not only the first thinker to seek definitions; he also had definite ideas about what sorts of things definitions are, what definitions are for, and what makes for an adequate definition. In this chapter we shall attempt to give an accurate description of Socrates' theory of definition; we shall also include a critical discussion of some problems in Socrates' theory and a comparison to modern theories of definition.

We shall begin by listing in section 1 all the definitions found in the Socratic Dialogues; we shall use the definitions on this list as data for various generalizations we make about Socratic definitions and as a basis for correcting various common misunderstandings about them. In section 2 we shall describe the various forms and syntax that Socrates allows definitions to take, and the forms that he excludes; in modern terminology, we shall be describing the syntactics of Socrates' definitions. In section 3 we shall ask what Socratic definitions are about and whether Socratic definitions are true or false; in modern terminology, we shall try to describe the semantics of Socratic definitions. The last two sections should give us a fairly accurate and detailed idea of what sorts of things Socratic definitions are. In section 4 we shall describe the uses to which Socrates puts definitions and the purposes for which he seeks definitions; in modern terminology, we shall describe the pragmatics of Socratic definitions. In section 5 we shall try to formulate the criteria for an adequate Socratic definition.

1 *A list of all the definitions in the Socratic Dialogues*

The following is a list of all the definitions in the Socratic Dialogues, which are accepted by Socrates as syntactically or formally correct though not necessarily as true or adequate. I divide these definitions into two groups. Group A contains all the definitions offered by interlocutors, accepted by Socrates as syntatically or formally correct, but which at the same time he rejects as untrue or inadequate. These definitions are usually rejected either on the basis of counter-examples that show the definitions to be either too broad or too narrow; or on the basis of arguments that show that a proposed definition, together with other propositions accepted by Socrates and/or the interlocutors, lead to a contradiction of some propositions that Socrates and/or the interlocutors believe and which they are not willing to give up. Socrates' rejection of Laches' definition of courage in the *Laches* is an example of the first type of rejection; Socrates' rejection of Euthyphro's first (formally correct) definition of piety is an example of the second type of rejection. Group B contains all the definitions offered by Socrates himself, either as examples of the sorts of definitions he wants or as correct definitions which he uses as premises in arguments. The definitions of 'quickness' in the *Laches* and of 'figure' in the *Meno* are of the first kind; the definition of 'fear' or 'dread' in the *Laches* and the *Protagoras* is of the second kind.

Group A

1 What is dear to the gods is the holy, what is not dear, the unholy. [*Euthyphro*, 7A]
2 That which all the gods love is the holy, that which all the gods hate the unholy. [*ibid.*, 9D]
3 The part of the just that pertains to the gods' service is the holy. [*ibid.*, 12D]
4 Holiness is the art (science) of asking of and giving to the gods. [*ibid.*, 14D]

5   Courage is a certain endurance of the soul. [*Laches*, 192B]

6   Courage is wise endurance. [*ibid*., 192D]

7   Courage is the knowledge of what is to be dreaded or dared in war or in anything else. [*ibid*., 195A]

8   Temperance is the doing of everything orderly and quietly. [*Charm*., 159D]

9   Temperance is a kind of quietness. [*ibid*., 159B]

10   Temperance is modesty. [*ibid*., 160E]

11   Temperance is the doing of one's own business. [*ibid*., 161B]

12   Temperance is the doing of good things. [*ibid*., 163E]

13   Temperance is the knowing of oneself. [*ibid*., 164DE]

14   Temperance is the science of the other sciences and itself. [*ibid*., 166E]

15   Virtue is (the) rejoicing in fair things and the being able to get them. [*Meno*, 77B]
Virtue is the wanting of good things and the being able to get them. [*ibid*., 78B — a restatement of 15]

16   Virtue is the power to get good things. [*ibid*., 78C]

17   Rhetoric is a creator (producer) of persuasion. [*Gorg*., 453A]
(Rhetoric is the persuading through speeches, judges in courts, councilmen in councils, assemblymen in the assembly, or any others at any meeting that may be held in public affairs.) [Georgias' first definition at 452E — a restatement of 17]

18   Rhetoric is the art of creating persuasion in law courts and public meetings concerning what is just and unjust. [*ibid*., 454B]

19   The just (by nature) is the ruling and the advantage of the stronger over the weaker. [*ibid*., 483D — amplified by Socrates at 488B]

20   The just and the fair by nature is this — I tell you now quite frankly — that the man who lives correctly must let his desires be as strong as possible and not chasten them, and must be able to minister to them when they are at their height through manliness and intelligence, and must fulfil each desire in turn with what it desires. [*ibid*., 492A]

21   The sophist is the knower of wise things. [*Prot.*, 312C]

22   Justice is truth telling and paying back what one has received from anyone. [*Rep*., 331C]

23   The just is the giving back to each the things owed him. [*ibid*., 331E]

24   The just is the rendering to each what is appropriate to him. [*ibid*., 332C]

25 Justice is the treating of friends well and enemies badly. [*ibid.*, 332D]

26 The just is nothing else than the advantage of the stronger. [*ibid.*, 338C]

27 The beautiful is the appropriate. [*Hip. Maj.*, 293E]

28 The beautiful is the useful. [*ibid.*, 295C]

29 The beautiful is the beneficial. [*ibid.*, 296E]

30 The beautiful is the pleasant through hearing and sight. [*ibid.*, 298A]

31 The beautiful is useful pleasure.[2] [*ibid.*, 303E]

Group B

32 I call quickness the power that gets many things done in a little time, whether in speech or in a race or all other things. [*Laches*, 192AB]

33 Fear is the expectation of future evil. [*ibid.*, 198B; *Prot.*, 358D]

34 Figure is the only existing thing that always follows color. [*Meno*, 75B]

35 That in which the solid ends, that is figure. [*ibid.*, 76A] (Figure is limit of solid)

36 Color is effluence of figures, commensurate with sight and sensible. [*ibid.*, 76D]

37 Cowardice is ignorance of what is dreadful and not dreadful. [*Prot.*, 360CD]

38 Courage is the wisdom of dreadful and non-dreadful things. [*ibid.*, 360D]

39 The fair is the pleasant or the good or both. [*Gorg.*, 475A]

40 The foul is the painful or the evil or both. [*ibid.*, 475A]

41 The function of a horse or anything else is that which one can do only with it or best with it. [*Rep.*, 352E]

Sometimes the reader of Plato, having gone through dialogue after dialogue in which Socrates refutes all the proposed definitions, forms the impression, not entirely unreasonably, that it is impossible to give a definition that will satisfy Socrates; perhaps even the impression that Socrates is trying to show that it is impossible to define anything. The definitions in group B serve to correct these impressions. The refutations of definitions in group A serve many purposes: they show that Socrates objected to some of the most dominant ethical ideas of his contemporaries (e.g., the ideas represented by the definitions of piety and justice); they show that Socrates found that his contemporaries had very unclear ideas of the ethical qualities they praised; the refutations also reveal some of the conditions that Socrates thinks a good or adequate definition must satisfy; and the refutations certainly show that it is difficult to discover and construct adequate definitions of ethical and other properties. But they do not show that it is impossible to satisfy Socrates or that Socrates thought it impossible to discover adequate definitions. The existence of definitions of group B, as well as later dialogues such as the *Republic*, in which Plato constructs and defends complex definitions of ethical qualities, shows that Socrates thought that the search for definitions is a viable and fruitful philosophical enterprise.

2 *The syntax and forms of Socratic definitions*

I have tried to make the translations of the definitions in our groups as literal as possible; even so the English does not always reflect faithfully the grammar and syntax of the Greek. The remarks below about the syntax of Socratic definitions hold true of the Greek, but not necessarily of the English translations.

In all the definitions the *definiendum term* (i.e., the term or expression used to denote what is defined) is a singular term or expression; i.e., it is a term or expression in the singular, which usually begins with the definite article, and which purports to refer to one and only one thing. In all our definitions the definiendum term is a feminine abstract noun or a neuter adjective with the definite article or a noun with the definite article; and it is substantive.

In all our definitions the *definiens term or expression* (i.e. the expression used to denote that by which what is defined is defined) is also a singular term, i.e. a term in the singular which usually begins with the definite article and which purports to denote one and only one thing (though not necessarily a simple or non-complex thing); and it is also substantive. There seems to be no further grammatical or syntactical agreement between definiendum and definiens; though some definiens are feminine abstracts or neuter adjectives with the definite article, other definiens are articular infinitives, relative clauses, and so on. So long as the definiens expression is a singular expression or term, Socrates seems content to allow considerable grammatical and syntactical variety.

A partial agreement that obtains between definiendum and definiens is that both are in the nominative case, except where the definitions are introduced by verbs of saying or thinking; in these cases, where the definitions occur within indirect discourse, the definiendum expression is in the accusative, as usual.

Finally, it should be noted that in all the definitions both the definiendum expressions and the definiens expressions appear to be abstract expressions, though it is not clear that the distinction between abstract and concrete expression is a matter of syntax rather than semantics.[3]

These brief general remarks about the grammar and syntax of Socratic definitions contain no surprises. They are in complete agreement with the way in which Socrates characterizes what is to be defined. In the case of piety, for example, the long version of his primary question, i.e. the question by which he requests a definition of piety, is:

> What is the kind which (a) is one and the same in all pious things, (b) is that by which all pious things are pious, (c) is that by which all pious things do not differ at all but are all the same, and (d) is that which in all pious things you call 'piety'? (see chapter III)

Clearly, Socrates presupposes that piety is a quality, property, or universal, and that there is one and only one such quality; given this, and given Smyth's explanation of an abstract word, we should clearly expect that in a definition of piety the definiendum expression will be an abstract singular term and the definiens expression will also be an abstract singular term. And this is exactly what we get.

Next I will consider the various forms that the definitions in our list have, and forms of definition excluded or simply missing.

All the definitions in our list are what Pap calls general (connotative) definitions. None of the definitions are definitions by example (denotative), whether ostensive or non-ostensive.[4] Moreover, definitions by example are explicitly excluded by Socrates, on the ground that they are not answers to his question — which is true of the long version of his primary question. This is what he seems to do in the case of the very first answers that Euthyphro, Laches and Meno give to the questions, What is piety? What is courage? and What is virtue? We saw in the last chapter that the way in which Socrates rejects a list of examples as an answer is by amplifying his primary questions into their long version; and to these questions a list of examples would not count as an answer (true or false, correct or incorrect).

Within general definitions, Socrates allows a considerable variety, a greater variety than Aristotle allows, who seems to confine definitions to those having the form of genus and difference. He also allows a greater variety than Plato allows in middle and late Dialogues. In his useful paper on Socratic definitions Nakhnikian notes that:[5]

the method of division is not merely a new recipe for discovering definitions. It is also a somewhat new theory of what a definition is. For Plato definition is analysis by a genus and a specific difference. For Socrates it is that, but not exclusively.

Whether or not Nakhnikian is correct about Plato, he is certainly correct about Socrates, that is, of course, Plato's Socrates. In our groups we have definitions by genus and difference: 3, 6, 31 seem clear examples of such definitions. We also have several definitions by simple synonym (as distinct from a definition in which the definiens is an analysis of the definiendum): 10, 27, 28, 29 are clear examples. We also have several disjunctive definitions, including some that Socrates himself offers: 39, 40 are clear examples of disjunctive definitions. Finally, there is a group of definitions that we might call definitions by conjunctive enumeration as distinct from definitions by genus and difference.[6] Definition 8 ('Temperance is the doing of everything orderly and quietly') is clearly a conjunctive definition which is not of the genus-difference type; so are 14, 15, 19, 22, and 25.

There are definitions in our list, perhaps the majority of them, that it is difficult to place within the four groups of the last paragraph. Perhaps Nakhnikian is right in saying that 'the vast majority' of these definitions are by genus and difference: thus, in addition to 3, 6, and 31 that were previously mentioned, 4, 7, 16, 17, 18, 21, 26, 30, 32, 33, 35, 36, 37, 38 may plausibly be thought to be definitions by genus and difference. Still, there remain some on our list that resist classification; witness 1, 2, 11, 12, 13, 23, 24. This suggests, once more, that within the class of general definitions Socrates allows almost unlimited freedom of expression.

All of the definitions in our list are explicit definitions; none are contextual definitions, recursive definitions, or axiomatic definitions. Unlike definitions by example, however, these last three groups of definitions are not excluded by Socrates; they are simply missing. This suggests that Socrates is not aware of definitions of this kind — not a surprising fact if Aristotle is right in saying that Socrates was the first to be concerned with definitions; whether, had he been aware of them, he would have allowed them we do not know.

We can summarize our results by presenting Pap's formal classification of definitions, adding to it, however, our class of definitions by conjunctive enumeration (see Figure 1).

We end this section by noting that the presence of the two disjunctive definitions in our list, 39 and 40, is surprising. Definitions of this kind do not seem to conform to the Socratic conception of

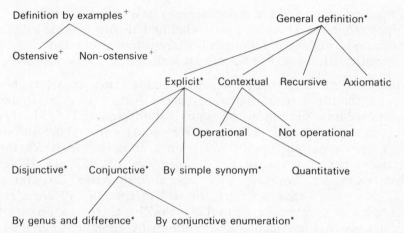

Figure 1 Formal classification of definitions, and summary of our results

+ = definitions of this kind are excluded by Socrates and not found in our list
* = definitions of this kind allowed by Socrates and found in our list
unmarked categories = definitions of this kind not found in our list

definition as revealed by the long version of the primary question by which Socrates asks for definitions. Consider definition 39: 'The fair is the pleasant or the good or both.' If Socrates were to ask for a definition of the fair, he would be asking the following question:

> What is the kind that (a) is one and the same in all fair things, (b) is that by which fair things do not differ, (c) is that by which in all fair things are fair, and (d) is that which in all fair things you call the fair?

Socrates plainly is asking for something, a kind or property or a complex of kinds or properties, that is common to all fair things. But definition 39 can be true even though neither the pleasant nor the good is common to all fair things; the definition would be true if some fair things were pleasant but not beneficial and the remaining fair things were beneficial but not pleasant. And similarly with any other disjunctive definition: the definiens of a disjunctive definition does not give us something that is common to all members of the class denoted by the definiendum; the definition does not therefore satisfy the Socratic demand for something common. It may be objected that even though none of the disjuncts that form the definiens of a disjunctive definition may be common to all members of the definiendum class when the definition is true, nevertheless the total disjunction of properties is common to all members of the definiendum class when the definition is true. Thus, assuming the definition of the fair to be true, even though it does not follow that being pleasant is common to all fair things, nor does it follow that being beneficial is common to all fair things, nevertheless it follows that being pleasant or beneficial is common to all fair things: the simple property of being pleasant may not be common and the simple property of being beneficial may not be common, but the complex disjunctive property of being pleasant or beneficial is common to all fair things. Therefore, definitions of this kind do satisfy the Socratic request for something common. This objection, however, seems unsatisfactory: for it seems to employ a sense of 'common to all' that is not the Socratic sense and appears indeed to be trivial. For if we allow the Socratic demand for something common to all instances of a kind to be satisfied by a complex disjunctive property, the demand can be met trivially by simply finding a property for each instance and then listing these properties disjunctively. All the instances of any kind you please will have as many of these disjunctive properties in common as you please; and all the members of any set you please will have as many of these disjunctive properties in common as you please. This is clearly not what Socrates means by 'having something in common.' We may avoid some of the triviality of disjunctive definitions if we confine the disjuncts to species of the definiendum: in a disjunctive definition we list disjunctively all the species of the definiendum, as for example in the definition: a sibling is a brother or a sister. It is possible that this is a restriction Socrates had in mind; the two disjunctive definitions he offers could be viewed as giving a disjunction of the species of the definiendum; in that case he could have regarded the total complex disjunctive property as being something all instances of the definiendum have in common, without seeing the threat of trivialization of the notion of having something in common.

To avoid misunderstanding, it should be said that the difficulty we noted regarding disjunctive definitions is a difficulty only relative to the Socratic demand that a definition give something that is common to all instances of the definiendum. It is not a difficulty in any absolute sense. It should also be said that this difficulty does not arise with regard to conjunctive definitions, since in the case of such definitions each conjunct must be common to all instances of the definiendum. It is also possible of course that Socrates would not accept disjunctive definitions, though the fact remains that 39 and 40 are definitions he himself offers and also uses in arguments.

3 *The semantics of Socratic definitions*

In this section we will attempt to answer three questions: (1) What is defined in a Socratic definition, according to Socrates? (2) Does a Socratic definition have a truth-value, according to Socrates? (3) What is the relation between definiendum and definiens, according to Socrates?

(1) It is clear from the various characterizations that Socrates gives of what is to be defined (quoted below) that it is not a word or an expression that Socrates seeks to define or invites the interlocutors to define. Socratic definitions are not, therefore, nominal definitions. For a nominal definition is always a definition of a word or expression of a given language and it is always relative to a language.[7] A nominal definition may be either a proposal that a word be used in a certain way by speakers of a given language, or a proposition, true or false, purporting to describe how speakers of the language of that word actually use that word. An example of the former type is: Let us use the word 'sterspin' to refer to all women over forty who have never been married and only to such women. This is obviously a stipulation, and has no truth-value. An example of the latter type is: In English competent speakers of that language use the word 'sibling' to refer to a brother or sister and to nothing else. This is clearly an empirical proposition of the sort found in dictionaries; it is true or false, and its truth or falsity can be determined by investigating how competent speakers use the word in speech and writing. In none of the passages in which Socrates asks for and discusses definitions is there the slightest evidence to suggest that Socrates is concerned with nominal definitions, either of the stipulative variety or the variety found in dictionaries (called by Copi 'reportive definitions').

In the *Meno*, in which a definition of virtue is sought and which contains the most sophisticated discussion of definition in the early Dialogues, Socrates gives us a number of characterizations of what is to be defined. These characterizations are the same as those found in the long version of his primary question – which would be, in the case of virtue, as follows:

> What is the kind that (a) is one and the same in all virtues, (b) is that by which all virtues are virtues, (c) is that by which all virtues do not differ but are the same, and (d) is that which in all virtues we call by the name 'virtue'?

Thus at 72B he says that if one were to ask what a bee is, one would be asking what that is 'by which they [bees] do not differ but are all the same.' At 72C he says that, though the virtues are many and various, 'they all have some form [kind, property – εἶδος] one and the same, through which they are virtues, at which one would do well to be looking who is answering someone who asks that this be made clear — what virtue really is.' And at 74D he says:

we are always arriving at many things, but let me have no more of that; but since you call these many things by some one name, and say of none of these that it is not figure, even though these are opposed to one another, what is it, which comprises the round no less than the straight, which you name figure, and say of the round that it is not less figure than the straight?

Clearly, then, Socrates seeks a definition of virtue in which what is defined is, he thinks, an εἶδος (form, kind, property) which is one and the same in all the virtues, by which virtues do not differ but are all the same, by reason of which the virtues are virtues, and which we call by the name 'virtue.' He does not always characterize what is to be defined as an εἶδος: in the *Euthyphro* he does, but in the *Laches*, for example, he characterizes courage, which he asks the interlocutors to define, and quickness, which he himself defines, as powers; and in other places he is silent as to what sort of thing it is, beyond (a), (b), (c), and (d). We should then perhaps be wary of attributing to Socrates, as Nakhnikian does, the view that what is defined in the sort of definition he seeks is always an εἶδος or a property, especially in view of the fact that, again as Nakhnikian points out, we have no criterion for identity of properties. Further, we have noted that Socrates uses two sorts of definiendum terms: an abstract feminine noun and a singular term formed by a neuter adjective preceded by the definite article; in some cases Socrates uses both kinds of terms within the same context, as in the case of the *Euthyphro*, where what is defined is sometimes piety and sometimes the pious. This may reflect a vacillation between thinking of what is to be defined as an attribute (quality, property, or relation) which serves to collect all the objects that have that attribute into a set; and thinking of what is to be defined as a pre-eminent or paradigmatic member of a set, which again may serve to collect all the other members of the set by some such relation as resemblance. Such a vacillation would not be suprising since we find just such a vacillation later in Plato's theory of forms, in the case of beauty, for example.[8]

There is no evidence in the Socratic dialogues with which we are concerned that Socrates thought of what is to be defined as existing apart from its instances; he speaks of it as something that all its instances have[9] and as something that is in all its instances.[10] Socrates does sometimes raise the question whether what is to be defined exists; at any rate he makes sure that its existence is granted[11] or he gives an argument that it exists.[12] But he does not raise the question whether what is to be defined exists separately from its instances. Nor does Socrates tell us what he means by characterizing what is to be defined as something that is one and the same in all its instances. In *Meno*, 72A, he does make a try: by saying that it is by the same εἶδος and the same strength that women and men are strong, he means, he says, that 'the strength does not differ with respect to strength, whether in a man or in a woman.' This does not help much in understanding what he means by 'the same in all' or 'one and the same in all.' But his language suggests that what is defined is an attribute, something that is common to all members of a class, rather than a pre-eminent or paradigmatic member of a class; for the latter could hardly be said to be something that 'is in all the members of the class' or something 'which is one and the same in all the members of the class.'

All things considered, then, perhaps the best answer we can give to our question — What is defined in a Socratic definition, according to Socrates? — is this: the definiendum of a Socratic definition of F-ness or the F is probably an attribute, which (a) is one and the same in all things that are F, (b) is that by reason of which all F things are F, (c) is that by which all F things do not differ but are all the same, and (d) is that which in all F things we call 'F-ness' or 'the F'.[13]

(2) In the *Euthyphro* (7A), after Euthyphro has understood that Socrates wants a general definition of piety, not a definition by examples, and he has produced his first definition ('The pious is the loved by the gods'), Socrates makes the following comment:

> Excellent, Euthyphro; now you have answered as I asked you to answer. However, whether it is true, I am not yet sure; but you will, of course, show that what you say is true.

This is the most explicit passage in which Socrates speaks of the truth (or falsity) of a definition. Clearly he thinks that definitions of the kind he seeks to discover are true or false. In other places, though he does not use the notion of truth, he uses related concepts; thus at *Laches* 192B we are told that Socrates' definition of quickness is correct (ὀρθῶς γε σὺ λέγων), and at 193D Laches' definition of courage as wise endurance is said not to be correct (οὐ καλῶς λέγειν). In addition to these explicit statements, Socrates' treatment of proposed definitions shows that he thinks them to be statements that are true or false, correct or incorrect: for the minute a general definition is given by an interlocutor

Socrates proceeds to test it, either by trying to imagine counter-examples or by investigating whether the definition is consistent with other statements that the interlocutor affirms as true. In answer to our question (2) — whether definitions are true or false statements according to Socrates — we can say, then, that Socrates clearly believes that the kind of definitions he seeks are true or false, correct or incorrect.

(3) What is the relation between definiendum and definiens in a Socratic definition, according to Socrates? This is a difficult question which Socrates does not give us much help to answer. There appear to be two main alternatives. (a) In a Socratic definition what is asserted is that the class of things that have the definiendum as an attribute is identical to the class of things that have the definiens as an attribute; or, that the definiendum term and the definiens term are extentionally equivalent. This alternative is compatible with the two attributes not being identical. (b) In a Socratic definition what is asserted is that the attribute that is the definiendum is identical with the attribute that is the definiens. If the two attributes are identical, then of course the corresponding classes are identical.

Socrates supposes that at least extentional equivalence is asserted in a definition of the proper form. This is shown by the fact that he asks for what is common to all instances of the definiendum and by the fact that he often criticizes a proposed definition for being too wide. Thus he does not question that Laches' first definition — (5) Courage is a certain endurance of the soul (192B) — contains an element, endurance of the soul, that is common to all cases of courage. But he does criticize the definition for being too wide; for, he says, there are cases of endurance of the soul that are not noble whereas courage is always noble. Similarly, Gorgias' definition (17) is criticized for being too wide. If the attribute that is the definiens must be common to all instances of the attribute that is the definiendum, and if there must be nothing that is an instance of the definiens and not an instance of the definiendum, it follows that for a definition to be true the definiendum and the definiens attributes must collect classes that are identical, i.e. have exactly the same members; or, to put it in an equivalent way, it follows that for a definition to be true the definiens expression and the definiendum expression must be extentionally equivalent. This much is fairly clear.

Does Socrates also suppose that in a Socratic definition — assuming that what is defined is an attribute — it is asserted that the attribute that is the definiens is identical with the attribute that is the definiendum? This is the difficult question. Nakhnikian argues that 'Socrates construes the relation between *definiens* and *definiendum* as one of property identity. . . .'[14] Nakhnikian cites as evidence the refutation of the definition of temperance as modesty in the *Charmides*, 160E—161B, arguing that[15]

> Socrates is not content merely with the observation that there is no perfect coincidence between the class of temperate men and the class of modest men. He goes on to argue to the conclusion that the *property* of temperance is not the same as the *property* of modesty.

The argument is not as clear, perhaps, as Nakhnikian supposes; nor is the next similar argument against the definition of temperance as quietness; nor is the similar argument in the *Laches*, 192CD, against the definition of courage as endurance. Consider the last of these arguments: courage is praiseworthy (*kalon*). Endurance with wisdom is praiseworthy and good, whereas endurance with folly is bad and harmful and hence not praiseworthy. Therefore, endurance is not courage, since endurance is not [always?] praiseworthy whereas courage is [always?] praiseworthy. We do not know whether this argument amounts to a denial of extentional equivalence between courage and endurance, which would be sufficient for overthrowing the definition, or to a denial of the identity of the property of courage and the property of endurance. We do not know this because the predications ('Courage is praiseworthy' and 'Endurance with folly is not praiseworthy') in the argument have just the kind of ambiguity recently noticed by Professor Gregory Vlastos.[16] 'Courage is praiseworthy' may mean that whatever is courageous is also praiseworthy, or it may mean that the property itself, courage, is praiseworthy, and similarly with the other predications in the argument. Taken in the first way, the argument would amount to a denial of extentional equivalence; taken in the second way, the argument would amount to a denial of identity. It is of course true that a denial of extentional equivalence entails a denial of property identity. But the point is that if we take the argument in the second way we have Socrates denying property identity *directly*, i.e. without bothering with extentional equivalence at all, and this *would* show that he took the definition to be asserting property identity. The same comments are true of the other arguments we cited since they have the same ambiguity.

Richard Sharvy, in a fine recent paper, denies that property identity is involved in Socratic definitions:[17]

> When Moore and Hare are talking about defining good or saying

110

what 'good' means, they are sometimes talking about saying what good *is* (*identical to*) or about what 'good' is synonymous with. When Socrates and Aristotle talk about defining something or saying what it is, they are not talking about what it is (identical to) or about meaning as synonymy; rather, they are talking about what it *is* (*by analysis*), or, meaning as analysis. The question of *what piety is* is not a question about what piety is identical to, for, as everybody knows, piety is identical to piety and is not identical to anything else. The question is what piety *is by analysis*; that is, what is the what-it-is-to-be of piety; that is, what is it to be pious?

Earlier, Sharvy denies that 'is defined as' is symmetric, and adds:[18]

The concept *male parent* is the analysis or definition of the concept *father*, but not vice versa. . . . So this relation ['=df'], or the relation 'is the analysis of', does not entail identity, and is not symmetric . . . . I believe that (5P) and (6P) can be justified by a theory of definitions as a species of formal cause. Roughly, the justification for (5P) and (6P) is that '=df' entails a kind of 'because', and that a 'because' of that kind is transitive.

Sharvy's paper is subtle and complex and deserves a special study; and the same is true of S. Mark Cohen's related paper on the same argument.[19] We cannot do justice to these papers here; the reader will have to study them separately to understand the issues and the controversy. We can take note of certain points, however, which enhance our understanding of Socratic definitions.

First, Sharvy is probably right in thinking that Socratic definitions, at least some of them, are 'a species of formal cause'; more exactly, perhaps, that the definiens of a Socratic definition is supposed to give the formal cause of something being an instance of the definiendum. The chief evidence for this is that, as we saw, Socrates usually expands his primary question 'What is the F or F-ness?' into a longer version that includes the following characterization of the definiens: 'that by which (by reason of which) whatever is F is F.' As Cohen notices, in the *Euthyphro* (5D7) Socrates begins by asking 'Euthyphro to "say what the pious is"; later, Socrates asks for "the characteristic in virtue of which everything pious is pious".'[20] Cohen and Sharvy agree that Socrates is arguing that the definition, *the pious is the god-loved*, fails precisely because the god-loved fails to be (the?) a characteristic by virtue of which everything that is pious is pious. This interpretation of Socratic definitions coheres very well with the interpretation Vlastos has recently given of Plato's Forms as formal causes or, better, reasons.[21] In Plato's philosophy, presumably, a Form will be defined as a conjunction of Forms, one conjunct being the genus and the other the specific difference. Thus, presumably, if we ask 'Why is this thing figure (rather than, say, color)?' the answer will be 'Because it participates in the Form Limit of Solid, and therefore participates in the Form Figure, since the Form Figure = df. the Form Limit of Solid.' All in all, then, it makes good sense to suppose that Socrates, sometimes at least, supposed that a definition of a kind gives a reason, perhaps *the* reason in the sense of the most conclusive reason, why a thing that is of the defined kind is of that kind. Surprisingly, this important point is not noted by Nakhnikian.

Second, Sharvy seems to be right, in an important sense, in thinking that the relation 'is defined as' ('=df.') or 'is an analysis of' (and we could probably add the relation 'is an explanation of') is not symmetric. The sense is, I think, clearly this: within the same body of knowledge, say Euclidean geometry, if *line* is defined as *length without breadth*, it is not also the case that *length without breadth* is defined as *line*; to have both of these definitions within the same body of knowledge is to have two viciously circular definitions. And possibly the same is true with 'is an analysis of' (and 'is an explanation of'). So far, this is to say that we can have either definition but not both. However, in the case of 'is an analysis of' not only is it false that we can have both; it is also false that we can have either. *Length without breadth* is clearly *an* analysis of *line*; but it is certainly not true that *line* is an analysis of *length without breadth*; whereas, conceivably, depending on what the body of knowledge is and what one uses definitions for, *length without breadth* could be defined as line.[22] We might well use the last definition in order to get someone to understand the notion of length without breadth who already understood the notion of a line, or in a case where we had in our vocabulary the term 'line' but not the term 'length without breadth.' Definitions being many and various and being used for many purposes, clearly the notion of 'is defined as' is wider than the notion of 'is an analysis of.' Presumably, Sharvy does no mean to say that the two notions are co-extensive, but only that 'is an analysis of' is one kind of 'is defined as,' the kind in which definitions are conceived as formal causes. And this perhaps is so.

Sharvy does, however, claim as we saw in the first quote from his paper, that (a) in Socratic definitions the relation 'is defined as' is the relation 'is an analysis of'; that (b) Socratic definitions are not by synonym; and that (c) Socratic definitions do not assert identity of properties. Claims (a) and (b) are partly false, and (c) also may be false.

We can see that claims (a) and (b) are partly false, because definitions 10, 27, 28, 29 are not analyses of the definiendum, and they appear to be definitions by synonym. It will be remembered that Socrates questions the truth of these definitions, he does not question their being definitions; he clearly allows them as candidates for legitimate definitions in contrast to definitions by example which he does not allow. This having been said, however, it must also be said that the great majority of definitions that the interlocutors offer and Socrates allows are definitions by analysis not by synonym; and that *all* the definitions that Socrates himself offers are definitions by analysis. Moreover, in the middle and later Plato all the definitions are by analysis, rather than synonym, and this is true also of all the definitions in Aristotle. Clearly Socrates prefers definitions that analyze the definiendum, and Plato and Aristotle confine definitions to that. When we discuss the pragmatics of Socratic definitions, the uses and purposes of such definitions, we shall see that there is good reason for this preference.

Sharvy's claim (c), that Socratic definitions do not assert identity of properties, is more difficult to assess. I would like, first of all, to observe that while it may be true, as Sharvy says, that the relations '=df.' and 'is an analysis of' do not entail identity, nevertheless these relations are not incompatible with identity. To say what a thing is, or to define a thing by analysis, is to say what the constituent parts of that thing are or that the constituent parts are related in a certain way. This is certainly not incompatible with identifying a thing with the totality of its constituent parts related in a certain way. When Moore was seeking for a definition of goodness he was seeking for the constituent parts of that property; and this is compatible with supposing that a resulting definition would state that the property goodness is identical with the complex of such and such properties related in such and such ways. Socrates' definition of figure may be looked at in that way; it asserts that the property *figure* is identical with the complex property *limit of solid*. The definition, in addition to asserting this identity, is also asserting that figure is defined as limit of solid — this is the point of adding 'df.' to the sign '=.' I do not see then why we could not suppose that the definition, Figure =df Limit of Solid, can be asserting both that figure is identical with limit of solid and also that limit of solid is the definition of, in the sense of an analysis of, figure. The relation '=', which may be extentional equivalence or identity, is symmetrical, but the total relation '=df.' is not symmetrical. In the second place, I wish to point out that questions of identity may be separated in part from questions of synonymy, at least in the following sense: the identity statement, 'Courage is identical with the virtue Socrates sought to define in Plato's *Laches*,' certainly does not entail that the expressions 'courage' and 'the virtue Socrates sought to define in Plato's *Laches*' are synonymous. Similarly, if we interpret Socratic definitions as involving assertions of property identity, this does not commit us to saying that Socratic definitions involve assertions of synonymy between the definiendum expressions and the definiens expressions.

Theoretically, then, we are free to accept Sharvy's claim (modified) that the great majority of Socratic definitions are conceived by Socrates as giving an analysis of the definiendum, and that the definiens is conceived by Socrates as a formal cause of something being an instance of the definiendum; and also Nakhnikian's claim that Socratic definitions assert property identity. The evidence, however, on the question of identity is, as we noted, very much inconclusive. On the whole, the evidence favors Nakhnikian (on the question of identity): especially the consistent use of abstract terms to signify both definiens and definiendum, the widespread use of the feminine abstract (which is clearly the name of a property), and the existence of several definitions by synonym (which would be difficult to interpret as anything but assertions of property identity, especially when the terms used are feminine abstract, as in the case of the definition of temperance as modesty).

We may summarize the results of our discussion in the last two sections as follows. (1) In a Socratic definition the expression used to refer to what is defined is always a singular term, always substantive, and probably always abstract; and the expression used to refer to that by which what is defined is defined is always an expression in the singular, always substantive, and also probably always abstract. (2) A Socratic definition is always a general definition, never a definition by example; it is always an explicit definition, either by genus and difference, or by disjunctive enumeration, or by conjunctive enumeration, or by synonym. (3) In a Socratic definition what is defined is an εἶδος (a kind of attribute), i.e. something that is common to or the same in several things (as distinct from a class or an individual, neither of which can be said to be common to or the same in several things). (4) A Socratic definition states what an εἶδος (kind of attribute) is, i.e., it gives something (a) that is common to all instances of that εἶδος, (b) with respect to which all instances of that εἶδος do not differ, but are the same, (c) by reason of which all instances of that εἶδος are instances of that εἶδος, and (d) which in all instances of that εἶδος we call by the name of that εἶδος. (5) A Socratic definition seems to identify an εἶδος or attribute with a disjunction of attributes neither of which is identical with the defined attribute; or with a conjunction of two attributes neither of which is identical with the defined attribute and one of which is the genus of the defined attribute and the other of which is the specific difference of the defined attribute; or with a conjunction of several attributes none of which is identical with the defined attribute; or with another εἶδος or attribute which is not itself a conjunction or disjunction or any other union of attributes. (6) A Socratic definition has a truth-value. It is true when the asserted identity between definiens and definiendum obtains.

This statement may be regarded as our definition of Socratic definition.

4 *The pragmatics of Socratic definitions*

Why did Socrates seek definitions? We may say confidently that Socrates saw definitions as essential instruments in the search for knowledge.

There are several Dialogues in which Plato has Socrates tell us why he sought definitions, and the uses to which he would put definitions. We may, I think, distinguish three such uses: what I shall call the *diagnostic*, the *aitiological* (or formal cause), and the *epistemic* use.

The diagnostic use

Having made clear to Euthyphro what kind of definitions of holiness or piety he is after, Socrates proceeds to tell us why he wants such a definition (*Euthyphro*, 6D):

> Well then, teach me this *idea* (kind, attribute) itself, what it is, so that by looking at it and using it as a paradigm I may be able to say that that, of the things that you or others do, which is similar to it is holy, and that which is not similar I am able to say is not holy.

Socrates is saying (1) that he wants a definition of holiness so that he may be able to tell whether any given action is holy; and (2) that he would be able to tell by looking at the defined kind, using it as a paradigm or model, and 'seeing' whether the action in question is τοιοῦτον, i.e. similar to it.

Several things need to be noticed about this use. First, Socrates does not tell us how he would be able to tell whether a given action

115

is similar to the defined kind. The phrase, 'by looking and seeing and using as a model,' suggests perhaps something like a comparison between, say, a statue and alleged copies of it to see whether they really are copies. But of course holiness is not a physical thing, so this comparison cannot be meant literally. If we are right in thinking that what is defined is a kind or attribute, then presumably Socrates would be able to say whether a given action is holy by 'seeing' whether the action has the attribute(s) that constitute the *definiens* of the definition. Thus if the definition were, say, the (later rejected) definition of holiness as that which all the gods love, Socrates would be able to say whether, for example, Euthyphro's action of bringing suit against his own father for murder is holy by determining whether this action has the attribute of being loved by all gods.

Second, Socrates does not say or imply that without having a definition of holiness it would be impossible for him to say, in the sense of forming a judgment or belief, that a given action is holy. He only says that by using such a definition he would be able to tell whether a given action is holy. In short, the use of such a definition would be sufficient for determining whether a given action is of the defined kind; it is not necessary, at least not relative to what Socrates says. This is a fundamental point. If Socrates had held the view that the use of a definition of a given kind is necessary to determining whether a given thing is of that kind, he would have committed himself to consequences that are indeed very bad for anyone who makes the discovery and use of definitions an essential part of the search for knowledge. The view would imply, in the first place, that we could not, theoretically, determine whether *all* the kinds or attributes there are have instances unless we had definitions of *all* the kinds of attributes there are — something we cannot have without resorting to viciously circular definitions. In the second place, the view would imply that we could not use instances of a kind as data from which, by generalization or abstraction, we could discover a definition of that kind — since we could not determine whether these things were instances of the kind to be defined without already having that definition. And in the third place, the view implies that we could not use instances of the kind defined as confirming instances or as counter-examples to a proposed definition, since, given this view, this procedure would be viciously circular: for we would be using instances of the defined kind to test the correctness of the definition and also using the definition to test whether the same instances are instances of the defined kind. Fortunately, Socrates does not hold this view, contrary to what Robinson says, and Geach sometimes seems to imply.[23] The diagnostic use, then, implies that the use of a definition of a given kind is a sufficient condition for determining whether a thing is of that kind; it does not imply that it is a necessary condition.

Third, it is noteworthy that Socrates describes the diagnostic use in the context of an ethical controversy as to whether a particular action (Euthyphro's bringing suit against his father for murder) is of the kind whose definition is sought. Euthyphro has already stated that he and his relatives disagree as to whether his action is holy: they heatedly accuse him of *un*holiness while he is sure that what he is doing is holy. Socrates is dubious about the holiness of Euthyphro's action, but he is not sure one way or the other. So we have here a controversy as to whether a particular action is of a given kind, and it is an ethical controversy. This is the context in which Socrates tells us why he wants a definition of holiness. When we couple this with the fact that Socrates sought chiefly definitions of the Greek virtues, and with the fact that in the second half of his life he lived during an age in which the traditional virtues and ideals came under attack (witness the sophists, Aristophanes, and Euripides), we can fairly say that, though the diagnostic use of Socratic definitions is quite general, in all probability Socrates thought of this use chiefly in connection with ethical disputes and uncertainties. In such cases the diagnostic use makes excellent sense: it is like the appeal to an ethical standard or rule or principle, or to a positive law, in order to resolve a dispute as to whether a given action has a certain ethical quality (goodness, rightness, honesty, justice, etc.); and this makes good sense, provided that the definition is not conceived as an arbitrary one, i.e. one that is made up on the spot, as one pleases, and to which one refuses to apply any standard of correctness. To say that it makes good sense is not of course to say that it is without difficulties.

Finally, with respect to determining whether something is of a given kind, the diagnostic use implies that we are better off after we have discovered a definition of that kind than we are beforehand. This is not surprising, especially in the cases where definitions offer an analysis of the definiendum, and in view of the fact that in the case of most attributes we can have borderline and controversial cases. For example, I can generally tell a plane tree from other kinds even though I do not know the definition of plane tree. But if I were asked to pick out all the plane trees in a given forest, I probably would do a lot better if I had a definition of plane tree, i.e. an enumeration of the characteristics on the basis of which trees are classified as plane trees. Again, if a dispute arose as to whether a given tree were a plane tree, or, say, a sycamore tree (which is a very similar species), a definition of at least one species would certainly be helpful, since given the definition we could examine the tree to see whether in fact it had all the characteristics enumerated in the definiens. Again, suppose I were presented with a number of different kinds of things and asked to determine what their functions were; I might or might not be able to do it, but I would certainly be better off if I had Socrates' definition of function: the function of a thing of a given kind is that work that only that kind of thing can do or that work that that kind of thing can do better than any other kind of thing can do. Given this definition I can make observations and conduct experiments to determine whether the various kinds of things presented to me had this or that work as their function. This is a beautiful example of the discovery of a definition enhancing our diagnostic powers, partly perhaps because our preanalytic concept of function is vague, partly because the concept is fairly abstract, complex, and even subtle. Again, in cases of technical or semi-technical concepts, such as, say, the concept of polluted water, the definition of the attribute of being polluted water would help us greatly in determining whether something is polluted water. Even in cases of perfectly familiar, non-technical, and apparently non-vague concepts, such as the concept of water, one would be better off, with respect to determining whether a given volume of liquid is water, knowing the definition of water is H_2O than without it. I have been able to tell whether something is water without ever resorting to chemical analysis to see whether the liquid in question had the composition H_2O. But if someone presented me with a volume of liquid that had the visual, tactile, and taste characteristics by which I usually tell that something is water, and yet claimed that the substance in question were not water, I would certainly be better off in deciding one way or the other if I had the definition; for by analyzing chemically the liquid we can use the results to settle the matter by appeal to the definition. In Euthyphro's own case, a definition would help in a similar way. In a variety of cases, then, some of which we have tried to illustrate, and for a variety of reasons, some of which we have tried to indicate, Socratic definitions (especially those that offer an analysis of the definiendum) enhance our diagnostic powers.

The aitiological use of Socratic definitions

In the *Hippias Major* Socrates introduces his primary question, 'What is the beautiful?' in the following context:

Now, however, give me a brief answer to a question about your discourse, for you reminded me of the beautiful just at the right moment. For recently, most excellent friend, as I was finding fault with some things in certain speeches as ugly and praising other things as beautiful, a man threw me into confusion by questioning me very insolently somewhat after this fashion: 'How, if you please, do you know, Socrates,' said he, 'what sort of things are beautiful and ugly? For, come now, could you tell me what the beautiful is?' And I, being of no account, was at a loss and could not answer him properly; and so, as I was going away from the company, I was angry with myself and reproached myself, and threatened that the first time I met one of you wise men, I would hear and learn and practice and then go back to the man who questioned me and renew the wordy strife. So now . . . teach me satisfactorily what the beautiful is . . . that I may not be confused a second time and be made ridiculous again.

And at the end of the *Lysis*, after several definitions of friendship have been found unsatisfactory, Socrates remarks:

Today, Lysis and Menexenus, we have made ourselves ridiculous — I, an old man, as well as you. For these others will go away and tell how we believe we are friends of one another — for I count myself in with you — but what a friend is, we have not yet succeeded in discovering.

In the first passage Socrates describes himself as having made some judgments that some things in certain speeches were beautiful, and as having being *challenged* to defend those judgments. The challenge took the form, 'Do you know what the beautiful is?' Socrates describes himself, further, as being unable to answer this question, and in consequence as being unable to defend his judgments. (The passage is to some extent ironic, but this does not affect the points we are making.) Since knowing what the beautiful is (which Socrates distinguishes from what is beautiful) would be knowing the definition of the beautiful, Socrates seems to be suggesting that knowing this definition would help one to *defend* or *support* a judgment that something is beautiful; and possibly that without knowing the definition one would be unable to defend such a judgment. This is not surprising and coheres well with the theory of Socratic definitions we have been expounding. For we saw that, according to that theory, a definition states that by reason of which a thing is of a given kind. A definition of, say, a plane tree states that by reason of which something is a plane tree;

119

i.e., the definiens will be the reason on the basis of which we classify this tree as a plane tree rather than some other species. And if this is so, clearly knowledge of the definition of plane tree will help us defend or support the judgment that this is a plane tree, and, possibly, without such knowledge we would be helpless to defend this judgment. This defence would take the form: a is a plane tree because a plane tree = df. a tree that has F, G, and H, and a has F, G, and H (where 'a' is the name of a particular thing, and 'F,' 'G,' and 'H' are names of properties). This use of definition in such an argument is what I have called the aitiological use of Socratic definitions: the definition being conceived as giving the formal cause (one kind of *aitia*) of a thing's being an instance of the definiendum, the definition is being appealed to *show* that a given thing is such an instance.

The passage from the *Lysis* is clearly to be interpreted in the light of this theory. Socrates and Lysis and Menexenus believe that they are friends, but what a friend is they do not know, having failed to discover the definition of friend. By putting ourselves in this condition, we have made ourselves ridiculous (literally: completely laughable), says Socrates. The idea is that if someone were to question them about their belief that they are friends, in the manner in which Socrates' insolent stranger questioned Socrates about his judgments of beautiful things, the results would be similar; not knowing the definition of friend, they would not be able to answer the question, 'How do you know you are friends?' and so would go away confused and ridiculous, unable to defend their belief that they are friends.

It is important to notice that in both passages Socrates represents himself as having made the judgment or as having the belief that some particular thing is of a certain kind without having or knowing the definition of that kind. Clearly he does not think that knowing the definition is a necessary condition to making such judgments and forming such beliefs. (And he is right: for example, we are able to teach children how to use successfully color and shape words without having to teach them definitions of the corresponding attributes.) For diagnosing a thing as being of a certain kind, knowledge of the definition is a help, and perhaps a sufficient condition; but it is not a necessary condition. However, in the *Hippias Major* and *Lysis* passages he seems to be arguing that knowledge of a definition of a given kind is a necessary as well as a sufficient condition for *defending* a judgment that a particular thing is of that kind or for *showing* that such a judgment is true. We cannot be sure that this is exactly his view since he does not state it exactly. And we also have to keep remembering that the Socratic Dialogues are works in progress. Nevertheless, it is understandable that this should be Socrates' view, since he seems to think that to show that a thing is of a certain kind is to give the reason by virtue of which things are of that kind, and he thinks that it is definitions that capture the characteristics that constitute such reasons.

It is also worth noticing that the question by which Socrates is challenged in the *Hippias Major* is a question that employs the concept of knowledge:

> How, if you please, do you know, Socrates, what sorts of things are beautiful and what ugly? For, come now, could you tell me what the beautiful is?

There is definitely a suggestion here that (a) one *can* know that, e.g., a part of a given speech is beautiful; and that (b) one *would* know this if (i) one possessed the definition of the beautiful and (ii) one were able to show that the particular part of the speech possessed the characteristics captured in the definiens. Part (b) of this suggestion coheres well with the view of knowledge implied in *Meno*, 98A: that knowledge is true belief 'made fast with causal reasoning.' To defend a belief that a thing is of a certain kind by appeal to the definition of that kind is, as we have seen, to give the formal cause of a thing's being of that kind; and the αἰτία of the *Meno* passage is almost certainly formal cause, given the mathematical and definitional questions and examples that are the concerns of the *Meno*.[24] Part (a) of the suggestion, which implies that we can have knowledge of sensible things, is also a possible view for Socrates to have held: for, as we have seen, there is no evidence whatsoever that Plato's Socrates, as distinct from Plato (middle and late Dialogues), thought of kinds (εἴδη) as existing separately from their instances; it is, therefore, likely that he did not see the reasons that Plato saw for restricting the class of things that can be known to εἴδη (forms) existing separately from and independently of their instances.[25]

Finally, the aitiological use of a Socratic definition must not be confused with the diagnostic use. The confusion might be made because a diagnosis that a thing is of such and such a kind may be arrived at by the use of the same argument that is used for the aitiological purpose. It must be remembered that the distinction is a pragmatic one: it is a distinction relative to the purpose for which we use a definition: in the diagnostic case the purpose is to arrive at a judgment that this thing is of that kind or to discover what kind of thing this is; in the aitiological case, the purpose is to prove that a judgment or belief already formed, that this thing is of such a kind, is true. The diagnostic use may or may not involve the use of an argument; the aitiological use always involves the use of an argument. Moreover, we have argued that Socrates holds different views with regard to the diagnostic and aitiological use: that knowledge of a definition of a kind is not necessary for diagnosing that a thing is of that kind, though it may be sufficient; whereas knowledge of the definition of a kind is, possibly, a necessary as well as a sufficient condition for showing or proving or knowing that this is a thing of that kind.[26]

The epistemic use of Socratic definitions

So far we have discussed Socrates' conception of the relation between knowing a Socratic definition of a given kind and making or defending singular judgments that a particular thing is of that kind. In several other passages Socrates states or implies that knowledge of *general* truths about a given kind depends on knowledge of the definition of the kind. The *Meno* opens with the question:

Can you tell me, Socrates, whether virtue can be taught, or is acquired by practice and not teaching? Or neither by practice nor by teaching, but by nature or in some other way?

Socrates answers this question as follows (71AB):

Stranger, you must think me a specially favored mortal, to be able to tell whether virtue can be taught, or in what way it comes to one: so far I am from knowing whether it can be taught or not, that I actually do not even know what the thing itself, virtue, is at all . . . that which I do not know what it is, how could I know what qualities it has? Or do you think it possible that one who does not know at all who Meno is can know this, whether he is beautiful or rich or noble or the opposite of these?

In the *Laches* 190BCD Socrates seems to be making a similar point:

And you know, Laches, at this moment our two friends are inviting us to a consultation as to the way in which virtue may be joined to their sons' souls, and so make them better? [*Laches*: Yes, indeed] Then it is necessary that this exist, the knowing of what is virtue? For if we did not know at all what virtue is, in what way could we become consultants in what way one might best acquire it? . . . Then let our first endeavor be, Laches, to say what courage is; after that we can proceed to inquire in what way our young men may obtain it, in so far as it can be obtained by means of pursuits and studies.

And at the end of *Republic*, Book I, again Socrates makes a similar point:

I have not dined well, however — by my own fault, not yours. But just as gluttons snatch at every dish that is handed along and taste it before they have properly enjoyed the preceding, so I, methinks, before finding the first object of our inquiry — what justice is — let go of that and set out to consider something about it, namely whether it is vice and ignorance or wisdom and virtue; and again, when later the view sprung upon us that injustice is more profitable than justice I could not refrain from turning to that from the other topics. So that for me the present outcome of the discussion is that I know nothing. For if I don't know what the just is, I shall hardly know whether it is a virtue or not, and whether its possessor is or is not happy.

In the *Meno* passage Socrates seems to be implying that certain general statements about virtue could not be known to be true unless the definition of virtue were known: the statements that virtue can be taught, and that virtue can be acquired by practice or by habitation. Perhaps Socrates is implying that any general statement as to how virtue can be acquired cannot be known unless the definition of virtue is known. In the *Laches* passage he seems to be implying that no statement about how virtue can best be acquired by young people can be known unless the definition of virtue is known. And in the *Republic* passage he implies a less clear-cut view: that when one does not know the definition of justice one 'will hardly know' whether justice is a virtue or whether the possessor of it is happy. In general, then, we may say that Socrates seems to hold the view that one cannot know certain general truths about virtue unless one knows the definition of virtue. Unfortunately, though Socrates *lists* the general statements about virtue, which he claims we cannot know unless we know the definition of virtue, he does not tell us, and we cannot tell, whether he means to assert (1) that no general statement about virtue can be known unless the definition is known; or (2) that just the general statements he listed cannot be so known; or (3) that some subset of general statements, of which the statements mentioned are members but which has other members and which can be specified in some general way, is such that no statement that is a member of it can be so known. Further, if we try to generalize the view, since we have no reason to believe that Socrates means to

hold such a view only with respect to virtue, we will meet with the
same kind of ambiguity as to the set of general statements meant.
The best we can do, it seems, is to say that Socrates seems to hold
the view that there are certain general true statements about each
kind (εἶδος, attribute) such that one cannot know them unless one
knows the definition of the kind. If we were to venture a general
characterization of such a set of general statements with reference
to a particular kind, we would suggest the following: the set of
true general statements about the F or F-ness, such that none of
them can be known unless the definition of 'the F' is known, is
the set of general statements such that none of them can be validly
deduced from any set of statements that does not contain the
definition of the F as a premise.

If this suggestion is near the mark, we can say that the use of
definitions that Socrates had in mind in the passages quoted is the
use of definitions in arguments: a definition of a kind is used as a
premise, which together with other premises yields new *general*
knowledge about that kind, knowledge that cannot be obtained,
or would be difficult to obtain, without the definition. This is
perhaps also the chief use of definitions in axiomatic systems,
such as Aristotle's system of syllogistics in the *Prior Analytics*, and
Euclid's system in *The Elements*: in these systems definitions
come at the beginning and are used as premises, together with
axioms and postulates, to derive theorems. The use of definitions
as premises in deductive arguments to yield new *general* knowledge
about the kind defined is the use I have called the *epistemic use* of
Socratic definitions. Though Socrates cannot be credited with
seeing clearly the use of definitions in axiomatic systems, since so
far as we know the first such system is Aristotle's, he can be
credited with a vision of definitions used in arguments to yield
new general knowledge. Let us consider some examples of such a
use.

We can construct a hypothetical example of an epistemic use of
a definition of virtue, based on evidence from the *Meno* and the
Laches. As we saw, in the *Meno* Socrates says that to find out
whether virtue can be taught they must first discover the definition of virtue. But he and Meno fail to discover it. Meno persists
in his original question, however, and Socrates, under protest, tries
to answer it in another way: Meno and Socrates agree without
argument that knowledge is the one and only thing that can be
taught (87C), and in that case, Socrates says, virtue can be taught
only if it is a kind of knowledge. After that he launches into a long
and dubious argument designed to show that virtue is knowledge
of some sort. Now from the *Laches* (199DE) it would appear that

a Socratic definition of virtue might plausibly be: Virtue = df. the knowledge of goods and evils and the causes of their production and destruction in the past, present, and future. Had Socrates and Meno arrived at this definition of virtue in the *Meno*, clearly they could have used the definition in the following valid deductive argument to obtain new general knowledge about the teachability of virtue:

(1) Virtue = df. the knowledge of goods and evils and the causes of their production and destruction in the past, present, and future.
(2) All knowledge and only knowledge can be taught.
Therefore
(3) Virtue can be taught.

Here is an actual epistemic use of the definition of dread or fear (33) which is given both in the *Laches* and the *Protagoras* (358DE):

Well, I said, is there something you call dread or fear? And is it what I say it is? I address you, Prodicus. This I call an expectation of evil, whether you call it fear or dread. . . . If our former statements are true, will any man want to go after what he dreads, when he may pursue what he does not? Or is it impossible from [given] what we have admitted? That he thinks those things which he dreads evil. And those he thinks evil no one will go after or take willingly.

The argument here is as follows:

(1) No one will go after or take willingly those things he thinks are evil. (conclusion of a previous argument)
(2) Dread = df. an expectation of evil.
Therefore
(3) If one dreads something, he thinks that thing is evil. (from (2))
Therefore
(4) No one will go after or take willingly those things which he dreads. (from (1) and (3))

(A somewhat similar use of the same definition is made in *Laches*, 198B.) Here a definition together with a general proposition already reached by argument are used as premises that yield another general proposition. In turn, the new proposition is used to reach the definitions of courage and cowardice at 360CD.

In the *Gorgias* 474C—375D we have another example where the definitions of the fair and the foul are used as premises in an argument against Polus (cf. chapter VIII, pp. 233—4).

Socrates uses several of his own definitions in arguments, particularly the definitions of function, of courage, and of cowardice. In fact, we can say of *all* of his own definitions (our group B) that he uses them either as premises in arguments that yield new general statements, or as examples of the kind of definitions he wants. He also uses several of the definitions he rejects in indirect or *reductio* arguments, for example, definitions 1, 7, 25.

It is noteworthy that in none of the cases where Socrates uses a definition as a premise in an argument does he even attempt to show that without knowing and using the definition one could not come to know the truth of the conclusion of the argument. Moreover, though he might have been able to show this in some cases, it is by no means clear that he could show it in general. This is perhaps why in the *Meno* and the *Laches* the view is put in the form of questions. It is possible that the epistemic use of definitions, then, should be described in a more cautious way that reflects more accurately Socrates' use of definitions in arguments and his remarks about such a use. This more cautious view is as follows: Socratic definitions of kinds, besides themselves representing knowledge of kinds, help us reach new general truths by being used as premises in arguments. Moreover, it is difficult to see how these new general truths could be known without so using the definitions as premises. Hence, if one wishes to gain general knowledge of kinds, one is well advised to begin with discovering definitions of these kinds. This more cautious view, besides being more accurate, shows the value of Socratic definitions relative to the search for knowledge of general truths, and it makes sense of Socrates' procedure of insisting that an inquiry into general truths about a given kind begin with trying to discover the definition of that kind. Commentators have tended to attribute to Socrates the stronger view we stated at the beginning of this section.[27] I am inclined, all in all, to ascribe to him the more cautious view.

5 *Criteria for adequate Socratic definitions*

One of the most frequent things that Socrates does in Plato's early Dialogues is to criticize definitions offered by the interlocutors. From these criticisms we can gather some of the conditions that Socrates seems to have thought must be satisfied if a definition is to be acceptable. Most of these conditions relate to his conceptions of *what a definition is* and *what a definition is for*.

(1) Socrates clearly supposes that the definitions he is after are true or false, and that a definition must be rejected if it is not

126

true (*Euthyphro*, 7A). What it means to say that a given Socratic definition is true depends on how one conceives the relation between the definiendum and the definiens: if the relation is one of property identity, then a given definition is true if and only if the alleged identity actually obtains. Socrates does not tell us clearly how he conceives the relation of definiendum to definiens, or how he conceives the truth of a definition. From Socrates' criticisms of definitions we can get a bit clearer about a related point: the many different *ways in which a definition may fail to be true*.

(a) A definition may not be true because it is too narrow or too wide or both. For example, the definition that Meno gives of virtue at 73D, virtue = df. the ability to govern mankind, has both these faults. Socrates objects that this definition excludes slaves and children from being virtuous — he and Meno agree they can be — and therefore the definition is too narrow. Second, Socrates objects that one may be able to govern mankind justly or unjustly; therefore, the definiens includes too much (unjust as well as just governing), and hence the definition is too wide. The last criticism is also made of another of Meno's definitions of virtue at 78C: virtue = df. the power to obtain good things. Socrates points out that one may obtain good things unjustly as well as justly, and therefore the definition is too wide.

(b) A definition that may not fail in being too narrow or too wide may fail in another way: the definiens might not include the characteristic or attribute by reason of which something is an instance of the definiendum; or in Aristotelean language, the definition may fail because the definiens fails to include the formal cause of something being an instance of the definiendum. This is precisely the criticism that Socrates makes of Euthyphro's definition of piety at 9D: that which all the gods love is holy — later restated as, the holy = df. the god-loved. In asking for a definition of holiness earlier, Socrates asked for that by reason of which something that is holy is holy. Now he criticizes the present definition as not giving this: whether or not everything holy is god-loved and everything god-loved is holy, it is not the case that something is holy because it is god-loved. Being god-loved is not the reason or the formal cause for something being holy. Hence, the definition fails.

(c) A definition may fail to be true, or at least may be judged unacceptable, by being inconsistent with certain pre-analytically known general truths. For example, the definition of temperance as quietness in the *Charmides* is rejected on the ground that temperance is something of high praise whereas quietness is not.

In the *Laches* the definition of courage as endurance is rejected on the ground that courage is *always* praiseworthy whereas endurance is not. Again, Nicias' definition of courage is rejected on the ground that courage is part and not the whole of virtue. Critias' definition of temperance as knowledge of knowledge is rejected on the ground that temperance is something beneficial whereas knowledge of knowledge apparently is not. In the *Laches, Charmides*, and *Meno*, certain general propositions about virtue are regarded as known truths; that the virtues are praiseworthy (καλά), that they are beneficial (ὠφέλιμα), and that each virtue is a part and not the whole of virtue. And several definitions are rejected as being inconsistent with these known truths. Here we must be careful. For we saw earlier that Socrates also holds the view that there are certain general truths about a given kind that cannot be known before a definition of the kind is known. It was not clear then what these general truths were about a given kind; and it is not clear now what the general truths are that can be known before a definition is known. Apparently, whether virtue can be taught cannot be known before a definition of virtue is known; but that virtue is praiseworthy can be known — and indeed any proposed definition must agree with this pre-definitional knowledge. Perhaps so; but why this is so is certainly not clear. Moreover, it is noteworthy that in the Dialogues before the *Republic* the virtues are said to be beneficial, and this is put forward as a general truth by which to test definitions of virtues. But in the *Republic*, at least the proposition that justice is beneficial (to the possessor) comes under attack; and at the end of Book I Socrates says that one must first discover the definition of justice before one can know whether justice is beneficial.

(d) In the *Charmides*, 167B, 169C Socrates criticizes Critias' definition of temperance as knowledge of knowledge by raising certain questions about possibility or existence. Thus he says that knowledge of knowledge is a puzzling notion and it is doubtful that there is or can be such a thing. The doubt is raised by the fact that such parallel notions as seeing of seeing and hearing of hearing are also puzzling and it does not seem possible that there are such things. It is not entirely clear whether Socrates is talking about possibility or existence. What he seems to imply is that Critias' definition fails or at least is doubtful (the discussion of this point is broken off inconclusively) either because temperance is something possible whereas knowledge of knowledge is not (or at least does not seem to be) or because there are instances of temperance but not of knowledge of knowledge. In general then, we might say that for a definition to be correct, Socrates implies, the definiens must be something possible or the definiens must match the definiendum on questions of existence (the corresponding classes must be either both empty or both non-empty) or both.

In sum, it is clear that Socrates thinks that a definition of the kind he is seeking must be true or correct if it is to be acceptable. This implies that there are or can be standards of correctness by which a definition can be evaluated. And his practice of criticizing definitions reveal some of the standards of correctness. These standards consist of truths or judgments, known or at least accepted, before a definition is known or accepted: some are judgments that something is or is not an instance of the definiendum or the definiens; judgments that having such and such an attribute is or is not the reason why a particular is of a certain kind; and general judgments about a given kind, including statements about possibility or existence. We note that Socrates has no theory and no clear view as to what propositions about a given kind can be known to be true before the definition is known. But he seems clearly to hold the view that some propositions can be known before the definition is known, and also the view that the learning of the definition helps us to acquire knowledge of new singular, (formal) causal, and general truths. We note, further, that some of the judgments that are accepted without question prior to definition in the early Dialogues come under fire in the *Republic* I, and Socrates says that these too must not wait till a definition is discovered. Socrates' criticisms of definitions seem to work well on a piecemeal basis, but it is doubtful that he appreciated all the difficulties involved in standards of correctness for definitions.[28]

(2) In the *Meno* 75B—E Meno challenges a definition that Socrates has given of figure, and Socrates replies to him as follows:

> *Meno*. According to your account figure is what always follows color. Very good. But if someone said he did not know color, and was puzzled about color as he was about figure, how would you answer him?
> *Soc*. The truth from me. And if my questioner were a professor of the contentious and eristic sort, I should say to him: I have made my statement; if it is wrong, your business is to examine and refute it. But if, like you and me on this occasion, we were friends and chose to have a discussion together, I should have to reply in some milder tone more suited to dialectic. The more dialectical way is perhaps not only to answer with what is true, but also with those things that the questioner admits he already knows. And this is the way in which I shall now try to speak with you.

Socrates proceeds immediately to ask Meno whether there is something he calls limit and something he calls solid, and having received affirmative answers, he defines figure as the limit of solid. Meno's response is to demand, once more, that Socrates tell him what color is. Socrates seems to imply that this demand is unreasonable, but proceeds to give Meno a definition of color anyway, first making sure, once more, that Meno already understands the new definiens. The passage is unclear on two points. First, Meno supposes that someone may have a difficulty about color like the difficulty he and Socrates have about virtue; the latter difficulty called for a definition of virtue. Though Socrates does produce a definition of color, and color was part of the definiens of his first definition of figure, he does not produce definitions of the definiens of his second definition of figure or of his definition of color. Rather he makes sure that Meno already understands either the definiens he is about to refer to or the definiens *expressions* he is about to use. Second, it is not clear what Socrates is making sure Meno understands before he gives a definition: is he making sure Meno knows, in the sense of being acquainted with, the definiens attributes, or that Meno understands the definiens expressions? The passages (75E, 76A and 76CD) perhaps favor the second alternative, but this is not clear.

Having noted these unclarities, we can say, nevertheless, that Socrates believes not only that a definition must be true, but also that it must refer to attributes that we are acquainted with or use terms that we understand or both.

(3) In the *Meno* (78D—79E) there may be a reference to another defect in definitions, circularity. At 78C Meno defined virtue as the power to acquire goods. Socrates objects to this definition as being too wide, since goods may be acquired justly or unjustly, piously or impiously. Socrates asks Meno if he wants to remedy this defect by adding to his definition 'justly and piously,' so that the new definition is: Virtue = df. the ability to acquire goods justly and piously. Meno replies in the affirmative, and *one* of the criticisms that Socrates makes of this new definition is as follows:[29]

> Or do you not agree that you have to meet the same question
> What is virtue? afresh? Do you suppose that anyone can know a
> part of virtue when he does not know virtue itself?
> *Meno*. No, I don't.
> *Soc*. And I daresay you remember, when I answered you a
> while ago about figure, how we rejected the sort of answer that
> attempts to proceed in terms which are still under inquiry and
> have not been admitted?

Meno. Yes, and we were right in rejecting it, Socrates.

Soc. Well then, my good sir, you must not in your turn suppose that while the nature of virtue as a whole is still under inquiry you will explain it to anyone by replying in terms of its parts, or by any other statement on the same lines: you will only have to face the same question over again — What is this virtue, of which you are speaking all the time?

Socrates' argument seems to be this:

1　One who does not know virtue cannot know a part of virtue (e.g. justice).
2　One who inquires what virtue is does not know virtue.

Therefore

3　One who inquires what virtue is does not know a part of virtue.
4　One who is seeking to define virtue is inquring into virtue.
5　Therefore, one who is seeking to define virtue does not know a part of virtue.
6　One should not try to define anything in terms of what one does not know.
7　Therefore, one who seeks to define virtue should not do so in terms of a part of virtue.[30]

It is not clear that this argument is intended to show that Meno's definition is circular. It can plausibly be interpreted as an argument that shows that Meno's definition violated the principle previously admitted, that one should not define anything in terms one does not know or in terms that an interlocutor does not know or has not admitted to know. This is probably how the argument is intended, especially since the definition is not *obviously* circular and since premise 1 is necessary to the argument.[31] However, it is clear that statements 2, 4 (or rather these statements generalized to apply to anything) and 6 exclude circularity in definitions. We can arrive at a statement that excludes circularity by using the generalized versions of 2 and 4 and also 6 as follows:

1　One who is seeking to define something is inquiring into that thing. (4, generalized)
2　One who is inquiring into something does not know that thing. (2, generalized)
3　Therefore, one who is seeking to define something does not know that thing.
4　One should not define anything in terms of what one does not know. (6)
5　Therefore, one should not define anything in terms of that thing itself.

131

Thus, if one defined virtue as, say, the power to acquire goods by virtuous means, this would be defining virtue in terms of itself ('virtuous means'), and this would violate rule 5, the conclusion of our last argument. So, if one produced this definition in response to someone who wanted to know what virtue is, he would not be producing the knowledge that the man wanted to have. And this is why Socrates keeps saying that the queston, What is virtue? would arise afresh.

The actual argument, then, that Socrates uses, even though it may not directly show that Meno's definition is circular, nevertheless contains in it premises that are strong enough to exclude circularity, and the argument shows why circularity should be excluded (a circular definition does not answer the request for knowledge and the request arises all over again).

(4) Though to my knowledge Socrates never discusses this point explicitly it is clear that, since, according to him, definitions of the kind he seeks are used for several purposes, such definitions can be good or bad, better or worse, *relative to those purposes*. We have seen that Socrates thinks his definitions can be used for at least three purposes: to tell whether a particular thing is of a given kind (the diagnostic purpose); to prove a judgment that a particular thing is of a certain kind (the aitiological purpose); and to obtain new knowledge, through arguments in which the definitions are used as premises, of general truths (the epistemic use). Clearly then, definitions can be evaluated and compared with respect to how well they serve these purposes: the better they serve these purposes, the better or more adequate they are. To put this point in Socratic terms, definitions have functions, and their virtue or goodness consists in whatever features enable them to do their work well. The question is, What are these features? Socrates unfortunately does not tell us, but we can make some educated and reasonable guesses.

Relative to the diagnostic use, it is reasonable to suppose that a definition of a kind that enhanced our diagnostic ability more than another definition of the same kind would be a better definition, other things being equal. By 'enhancing our diagnostic ability' I mean that the definition would make it easier for us to recognize an instance of a kind or would give us a more reliable test as to whether something is an instance of a kind. It will be remembered that Socrates said that he was going to tell whether an action was pious or not by comparing the action and the defined kind, the pious or piety. The definition, then, must be such that by such a comparison one can tell. Consider the diagnostic value of one of

Euthyphro's definitions of piety: the pious is whatever all the gods love. Clearly, unless one has a way of telling whether all the gods love a given action, the definition will be of no diagnostic value to him. Even though the Greeks relied on oracles, seers, and stories about the gods — which apparently they at least half believed — to divine what the gods loved, all these tests were notoriously enigmatic, inconsistent with each other, and generally unreliable. Even for the Greeks, therefore, Euthyphro's definition, aside from its other defects, had very little diagnostic value. Consider next the two definitions of figure, the only instance known to me where two apparently true definitions of the same kind are given in the Socratic Dialogues: figure = df. the only existing thing that always follows color, and figure = df. the limit of solid. Now it would be difficult, to say the least, to determine whether something was such that (a) it *always* follows color, and (b) it is the *only* thing that always follows color. It is difficult to see how the first definition of figure enables us to tell whether something is a figure or not. In sharp contrast the second definition of figure is illuminating: we can tell at once, for instance, that the limit of a cube is a figure. The second definition of figure is, therefore, immensely better than the first, relative to the diagnostic use.

Relative to the aitiological use, again it is reasonable to suppose that a definition would enhance our power to defend or prove a judgment that something is an instance of the defined kind. Let us compare the aitiological powers of the two definitions of figure relative to the judgment: roundness is a figure (the very instance of species of figure that Socrates uses in *Meno* 74B). How would we support this judgment using the first definition? Perhaps as follows:

1   Figure = df. the only existing thing that always follows color.
2   Roundness is an instance of (or, a species of) the only thing that always follows color.
3   Therefore, roundness is an instance of (or a species of) figure.

How would we support the same judgment using the second definition? Perhaps as follows:

1   Figure = df. the limit of solid.
2   Roundness is the limit of sphere.
3   A sphere is a (species of) solid.
4   Therefore, roundness is a (species of) figure.

The second defence is far superior to the first because premise 2 of

133

the first defence is not known to be true and it would be very difficult to demonstrate, whereas premises 2 and 3 of the second defence are known to be true and beyond dispute. Thus the second definition enables us to take advantage of knowledge we already have to defend the judgment in question; whereas the first definition does not. Hence, the second definition is superior to the first relative to the aitiological uses.

We may note in passing that, relative to both the diagnostic and the aitiological use, definitions by synonym are probably in general inferior to definitions by analysis. Compare, for example, definitions 27, 28, and 29 (all by synonym) with definition 30: respectively, the beautiful = df. the appropriate; the beautiful = df. the useful; the beautiful = df. the beneficial; and the beautiful = df. the pleasant through hearing or sight. The first of these would be completely useless for telling whether something is beautiful or for supporting a judgment that something is beautiful: for there is at least as much difficulty in telling, and supporting a judgment, that something is appropriate as there is in telling and supporting a judgment that something is beautiful. The second and third definitions are perhaps not as useless as the first but come close to it. The last definition, on the other hand, is in sharp contrast to the others in these respects: we can tell easily whether something gives us pleasure through hearing or sight or both, and we can see easily how we might support a judgment that, say, the statue of Venus of Milo is beautiful:

1   The beautiful = df. the pleasant through hearing or sight or both.
2   The statue of Venus of Milo gives pleasure through sight to everyone who sees it.
3   Therefore, the statue of Venus of Milo is beautiful.

Though premise 2 may not be known to be true, it at least can be tested for its truth.

It is also worth noting that relative to the diagnostic and aitiological uses criteria 2 and 3 (the definiens must be known or admitted to be known and the definition must not be circular) make good sense: if the definition is circular, it will not enhance our diagnostic powers; and if the definiens is not known, we will not be able to use the definition for diagnosis or support. Generally, the more easily recognizable and the more perspicuous the definiens the better the definition; and the more known about the definiens the better the definition. What makes the definition of Figure as the limit of solid so useful is the fact that we already know a great deal about solids, and that the notion of limit as applied to solids is clear and perspicuous.

Relative to the epistemic use, it is perhaps most difficult to say what features of a definition would serve this purpose well. Since the epistemic use consists in using the definition as a premise together with other premises to reach new knowledge of general truths, we can say that, the more a definition can relate to our pre-existent knowledge, the more useful it will be. Thus, the Socratic definition of virtue as knowledge of goods and evils is useful epistemically in so far as we already know some properties of knowledge, for example that knowledge can be taught and how it can be taught. Again, the definition of water as H_2O (water is a substance composed of molecules consisting of two hydrogen atoms and one oxygen atom) is epistemically useful because it relates the substance water to our pre-existent knowledge of the atomic theory of matter. Socrates' definition of function is useful because it relates the notion of function to our pre-existent knowledge of the uses of artifacts, organs, professions, and so on. It seems clear, then, that the epistemic use of a definition depends on pre-existent knowledge, and that the more a definition relates to pre-existent knowledge, the better the definition will be.

6 Conclusion

In conclusion, we must remember, in order to avoid misunderstandings of Socrates' work and of this chapter, that Socrates did not have many of the distinctions we have used in this chapter. For example, he did not have the distinctions between the syntactic, pragmatic, and semantic features of a definition. We have tried to use these distinctions to clarify his thought without distorting it. Again, Socrates was not acquainted, so far as we know, with axiomatic systems in which the epistemic use of definitions is systematic. Nor was he aware of several types of definitions which we find used in scientific theories and in logic and mathematics. We find relatively little theory of definition in the Socratic dialogues. What we find is a consistent and persistent search for definitions, a fairly clear conception of several systematic techniques of searching for definitions and of testing definitions, an awareness of several important uses of definitions, and some awareness of criteria for good definitions. When we remember the limitations of knowledge stated above within which Socrates worked, and the fact that he was the first thinker in the history of man to investigate the concept of definition, this is a remarkable achievement, which need not be exaggerated to be appreciated.

V

Socratic Arguments

Introduction

In most rounds of conversation with various interlocutors Socrates does three sorts of things: he raises questions, he obtains definitions or theses from the interlocutors, and he constructs arguments by which he tests the theses or definitions. Socrates' contribution to philosophic method consists not only in his elaboration of the art of asking questions and his discovery of the art of constructing definitions, but also in his art of constructing arguments and using them to test definitions and to try to settle issues. It would be difficult to find a round of conversation in which Socrates does not construct at least one argument — to my knowledge there is none. As Vlastos puts it, his talk is 'wiry argument' and that is its beauty for the philosopher. Our understanding of Socrates' philosophic method should be enhanced, therefore, by an examination of a representative sample of the arguments Socrates contructs. While we have of course examined many of Socrates' arguments in other chapters, our concerns in this chapter are different. First, we shall try to exhibit the variety and richness of Socrates' arguments by constructing a sample that includes several kinds of argument that Socrates uses; and second, in the case of each example, we shall try to practice and exhibit clearly a method of analysis by which we can try to understand and assess Socrates' arguments. The overriding aim here is not to settle issues between Socrates and the interlocutors, but rather to exhibit clearly the arguments that Socrates uses as instruments for testing truth or falsity; in particular, to exhibit those features of the arguments that determine whether the arguments are successful as such instruments, the features of validity, soundness, and the presence or absence of informal fallacies such as equivocation.

1 *Variety of arguments*

We shall find that Socrates uses arguments of nearly every form. First, he constructs a great number of *inductive* arguments; some of these are inductive arguments from analogy, which we shall call *inductive analogies*; others are inductive arguments to a generalization, which we shall call *inductive generalizations*. He also constructs a great number of *deductive* arguments. Many of these are *direct* arguments, others are *indirect* or *reductio ad absurdum*. In the category of direct arguments we find many varieties: *syllogistic* arguments of various forms, *truth-functional* arguments of various forms, and some that are neither but would properly be analyzed by using the *non-syllogistic* parts of the *predicate calculus*. Finally, most of Socrates' most significant and most controversial arguments are *reductio ad absurdum* arguments, and we shall analyze some varieties of these.

2 *Method of analyzing arguments*

Socrates uses arguments to test the *truth* of a given definition, or to settle an issue between himself and an interlocutor by testing the *truth* of the interlocutor's view. The method of analysis described below is designed to bring out those features of Socrates' arguments that are central and decisive in understanding and assessing arguments considered as instruments for testing truth. (The use of arguments as instruments for causing or inducing belief — the use that Gorgias makes of them (*Gorgias* 456—9) — would require an analysis of different features.) Given this understanding, in the case of each argument I will try to do the following things in order.

The context. I will explain the *context* of the argument: this will include stating the issue(s) between Socrates and the interlocutor, the proposition or definition whose truth the argument is designed to test, and previous or subsequent agreements between Socrates and the interlocutor that affect the argument (for example, previous agreements which function as implicit premises).

The argument. I will put the argument in Gross Standard Form: this includes changing questions into statements (according to the answers given in the text), rearranging the order of the statements if necessary so that the premises appear before the conclusion and the conclusion appears as the last line, and, where there are sub-arguments, indicating the intermediate conclusions that are used as premises in the next sub-argument. A symbol such as 'Pn' (where 'n' is substituted by a numeral) indicates that a statement so marked is used as a premise, and '*Cn*' indicates a conclusion (which in a chain argument can be also a premise for the next sub-argument). In putting the argument in Gross Standard Form we shall stay as close to Plato's text as possible.

Validity. In many cases we shall next re-write the argument so as to show clearly its logical form and state its premises unambiguously; we shall also add premises as it is necessary and as the context warrants. In some cases of re-writing, we shall put the argument in symbolic form and indicate what is derived from what and by what rules of inference. This makes the form of the argument crystal-clear and helps us to determine validity. The rules of inference used as those of I. M. Copi.[1] In symbolizing an argument, we shall use capital letters from the English alphabet as predicated abbreviations, and small letters from the end of the alphabet as sentence variables, except for 'x' and 'y' which we shall use as individual variables; we shall use small letters from the beginning of the alphabet as names of individuals; and finally, we shall use '(Ex)' and '(x)' as the existential and universal quantifiers respectively, to be read 'there is at least one x such that . . .' and 'for all x . . .' respectively.

Soundness. An argument is sound if and only if it is valid and all of its premises are true. An argument is valid if and only if it is impossible for all its premises to be true and its conclusion to be false at the same time. A conclusion is proved to be true if and only if the argument whose conclusion it is is sound; it is not sufficient that it be valid, nor is it sufficient that it have all true premises; both conditions must obtain if the truth of the conclusion is to be demonstrated. After we have put the argument in Gross Standard Form and have restated or have symbolized it, we shall discuss its soundness. Validity will be relatively easy to determine once we have symbolized it. The truth or falsity of the premises is much more difficult to decide and depends in many cases on empirical knowledge that we do not have. In cases of informal fallacies, such as ambiguity, we shall always try to give Socrates the benefit of the doubt; that is, we shall take the most favorable interpretation to his argument provided this is allowed by the questions at issue, by the text, and by considerations of consistency.

3 *Inductive analogies: from the arts-crafts-sciences to ethics*

One of Socrates' most characteristic beliefs is that conclusions and decisions about what is good or bad, right or wrong, noble or disgraceful should be reached not by consulting what society approves or disapproves or what society will praise or punish, nor by the procedure of casting votes. Rather, such conclusions and decisions should be reached in the same way as conclusions and decisions are reached in the arts, crafts, and sciences (*technai*), that is, on the basis of expert knowledge and reasoning. Plato presents this belief as a controversial view, at variance with the beliefs and practices of the Athenians, and he often has Socrates support this belief by arguments from analogy. This belief still remains controversial, and in modern times the controversy takes the form of the question whether ethics can be a science. Moreover, this belief seems to have influenced Plato considerably, since in his epistemology and metaphysics no significant distinction seems to be made between knowledge of values and knowledge in the sciences such as arithmetic and medicine, other than a distinction in terms of subject matter. In this section we shall examine two arguments from analogy that Socrates presents in support of his belief, one from the *Laches* and one from the *Crito*.

Laches *184D—185A*

The context. The two generals, Laches and Nicias, disagree as to whether a new military exercise, fighting in armour, 'is in many ways useful for young men to possess' (181E). After the two generals have finished their speeches, Lysimachus, who is considering whether to have his son acquire this accomplishment, asks Socrates to decide the matter by casting his vote on one side or the other (184CD). Lysimachus wants to decide the issue as it is decided in the assembly courts: two or more speakers speak on opposite sides of the issue and the matter is then decided by vote. Socrates proceeds to give an argument from analogy which implies that this is a wrong method for deciding the issue and that a different method should be followed. Socrates seems to be making an inference from the way we would and/or should proceed in a consultation about what our sons' exercise should be, to prepare them for a future contest, to the way we would and/or should proceed in the consultation as to whether our sons should be taught the exercise of fighting in armour. The argument then seems to be as follows:

P1 In consulting as to what exercise our sons should do to prepare for a coming contest, we must be guided by one who has trained and exercised under a good master, an expert on the subject at hand, not by the majority of us (non-experts).

C1 Therefore, in consulting as to whether our sons should

learn the exercise of fighting in armour, we must also be guided by an expert on the subject, and not by the majority of us (non-experts).

This however, cannot be the whole argument, since the similarity between the two cases, on the basis of which an inference is made about the second case, is not explicitly stated. An argument from (inductive) analogy has the form:[2]

P1   a,b,c, each is known (observed) to have S and P
P2   d is an S
C1   Therefore, (probably) d is P.

Now in the argument Socrates gives, P is clearly the property of being guided by experts, rather than by a majority of non-experts, in a given subject of consultation. But what is property S? What we are given in the passage quoted is that both cases are cases of consultation as to whether certain exercises, or as to what exercises, should be learned by our sons. In addition, in the first case the consultation is as to what exercises our sons should learn relative to achieving the end of being prepared (or, possibly winning) in a coming contest. And in the passage immediately following the quoted argument Socrates indicates that he conceives the consultation about fighting in armour to be whether our sons should learn this accomplishment relative to attaining a certain end, which he claims is the possession of the virtue of courage (185B—E, 189E—190E). In all probability, this is the similarity between the two cases on which his argument relies. If so, his argument can be set out more fully as follows:

P1   The consultation as to what exercises our sons should learn for a coming contest is a consultation about means to ends, and in it we must be guided by experts on those means and ends and not by majority (vote) of non-experts.
P2   The consultation as to whether our sons should learn fighting in armour is a consultation about means to ends.
C1   Therefore, in it (the consultation as to whether our sons should learn fighting in armour) we must be guided by experts and not by a majority (vote) of non-experts.

This argument does have the form of inductive analogy given above.

Strength.[3] How strong is this argument? It is an inference from only one instance, and for that reason it may be considered weak. On the other hand, the similarities between the two cases are considerable, and this strengthens the argument: both consultations are about means to ends, both are about physical exercises or accomplishments and their effects, both are about accomplishments of youths or educational accomplishments, and both are about accomplishments about which we can and do have experience and about which we can experiment. Finally, the argument is strong because Socrates asserts a proposition that, if it is true as it seems to be, explains the connection between properties S and P: the properties of a consultation being about means and ends and the consultation being decided by experts are not just accidentally connected in the first case. For in deciding a question about means to a certain end we wish to find out what is in fact or in truth the best means to that end; and if this is our purpose in consulting we will consult well when we are guided by experts on that subject — that is, by those who have learned and practiced and experimented on the subject. Whereas we shall not consult well if we are guided by the majority or the vote of non-experts (we could of course reach the correct decision by voting, either by chance or by voting only whatever the experts tell us, but the first procedure cannot be a case of consulting well and the second amounts pretty much to what Socrates is recommending). This is what I take to be the point of the proposition that Socrates asserts in the middle of the argument, that if one is to decide well about an outcome one must decide by knowledge, not by numbers.

It may be objected that to say that in both cases the issue is what is the best means to a given end, or is whether a given means is the best to a given end, is to say something vague; something that may hide the complexity of the cases, and may make it seem that the issues are purely empirical or experimental ones. In particular, though the question whether learning fighting in armour fosters courage may be an empirical or experimental one, the question whether fighting in armour is a useful or beneficial (ὠφέλιμον) thing for the young to learn may not be *entirely* an experimental question (and it is the latter question with which Nicias begins his debate — 181E). For to answer the latter question, we may need to know not only what courage is, itself not an experimental question, but also whether it is good or useful for the young to possess courage. The point is important not because there was in the Greek society controversy as to whether courage is good or useful (there was not), or because there is such controversy in our culture, but rather because this question is at least in part a value question. It would appear then that the answer to the question (1), whether fighting in armour is a useful or beneficial thing for the young to learn, depends on answers to the questions (2), what courage is, (3), whether fighting in armour fosters courage, and (4), whether courage is a good or useful thing for the young to possess. Of these, (2) appears to be a question of definition, (3) an empirical or experimental question, and (4) a question about value. This, however, does not invalidate Socrates' argument, perhaps it does not even weaken it; for it can be argued convincingly that the question about exercising for a coming contest that is parallel to (1), that is, whether it is useful or beneficial for the young to exercise in a certain way for a coming contest, has a parallel complexity. But the complexity is, nevertheless, important to notice, for it shows that it would be inaccurate to suppose that the issue for which Socrates proposes a method is purely an empirical or experimental issue. And it would probably be misleading to suppose that Socrates is implying by his argument that the proper method for deciding (1) is *confined* to the method of observation and experimentation. His point rather seems to be the more general one that the proper method is to decide the issue on the basis of knowledge, rather than by a voting procedure. If for example there is a method that leads to, say, knowledge of what courage is, that method is to be *included* in the methods by which (1) is to be decided. And if, again, there is a method that leads to knowledge of whether courage is a good thing for the young to possess, that method also is to be included in the methods by which (1) is to be decided. The argument of course does not show that there are such methods. But if the complexity of (1) is parallel to the complexity of the issue whether it is useful or beneficial for the young to exercise in a certain way for a given contest, then the argument shows that voting procedures, as normally practiced, would *not* be proper methods for deciding (1), and that methods that lead to knowledge would be.

Crito 46B—48B

The context. Crito is urging Socrates, who is in jail waiting execution, to escape. Crito begins (44BC) by saying that if Socrates does not escape many people will think that Socrates' friends were not willing to help and this will be a disgraceful reputation. Socrates protests this kind of consideration (44C):

> But, my dear Crito, why do we care so much for what most people think? For the most reasonable men, whose opinion is more worth considering, will think that things were done as they really will be done.

Crito replies that the opinion of the public cannot be disregarded, for the very trouble Socrates is in now shows the power of the public if one has a bad reputation (44D). And later he again appeals to public opinion (45E–46A). It is not clear whether Crito appeals to public opinion as something powerful which can be disregarded only at great risk, or also as an arbiter of what is good or evil, praiseworthy or disgraceful, right or wrong. Possibly both, but in any case Socrates takes up Crito first on the latter. He says that they ought to consider whether he must escape, and asks (46B–47A):

> Now how could we examine the matter most reasonably? By taking up first what you say about opinions and asking whether we were right when we always used to say that we ought to pay attention to some opinions and not to others? . . . Now say, do you not think we were correct in saying that we ought not to esteem all the opinions of men, but some and not others, and not those of all men but only of some?

The ultimate issue at stake is whether Socrates ought to escape. The immediate issue is whether to decide the ultimate issue on the basis of public opinion about what is good or bad, praiseworthy or disgraceful, right or wrong. Socrates' last question quoted is about this immediate issue. And when Crito answers that they must not esteem and follow all opinions but only some and not the opinions of all men but only of some, the next question becomes: which opinions, and whose opinions? The argument Socrates gives next is meant to answer these last questions.

The argument (478A–E). Socrates' argument seems to consist of an inference by analogy from the case of athletics (matters pertaining to the body) to the case of matters pertaining to right and wrong, noble and disgraceful, good and bad, matters that pertain to the soul. So far the argument seems to be as follows.

P1 When one is engaged in athletics or training of the body (a) he pays attention not to every man's praise and blame and opinion but only to those of the one man who is a trainer or physician, and (b) he must fear the blame and welcome the praise not of the multitude but of the trainer or physician, and (c) he must act and exercise and eat and drink not as everyone thinks but as the trainer or physician who knows the business best thinks, and (d) he will harm his body if he disregards and disobeys the opinion and praise of the physician and trainer and instead regards the opinion of the many who have no knowledge of the business.

143

C1 Therefore, when one is engaged in questions pertaining to right and wrong, noble and disgraceful, good and bad, or to matters pertaining to the psyche, (a) he must follow and fear not the opinion of the many but of the one who knows about these things if there is any, and (b) he must revere and fear him (who knows about these matters) more than all the others (who do not know), and (c) he will harm that which is benefited by the right and harmed by the wrong (his psyche) if he does not follow him (who knows and follows instead the many who have no knowledge).

Once more Socrates does not explicitly state the analogies or similarities between the two cases on the basis of which he draws the inference that, since in the case of athletics we consult and follow the opinion of the man who knows, so in the other case we must consult and follow the opinion of the man who knows. We have, therefore, to reconstruct these similarities from what we find in the text and what we know from other Dialogues (in this case chiefly *Gorgias*, 464A—466A). We may begin with the point that Socrates and Crito are clearly right in agreeing that, in the matters of training the body to be strong and swift (the matters of athletic training) and in the matters of health and disease (the matters the physician attends to), one does and should follow the advice of the athletic trainer and the physician — i.e. those who have special knowledge of these matters — and not the advice of the many who do not know. The opinion of the public (the opinion of non-experts who happen to be the majority of a society, usually) on what one should and should not do in order to have a strong and swift body and in order to be healthy and avoid diseases is worthless as compared to the opinion of experts on these matters. And why this is so is clear enough. Certain actions will promote strength and speed in the body, and many other actions will not; certain diets will, and many other diets will not; certain actions and diets and regimes will promote health, and many others will not; and certain drugs and treatments will cure disease and many others will not. And it takes experience, systematic observation, and systematic experimenting under controlled conditions to discover which do and which don't. Clearly the people who have conducted and/or have become acquainted with these observations and experiments and have put them to use successfully are the people one should consult and whose advice one should follow in these matters; not the people who have no knowledge of these matters.

But why should Socrates hold that in seemingly very different

144

matters of right and wrong, noble and disgraceful, good and bad, we should consult and follow the advice of experts on these matters rather than the advice and opinion of the public? Clearly Socrates is supposing that some significant analogy or similarity exists between the two cases that is the basis for his inference. We get a clue of it in the passage immediately following the argument. In this passage Socrates thinks there is an analogy between the healthy and the diseased relative to the body, on the one hand, and the right and the wrong relative to the psyche (soul), on the other. And from the *Gorgias* (464A—466A) we know in some detail what he thinks the analogy is. There is a certain good condition of the body, called health and strength, and several bad conditions; and there are two science-crafts, gymnastics and medicine, the first of which aims at developing and promoting health and strength, and the second at destroying disease and restoring health. Similarly, there is a good condition of the psyche, called virtue, and several bad conditions, called vices; and there are two science-crafts, legislation and justice, the first of which aims at developing and promoting virtue, and the second at destroying vice and restoring virtue in the psyche. Just as some actions promote health and strength in the body and others destroy it, so some actions promote virtue in the psyche and others destroy it; and just as it takes experience and systematic observation and experiment to discover which actions promote health in the body and which disease, so it takes observation and experiment to discover which actions develop virtue in the psyche and which destroy it. And, consequently, just as one should consult and take the advice of the experts on what actions promote health and strength, so one should consult and take the advice of experts on what actions promote virtue in the soul and what actions destroy it, i.e. what actions are right (just) and what wrong (unjust). Further, Socrates assumes that people want to avoid the bad condition of the body and the bad condition of the soul. Life is not worth living when the body and soul are harmed, he says, and it is relative to wanting the avoidance of these bad states, at the very least, that it is argued that one should consult and follow the advice of experts. Given all these points, we can try to reconstruct Socrates' argument so as to reflect more accurately what seems to be his thought (we will collapse (a), (b), and (c) in P1 into one point, for convenience, and (d) will be relocated to the base of the analogy).

P1   In the matters of what actions promote the good condition of the body, health and strength, and what actions destroy the bad condition of the body, disease, (a) it takes experience and knowledge to determine which actions promote health and which destroy disease, i.e. which actions benefit and which harm the body; and therefore (b) if one wants to develop health and strength, the good condition of the body, and to avoid diseases, the bad conditions of the body, one should consult and follow the advice of those who have experience and knowledge of these matters and one should disregard the opinions of the public (the non-experts on these matters).

P2   In the matters of what actions promote the good condition of the psyche, virtue, and what actions destroy the bad conditions of the psyche, the vices, (a) it takes experience and knowledge to determine which actions promote virtue in the psyche and which destroy vice, i.e. which actions benefit the psyche and which harm it.

C1   Therefore, (b) if one wants to develop virtue, the good condition of the psyche, and avoid vices, the bad conditions of the psyche, one should consult and follow the advice of those who have experience and knowledge of these matters and one should disregard the opinions of the public (i.e. the non-experts on these matters).

Strength of the argument. How strong is the argument? It has the form of an argument by analogy, and in so far as it proceeds from only one instance it is weak. However, despite this, it appears to be a very strong argument because the connection between (a) and (b) in P1 is not simply conjunction but a much stronger connection: (a) appears to be the ground or reason for (b), or (a) seems to imply (b). Therefore, if P2 is true, and there are no problems connected with vagueness and ambiguity undermining the parallel between P1(a) and P2(a), the argument is very strong indeed. If we grant P1(b) on the basis of P1(a), it appears that by parity of reasoning we should grant C1(b) on the basis of P2(a). Is then P2 true, and at the same time is P2 analogous to P1(a)? There are at least two important differences between P1(a) and P2, which make P2 a very controversial proposition, and both differences are brought up by Socrates himself. The first difference is hinted by Socrates in the very passage we are discussing when he says that in matters of right and wrong, noble and disgraceful, good and bad, one should follow not the opinion of the many but of the one, *if there is one who knows about them* (47D). This of course can be related to the discussions in the *Protagoras* and the *Meno* as to whether virtue can be taught and whether there are teachers of virtue. In the *Meno* Socrates finds that there are no teachers of virtue, or at least that the usual candidates do not pass the tests. It appears then that, while in the matters of strength and health and disease there were experts in the Greek society, in the matters of what is right and wrong and noble and disgraceful and good and bad there seemed to be none. This difference does not invalidate the argument, since one might argue that even though there were none there could and ought to be some, and perhaps, as in the case of many other science-crafts, in time there would be some. But this difference may be of some importance in so far as its existence may cast doubt on the parallel between P1(a) and P2 or on the truth of P2: for one possible explanation for this difference is that the matters of what is right and wrong, noble and disgraceful, and good and bad, are not matters of special knowledge or special expertise at all, or at any rate that they are matters knowledge of which every member of the society has, more or less, by education and training common to all members of the society (a position that Protagoras takes in his great speech).

The second difference is that it can be taken for granted that the set of actions that benefit one's body is the same as the set of actions that promote one's health; whereas it cannot be similarly taken for granted that the set of actions that benefit one's psyche is the same as the set of actions that promote one's virtue or justice. That the latter cannot be taken for granted is shown by the great controversy in the *Gorgias*, whether justice brings happiness to the agent. Consequently, Socrates' argument may show that one should consult and follow the advice of experts as to whether a given action or set of actions benefits one's psyche; but it does not show that one should consult and follow the advice of experts as to whether a given action or set of actions are just or virtuous or promote virtue.

4 *Inductive generalizations: from the art-crafts-sciences to ethics*

Socrates often generalizes about the science-crafts (τέχναι); that is, he draws conclusions about all the science-crafts from an examination of several science-crafts; and almost invariably he proceeds to apply these generalizations to ethics, usually with startling results. Though it is these applications that make his remarks about the science-crafts philosophically interesting, in this section we are interested primarily in exhibiting the inductive generalizations themselves. We shall examine two instances; and in the second instance we shall extend the discussion to the application of the

147

generalization to ethics since this is the whole point of making it and since it is intended to support a famous Socratic thesis in ethics.

Hippias Minor 366C–369A: intentional incompetence

The context. The immediate issue between Socrates and Hippias is whether those who are able voluntarily to utter falsehoods always and uniformly in a given subject are the same as those who are able voluntarily or intentionally to utter truths always and uniformly in the same subject[4] (366AB). Socrates gives an inductive argument for an affirmative answer to this issue (Hippias had taken the negative side). He then uses the conclusion in order to argue for another conclusion: that those who utter falsehoods voluntarily are better than those who do so involuntarily (371E). And, in turn, he uses this last conclusion to argue that, more generally, those who err or do wrong voluntarily are better than those who do so involuntarily (373C, 375D)!

The argument

P1 In the science-craft of arithmetic those who have the most power to tell falsehoods voluntarily about calculation and number are the same as those who have the most power to tell the truth voluntarily about calculation and number. (367C)

P2 In the science-craft of geometry those who have the most power to tell falsehoods voluntarily about diagrams are the same as those who have the most power to tell the truth voluntarily about diagrams. (367E)

P3 In the science-craft of astronomy those who have the most power to speak falsehoods voluntarily about the heavenly bodies are the same as those who have the most power to speak the truth voluntarily about the heavenly bodies. (368A)

P4 No science-craft is known (to Hippias, a great master of science-crafts, and to Socrates) in which those who have the power to speak falsely voluntarily are not the same as those who have the most power to speak the truth voluntarily. (368E–369A)

C1 Therefore, in all the science-crafts those who have the most power to speak falsely voluntarily are the same as those who have the most power to speak the truth voluntarily. (368B, 369A)

This is a perfect example of an inductive generalization. An inductive generalization is the form:[5]

P1   a,b,c . . . each has been observed (is known) to be S and P.
P2   Nothing has been observed (is known) to be S and not P.
C1   Therefore, probably, all S are P.

Socrates' argument has this form (the only difference being the unimportant one that the first three premises are not stated together as one premise).

Strength. How strong is this argument? First, the sample is fairly small, and this weakens the argument. Second, the whole sample comes from the so-called theoretical science-crafts, and none of the practical crafts are inspected; and this again weakens the argument, since for all we know (that is, given the evidence presented) the conclusion may not hold for *any* practical science-crafts. Nevertheless, despite these weaknesses, the argument is strong: for Socrates shows (367E) that the power of intentionally uttering falsehoods always (whenever one wished) and uniformly (without error — i.e., without mistakenly telling the truth) depends on knowing the truth in all the cases of the science-crafts examined. For example, to have the power intentionally to tell falsehoods always and uniformly about calculation and number one must know the true answers about calculation and number; and if one knows the true answers one has the power intentionally to tell the truth always and uniformly about calculation and number (366E–367A). And the same is true of the other science-crafts examined. It is possible, of course, that one might set out to give just false answers about calculation and number, and that he might succeed *by chance* and without knowing the true answers in giving always and uniformly false answers. But the chances that he can do so are very small in the long run (though perhaps better than one might initially suppose since the question 'what is 568×512?' has one true answer and infinite false ones). And, in any case, if we knew that he was doing this without knowing the true answers we might be inclined to say that he did not have the power to give false answers always and uniformly; and Socrates' explanation of power supports this — 'he has power [relative to doing F] who does what he wishes whenever he wishes [relative to doing F]' (366C). A man who gives false answers by chance does not have the power to give false answers if he wishes to give false answers and whenever he wishes to give false answers. We can certainly say, at the very least, that if a man is voluntarily giving false answers always and uniformly in a given subject matter, that is strong evidence that he knows the true answers. And in that case the connection between voluntary incompetence and competence in a given science-craft is a lot stronger than conjunction: that is, voluntary incompetence is very strong evidence of competence. Moreover, even though the practical sciences, such as medicine, have not been examined in the argument, it seems that the conclusion holds in their case also. In medicine, for instance, if one has the power voluntarily to use wrong techniques always and uniformly and voluntarily to produce wrong results (disease rather than health) always and uniformly, that would be strong evidence that he is competent in medicine. All in all, then, even though the premises cover only three instances, and even though all the instances are from the theoretical science-crafts, the argument is strong, and the conclusion seems to apply equally well to the practical science-crafts.

Gorgias 460C: knowledge in the practical crafts and justice

The context. The immediate issue between Socrates and Georgias is whether learning a science-craft renders a man a qualified (or, perhaps, successful) practitioner of that science-craft. The argument by inductive generalization to C1 settles this issue affirmatively. The intermediate issue, which is made to depend on the issue above, is whether a man who knows what is just is a just man. This issue is settled affirmatively by an additional argument, a deductive one with C1 as a premise, to C2. And the ultimate issue which is made to depend on these two issues is whether the rhetorician is a just man, and this issue is settled affirmatively by an argument that uses C2 as a premise. This last settlement shows Gorgias to be inconsistent since he had previously said that the rhetorician is sometimes unjust and also that the rhetorician knows what is just, and now he is forced to agree to conclusion C2, that if a man knows what is just he is a just man. Though the issue about the rhetorician is the widest context, the philosophical interest of the argument centers on C2, since C2 is an instance of the Socratic paradox that knowledge is sufficient for virtue, and the argument from P1 to C2 is given as a demonstration of this paradox. For this reason, we shall consider the chain of argument from P1 through C2, rather than the inductive generalization P1 to C1 alone. A previous agreement between Socrates and Gorgias that is relevant to the argument occurs at 454CE: Socrates distinguished between 'having learned' and 'having believed'; both are forms of 'having been persuaded' but the former results in having knowledge and the latter in having belief only.

The argument

P1   He who has learnt the things pertaining to the science-craft building is a builder.

P2   He who has learned the things pertaining to the science-craft music is a musician.

P3   He who has learned the things pertaining to the science-craft medicine is a physician.

C1   And the others similarly according to the same principle: whoever has learned the things pertaining to a science-craft is such as that science-craft makes him.

(P4   Justice is a science-craft.)

C2   Then, according to this principle (C1), he who has learned the things pertaining to the science-craft justice is a just man.

P4   The just man does what is just.

P5   The just man of necessity wishes to do just things.

C3   Hence, the just man will never do injustice.[6]

The two arguments to C2 appear to have the following form:

a   (the science-craft) building
b   (the science-craft) music
c   (the science-craft) medicine
d   (the science-craft) justice
Ty   y is a science-craft
Mxy x has learned science-craft y
Sxy x is a scientist-craftsman of science-craft y

P1 $Ta. (x)(Mxa \supset Sxa)$
P2 $Tb. (x)(Mxb \supset Sxb)$
P3 $Tc. (x)(Mxc \supset Sxc)$
C1 $(y)[Ty \supset (x)(Mxy \supset Sxy)]$ (inductive generalization from P1, P2, P3)
P4 Td (supplied premise)
C1.1 $Td \supset (x)(Mxd \supset Sxd)$ (supplied conclusion from C1 by universal instantiation)
C2 $(x)(Mxd \supset Sxd)$ (from P4 and C1.1 by *modus ponens*)

Strength of P1—C1. How strong is the inductive generalization P1—C2? Despite the fact that only three instances are considered, and despite the fact that all the instances are from the practical science-crafts, the argument is very strong. For the connection between something being a science-craft and the fact that someone who learns its subject matter becomes a successful practitioner of it is not simply conjunction; it is an evidential connection. A science-craft is a specialized body of knowledge of principles and practices and techniques about a given subject matter, say building, such that their application leads to a certain object, say the construction of sound, functional, and beautiful buildings; given this, the fact that a man has mastered these ('learned' in the sense in which learning leads to knowledge) is strong evidence that he is or will be a successful practitioner of that science-craft. The argument, then, to C1 is strong and sound. It should be noted that when Socrates says that he who has learned the things pertaining to building is a builder, I take him to mean that he who has knowledge of the relevant principles and techniques and practices has the power to be a successful practitioner of the science-craft of building; and if one has that power one will, in the appropriate circumstances, design and construct sound, functional and beautiful structures. Premises P1, P2, and P3 are not tautologies; rather they tell us what the power of knowledge is in the science-crafts.

Soundness of C1–C2. The argument C1–C2 is a deductive argument of the form given above. It is valid since C2 can be derived from C1, P4, and C1.1 by the rules of universal instantiation and *modus ponens*. However, it is doubtful that it is a sound argument, that is a valid argument with all its premises true, for it is doubtful that P4 is true. How so?

What seems to be wrong with P4? It seems that justice, considered as a science-craft, fails to pass the test of voluntary or intentional incompetence which, Socrates has argued, as we saw in the *Hippias Minor* 366C–369 argument, is characteristic of the science-crafts. If we look at generalization C1 of *that* argument it may at first seem that justice falls under it. That generalization is (*Hippias Minor* 368B, 369A):

C1   In all science crafts those who have the most power to speak falsely voluntarily or intentionally are the same as those who have the most power to speak the truth voluntarily or intentionally.

We might well argue that in the case of justice those who have the most power to speak falsely intentionally are the same as those who have the most power to speak the truth intentionally. For speaking falsely in this case would be saying of what is just that it is unjust or of what is unjust that it is just; and in order to do either intentionally and successfully (always and uniformly) it would seem that one would have to know what is just and what is unjust. So here too, it would seem, intentional incompetence would be strong evidence, if not proof, of competence. This is so, but a problem remains about P4 because justice would seem to be a practical rather than a theoretical science craft (as the analogies with medicine, building, and music suggest); and in the case of practical science crafts the principle of intentional incompetence would presumably apply to doing as well as to saying. So expanded the principle would be:

C1.2   In all the science-crafts, practical or theoretical, those who have the most power to intentionally speak falsely or do the wrong thing (use a mistaken technique or administer poor treatment, etc.) always and uniformly are the same as those who have the power to intentionally speak the truth or do the right thing always and uniformly.

Thus in medicine, say, those who have the most power to say intentionally what is false (e.g. give false diagnosis) or to prescribe and practice wrong treatment always and uniformly are the same as those who have the most power to speak truly or prescribe and practice the right treatment always and uniformly. Thus if a man intentionally gives false diagnoses or prescribes and practices wrong treatment always and uniformly that would be strong evidence if not proof that he knows the true diagnosis and knows the right treatment; and if he knows the true diagnosis and the right treatment, then, by principle C1 of the *Gorgias* argument, he is a physician. But if we make a similar application of these two principles (C1.2 of the *Hippias Minor* and C1 of the *Gorgias*) to justice, we shall contradict not only our idea of a just man but also the conception of a just man that Socrates has (as revealed by P5, P6, C3 of the *Gorgias* argument). According to C1.2, those who have the most power to do intentionally what is unjust always and uniformly (the parallel to practicing wrong medical treatment) are the same as those who know what is just. Thus, if a man intentionally does what is unjust always and uniformly that is strong evidence if not proof that he knows what is just. And if he knows what is just, then, by C2 of the *Gorgias* argument or by an application of C1 of the *Gorgias* argument to justice, he is a just man. And if he is a just man, then, by C3, he never does what is unjust. Therefore (it follows from the last three statements by hypothetical syllogism), if a man intentionally does what is unjust always and uniformly then he never does what is unjust! Thus when we put together the principles of the *Hippias Minor* argument and those of the *Gorgias* and apply them to justice we obtain a contradiction (the only thing that softens this is the qualifying phrase 'that is evidence if not proof' — but this presents no way out).

We shall end this section by indicating several possible ways out of this contradiction. One way is to deny that justice is a science-craft, but this is not Socrates' way out as we know both from the argument we have examined and from *Gorgias* 464B—466 where justice is explicitly said to be a science-craft. Another way is to deny that justice is a *practical* science-craft, but this too does not seem to be Socrates' way out since in the passage just cited justice is said to be a science-craft which is analogous to medicine. Yet a third way is to try to restrict principle C1 of the *Hippias Minor* to the theoretical crafts. It is perhaps not clear on what grounds this would be recommended, but there does seem to be an important difference between the theoretical science-crafts and the practical ones with respect to the principles we have been discussing. The difference might be brought out as follows. If a man intentionally gives false answers about geometrical figures always and uniformly, this is evidence if not proof that he knows the true answers; and if he knows the true answers he is a geometer. Here it seems that there is no difficulty in saying both that he intentionally gives false answers always and uniformly and that he is a geometer. But the parallel in the case of, say, medicine seems problematic. If a man intentionally gives false diagnosis always and uniformly that is evidence if not proof that he knows the true diagnosis; and if he knows the true diagnosis he is a physician. This seems to be also all right. And, again, if a man intentionally prescribes and practices the wrong medical treatment always and uniformly that is evidence if not proof that he knows the right medical treatment; and if he knows the right medical treatment he is a physician. Here there seems to be a problem: it seems problematic to say both that a man intentionally prescribes the wrong medical treatment always and uniformly and at the same time that he is a physician. The reason this seems problematic may be that it may be part of the defini-tion of a physician that he not only knows health and disease and right treatments but also that he aims at and practices correct treatments. Further, while in the case of geometry it seems all right and in the case of medicine problematic, in the case of justice it seems to be a clear-cut mistake to suppose that we can say both that a man intentionally does injustice always and uniformly and also that he is a just man. But though this is clear enough, it cer-tainly is not clear that it constitutes a ground for excluding justice, and possibly all the practical science-crafts, from the principle of intentional incompetence of the *Hippias Minor*. The dis-analogy we have brought out between the theoretical and the practical science-crafts may be taken with equal plausibility as pointing to the necessity to give up the inductive generalization C1 of the

Gorgias argument in the case of practical crafts. That would mean that in the case of the practical crafts possession of knowledge of, say, health and disease and their causes would not be sufficient for a man to be a physician; successful performance would also be required. And in the case of justice, this would mean that knowledge of justice would not be sufficient for being a just man; successful performances — doing just acts — would also be required.

5 *Deductive arguments: two indirect arguments from the* Lysis

Context. The main question of the *Lysis* is raised by Socrates at 212A: in what way does one person become a friend of another? At the end of the dialogue Socrates says that the question they failed to aswer is: what is a friend? The two questions are closely related, perhaps as follows. If we find that, say, to be a friend of y is to love y, then one becomes a friend of y by coming to love y. Socrates and the interlocutors try to answer mostly the second question by taking up a series of hypotheses that specify what is the relation 'x is friend of y.' The first candidate is 'x loves y'.[7] By argument the following hypotheses are *refuted*: (1a) If x loves y, x is friend of y; (1b) if x loves y, y is a friend of x; (1c) if x loves y, x is friend to y and y is friend to x (212B–213D). The second candidate taken up is the relation 'x is like y' or possibly 'x and y are alike.' Two people can be alike in many different ways, but only the cases of two people being both good and two people being both bad or wicked are considered, these properties possibly being considered the most relevant ones to being friends; but the general relation of one person being like another, without specification of respect, is also taken up. Thus the second series of hypotheses *refuted* is: (2a) If x is like y then x [is] can be friend of y; (2b) if x is like y in that x is bad or wicked and y is bad or wicked, then x [is] can be friend to y; and (2c) if x is like y in that x is good and y is good, then x [is] can be friend to y (214A–215C). The third major candidate is the relation 'x is opposite to y,' on the ground that everything is desired by its opposite (rather than its like). Again, two things may be opposites in many different ways, but the particular opposites taken up are hatred and friendship, the just and the unjust, the temperate and the profligate, and the good and the bad. Thus the third series of hypotheses *refuted* is: (3a) If x and y are opposites in that x is hatred and y is friendship, then x [is] can be friend to y; (3b) if x and y are opposites in that x is just and y unjust, then x [is] can be a friend to y; (3c) if x is opposite to y in that x is temperate and y profligate, then x [is] can be friend to y; and (3d) if x is opposite to y in that x is good and y is bad, then x is friend to y (216A–216C). Finally, a fourth hypothesis is taken up: (4) if x is neither good nor bad and y is good and beautiful, then x [is] can be friend to y (216D–217). This hypothesis is elaborated and eventually also refuted in the rest of the dialogue. Many of the arguments in the *Lysis* are interdependent, and so it is advisable to keep in mind this whole context of the whole dialogue. In this section we shall analyze two indirect or *reductio ad absurdum* arguments, one against hypothesis (2a) and one against (2c). And in the next section we shall analyze a direct deductive argument *for* hypothesis (4).

The hypotheses (2a)–(2c) are introduced as follows. The first hypothesis having been refuted, Socrates appeals to the poets for wisdom and takes a hint from Homer (*Odyssey* 218):

Yea, every like and like together God doth draw.

He takes this to mean 'the like of necessity is always friend to the like' (214AB). Next Socrates argues that what he calls 'half' of this saying cannot be true: for, he says, the wicked cannot be friends to the wicked, since they injure or do injustice to each other, and people that injure each other cannot be friends. So, he concludes, 'half of the saying cannot be true, if the wicked are like one another' (214C). The other 'half' of the saying is then taken up as being what the poets really mean:

P1   The good are like one another and are friends.

Socrates proceeds to interpret P1 in two different ways and gives an argument against each:

P1.1   The like is friend to the like in so far as he is like (214E)
and
P1.2   The good is friend to the good in so far as he is good, not in so far as he is like. (215A)

It is not perhaps too clear what P1.1 and P1.2 mean. Perhaps P1.1 means that if two people are like each other and they are both good and they are friends, it is their being like each other that accounts for their being friends, not their both being good; whereas what P1.2 perhaps means is that if two people are like each other and are both good and are friends, it is their both being good that accounts for their being friends, not their being like each other. In any case, it is clear enough that P1.1 implies hypothesis (2a) and that P1.2 implies (2c); if so, it is sufficient to consider the argument as being against (2a) and (2c).

156

The argument against (2a) or P1.12. The argument presented by Socrates at 214E—215A seems to be as follows:

SP2   When anything is like to another thing it cannot offer any benefit (or harm) to its like which it (its like) cannot offer to itself; and nothing can be done to it, by its like, which could not be done to it by itself.

SP3   If things cannot be of mutual benefit (or help or usefulness), they cannot cherish each other.

SP4   What cannot be cherished cannot be friend.

SC1   The like is no friend to the like.

To bring out the structure of this argument as a *reductio ad absurdum* we shall recast it, starting from the hypothesis to be refuted, changing the order of the premises where convenient, and drawing intermediate conclusions by standard rules of inference.

P1.12   (x)(y)[(x is like y)⊃(x [is] can be friend to y)] (hypothesis)

P2   (x)(y)[(x [is] can be friend to y)⊃(x can cherish[es] y and y can cherish[es] x) (from SP4 by transposition)

P3   (x)(y)[(x can cherish[es] y and y can cherish[es] x)⊃ (x can offer benefit to y and y can offer benefit to x)] (from SP3 by transposition)

P4   (x)(y)[(x can offer benefit to y and y can offer benefit to x) ⊃ (x cannot be like y)] (from SP2 by transposition)

C1   (x)(y)[(x is like y)⊃(x can cherish[es] y and y can cherish[es] x)] (from P1.12 and P2 by hypothetical syllogism)

C2   (x)(y)[(x is like y)⊃(x can offer benefit to y and y can offer benefit to x)] (from C1 and P3 by hypothetical syllogism)

C3   (x)(y)[(x is like y)⊃(x cannot be like y)] (from C2 and P4 by hypothetical syllogism)

Soundness. A sound argument is a valid argument with all true premises. Is the argument sound? It is certainly valid. In fact it is a perfect *reductio ad absurdum* argument, so far as its logic is concerned: starting from the hypothesis to be tested, with the help of auxiliary premises and by using standard rules of inference, we arrive validly at a contradiction. Given this, if we know our auxiliary premises to be true we have no choice but to reject the hypothesis. Of course Socrates does not state the argument in the form in which I have recast it. But the recasting is perfectly legitimate as interpretation; for it uses nothing more than the premises

157

Socrates actually supplies and standard rules of inference. Are the auxiliary premises true? This is a far more difficult question to answer. We can only note two major points here about the auxiliary premises. SP3 and SP4 or their near equivalents seem to be almost axiomatic in the *Lysis*: as Vlastos has recently noticed,[8] intimate connections between love and friendship on the one hand and usefulness or benefit on the other are asserted very early in the *Lysis* (210CD), way before our refutations begin:

> And shall we be friends of anyone, and will anyone love us, in those respects in which we are unprofitable?
> Of course not, he said.
> So your father does not love you now, nor do others love anyone so far as he is useless.

This exchange affirms the near equivalents of SP3 and SP4. The readiness with which these propositions are affirmed, without argument and without the least hesitation, suggests that friendship and the love involved in friendship were perhaps largely conceived in terms of benefit or valuable assets. The second major point is about SP2. SP2 can be taken in an absolute or a relative sense:

SP2a   When x is like y in every respect, x cannot offer to y any benefit that y cannot offer to itself . . . (similarly with the rest of SP2)

or

SP2r   When x is like y with respect to being F, x cannot offer to y any benefit with respect to F that y cannot offer to itself.

SP2a is presumably true because, given that x and y are alike in every respect, y already has anything that x has to offer. And similarly with SP2r: for example, if x is like y with respect to possessing medical knowledge, x cannot offer any benefit to y with respect to medical knowledge because y already has anything that x has to offer. The absolute version SP2a would seem to be pretty idle since hardly any two people are alike in every respect. Fortunately, however, the relativized version SP2r is sufficient for Socrates' argument. For what Socrates is trying to show is not that it cannot be the case that two people are alike in respect F and also that they are friends. Rather, he is trying to show that if two people are alike with respect to both being F and are also friends, it is not their being alike with respect to being F that accounts for their friendship; or, it is not the case that they are friends *because* they are alike. It is clear enough that this is what he intends to show from the way he states the hypothesis to be refuted (P1.1

at 214E above). And this is sufficient for his argument, since what he ultimately intends is to show that friendship cannot be *defined* or accounted for in terms of being like.

The argument against P1.2. The good is friend to the good in so far as he is good, not in so far as he is like. We took this to imply that for any two people that are both good and friends (and are like each other), they are friends because they are both good (not because they are like each other). Dropping the parentheses for simplicity, the argument against this hypothesis that Socrates gives is as follows (215AB):

SP2   The good (whoever is good), in so far as he is good, is to that extent sufficient to himself.

SP3   The sufficient (whoever is sufficient to himself) has no need with respect to that in which he is sufficient.

SP4   Whoever does not need something would not cherish that thing.

SP5   Whoever does not cherish (something) does not love (that thing).

SP6   Whoever does not love something is no friend (of that thing).

It can be seen that some of these premises also can be interpreted in an absolute or relative way. It will be easier to recast the argument so as to see clearly its *reductio* form if we first interpret it in an absolute way.

P.12 $(x)(y)[(x$ is good and y is good and x is friend to $y)\supset(x$ is friend to y because x is good and y is good)]. (hypothesis)

Let a and b be any two arbitrarily selected individuals such that

P1.21   a is good and b is good and a is friend to b. (assumption)

P1.22 $(x)(y)(x$ is good and y is good and x is friend to y). (from P1.21 by Universal Generalization)

C1 $(x)(y)(x$ is friend to y because x is good and y is good). (from P1.2 and P1.22 by *modus ponens*)

C2 $(x)(y)[(x$ is good and y is good$)\supset(x$ is friend to y)]. (from C1 on the assumption that (p because q) implies $(q\supset p))$

P2 $(x)(y)[(x$ is friend to y$)\supset(x$ loves y)]. (from SP6 by transposition)

C3 $(x)(y)[(x$ is good and y is good$)\supset(x$ loves y)]. (from C2 and P2 by hypothetical syllogism)

P3 $(x)(y)[(x$ loves y$)\supset(x$ cherishes y)]. (from SP5 by transposition)

C4 (x)(y)[(x is good and y is good)⊃(x cherishes y)]. (from C3 and P3 by hypothetical syllogism)

P4 (x)(y)[(x cherishes y)⊃(x needs y)]. (from SP4 by transposition)

C5 (x)(y)[(x is good and y is good)⊃(x needs y)]. (from C4 and P4 by hypothetical syllogism)

P5 (x)(y)[(x needs y)⊃(x is not sufficient to himself)]. (from SP3 by transposition)

C6 (x)(y)[(x is good and y is good)⊃(x is not sufficient to himself)]. (from C5 and P5 by hypothetical syllogism)

P6 (x)[(x is not sufficient to himself)⊃(x is not good)]. (from SP2 by transposition)

C7 (x)(y)[(x is good and y is good)⊃(x is not good)]. (from C6 and P6 by hypothetical syllogism)

Soundness. Is this argument, P1.2–C7, sound? It is a valid *reductio ad absurdum*: from the hypothesis and auxiliary premises a contradiction is validly derived by standard rules of inference and a minimal interpretation of 'p because q.' So, if the auxiliary premises are true, the hypothesis must be false. Are the auxiliary premises true? Offhand it would seem that P5 and P6 are false. It should be remembered, however, that P1.2 through C7 is constructed on the assumption of an absolutist interpretation of Socrates' premises SP2 and SP3: this means that in P5 and P6 we take the expression 'x is good' to mean 'x is good in all respects,' and the expression 'x is sufficient' to mean 'x is sufficient in all respects.' So understood, P6 becomes very plausible: for if x is good in all respects (a good huntsman, a good carpenter, a good doctor, and so on) he will be also sufficient in all respects (where sufficiency at any rate is understood in terms of need and benefit rather than in terms of desire or impulse); and if x is sufficient in all respects he needs no one, since no one would have any benefit or need satisfying any object that x lacks. Premises SP4 and SP5 reflect the connections between loving and cherishing and needing which we pointed out earlier seem to be taken for granted in the *Lysis*, and they are certainly controversial statements.

It may be objected that taking premises P5 and P6 in an absolutist way makes the argument idle or inapplicable to anything since no one is good or sufficient in all respects; and the hypothesis itself, interpreted in an absolutist fashion, would appear to be outlandish. The answer is that, once we understand the argument on the absolutist interpretation, we can construct a relativized version, which in all probability is the version Socrates meant given the way SP2 and SP3 are phrased. The relativized version can be produced by taking the expression 'x is good' to mean 'x is a good F,' and the expression 'x is sufficient to himself' to mean 'x is a self-sufficient F' where 'F' can be substituted by such expressions as 'carpenter,' 'physician,' 'citizen,' 'man,' 'hunter,' 'father,' and so on. Thus SP2, SP3, SP4, SP5, SP6, in their relativized version would read:

SP2R   Whoever is a good F is a self-sufficient F.
SP3R   Whoever is a self-sufficient F has no need of possessing or becoming an F.
SP4R   Whoever has no need of possessing or becoming an F would not cherish an F.
SP5R   Whoever would not cherish an F would not love an F.
SP6R   Whoever does not love an F is no friend of an F.

So interpreted, SP2R and SP3R appear to be true. For example, it would appear to be true that whoever is a good potter (that is, possesses knowledge of the principles and techniques of pottery and is able to make functional and beautiful pots and vases) is a self-sufficient potter; and if he is a self-sufficient potter then he has no need of becoming a good potter or of acquiring knowledge of the principles and techniques of pottery. SP4R, SP5R, and SP6R, though, still appear to be troublesome. For, to take SP4R, someone who has no need of becoming a potter (if, say, he already is one) may nevertheless cherish another potter though not necessarily because he (the latter) is a potter; a potter obviously is many other things besides being a potter and he may be cherished by another potter for some of these other attributes; and similarly with loving. Socrates' language, once more, would seem to allow for this, and so we need to restate these three premises as follows:

SP4R   Whoever has no need of possessing or becoming an F would not cherish something which is F *as an F* (*or because it is an F*).
SP5R   Whoever would not cherish something because it is an F or as an F would not love that thing because it is an F or as an F.
SP6R   Whoever would not love something because it is an F or as an F would not be friends to that thing because it is an F or as an F.

These interpretations obviously allow that someone who is a good carpenter can cherish and love and be friend to a good carpenter, but disallow that he is friend to him as a good carpenter or because he is a good carpenter. And this is sufficient for Socrates' purposes given the hypothesis he has set out to refute. Allowing for this, still why should we suppose SP4R to be true? Can't one cherish something even though one does not need to possess it or become it (because he already has it or is it)? An answer is that for Socrates all desiring, including cherishing, loving, wanting, is desiring for the possession of something one lacks or for becoming something one is not; thus if one already possesses something or is something, he cannot desire, cherish, love, or want that thing (see, e.g. *Lysis* 221).

We are ready now to give the relativized version of Socrates' argument against hypothesis P1.2 understood as relativized. We shall skip steps P1.2R—C1R. Further, we can reconstruct Socrates' argument so as to reflect the way Socrates argues (the order of his premises and conclusion) by taking C1R to imply:

C2.1R (x)(y)[(x is friend to y)⊃(x is a good F and y is a good F)].[9]

P2R (x)(y)[(x is a good F and y is a good F)⊃(x is a self-sufficient F)].

P3R (x)(y)[(x is a self-sufficient F)⊃not (x needs y because x is a good F and y is a good F)].

P4R (x)(y) [not (x needs y because x is a good F and y is a good F)⊃ not (x cherishes y because x is a good F and y is a good F)].

P5R (x)(y)[not (x cherishes y because x is good and y is good)⊃ not (x loves y because x is a good F and y is a good F)].

P6R (x)(y)[not (x loves y because x is a good F and y is a good F)⊃ not (x is friend to y because x is a good F and y is a good F)].

C3R (x)(y)[(x is friend to y)⊃ not (x is friend to y because x is a good F and y is a good F)]. (from C2.1R—P6R by successive applications of hypothetical syllogism)

CR3 is not of course a contradiction; rather it is the contradictory of the hypothesis P1.2R. Thus from the original hypothesis and auxiliary premises we have derived the contradictory of that hypothesis by successive applications of the rule of inference by hypothetical syllogism. If the auxiliary premises are all true, it follows that the original hypothesis is false.

6 *Deductive arguments: a direct argument from the* Lysis

Context. After hypothesis (1), (2), and (3) have been refuted in all their different versions, Socrates brings up a new hypothesis about what a friend is. The previous hypotheses had been suggested by considerations of language or by various poetic traditions, but this new hypothesis is argued for, and it is argued for partly on the basis of previous refutations, especially the refutations of hypotheses (2) and (3). In a somewhat Delphic mood, Socrates reminds the interlocutors of the old proverb that 'the beautiful is a friend' and secures their agreement that 'the good is beautiful.' Then he says: 'Then I will be a diviner for once, and state that what is neither good nor bad is friend to what is beautiful and good' (216D). We can see intuitively how this hypothesis is suggested by previous arguments and by the introduction of the beautiful: the beautiful was universally thought as an object of love and attraction, and previous arguments preclude the supposition that what is beautiful or good (or bad) can be the subject of love and attraction, and hence the subject 'what is neither good nor bad' is introduced (by the 'subject' here we mean what is referred to by the first term in 'x loves y' or 'x is friend of y'). Socrates proceeds to give a deductive argument, an argument by elimination, which captures these intuitions.

The argument

SP1   There are three kinds (of things), what is good, what is bad, and what is neither good nor bad. (216D)

SP2   What is good is not friend to what is good, and what is bad is not friend to what is bad, and what is good is not friend to what is bad. (216E)

SP3   Nothing is friend to what is bad. (216E)

SC1   If anything is friend to anything, then that which is neither good nor bad is friend to what is good, or that which is neither good nor bad is friend to what is like itself (= to what is neither good nor bad). (216E)

SP4   Like cannot be friend to like. (216E)

SC2   What is neither good nor bad is not friend to what is like itself (= to what is neither good nor bad). (216E)

SC3   Only what is neither good nor bad is a friend only to what is good. (216E—217A)

This is clearly an argument by elimination whose main rule of inference is disjunctive syllogism: the idea is that, given SP1 and the fact that being a friend is a two-term relation, there is a definite number of possibilities as to how the three kinds of things listed in SP1 can be so related, namely exactly nine possibilities; previous arguments and agreements have eliminated eight of these possibilities; therefore, the remaining is the one to be examined.

Socrates does not state all the possibilities at the outset, nor does he eliminate eight of them explicitly; in recasting his argument we shall do both of these things by supplying additional premises which are needed; these can be found explicitly or implicitly in previous texts. The argument can be recast as follows:

P1   (x)(x is good or x is bad or x is neither good nor bad). (assumption)

P1.1   (x)(y) [(x is friend to y⊃x is good and y is good)]
        or [(x is friend to y⊃x is good and y is bad)]
        or [(x is friend to y⊃x is good and y is neither good nor bad)]
        or [(x is friend to y⊃x is bad and y is bad)]
        or [(x is friend to y⊃x is bad and y is good)]
        or [(x is friend to y⊃x is bad and y is neither good nor bad)]
        or [(x is friend to y⊃x is neither good nor bad and y neither good nor bad)]
        or [(x is friend to y⊃x is neither good nor bad and y is bad)]
        or [(x is friend to y⊃x is neither good nor bad and y is good)].   (supplied assumption)

P2   (x)(y) [x is friend to y⊃not (x is good and y is good)]. (SP2)

P2.1   (x)(y) [x is friend to y⊃not (x is bad and y is bad)]. (SP2)

P2.2   (x)(y)[x is friend to y⊃not (x is good and y is bad)]. (SP2)

P3   (x)(y) [x is friend to y⊃not (x is neither good nor bad and y is bad)].   (SP3)

P3.1   (x)(y) [x is friend to y⊃not (x is good and y is neither good nor bad)].   (supplied)

P3.2   (x)(y) [x is friend to y⊃not (x is bad and y is good)]. (supplied)

P3.3   (x)(y) [x is friend to y⊃not (x is bad and y is neither good nor bad)].   (supplied)

C1   (x)(y) [(x is friend to y⊃x is neither good nor bad and y is neither good nor bad)]
        or [(x is friend to y⊃x is neither good nor bad and y is good)].   (from P1.1 through P3.3 by dis/junctive syllogism)

P4   (x)(y) [x is friend to y⊃not (x is neither good nor bad and y is neither good nor bad)].   (SP4 and SC2)

C2   (x)(y)(x is friend to y⊃x is neither good nor bad and y is good).   (from C1 and P4 by disjunctive syllogism)

Soundness. The argument as Socrates states it is not valid, for he neglects to eliminate three possibilities, the possibilities eliminated by the premises I have supplied. The argument as I have recast it is valid: it consists of two disjunctive syllogisms. Are all the premises true? P1 is false if something can be both good and bad; and if so P1.1 is also false, since if something can be both good and bad there are more than nine possibilities as to what sort of thing can be friend to what sort of thing. Possibly, Socrates does not consider the possibility that something is both good and bad because by 'good' and 'bad' he means something like 'good on the whole' (or 'good on balance') and 'bad on the whole' (or 'bad on balance'); in that case he is justified in assuming that there are only things that are good, things that are bad, and things that are neither good nor bad; and consequently he is justified in assuming, implicitly, P1.1. (We find assumption P1 explicitly stated also in *Gorgias* 467E.) Premises P2, P2.1, P2.2, and P3 relate to previous refutations, some of which we have considered in previous sections, and their truth depends on the soundness of these refutations. P3.2 eliminates the fifth possibility stated in P1.1, and that possibility is explicitly eliminated at 214D. It is not entirely clear there why the bad cannot be friend to the good, but apparently the reason is the same as that given at 214C as the reason why the bad cannot be friends to the bad; namely, whoever is bad injures or does injustice to those he associates with, and whoever does injury or injustice to another cannot be friend to that other. If so, this reasoning eliminates the sixth possibility as well, the possibility eliminated by P3.3. What about the third possibility, the possibility eliminated by P3.1? Why cannot one who is good not be friend to one who is neither good nor bad? So far as I know no explicit reason is given for P3.1. Possibly principles used in previous refutations can be used to derive P3.1. In particular, the principles that whoever does not cherish something does not love it, and whoever does not love something is not friend to that thing, can be appealed to here, on the very plausible Socratic assumption that what is neither good nor bad is neither cherished nor loved.

7 *Deductive arguments: a direct argument from the* Protagoras

Context. At 359AB Socrates reopens a dispute he had with Protagoras earlier in the dialogue. The widest dispute he had with Protagoras was whether a man can have any one of the five virtues, holiness, justice, temperance, wisdom, and courage, without having all the rest (330 ff). By a series of arguments Socrates appears to have convinced Protagoras that a man cannot have any one of *the first four* of these virtues without having the remaining three of *them*.[10] Now (359AB) Socrates takes up the connection between the first four virtues and courage and undertakes to refute what remains of Protagoras' view, which he states as follows:

> You will find, Socrates, said he, that men may be most unholy, most unjust, most dissolute, and most ignorant, yet most courageous; whence you may judge that courage is very different from the other parts of virtue.

Since Socrates has already argued for the connection we stated above among the first four virtues, it is sufficient for him now to argue that one cannot have courage without having wisdom. He proceeds to give a long and complex argument whose last conclusion appears to be his favorite *definition* of courage, 'that courage is the knowledge [wisdom, *sophia*] of fearful and non-fearful things' (360D). And from that he compels Protagoras to draw the conclusion that a man cannot be most ignorant (of fearful and non-fearful things) and yet most courageous. Here we are interested in the argument whose last conclusion is the definition of courage.

This is a very long and complex argument: it contains no fewer than *nine sub-arguments*, and it relies a lot on several agreements reached in a previous argument, at *Protagoras* 352—358.[11] In order to try to get clear about his argument, we shall first stay very close to Socrates' statement, marking our premises and conclusions clearly and stating them in order, and making clear what the nine sub-arguments are. Secondly, we shall analyze each sub-argument, precising and dis-ambiguating premises and conclusions where necessary, marking out clearly reliance on previous agreements, and using symbols where necessary to bring out clearly the form of each sub-argument, and the rules of inference on which each relies. This procedure will make possible a decision on the validity of the argument. However, we shall not attempt to determine the truth or falsity of all the premises: this would be too vast a task, relative to both the knowledge we possess and the space and time at our disposal.

The argument as Socrates presents it

P1   Fear or dread is an expectation of evil (something bad for one). (358D)

P1.1   What one fears one thinks evil. (358E)

P1.2   No one pursues (goes after) or accepts (takes) willingly those things he thinks evil. (358E — by previous agreement 358CD)

C1	No one wants to pursue the things he fears when he can pursue those he does not. (358E)
P2	Courageous men are daring ($\vartheta\alpha\rho\rho\alpha\lambda\acute{\epsilon}o\upsilon\varsigma$) and eager ($\acute{\iota}\tau\alpha\varsigma$). (359B)
P3	Cowards pursue (go after) dared things ($\vartheta\alpha\rho\rho\alpha\lambda\acute{\epsilon}\alpha$). (359C)
P4	Courageous men pursue (are impetuous towards) fearful things ($\delta\epsilon\iota\nu\acute{\alpha}$). (359C)
P5	Courageous men pursue fearful things thinking they are fearful or pursue non-fearful things (and/or things they do not think are fearful). (359D)
C2	Courageous men pursue non-fearful things (and/or things they do not think fearful). (359D)
C3	All men, cowards and courageous, pursue the things they dare ($\vartheta\alpha\rho\rho o\tilde{\upsilon}\sigma\iota$), and in this manner cowards and courageous men pursue the same things. (359DE)
P6	What courageous men pursue is the very opposite of what cowards pursue: for instance, courageous men are willing (want) to go to war, whereas cowards are not willing. (359E)
P7	Going to war is (an) honorable (action) ($\kappa\alpha\lambda\acute{o}\nu$). (359E)
P7.1	All honorable actions are good. (359E — previous agreement 358B)
C4	Going to war is a good action. (359E)
P7.2	If going to war is honorable and good, it is also pleasant. (360A — previous agreement 355AB)
C5	Going to war is pleasant. (supplied)
P8	Everyone is willing (wants) to go to (pursue) (what he thinks is) the more honorable and the better and the pleasanter. (previous argument 356BC, 358BC)
C6	The cowards are not willing to go to what is more honorable and better and pleasanter not knowing (that it is more honorable and better and pleasanter). (360A)
C7	The courageous man pursues the more honorable and better and pleasanter. (360AB)
P9	Courageous men do not fear base ($\alpha\iota\sigma\chi\rho o\acute{\upsilon}\varsigma$) fears when they fear, nor do they dare base darings. (360B)
P9.1	If not base, then honorable. (360B)
P9.2	If honorable, then good. (360B)
P10	The cowards and the bold and the mad, on the contrary, feel base fears, and dare base darings. (360B)
P11	The cowards dare base and bad things through (because of) nothing else than ignorance and lack of learning. (360BC)

P12   That through (because of) which the cowards are cowards is cowardice. (360C)

P13   The cowards were found to be cowards through (because of) the ignorance of fearful things. (360C)

C8   The ignorance of fearful and non-fearful things is cowardice. (360C)

P14   Courage is the opposite of cowardice. (360D)

P15   The knowledge (wisdom) of fearful and non-fearful things is the opposite of the ignorance of fearful and non-fearful things. (360D)

C9   The knowledge (wisdom) of fearful and non-fearful things is courage. (360D)

This is the argument pretty much as we find it in Plato's text. There are many unclarities in it, including unclarities as to the meaning and form of particular sentences, unclarities as to whether some sentences, such as P8, P9, P10, are premises or conclusions, and unclarities as to what is derived from what. By modern logical standards the argument is indeed very badly written, which is not suprising considering its length and complexity and the non-existence at the time of any logical standards. We shall have to do the best we can, on the basis of relevant texts, to resolve the problems in it. We shall have to do this piecemeal, taking up each sub-argument in turn.

First sub-argument. P1 is clearly of a definitional character, and P1.1 seems clearly to be based on P1; if so, P1 is best recast so as to make possible the derivation of P1.1 from it. Further, in all probability we should expand 'willingly' in P1.2 so as to reflect the clause 'when he can pursue those he does not' in C1; in any case the previous argument (*Protagoras* 352—8) makes it clear in many places that actions are being considered in relation to the agent's alternatives (cf. chapter 9); and the abrupt switch to a comparative form of 'honorable,' 'good', and 'pleasant' in the middle of our argument (P8, C6, C7) also makes it clear that a comparison to the agent's alternatives is always being assumed in the background. Taking all these points into account, we recast the first sub-argument as follows:

P1 $(x)(y)(x$ fears y = x thinks y is evil and x foresees that y will happen to x or that y will happen to x if x goes to meet y).

Co[=P1.1] $(x)(y)(x$ fears $y \supset x$ thinks y is evil). (from P1 by UI, equiv., simp., and UG)[12]

P1.2 $(x)(x)[(x$ thinks y is evil) $\supset (z)(x$ thinks z is less evil than y and x can do z instead of y⊃x does not pursue y)] .

C1   (x)(y)[(x fears y)⊃(z)(x thinks z is less evil than y and x can pursue z instead of y⊃x does not pursue y)] . (from Co and P1.2 by U1, HS, and UG)

Second sub-argument. In this argument 'fearful things,' 'dared things,' 'x dares y,' 'x thinks y is fearful,' and 'x thinks y is a dared thing' are used. We take 'fearful things' to mean not necessarily 'things that are feared' but rather 'things to be feared,' and we take the latter to imply at least 'future evils' (things that are evil and may be or will be forthcoming). Further, we take 'x thinks y is fearful' to imply 'x thinks y is evil.' We take 'dared things' to mean 'things that are to be dared,' and we take the latter to imply at least 'future goods;' further, 'x thinks y is a dared thing' implies 'x thinks y is a good thing,' and we analyze 'x dares y' in a parallel way to 'x fears y'. It should be noted that Protagoras presents P2, P3, and P4, as if these were what was characteristically thought about courageous men and cowards: courageous men are thought of as daring men, and, further, as men that dare to pursue fearful things, and this is presumably part of the reason why they are admired. On the other hand, cowards are thought of as not pursuing dared things, that is future goods, that is things that are safe to pursue, and this is presumably the reason why, in part, they are not admired.

This sub-argument proceeds by Socrates pointing out that P4 is ambiguous and that it can be disambiguated by the two alternatives presented by P5; one of these alternatives is then found inconsistent with previous agreements, and the other alternative is inferred in C2. A parallel ambiguity exists in P3; and a parallel argument would conclude that P3 is to be taken in the sense that cowards pursue dared things thinking that they are dared things (or, dared things are the *intended* objects of their pursuit; the *actual* objects may well be things to be feared — for this terminology cf. chapter VI). In disambiguating P4 we run into a problem. The alternatives seem to be: courageous men pursue fearful things thinking they are fearful or courageous men pursue fearful things not thinking they are fearful (or thinking they are non-fearful). In rejecting the first alternative as being inconsistent with Co, P1.2, and C1, and in affirming the second, Socrates would appear committed to the view that the courageous man is making a mistake (pursuing things that are in fact fearful thinking that they are not). The alternative disambiguation of P4, where we take the second alternative to be 'pursuing non-fearful things thinking they are not fearful,'

169

solves the problem, but it is clearly a fallacious disambiguation of P4. This problem perhaps can be overlooked at this stage of the argument since C3 clearly shows that what Socrates is interested in here is to show that the cowards and the courageous men pursue the same objects in the sense of *'intended* objects'; he wants to show that 'dared things' are the intended objects both kinds of men pursue, and that fearful things are not the intended objects that either pursues. Finally, it should be noted that, just as in the case of good and evil, so in the case of fearful and dared things, comparison to the agent's alternatives is always in the background; an agent may think that what he does is fearful and also think of the alternatives open to him as equally, or more, or less fearful. Given all these points, we state the second sub-argument as follows:

P4 (x)(y)(x is courageous and x pursues y⊃y is fearful).
P5 (x)(y)(x is courageous and x pursues y⊃y is fearful and x thinks y is fearful)
   or (x)(y)(x is courageous and x pursues y⊃x is fearful and y thinks not y is fearful).
P5.1 Not (x)(y)(x is courageous and x pursues y⊃y is fearful and x thinks y is fearful).[13]
C2 (x)(y)(x is courageous and x pursues y⊃y is fearful and x thinks not y is fearful) (= x thinks y is dared).[14]

Third sub-argument. Having shown that the intended objects of the courageous men's pursuit are not fearful things but rather dared things, Socrates now takes advantage of P3, that cowards pursue dared things, in the sense that dared things are the intended objects of their pursuit, to argue further that 'in a sense' both cowards and courageous men pursue the 'same things'; that is, the intended objects of pursuit of the courageous men are dared things, and the intended objects of pursuit of the cowards are also dared things. This of course is compatible with the view that the actual objects in the two cases may be different. Given all this, we can state the third sub-argument as follows:

C2.1 (x)(y)(x is courageous and x pursues y⊃x thinks y is dared). (from C2)
P3 (x)(y)(x is a coward and x pursues y⊃x thinks y is dared).
C3 (x)(y) [(x pursues y) and (x is courageous or x is a coward) ⊃(x thinks y is dared)] .

It should be noticed that C3 is different from another proposition which Socrates neither asserts nor implies, namely: (x)(y)(w) (z) [(x is courageous and x pursues y and w is a coward and w pursues z)⊃(y=z)]. This proposition says that the *actual* objects that cowards and courageous men pursue are the same. That Socrates neither implies nor asserts this proposition is shown by the fact that in the next sub-argument Socrates disputes the proposition that courageous men and cowards pursue opposite things, that is disputes this proposition in so far as it contradicts C3; but does not dispute Protagoras' assertion that courageous men are willing to go to war whereas cowards are not, thus allowing that going to war is an actual (and intended) object of the courageous men's pursuit but not an actual object that cowards pursue.

Fourth sub-argument. This argument begins with what seems an objection from Protagoras (359E):

> But still, Socrates, he said, what cowards go to meet is the very opposite of what the courageous go to meet. For instance, the latter are willing to go to war, but the former are not.

Socrates' handling of this objection and his strategy in the whole argument begin to emerge in the next three sub-arguments. We will proceed to state these:

P7 $(x)[(x = \text{going to war}) \supset x \text{ is honorable}]$
P7.1 $(x)(x \text{ is honorable} \supset x \text{ is good})$
C4 $(x)[(x = \text{going to war}) \supset x \text{ is good}]$ (from P7 and P7.1 by UI, HS, and UG)

Fifth sub-argument

P7.2 $(x)(x \text{ is honorable and } x \text{ is good} \supset x \text{ is pleasant})$.
C4.1 $(x)(x = \text{going to war} \supset x \text{ is honorable and } x \text{ is good})$. (conjunction of P7 and C4)
C5 $(x)(x = \text{going to war} \supset x \text{ is pleasant})$. (from C4.1 and P7.2 by UI, HS and UG)

Some of the statements in these two sub-arguments may appear preposterous, at least in the sense of being obviously false. Possibly some wars or some goings-to-war are honorable, and possibly some are good, but is it even plausible to maintain that all are? Worse yet, is it even plausible to maintain that any war or any going to war is pleasant? Perhaps the paradox can be lessened by two considerations, both of which derive from relevant texts. In this whole argument, as in the previous one, Socrates is operating within the hedonistic beliefs of the many, both ethical and psychological hedonism (cf. chapter VII below and Vlastos, 'Socrates on Akrasia'[15]). In expounding hedonism, not on his own behalf but

171

on behalf of the many, he says at one point: 'You call being pained a good thing as soon as it either rids us of greater pains than those it comprises or leads to greater pleasures than its pain' (354D). War then could be called good, even if always painful, if it helped us rid ourselves of greater pains than those it contains or led to pleasures greater than those it contains. If this is so, Socrates and the interlocutors may well be willing to call going to war pleasant even though it is painful provided that it rids us of greater pains than those it contains or brings us pleasures greater than the pains it contains; in view of the fact that at 345AB military service is cited as an example of a painful thing that brings us such things as 'deliverance of cities, dominion over others, and wealth,' this interpretation of C5, that war is pleasant, may well be correct. This makes these statements at least understandable as common beliefs, though not necessarily Socrates' beliefs.[16] It should of course be remembered that Socrates is arguing against the views of the many, and of Protagoras, that one can be ignorant and yet courageous; so he can use their beliefs as premises in his argument. The second consideration is that, though 'honorable,' 'good,' and 'pleasant' are not used in a comparative form in the fourth and fifth sub-arguments, a comparison to the agent's alternatives is in the background, as we noted earlier; and this is confirmed in the very next argument. So it is not being asserted that war is honorable and good and pleasant absolutely, but rather relative to the alternatives, which in this case is not going to war or refusing to go to war, the alternative the coward takes. This again lessens the paradox of these assertions: for in a given case, even though going to a given war is not honorable or good or pleasant, the alternative may be even less honorable, good, and pleasant if, for instance, *it* results in slavery and all its sufferings.

Sixth sub-argument. Socrates goes over this argument very fast: from a previous argeement which I have identified as P8, and from the second part of P6, he deduces that the cowards refuse (= are not willing) to go to war in ignorance of the (alleged) fact that going to war is more honorable and better and pleasanter (than not going). This is my reconstruction of the inference he makes to C6:

P8.1　$(x)(y)(z)(x$ is not willing to go to meet y instead of $z \supset x$ is not willing to go to meet y instead of z and x does not know or believe that y is more honorable and better and pleasanter than z). (contrapositive of P8 by Absorption)

P6.1　$(x)(y)(z)(x$ is a coward and y = going-to-war and z =

172

not-going-to-war ⊃ x is not willing to go to meet y rather than z).

C6   (x)(y)(z)(x is a coward and y = going-to-war and z = not-going-to-war ⊃ x is not willing to go to meet y instead of x and x does not know or believe or think that y is more honorable and better and pleasanter than z). (from P6.1 and P8.1 by UI, HS and UG)

Seventh sub-argument. Having shown that cowards are not willing to go to war, in ignorance of the (alleged) fact that going to war is more honorable and better and pleasanter, Socrates now apparently wishes to show that courageous men are willing to go to war knowing or at least truly believing that going to war is more honorable and better and pleasanter. Socrates goes very fast over this inference also: 'But what of the courageous man? Does he not go to the more honorable and better and pleasanter? — I am forced to admit that, he said' (360AB). It is from Protagoras' reply that we infer that what is being affirmed as a result of this exchange is being inferred from previous steps in the argument. But which steps? Apparently, from P6 (that courageous men are willing to go to war) and the conjunction of P7, C4, and C5 in comparative form (that going to war is more honorable and better and pleasanter). But these premises only support the conclusion that courageous men are willing to go to something that in fact is more honorable and better and pleasanter; not the conclusion that they do so knowing or believing that it is more honorable and better and pleasanter, and it is apparently this latter conclusion that Socrates means to draw. Looking around for premises or previous conclusions to derive this latter conclusion from, the only candidate that gives even a start is

C2.1   (x)(y)(x is courageous and x pursues y⊃x thinks y is dared).

In addition we need the following implications: 'x thinks y is dared' implies 'x thinks y is good'; and 'x thinks y is good' implies 'x thinks y is honorable'; and 'x thinks y is good' implies 'x thinks y is pleasant.' Assuming all this we have

C2.2   (x)(y)(x thinks y is dared⊃x thinks y is good and honorable and pleasant).

Assuming that alternatives open to the agent is an idea always in the background, we can proceed to relativize C2.1 and C2.2 as follows:

C2.12 (x)(y)(z)(x is courageous and x pursues y instead of

173

z⊃x knows or thinks that y is more dared than z).

C2.21 (x)(y)(z)(x thinks or knows that y is more dared than z⊃x thinks or knows that y is more honorable and better and pleasanter than z).

And from these two statements we can obtain by hypothetical syllogism the statement we need for the seventh sub-argument,

C2.3 (x)(y)(z)(x is courageous and x pursues y instead of z⊃x knows or thinks that y is more honorable and better and pleasanter than z).

We can state the seventh sub-argument as follows:

P6.2 (x)(y)(z)(x is courageous and y is a going to war and z = not-going to war ⊃ x is courageous and x pursues y instead of z). (from P6 by Absorption)

C2.3 (x)(y)(z)(x is courageous and x pursues y instead of z ⊃ x pursues y instead of z and x knows or thinks that y is more honorable and better and pleasanter than z). (from C2.3 by Absorption)

C7 (x)(y)(z)(x is courageous and y = going-to-war and z = not-going-to-war⊃x pursues y instead of z and x knows or thinks truly that y is more honorable and better and pleasanter than z). (from P6.2 and C2.3 by UI, HS and UG)

Eighth sub-argument. This argument is puzzling for several reasons, of which two are the most relevant here. The first is that Socrates elicits from Protagoras a number of admissions, P9, P9.1, P9.2, P10, all of which are unclear as to their source, their meaning, and their function in the argument. These statements do not seem to be derived from anything preceding them; and it is not very clear what they mean since the notions of a shameful or base fear or daring and good and honorable fear or daring have not been explained. Possibly, a base or shameful fear is a fear that causes one to act in a base or a shameful manner; the coward's fear or daring is shameful because it causes him to act in a shameful manner, that is, causes him to act cowardly, as presumably in the case of war his fear of war causes him to not be willing to go to war. And, possibly, his daring not to go to war is shameful since it causes him not to go to war, which is shameful; and similarly for the case of the courageous man and his fears and darings. Further, it is not clear what function these statements have in the argument, since they do not seem to be used subsequently. The second major thing that is puzzling about the eighth sub-argument is that P11 introduces a new relation (through or because of — δι' ὅ) which has not occurred previously in the argument, for which there is no warrant given, and which seems very dubious. P11 is a very strong statement: it says not only that cowards dare base and bad things through or because of ignorance and lack of learning, but also that it is through or because of nothing else that they dare base and bad things. If we take the case of war, and suppose plausibly that the relevant things that are asserted about cowards and courageous men in the case of war can be generalized to all cases of courageous and cowardly behavior, we can plausibly suppose that the bad and base things that the cowards dare include not going to war (not going to war would be bad and base according to the argument since going to war has been said to be more honorable and better and pleasanter). And we can take the ignorance and lack of learning to refer to the ignorance of the coward that going to war is better and pleasanter and more honorable and ignorance that not going to war is worse and less honorable than going; and we can refer to this ignorance collectively as ignorance of what is and what is not fearful. But, given all this, all that we find in the previous argument, specifically in C6 of the sixth subargument, is that cowards are not willing to go to war *and* they are ignorant of . . .; from this it certainly does not follow that they are not willing to go to war *through* or *because* of that ignorance; not to mention that it certainly does not follow that they are not willing to go to war through or because of *nothing else than* that ignorance. How then does Socrates get to this new relation? There may be at least two ways in which he can do so. One way is to begin with the plausible view that the cowards dare base and bad things (not going to war, say) because of nothing else than that they fear the things they are unwilling to meet (going to war, say). Now we can use Socrates' definition of fear and auxiliary premises already at our disposal as follows. The cowards fear the things they are unwilling to meet because of nothing else than that they are ignorant that these things are more honorable and better and pleasanter. Therefore, the cowards do base and bad things because of nothing else than that they are ignorant that the things they are unwilling to meet are more honorable and better and pleasanter (or, ignorant of fearful and non-fearful things, to use the Socratic formula). This way of bridging the gap is fairly attractive since it uses premises of the argument, and the only new premises it introduces could plausibly be described as a common belief or a belief of the many. The other way of closing the gap is also fairly attractive and it draws entirely on premises found in the argument for an inference to P11. From P1.2, relativized, we have it that no one pursues what he knows or believes is less honorable and worse and less pleasant than any alternative open to him. And from P8 we have it that every one pursues what he knows or believes is more honorable and better and pleasanter than any alternative open to him. In addition we have it that going to war is more honorable and better and pleasanter. Further, we have it that the courageous man is willing to go to war and the coward is not, and that the first knows or believes that war is more honorable and better and pleasanter and the second does not. Thus the motivations of the courageous man and the coward seem to be identical, or, more precisely, the intended objects they pursue *qua* courageous and *qua* cowards are the same. Yet their behavior is different, and the only difference that we have to explain this difference of behavior is the fact that one knows or believes truly what is better and more honorable and pleasanter than what, and the other does not. It seems, therefore, that we can (perhaps abductively, rather than deductively) infer that the coward does base and bad things (or, less honorable and worse and less pleasant) because of no other reason than that he is ignorant that these things are so, and similarly for the courageous man. If it be objected that the coward perhaps does base and bad things not because of his ignorance but because of his fear of the things he is not willing to do, it can be replied, on behalf of Socrates and his argument, that in turn he fears these things because he is ignorant that they are more honorable and better and pleasanter (that is, this objection is answered by appeal to the first way of bridging the gap). Given all this, the eighth sub-argument can be stated as follows:

P11　　All cowards do base and bad things because and only because of their ignorance of what is and is not fearful.

P11.1　All and only those who do base and bad things are cowards. (supplied)

P13　　All cowards are cowards because and only because of their ignorance of what is and is not fearful. (from P11 and P11.1 by equiv.)

P12　　That because of which cowards are cowards is called cowardice.

C8　　The ignorance of what is and is not to be feared is cowardice.

Skipping P11 and P11.1, we can symbolize P13–C8 as follows:

P13　　(x)(y)(x is a coward because and only because of y⊃. y = ignorance by x of what is and is not to be feared).

P12　　(x)(z)(x is a coward because of z⊃. z = cowardice of x).

P12.1   (x)(y)(z)(x is a coward because and only because of y and x is a coward because of z⊃.y=z).

C8   (x)(y)(z)(y=ignorance by x of what is and is not to be feared and z=the cowardice of x.⊃.y=z).

Ninth sub-argument. This argument uses C8 as a premise, and it is as follows:

C8   The ignorance of fearful and non-fearful things is (identical with) cowardice.

P14   Courage is the opposite of cowardice.

P15   The wisdom of fearful and non-fearful things is the opposite of the ignorance of fearful and non-fearful things.

C9   The wisdom of fearful and non-fearful things is (identical with) courage.

As it stands this argument is not valid; however, it clearly relies on a proposition agreed in previous arguments of this form, back at *Protagoras* 332CD, that 'to each single thing that is an opposite there is one opposite and not many.' This principle can be stated as follows:

P16   (x)(y)(z)(x is opposite of y and z is opposite of y⊃.x=z).

Given this, we can restate the argument fully as follows:

C8   The ignorance of fearful and non-fearful things is identical with cowardice.

P14   Courage is the opposite of cowardice. (assumption)

P15   The wisdom of fearful and non-fearful things is the opposite of the ignorance of fearful and non-fearful things. (assumption)

C8.1   The wisdom of fearful and non-fearful things is the opposite of cowardice. (from C8 and P15 by substitution of identicals)

P16   (x)(y)(z)(x is opposite of y and z is opposite of y⊃.x=z). (assumption)

C9   The wisdom of fearful and non-fearful things is identical with courage. (from P14 and C8.1 and P16 by *modus ponens*)

This is a valid argument. Is it sound? Aside from C8, there is some question about the three assumptions. What does 'opposite' mean in P16? Vlastos remarks, probably correctly:[17]

What 'opposite' means in this context is what is called 'complement' in set theory: for class K, its complement, $\overline{K}$, is such that

177

K and $\overline{K}$ are mutually exclusive and jointly exhaustive of their universe of discourse.

Now are courage and cowardice opposites in this sense? And are the wisdom and ignorance of fearful and non-fearful things opposites in this sense? It is not very clear. To say that courage and cowardice are opposites in this sense is to say that every man is courageous or a coward and that no man is both (at the same time); it is not clear that this is true, since conceivably a man may never be in circumstances in which courage or cowardice can be shown, and so may be neither courageous nor a coward. Further, to say that wisdom and ignorance of what is fearful and not fearful are opposites in this sense is to say that a man is either wise or ignorant of what is and is not fearful and that no man is both. At *Protagoras* 358C we are told that ignorance consists in false beliefs, and if so ignorance of what is and is not fearful consists in false beliefs as to what is and is not fearful. Now is it not possible that a man has no beliefs as to what is and is not fearful? Further, what is meant by 'wisdom of what is and is not fearful'? At least true beliefs of what is and is not fearful. But a man may have true beliefs without evidence or true beliefs with evidence. From all this, it would appear plausible to suppose that a man may have true beliefs with evidence or true beliefs or false beliefs or no beliefs at all as to what is and is not fearful. Perhaps the answer is that Socrates supposes that wisdom is true beliefs with evidence or true beliefs, and that ignorance is false beliefs or no beliefs at all. But this is not clear, since this notion of ignorance contradicts his explanation; and this notion of wisdom would require that σοφία (wisdom) is wider than ἐπιστήμη (knowledge), assuming that knowledge requires not only true belief but also evidence.[18]

8 *Conclusion*

In this chapter we have analyzed more than seventeen arguments that Socrates constructs. This represents only a very small sample of all the arguments that Socrates constructs in the early Platonic Dialogues. Yet it is sufficient to exhibit the rich variety of arguments that Socrates constructed, the ingenuity and sophistication with which he argued, and the variety of argument forms or rules of inference that he used. Of course we cannot say that he used all the rules of inference that we used in order to show validity; nor can we say that the rules of inference or argument forms that he did use he could have stated as rules of inference (any more than we can say that a man who uses English sentences grammatically can state the rules of grammar which the construction of his sentences satisfy). Plato did not write books on logic, nor do we have any evidence that Plato or Socrates concerned themselves systematically with formulating rules of inference. Nevertheless, Socrates makes systematic and complicated uses of argument forms or rules of inference to construct some very complex arguments, especially of such rules as *modus ponens*, hypothetical syllogism, disjunctive syllogism, and transposition or contraposition. He is not a logician, but neither is he like a man who argues without ever reflecting on arguments, their form, and their validity and soundness. And for one who was arguing before *any* rules of argument had been *stated*, he shows not only a remarkable skill in constructing arguments, but also a remarkable awareness of arguments as instruments for testing the truth of some of the dominant ideas of his time. The idea that, especially in ethics, we can test our beliefs by such arguments is almost entirely due to him, and the influence of this idea is almost entirely due to his putting it to practice so skillfully and resourcefully and persistently. And the discovery of logic by Aristotle and the Stoics can hardly not be indebted to the rich hunting grounds that Socrates' arguments provided. One can still learn much about arguments by studying his arguments.[19]

PART THREE

Socratic Ethics

VI

Virtue and Knowledge I:
The Socratic Paradoxes[1]

Introduction

Plato's ethics in the earlier dialogues (at least up to the *Republic*) is characterized by two doctrines commonly known as the Socratic paradoxes. The first of these is that no one desires evil things and that all who pursue evil things do so involuntarily;[2] the second doctrine is that virtue is knowledge and that all who do injustice or wrong do so involuntarily.[3]

Students of Plato have found these doctrines puzzling and paradoxical. It is not difficult to see why. We commonly think that men sometimes harm themselves knowing that they are doing so, and that often they do what is morally wrong knowing that it is morally wrong when it is in their power to do otherwise. Incontinence and moral weakness are supposed to be familiar facts of experience; yet the doctrines just mentioned seem to contradict these facts. How are we to account for this? Are we to suppose that Plato held, and held most persistently through several Dialogues, views that contradict facts with which presumably everyone is acquainted?

Most students of Plato have supposed just this. T. Gomperz, for example, writes:[4]

Such a thing as knowing what is right and yet disobeying that knowledge, believing an action wrong and yet yielding to the motives that impel to it, is for Socrates not merely a sad and disastrous occurrence; it is a sheer impossibility. He does not combat or condemn, he simply denies, that state of mind which his contemporaries called 'being overcome by desire.' . . .
Although the state of mind whose existence is denied by Socrates does really occur, its occurrence is a far rarer phenomenon than is generally supposed.

This opinion, that the Socratic paradoxes contradict facts, is shared by Aristotle, St Thomas Aquinas, W. Jaeger, F. M. Cornford, and others;[5] indeed it is no exaggeration to say that it is the received opinion about the paradoxes.[6]

An idea behind this widespread interpretation is that Plato over-emphasized the intellect and neglected — even entirely neglected — the will (this tendency in Plato's thought is usually labeled 'intellectualism').[7] Perhaps the best general statement of this idea has been made by John Gould who, in interpreting Aristotle's criticism, says:[8]

> Socrates was wrong in supposing that if a man achieved an understanding of what justice involves, he would necessarily become just in behavior, since the whole problem of choice intervenes between knowledge and action.

I think that this interpretation of the Socratic paradoxes is at the very least partly mistaken, though not at all for the reasons that Gould gives.[9] It is the aim of this chapter to show that Plato does not deny the fact of moral weakness and that his views concerning the relation of knowledge to conduct are far more plausible than they are usually supposed to be. I shall begin by drawing a distinction between the two doctrines stated in the beginning, calling the first a 'prudential paradox' and the second a 'moral paradox'; I shall then consider each of these in turn.

1 The distinction between the prudential and the moral paradox

There is excellent textual evidence, at least in the *Gorgias* and the *Meno*, for drawing a sharp distinction between the two doctrines stated at the beginning of this chapter. In the first place, Plato himself uses two distinct pairs of terms to state the two paradoxes. In the first paradox (and its corollary, that men desire only good things) he uses *agatha* (good things) and *kaka* (evil things); in the second *dikaia* (what is just) and *adika* (what is unjust). Moreover, there is an important difference in Plato's use of these two pairs of terms. The difference is as follows. Plato takes it for granted, and never argues, that *agatha* always benefit (*ofelein*) the possessor of them, and *kaka* always harm (*blabtein*) the possessor of them (for example, *Meno* 77D2—9, 87E; *Gorgias* 467A—B, 468B1—8). On the other hand, he *argues* that behaving justly (*dikaia prattein*) always benefits the agent, and that behaving unjustly always harms the agent; whether this is so, far from being taken for granted, is indeed the chief dispute between Socrates and Polus and Callicles,

184

as Olympiodorus rightly points out.[10] A passage in the *Meno* 77D–E further suggests the difference: '*Soc.* And do you think that they know the evil things to be evil, those who think that such things benefit? *Meno.* I do not think that at all.' The proposition that is being affirmed here with emphasis and not the least show of argument is that if someone thinks that something that is in fact evil benefits (the man who has or gets it) then he does not know that the thing is evil. To my knowledge Plato nowhere says, assumes, argues for, or implies that if a man thinks that something that is in fact unjust benefits (the agent) then he does not know that it is unjust. I shall say that for Plato it is in some sense definitional that *agatha* benefit whoever has them and that *kaka* harm; and I shall call this a prudential use of these terms. ('Evil' in view of these considerations becomes a poor translation of *kaka*, since the former word has moral connotations. I suggest as the least misleading translation 'things good for one' for *agatha* and 'things bad for one' for *kaka*; this now brings out the plausibility of supposing definitional connections with 'benefit' and 'harm.'[11])

It results from these considerations that we cannot 'lump together' the two doctrines and try to give the same account of both, as Cornford and others seem to do.[12] I shall call the first doctrine the prudential paradox, the second the moral paradox. The first is concerned with situations where no questions of justice and injustice (or, more generally, right and wrong) arise, and it appears to deny the fact of prudential weakness; the second is concerned with moral situations and appears to deny the fact of moral weakness.

2 *The prudential paradox*

In the course of refuting a definition of virtue proposed by Meno, Socrates offers what is the chief and yet much neglected argument for part of the prudential paradox, the argument that no one desires things that are bad for one. Socrates takes Meno's definition at 77B to imply that there are people who desire things that are bad for one, and Meno accepts this implication. Socrates immediately raises the question whether these people who, according to Meno, desire things that are bad for one *know* that these things are bad for one or *think* that they are things good for one. Meno replies that there are people in both these classes, and Socrates now undertakes to show by a deductive argument that both hypotheses are mistaken.[13] He begins arguing against the first hypothesis (there are people who desire things that are bad for one knowing that they are bad for one), interrupts this argument at

77D5—E4 in order to argue against the second hypothesis, and then resumes the argument against the first and concludes it at 78B. Instead of following this somewhat confusing procedure, I shall take up the argument against the first hypothesis, and then consider the much more difficult argument against the second.

Socrates' argument against the first hypothesis (itself the first premise in that argument that has the form of a *reductio*) is as follows. Meno agrees readily that desiring something is desiring to possess it,[14] and that a man who knows that a thing is bad for one also knows that it harms the one who has it. The people then who, according to Meno, desire bad things, knowing that they are bad, know that these things harm the one who has them and that they will be harmed by them (if they get them); they also think, Meno again agrees, that those who are harmed are miserable in proportion to the harm they suffer, and that the miserable are ill-starred. (Hence, the men who, according to Meno, desire bad things knowing that they are bad desire to be miserable and ill-starred.)[15] But, Meno agrees readily once more, no one wants (wishes) to be miserable and ill starred.[16] Hence, Socrates finally concludes, no one (that is, no one of the people of the hypothesis) wants things that are bad for one if no one (whatsoever) wants to be miserable and ill-starred.

To say that the passage in which Socrates argues against the second hypothesis is problematic is an understatement. This hypothesis, at 77C2—3, is that there are some people who desire bad things thinking (mistakenly, presumably) that they are good things; to this it may be added, as a result of what is agreed at 77D3—7, that these people do know that these things (that they desire) are bad. The problematic passage runs as follows:[17]

> Obviously they do not desire bad things, the people who are ignorant of them, but [they desire] the things which they supposed to be good things, even though these things are in fact bad; so that those who are ignorant of them and think them good really desire good things. Isn't that so? *Meno.* It would seem to be so in their case.

There are at least three problems here: (1) to see how Socrates can claim *consistently* both that these people do not desire bad things and also that they desire things that they thought to be good though *these things are in fact bad* (one might be tempted to infer from Socrates' last two claims that these people do desire bad things, and say that Socrates contradicted himself within the space of three lines); (2) to see on what grounds Socrates can assert the first of these statements; and (3) to see how Socrates can plausibly infer, as he seems to do, that these people really desire good things (not simply things they *thought* to be good).

The key to the solution of these problems and to a sound interpretation of the passage lies in the fact that statements of desire, wish, want ('He desires . . .') are cases of indirect discourse. A statement such as 'He desired to be the first European to land on the new continent' *may* change in truth-value if we substitute 'the first European to be killed by Indians' for 'the first European to land on the new continent' even though these two expressions in fact refer to one and the same person (and similarly with expressions of the form 'an *F*' or '*F* things' when substituted for coextensive expressions).[18] It follows that Socrates is in no danger of contradicting himself when he asserts that the people in the hypothesis desire what they thought to be good things, that these things are in fact bad things, and yet that these people do not desire bad things.

What lies behind the fact that statements of desire, among others, are cases of indirect discourse is that, as Frege puts it, 'a conviction or a belief is the ground of a feeling';[19] if a man desires something, it is his conception of what the object is that is the ground of his desire, not (necessarily) what the object in fact is (he may be under a misconception as to what sort of thing the object is or unaware that it has a certain property). If then a man reaches for something — say the salt shaker — does not express reservations or show reluctance in doing so, and we say 'He wants the salt shaker,' we might, even under these conditions, be mis-describing the object of his desire (want): mis-describing not in the sense that 'salt shaker' is not applicable to the object he reaches for, but in the sense that 'salt shaker' is not the description *under which* he desires it (this would turn out to be the case if the man was not aware that what he was reaching for was a salt shaker or if, for example, he mistook the salt shaker for the pepper mill).[20] It seems then that we ought to say that a statement of the form 'He desires (wants) . . .' is not to count as true unless the description that fills the blank is the description under which the object is desired; I shall call such a description the description of the *intended* object of desire. At the same time, this is compatible with regarding a certain kind of behavior toward an object and our knowledge of the object as reasonable evidence for saying that someone desires so-and-so; thus if a man reaches for (goes after, aims at) something, does not show reservations or reluctance in doing so, and what he is reaching for is, for example, a salt shaker, then we have reasonable evidence for saying (claiming) that he wants the salt shaker.[21] But of course we must remember that

187

when such is our evidence for making the statement, we run the risk of mis-describing the object of the man's desire; to mark this point, I shall say that when a statement of the form 'He desires (wants) . . .' is made on such evidence, the description that fills the blank is the description of the *actual* object of desire. It is clear that one and the same description could be the description of both the intended and the actual object of desire. It is also clear that there is no contradiction in saying, for example, both that the intended object of the man's desire was the pepper mill and that the actual object of his desire was the salt shaker.[22]

Now in the passage we are considering, we can say that what Socrates is denying is that bad things are the *intended* objects of these people's desires. For his only basis in the passage for saying that the people in the hypothesis do not desire bad things is the statement that these people do not know that the things, which according to Meno they desire, are bad; and the only relevant statement that follows from this is that bad things are not the intended objects of their desires. Further, the only basis that Socrates has in this passage for saying that the people in the hypothesis really desire good things is the statement that they thought that the things, which according to Meno they desire, were good things; and the only relevant thing that can follow from this is that good things are the *intended* objects of their desires (at any rate if they desire these things, which according to Meno they desire, because they think they are good things or *qua* good things). It is important to realize that Socrates is not denying (he certainly does not have to) that the actual objects of these people's desires are indeed bad things; his statement, that 'these things [which they thought to be good things] are in fact bad,' is good enough evidence for this, and in addition it is not part of his case that these people express reluctance or show reservations in pursuing (going after) things that are in fact bad. (On this see also n. 16.)

I am not of course claiming that Socrates (or Plato) was aware of the distinction between direct and indirect discourse on which the present interpretation is based. In this regard, all that can be safely inferred is that, unlike Meno, Socrates is unwilling to say that a man who pursues bad things desires bad things unless the man is aware that they are bad. In this Socrates is clearly correct, provided we do not take his unwillingness as a denial that the actual objects of some people's desires are bad things.

In sum, we can say (using the terminology introduced) that what Socrates has tried to show is that in no case are bad things the intended objects of people's desires, though in some cases they are the actual objects. In his arguments he has used three crucial premises, all readily agreed to by Meno without argument: that desiring something is desiring to possess it; that if one knows or believes that a thing is bad for one, he also knows or believes that it harms the man who has it and in proportion to the harm makes him miserable; and that no one desires to be miserable (in the sense that to be miserable is never the intended object of anyone's desire). Of these only the last is even a plausible candidate for a factual proposition, a proposition that is supposed to represent a general fact concerning 'human nature.'[23] It is far from obvious that this proposition contradicts any facts; indeed it, or some version of it, seems to be one of the most common presuppositions made in accounting for human behavior, at any rate in situations of prudential choice. If anyone supposes that the prudential paradox contradicts facts because it is based on this proposition, the burden of proof is on him, not on Plato.

3 The moral paradox

In the moral paradox we have two propositions: virtue is knowledge, and all who do injustice do so involuntarily. I shall concentrate on the first of these, and interpret the second in terms of it. The first is usually interpreted as a biconditional: if one has knowledge one is virtuous; if one is virtuous one has knowledge. Most commentators take 'knowledge' to mean 'knowledge of virtue,' so that the first part of the biconditional becomes 'If one has knowledge of virtue one is a virtuous man.' It is plausible enough to take the contrapositive of this to mean that if a man does something that is unjust (or intemperate, cowardly, or the like) then he does not know that it is unjust. And if it is a familiar, or even rare, fact of experience that men sometimes do injustice or wrong knowing that they are doing so, we do seem to have here a Platonic doctrine that contradicts facts. The strongest single piece of evidence for this interpretation is in the Gorgias 460B–D. Here Socrates asserts that 'he who has learnt what is just is a just man;' he then proceeds to make matters worse by adding that the just man always does what is just and never even desires to do what is unjust. This position seems to be even more extraordinary than the previous one, since it seems to deny also the fact that sometimes men have morally bad desires (that is, the fact that sometimes to do injustice or wrong is the *intended* object of men's desires).

I want to take as the main guide for the interpretation of the moral paradox the fact that it can be derived from three doctrines that Plato certainly holds. There is evidence that in the *Gorgias* Plato himself derives part of the paradox from these doctrines.

The first of these is the prudential paradox itself. The second is the view that no action (or, at any rate, no unjust or wrong action) is ever done for its own sake and that every action (or, at any rate, every unjust or wrong action) is done for the sake of possessing what the agent considers a good — that is, something beneficial to himself.[24] Finally, we need for the derivation of the moral paradox the well-known Platonic doctrine, argued in the *Gorgias* (and of course in the *Republic*), that doing what is just (and, more generally, right) always benefits the agent, and doing what is unjust always harms the agent; and consequently, that it is always better for the agent to do justice than injustice no matter what the circumstances.

I have given only a bare outline of the last two doctrines, but this is sufficient for my present purposes.

Consider now the most problematic part of the moral paradox: if one has knowledge, one is virtuous (or, knowledge is a sufficient condition for being virtuous). The basic difference between the traditional interpretation and the one I am about to suggest turns on what we take 'knowledge' to include and on the distinction between the items included in this knowledge. The traditional interpretation is that Plato meant 'knowledge of virtue,' so that the paradoxical statement becomes 'If one knows what is virtuous, one will do what is virtuous.'[25] I suggest, on the other hand, that Plato meant that if a man has knowledge of what is virtuous and *also* knowledge that it is always better for one to do what is virtuous, then he will always (so long as he has this knowledge and virtuous behavior is in his power) behave virtuously. I suggest, further, that these two items of knowledge are logically independent, in the sense that a man may have one without having the other.

The first advantage of this interpretation is that the Platonic thesis, that knowledge is sufficient for virtue, no longer contradicts the fact of moral weakness. The thesis is that if a man knows what is virtuous (and what is not) and also knows that it is always better for one to behave virtuously, then he will always do what is virtuous and will not even desire to do otherwise. What follows from this is that if a man commits injustice (or behaves in a cowardly or intemperate fashion), then he does not know either that he is committing injustice or that doing so is worse for him or both. It is clear that this proposition does not contradict the proposition that sometimes men do what is unjust (or wrong) knowing or believing that it is unjust. Hence, on this interpretation the main reason for thinking Plato's thesis paradoxical is removed.

The second advantage of this interpretation is that the moral paradox does really now follow from the three doctrines stated earlier. These doctrines are that men desire (to possess, to get) only good things (in the sense explained above), that they do what they do, not for its own sake but for the sake of possessing good things, and that justice (and, more generally, virtuous behavior) always benefits the agent whereas injustice harms him. It follows that if a man knows which actions are just (and which unjust) and also knows that it is always better for him to do justice rather than injustice, then he will desire to do what is just, and will do what is just (in the relevant situations) unless this is not in his power. If a man who had such knowledge desired to do injustice, this would imply that he desired to possess a bad thing, which contradicts the prudential paradox. The *Gorgias* provides evidence that Plato himself based the moral paradox on the three doctrines stated earlier. At 509E, where Socrates asserts a related part of the moral paradox — that no one does injustice willingly, but that all who do injustice do so involuntarily[26] — he explicitly cites as the basis for this his discussion with Polus. And what he and Polus agreed on, in the main, were the doctrines in question: that men desire only good things, that men do what they do not for its own sake but because they think it is better for them, and that doing what is just is not only honorable or fair, but also good for the agent (whereas injustice is harmful). In addition, it is worth noting that, when Polus brings up examples of extreme wrongdoers such as Archelaus, the dispute is not whether this man knew or believed that what he did was unjust (indeed, this issue never comes up!), but whether he was better off doing injustice, as he himself believed. This suggests that one explanation that Plato would give as to why people do wrong is that they do not know that it is worse for them. Of course, on the interpretation that is presented here Plato can give either one or both of two general explanations as to why people do wrong (when they are not forced to); that they do not know that it is wrong, or that they do not know it is worse for them; whereas on the interpretation I am criticising, only the first of these explanations is available to Plato.

I do not see, on the other hand, how the moral paradox, on the traditional interpretation, can be derived from Platonic doctrines: we are to suppose that knowledge that an action is just (or temperate, or courageous, and so forth) is sufficient for doing it (in the relevant situations) and even for desiring to do it. I do not think this proposition can be derived from Platonic doctrines. Plato argues, in effect, that there is a necessary connection between recognizing something as good for one and desiring (to have, to

191

get, to possess) it; but he does not argue, nor does he hold, in my opinion, that there is a necessary connection between recognizing an action as just and desiring to do it.

It may be objected that on Plato's view knowledge that an action is just (or unjust) presupposes a knowledge of justice (and injustice), and that the latter presupposes a knowledge that it is always better for one to behave justly rather than unjustly; so that it could not be the case that a man had knowledge that an action is just and at the same time did not know that it was to his greater advantage to do it. It would follow from this that, though both items are included in the knowledge that is sufficient for virtuous behavior, as I have suggested, they are nevertheless not logically independent.

There is some evidence that Plato holds that if a man knows the definition of justice in a man (justice in a man being a state of soul characterized by a certain kind of order and, perhaps, harmony), he cannot fail to see that it is always better for one to be in this state of soul rather than any other (see, for example, Glaucon's reply at *Republic* 445A–C after justice in the soul has been defined). But it does not follow from this, nor is it Plato's doctrine, that in order to know that an *action* is just one has to know the definition of justice in the soul. In the *Republic* 443, for example, Plato says that the definition of justice in the soul may be confirmed by 'commonplace and vulgar tests of justice'; this implies that there are 'commonplace and vulgar' standards of justice by which a man may know, for example, that it is unjust to embezzle gold that has been entrusted to him, without knowing the definition of justice in the soul. I suggest then that on Plato's view knowing or believing that an action is just is logically independent of knowing or believing that just actions benefit the agent and unjust ones harm him. And this is quite consistent with what I take to be also his view: that just actions necessarily benefit the agent and unjust ones necessarily harm him.

Incidentally, it cannot be taken for granted that Plato means to exclude the view that true *belief* (as distinct from knowledge) is sufficient for acting justly. Though he uses *sofia, episteme, mathesis* (all usually translated 'knowledge'), which he distinguishes from *pistis* or *doxa* (belief, opinion), in stating the moral paradox, he nevertheless contrasts these with ignorance or false belief (never with true belief) when he argues for the moral paradox.[27] It is reasonable to suppose that he would accept the view that true belief (that an action is just and that it is also to one's advantage or greater advantage to do it), if it is a firm conviction, would be sufficient for acting justly. It is even reasonable to suppose that

192

false belief, if it is a firm conviction, would be sufficient for acting *in accordance with the belief*, though of course if may not be sufficient for acting justly; at any rate it is difficult to see how the arguments given for knowledge would not apply here.

It is important to emphasize that on the interpretation I have suggested the condition that is sufficient for virtuous behavior includes not only knowledge but also the *desire* for things that are good for one (and the consequent desire to do always what is beneficial or more beneficial for oneself). This point emerged from the way I have derived the moral paradox, and it is worth emphasizing because it is sometimes thought that Plato did not see that there is a 'gap,' as it were, between knowledge and action; that, no matter what knowledge a man has, his desires and passions may prompt him to act against his knowledge. It is to take care of this very point that Plato argues that no man desires things that are bad for one, that men desire only good things, and that they do what they do for the sake of what they consider a benefit to themselves. Part of the reason this point is not usually emphasized in discussions of the Socratic paradoxes may be the fact that Plato holds that this desire is common to all men, whether virtuous or wrongdoers, and hence that what accounts for the difference between them is not presence or absence of this desire, but of knowledge. This is quite true; but it is also consistent with saying, as I am saying, that this doctrine of desire — what may be called an egoistic theory of motivation — is essential to the moral paradox. The form in which the paradox is usually stated — that virtue is knowledge or that knowledge is sufficient for being virtuous — is misleading in this respect: in considering it, one tends to forget the doctrine of desire or motivation that underlies it. But what Plato is saying is that, *given* this universal desire for possessing (having, getting) things that are good for one, *then* knowledge of virtue and vice and knowledge that it is always to one's greater advantage to behave virtuously is sufficient for such behavior.

It seems to me then that traditional accounts of the paradoxes have gone wrong in either one or both of two ways. In the first place, it was not always seen or properly emphasized that the doctrine of desire — what I have called Plato's egoistic theory of motivation — is part of the logical foundation of the moral paradox; and consequently it has seemed as if Plato ignored the role of desires and passions in the choice of right or wrong behavior and thought that this choice depended entirely on knowledge. If I am right, the truth of the matter is that Plato considered the central desire for the possession of things that are good for one as absolutely essential in any account of human behavior. If Plato has

193

gone wrong at all in this, it may be in the strong emphasis he seems to place on the dependence of one's desires and passions on one's convictions, and in the fact that he writes, in the early dialogues at least, as if there is no stronger desire or passion than this central desire for things that are good for one (or, perhaps more plausibly, the desire for one's own happiness). In the second place, it was not always seen or properly emphasized that the Platonic doctrine that virtuous behavior is always more beneficial to the agent than wrong behavior is also part of the logical foundation of the moral paradox; and consequently it was not seen that there is, at the very least, a possibility that on Plato's view the knowledge which, together with the desire, is sufficient for virtuous behavior includes two items that, as items of knowledge, are logically independent. On this possibility, as we have seen, the moral paradox does not deny the fact of moral weakness.

The interpretation I have sketched seems to me to constitute a resolution of the Socratic paradoxes in so far as it removes the two elements that traditionally have been the most puzzling — the extreme intellectualism and the alleged denial of moral weakness — and in so far as it renders, as I think it does, Plato's account of the relation of knowledge to conduct (a relation that is now mediated by the element of desire) far more plausible than it is usually supposed to be. But it is not, of course, part of my contention that the Socratic paradoxes are true, nor do I consider showing this part of such a resolution. I have not shown, or attempted to show, that the paradoxes do not contradict any facts, but only that they do not contradict what they are usually supposed to contradict. Nor have I claimed that the doctrines from which the paradoxes are derived are true, especially the doctrine that it is always to one's own greater advantage to do justice rather than injustice. If this doctrine is false, as it appears to be, then no one can have the knowledge or *true* opinion that Plato thought sufficient (together with the desire) for virtuous conduct. We shall examine Socrates' defence of this doctrine in chapter VIII. Aside from this, another objection arises to the Socratic paradoxes as conceived in this chapter. Even if we concede that our desires are directed by our knowledge or belief as to what is good for one, it may be objected that we do not always act accordingly because of the strength or intensity of conflicting desires, fears, or other passions. Socrates argues against this type of explanation in the *Protagoras*, and in the next chapter we shall examine this argument in detail.

VII

Virtue and Knowledge II:
An Argument against Explanations
of Weakness[1]

Introduction

Understanding the sorts of explanations that can be offered in
cases of weakness (weakness of will, weakness of character, and
moral weakness) is an important aspect of the philosophical problem of *akrasia*.[2] In a case of weakness a man does something that
he knows or believes he should (ought) not do, or fails to do something that he knows or believes he should do, when the occasion
and the opportunity for acting or refraining is present, and when it
is in his power, in some significant sense, to act in accordance with
his knowledge or belief. Because of the first of these characteristics,
which are the *given* characteristics of cases of weakness,[3] it always
makes sense to raise the question why the man acted in this way —
that is, contrary to his knowledge or belief. But, aside from this, it
is necessary to find a correct answer to it if we wish to understand
the man's behavior and to reach a reasonable evaluative attitude
toward the man. Finally, if we discover the sorts of explanations
that are (and the sorts that are not) available in cases of weakness,
we should be in a better position to understand the relation of
knowledge of value (or value beliefs) to conduct.

In this chapter I want to examine in some detail a long and
elaborate argument that Plato offers in the *Protagoras* (352—356C)
to the effect that certain explanations commonly offered in cases
of weakness are untenable or absurd. This passage has been discussed often,[4] but the issues and difficulties that it raises about
explanations of weakness have not been sufficiently appreciated;
I shall try to show that Plato's argument is at the very least a
serious challenge to those who think that the phenomenon of
human weakness, though perhaps common enough and familiar

195

enough, can be easily understood. In section 1, I set out the context and limitations of Plato's argument, and state the main questions that should be raised about in. In section 2, I try to reconstruct the argument as we find it in the text, and in the next section I indicate briefly how the argument may be freed from the severe limitations set to it and thus generalized. Finally, in sections 4 and 5, I try to unravel the main ambiguities in Plato's argument, assess their consequences to the argument, and follow out their implications concerning different kinds of explanations in cases of weakness. Different sorts of explanations employed recently by philosophers and psychologists are discussed.

1 *The context and the strategy*

Toward the end of a lengthy discussion about the unity of the virtues, Socrates raises a (relatively) new issue within which the argument against explanations is set: the role of knowledge in action. At 352B he sets out before Protagoras two opposite hypotheses:

> The opinion generally held of knowledge is something of this sort — that it is not a strong or guiding or governing thing; it is not regarded as anything of that kind, but people think that, while a man often has knowledge in him, he is not governed by it, but by something else — now by passion, now by pleasure, now by pain, at times by love, and often by fear.

and

> knowledge is something noble and able to govern man, and that whoever learns what is good and what is bad will never be swayed by anything to act otherwise than as knowledge bids, and . . . intelligence is a sufficient succor of mankind.

Protagoras, asked to reveal his own thoughts on the subject, politely agrees with the second hypothesis, which represents Socrates' own view, but Socrates is set on examining the first hypothesis — the hypothesis of the many — and proceeds to restate it with some additions and distinctions (352DE):

> Now you know that most people will not listen to you and me, but say that (a) many, while knowing what is best, refuse to perform it, though they have the power, and do other things instead. And whenever I have asked them to tell me what can be the reason for this, they say that (b) those who act so are

196

acting under the influence of pleasure or pain, or under the
control of one of the things I have just mentioned.

In this restatement of the hypothesis of the many, Socrates has
distinguished two parts: part (a) states that a certain phenomenon
occurs, and part (b) is given as an explanation of the occurrence of
that phenomenon. The significant point about this distinction is
that Socrates proceeds to give an argument against (b), *not*
(directly) against (a).[5] The conclusion of the argument that ends
formally at 355B is *not* that no one acts contrary to what he
knows to be best, but that (on the premises agreed on) the explanation 'overcome by pleasure' has been reduced to absurdity. Of
course, Socrates (and Plato) believe that part (a) of the hypothesis
is false, and he asserts this at the beginning and the end of the
argument (352B, 357D); these assertions indeed provide the wider
context within which the argument presented between 352D and
355C is set, but it is not these assertions (the denial of weakness)
that the argument attempts to prove, but the absurdity of the
explanation of weakness.

Understanding the argument in this way — as an argument
against (b) — is very different from understanding it as an argument against (a). Aside from the fact that this interpretation is
faithful to the text, it enables us to avoid a general difficulty,
noticed by Professor Vlastos in his excellent introduction to the
Protagoras, a difficulty that would seem to doom the argument to
failure from the outset. Commenting on Socrates' statements at
352A–C and 358D — statements that deny part (a) and that on
the present interpretation form the wider context of the argument,
not the conclusion of it — he writes:[6]

The words which are italicized show quite well what kind of
statement Socrates is making here: the kind which we would
call an empirical one. K, like its humbler cousin, C, purports
to tell us a fact of human nature — the kind of matter of fact
that can only be found out by observation. Where then is the
reference to such observation? Nowhere in the whole of this
elaborate argument. In the case of C Socrates at least went
through the motions of induction; here not even this: he is
quite content here with a purely *deductive* proof of it. Now
anyone who could excogitate by pure deduction a fact of
human nature would have to be more than a master of argument
— he would have to be a wizard. And as Socrates is only human,
we would not be risking much if we were to predict that his
attempt will fail.

I agree that it is difficult to see how one can show by a 'purely deductive proof' and no reliance on observations or empirical propositions that (a) is false. But there is no similar difficulty in showing that, given the description of weakness — as given in part (a) — and the hedonistic hypothesis, then the explanation given in (b) is absurd or untenable; for there is at least a possibility that the explanation in (b) is incompatible with the description of weakness and hedonism, and this of course could be shown by a purely deductive proof or by logical analysis alone. In interpreting the argument in this way I am not denying that Socrates was very much concerned to convince Protagoras and the *hoi polloi* that (a) or some version of it is false; indeed, his motive perhaps for attacking common explanations of weakness was to convince us that the weakness does not occur at all. But the falsity of (a) does not follow logically from the absurdity of the explanation (b); nor does Plato write that it does. The most we can say is that the absurdity of the common explanation paves the way to Socrates' own explanation, and that if we become convinced of the absurdity of the explanation (b) and of the absurdity of the other common explanations as well, we may reasonably come to doubt the truth of (a) or at least come to suspect its apparent innocence. In any case, Plato may not succeed here in convincing us that weakness does not occur, but he may succeed in showing that there are some difficulties with the ways we commonly explain weakness.[7]

There are two other points worth noticing about the actual argument that Socrates presents between 352D and 355C, and they are worth noticing because they constitute limitations on the scope and generality of the argument.

The first limitation is that, as Vlastos has pointed out, Socrates argues only against *one* of the five explanations of weakness that he first mentioned; he argues that 'overcome by pleasure' reduces to absurdity as an explanation of weakness, but he makes no clear move to show how his argument might be applied against the explanations 'overcome by' fear, love, hate, and passion. His argument, then, even if entirely successful, can refute only part of the opinion of the many; they might still be right about people being overcome by fear, love, and so forth.

The second important limitation of the argument is that it depends on the hedonistic hypothesis elaborated by Socrates between 353D and 354E. Not only is Socrates aware of this, but he emphasizes it. At the end of this passage he says that 'it is still possible to retract if you can somehow contrive to say that the good is different from pleasure, or the bad from pain.' The argument then is not intended to show that 'overcome by pleasure' is absurd as an explanation of weakness, but only that it is absurd if one assumes hedonism; that is, it only shows that a hedonist is logically prevented from giving such an explanation. And incidentally, it is quite clear that Plato can argue this without being himself a hedonist.[8]

The point of setting out the context and limitations of Socrates' argument, aside from faithfulness to the text, is that we must, first, try to reconstruct and assess the soundness of the argument within its context and limitations. If the argument fails within these narrow bounds, we need go no further, aside from determining the mistakes it contains. But if it has some measure of success, as I shall try to show, then we can, and must, raise the question whether it can be freed from those limitations, whether it can be freed from the hedonistic hypothesis, and whether it can be brought to bear against the other explanations of weakness. This is the strategy I follow in this chapter.

2 The argument

The argument that Socrates offers between 352B and 356C divides into three stages: (1) descriptions of cases of weakness and statements of the explanations commonly offered for the occurrence of weakness so described (352B—353D); (2) elaboration of the hedonistic hypothesis on which Socrates' argument depends (353D—355A); (3) substitution of 'good' for 'pleasure' in the explanation 'overcome by pleasure,' 'painful' for 'evil' in the description of the case, and argument that on either substitution the resulting explanation has been reduced to absurdity (355A—356C). (From 356C to 358E Socrates, apparently assuming that he has disposed of the explanations of the many, proceeds to elaborate his own familiar explanation, that what is called weakness is due to mis-estimation of the values of the alternatives, owing to their nearness or remoteness in time.) I shall discuss each stage of the argument in turn, concentrating on stage (3), which is the source of all the important difficulties that arise in trying to understand and assess the success of Socrates' argument. In doing this, I shall stay close to the text, but at the same time I shall give Plato the benefit of the doubt in cases of ambiguity and incompleteness of expression. My aim in this section is to reconstruct the argument so that any success that it may have, however limited, can be brought out, the only limitations in this being the text and the nature of the case.

In stage (1) Socrates offers four different descriptions of cases

of weakness, and lists five possible explanations of cases so described,[9] but at the beginning of stage (3) of the argument Socrates
picks out one of these descriptions and matches it with the
explanation 'overcome by pleasure,' and his subsequent argument
about the absurdity of the explanation concerns this pair (355B):

> It is often the case that a man, knowing the evil to be evil
> [knowing bad things to be bad things], nevertheless commits it
> [does them], when he might avoid it [them], because he is
> driven and dazed[10] by his pleasures.

The sorts of cases that the many have in mind when they give this
sort of explanation, according to Socrates, are those in which a
man is overcome by the pleasures of 'food or drink or sexual acts'
(355C).[11] There are obvious ambiguities in Socrates' description
of the case just quoted. In one sort of case a man may know
(believe) that what he does (A) is bad, but he may also know that
the alternatives to A open to him (B or C) are worse. This clearly
is a case of doing the lesser of several evils, not a case of weakness.
To get the latter we must suppose that the man thinks that either
B or C is a good or at least a lesser evil than A; in short, we must
suppose that he thinks that what he does is *bad in comparison to
the alternatives*. In a second sort of case a man may think of the
alternatives of what he is doing (A) as simply not doing or avoiding
A (rather than doing something else), and he may think of the
value of not doing A as simply the absence of the value contained
in doing A (nothing lost and nothing gained). Here of course the
man may think that A contains only good, or only evil, or both
good and evil. In the last (mixed type) case, he may think that the
good outweighs the evil (so that A is *good on the whole*) or the
converse (*bad on the whole*), or that neither outweighs the other.
It is in fact this mixed type of case that Socrates seems to be discussing, since throughout the passage he finds it necessary to compare with each other only the values contained in what the agent
does, not the value of what he does with the value of the alternatives open to him. And here quite clearly we must suppose that
the case Socrates is considering is one in which the man knows
that what he does is *bad on the whole*.[12]

In stage (2) of the argument we are invited to suppose that the
people who give the explanation 'overcome by pleasure,' the *hoi
polloi*, are hedonists. What kind of hedonists? We do not have to
classify them.[13] It is sufficient to notice that the following points
about them are agreed to by Socrates and Protagoras. (1) When
the *hoi polloi* assert that something that they say is pleasant is also
bad, the only reason they can give is that it results in pain which

outweighs the pleasure (so that it is painful on the whole); and when they judge something that they say is painful to be good the only reason they can give is that it results in pleasure which outweighs the pain (so that it is pleasant on the whole) (354C–E). (2) The *hoi polloi* pursue pleasure as a good, and avoid pain as an evil (354C). (3) The *hoi polloi* cannot contrive to say that the good is different from pleasure and the bad from pain (if they could the argument would not go through) (355A). (4) According to the hedonism of the *hoi polloi* we have two things and four names: the names 'good,' 'bad,' 'pain,' and 'pleasure' (the point being that 'good' and 'pleasure' are names for one and the same thing, and similarly with the other pair). In the next stage of the argument Socrates indeed proceeds to *substitute* 'good' for 'pleasure' and 'painful' for 'evil.'[14]

We come now to the final stage (3) of the argument (355C–356C), by far the most difficult. Plato's text here seems full of obscurities and ambiguities, but there are a few signposts in it, which have not been sufficiently noticed and which will help us to a sound interpretation of the passage and an appreciation of Plato's argument. The first of these is that at the beginning of this stage of the argument, having already said that without assuming hedonism his argument does not go through, Socrates says:

> I tell you that if this is so [that is, if we assume the hedonism described above], the argument becomes absurd, when you say that it is often the case that a man, knowing the evil to be evil, nevertheless commits it, when he might avoid it, because he is driven and dazed by his pleasures.

The complete dependence on hedonism in which Socrates places his argument against the explanation 'overcome (or driven and dazed by) pleasure' indicates clearly not only that this explanation is to be reconstructed along hedonistic lines but also that the alleged absurdity is to be found in a conjunction of the explanation and hedonism, not simply in the explanation. Second, shortly after the above passage, Socrates begins the long paragraph which contains stage (3) of the argument by announcing:

> The absurdity of all this will be manifest if we refrain from using a number of terms at once, such as pleasant, painful, good, and bad; and as there appeared to be two things let us call them by two names — first good and evil, and then later on, pleasant and painful.

Socrates completes both of these substitutions by the end of this long paragraph, and after that (356C) the absurdity of the explanation 'overcome by pleasure' is not even mentioned once. This suggests quite clearly that the absurdity that Socrates has in mind must be sought in the text of this paragraph, not in later text (when Socrates elaborates his own explanation) as some writers have supposed.[15] Finally, though in several places the expressions that Socrates uses that have been translated by 'because he is overcome by pleasure' are ambiguous and could be rendered by 'being overcome by pleasure,' in two passages (352D–E and 355C) Socrates makes it perfectly clear that being overcome by pleasure is given by the many as the reason or cause (*aition, to dia ti*) of the behavior of acting contrary to one's knowledge; and hence '*because* he is overcome by pleasure' is the correct translation of the expressions that Socrates uses, suggesting as it does that 'overcome by pleasure' is given as an explanation of the behavior of acting contrary to one's knowledge. The upshot is that — though Socrates does not *always* say this during stage (3) of his argument — it is the statement 'Sometimes men do what they know (or believe) is bad, when they can avoid it, *because* they are overcome by pleasure' that Socrates argues is absurd; not the statement 'Sometimes men do what they know (or believe) is bad, when they can avoid it, *and* (yet) they are overcome by pleasure.'[16] These two statements are of course of different logical form; in conjunction with hedonism the former may turn out upon analysis to contain an absurdity, while the latter may not. Moreover, the former directs our attention to the fact that Socrates is arguing against an explanation, not simply against a statement of fact — an explanation that needs reconstruction.

These preliminaries out of the way, we come now to the difficult matter of locating the absurdity that Socrates has in mind; it is worth giving in full here Socrates' argumentation (following the last quotation) during the first substitution:

> Let us then lay it down as our statement, that a man does evil in spite of knowing the evil of it. Now if someone asks us: Why? we shall answer: Because he is overcome. By what? the questioner will ask us; and this time we shall be unable to reply: By pleasure — for this has exchanged its name for 'the good.' So we must answer only with the words: Because he is overcome. By what? says the questioner. The good — must surely be our reply. Now if our questioner chance to be an arrogant person he will laugh and exclaim: What a ridiculous statement, that a man does evil, knowing it to be evil, and not having to do it, because he is overcome by the good! Is this, he will ask, because the good is not worthy of conquering the evil in you, or because it is worthy?

Clearly we must reply: Because it is not worthy; otherwise he whom we speak of as overcome by pleasures would not have offended. But in what sense, he might ask us, is the good unworthy of the bad, or the bad of the good? This can only be when the one is greater and the other smaller, or when there are more on the one side and fewer on the other. We shall not find any other reason to give. So it is clear, he will say, that by 'being overcome' you mean getting the greater evil in exchange for the lesser good. That must be agreed.

Socrates is here discussing a case of doing something or avoiding it (say, eating another serving of Athenian pastries or refusing to do so) where doing the thing in question contains both good and bad (harm and benefit) or both pleasure and pain (say, the pleasure of eating the pastries and the subsequent indigestion). Socrates is trying to give an analysis of 'overcome by good' so that it becomes absurd, on the hedonistic premises already agreed on, as a reason or cause of weakness. Vlastos has correctly pointed out that 'worthy' (*axion*) is used by Socrates here as a value term, so that the good (benefit, pleasure) contained in a course of action is 'worthy of conquering' the evil (harm, pain) also contained in it if and only if the good exceeds the evil in quantity so that the course of action is good on the whole.[17] Once we see this, it becomes clear from the two questions that Socrates raises and himself answers in this passage that he is taking 'overcome by good' in *one of two possible senses* — and this indeed is the most important ambiguity of the whole argument. In one sense (1) a man who does something that contains both good (benefit) and bad (harm) may be said to be 'overcome by the good' if the good is worthy of conquering the bad; that is, if the good outweighs the bad. In another sense (2) a man in similar circumstances may be said to be overcome by the good (pleasure) if his desire for the good (pleasure) that the course of action contains is *stronger* than his fear of (desire to avoid) the bad (pain) it contains. Socrates ignores the possibility of taking 'overcomes' in sense (2), and this is a serious fault in the argument. We must not be satisfied with this criticism, however; we need to follow out the argument with *each* of (1) and (2) if we are to appreciate the issues involved, and for the moment we must follow Socrates. Now once we grant Socrates' interpretation of 'overcome by . . .,' the explanation of the *hoi polloi* can be interpreted in three different ways, all untenable:

D1 Sometimes a man does something that is bad, knowing it to be bad, when he can avoid doing it . . .
because

E1   the good contained in what he does is worthy of conquering — that is, outweighs — the bad contained in what he does.

E2   the good contained in what he does is worthy of conquering — that is, outweighs — the bad contained in what he does, and the man knows this.

E3   the man takes (chooses, prefers, decides to take) the (known) greater harm (evil) contained in what he does in return for securing (as the price of) the (known) lesser good contained in what he does.

Socrates does not explicitly separate the first two interpretations but this does not damage his argument, for both E1 and E2 contradict the description of the case; this is what Socrates is pointing out when he says that we must suppose that the harm contained in what the man does outweighs the benefit, otherwise the man would not have erred or (in our terms) he would not have done something that was *bad on the whole*; by hypothesis our man does something that contains good and bad where the bad outweighs the good and by hypothesis again he knows this. Once we rephrase the description so as to make this clear, the conjunction of the description with either E1 or E2 is self-contradictory:

D2   Sometimes a man does something which contains good and bad where the bad outweighs the good, knowing that this is so, when he can avoid doing it, because E1 and/or E2.

There is one way in which E1 can be saved, and that is by adding 'the man thinks or believes' in front of it, and deleting 'knowing it to be bad on the whole' from the description; but this way out is Socrates' own, and impossible for the many, for it amounts to a denial of weakness, since the man is now acting in accordance, and indeed on the basis of, his value beliefs (though mistaken ones, of course). We may notice that E1 and E2 would not contradict D2 if 'good' had not been substituted for 'pleasure' in E1 and E2; similarly with the second set of substitutions. Here we see clearly what exactly ethical hedonism contributes to Socrates' argument.

Explanation E3 does not contradict the description. The absurdity it involves consists in E3 (considered as an explanation of the case described in D2) contradicting one of the principles of the hedonism of the *hoi polloi*; but before we go into this we must consider more carefully the line in Plato's text of which E3 is a translation.[18] This line is obscure mainly because of two difficulties, only the first of which has been resolved by writers on the passage. Gallop points out correctly that the preposition *anti*, normally rendered 'instead of' or 'in exchange of,' cannot be so rendered here because both these expressions suggest that the agent does not 'take' the good or benefit contained in the case, whereas quite clearly Socrates is discussing a mixed case where the course of action the agent follows contains both harm and benefit (this is made quite explicit at 353C among other places). Following J. L. Stocks, Gallop correctly suggests that we take *anti* in the sense of 'as the price of' or 'in return for securing,' and I follow this rendering which enhances our understanding of the argument. The second and more serious difficulty is how to understand the crucial verb *lambanein* in this line (this is the verb that replaces 'overcome' in the whole sentence; this replacement I shall discuss later): it has been translated as 'gets,' 'takes,' 'chooses.'[19] Now *lambanein*, and its literal translation 'take,' in the present context, may be understood in either one (or both) of two different ways: to refer to (1) what the agent in fact does, the actual execution of the action which contains more harm than benefit (say, the man's actual reaching for, taking hold of, and eating the pastries), or (2) to what the agent seeks, chooses, or possibly decides or prefers to do. In the latter case the use of the verb would introduce a referentially opaque or intensional context; in the former case it would not.[20] There are several excellent reasons for rejecting (1) and adopting *lambanein* in sense (2) as the correct interpretation of the text. The major reason against (1) is that, if we were to understand *lambanein* in the sense of (1), then E2 would not be an explanation at all, for it would simply (do nothing more than) *repeat* part of what we already have in the description of the case, namely that the man does what (he knows) is bad on the whole. It is not that E3 so interpreted involves absurdity or contradicts hedonism; it is not an explanation at all. This is not what Plato is talking about.[21] The major reason in favor of understanding *lambanein* in the sense 'seeks to' or 'chooses' is that it enables us to see the relevance of what Socrates proceeds to do immediately after this line when he takes up the second substitution, and to bring out the absurdity that Socrates is talking about. On the second substitution we obtain:

D3   Sometimes a man does something which is painful on the whole, knowing that this is so, when he can avoid doing it,
because
E4   he takes (chooses, prefers, decides to have) the (known) greater pain contained in what he does in return for securing the (known) lesser pleasure.

Socrates repeats once more interpretation (1) of 'overcome,' and

205

immediately after that proceeds to elaborate a principle that is implied by the hedonism of the *hoi polloi* (which we may remember is a premise of the whole argument) and which contradicts the explanation of E3 once we take *lambanein* in the sense of 'seeks,' 'chooses,' or 'prefers' (356B—C):

> For if you weigh pleasant things against pleasant, the greater and the more are always to be preferred [*leptea*] : if painful against painful, then always the fewer and the smaller. If you weigh pleasant against painful, and find that the painful are outbalanced (outweighed) by the pleasant — whether the near by the remote or the remote by the near — that action must be (is to be) done to which the pleasant are attached; but if the pleasant are outweighed by the painful, that action is not (must not) be done.[22]

The very last part of this hedonistic principle contradicts directly the explanation of the *hoi polloi* in its last substitution; and a similar principle, obtained by substituting 'good' for 'pleasant' and 'bad' for 'painful' in the above principle, contradicts directly the explanation of the *hoi polloi* that is obtained by the first substitution (that is, E3). This indeed is the absurdity that Socrates is talking about. But in order to appreciate this we must see at once that the hedonistic principle elaborated by Socrates does *not* assert a connection between a man's evaluations or ranking of the alternatives before him (the immediate results of the 'weighing' that Socrates is talking about) and his behavior (the execution of a particular action), but rather a connection between his evaluations and what (presumably as a result of the evaluations) he seeks or chooses to do. If Socrates' hedonistic principle were interpreted as asserting the former connection, Socrates would indeed at this point be begging the wider issue at stake within which the argument against explanations is set: the relation of knowledge to action. But Socrates need not rely on this. All that he needs at this stage is the latter connection, between a man's evaluations or rankings of the alternatives and what he seeks or chooses (decides, prefers) to do. This interpretation of the hedonistic principle on which Socrates relies to obtain the absurdity is perfectly consistent with — indeed, it is suggested by — the psychological hedonism that Socrates and Protagoras earlier attribute to the masses: people 'pursue pleasure as being a good and avoid pain as being an evil' (354C). 'Pursue' and 'avoid' (*diokein* and *pheugein*) must be understood to refer to one's seeking to obtain pleasures and seeking to avoid pains, not to one's actually obtaining pleasures and successfully avoiding pains.[23] The principle asserted is *not* that (1)

206

people always act in a way that maximizes their pleasures and/or minimizes their pains, but that (2) people always seek to act in such a way as to maximize pleasure and/or to minimize pain, where 'seek' is clearly opaque. Principle (1) is clearly and obviously false, since people often make mistakes, or lack the opportunity or the ability, or are prevented from maximizing and/or minimizing their pleasures. And it is clear that the psychological hedonism on which Socrates is relying here would employ (2), not (1), as a principle of explanation of human behavior: a typical explanation along these lines would include (2) as the operative principle, statements about the agent's knowledge or estimate of the amounts of pleasures and pains involved in the alternatives before him, and possibly statements about opportunity and ability to do or avoid the behavior at issue.[24] What Socrates has shown is that on the assumption of hedonism (ethical and psychological), one explanation of weakness commonly given by the masses, 'overcome by pleasure,' reduces to absurdity in the sense that (once we make the sustitutions allowed by ethical hedonism and interpret 'overcome' in the sense indicated) it contradicts the very principle of psychological hedonism that is universally employed by hedonists in the explanation of behavior.

Socrates is thus successful in reducing the explanation of weakness commonly given by the masses, 'overcome by pleasure,' to absurdity provided (1) that we allow him as premises the combination of ethical and psychological hedonism that he attributes to the masses, (2) that we grant him his interpretation of 'overcome,' and (3) that we understand the main verbs used in the various statements of psychological hedonism ('take,' 'pursue,' 'avoid') in an opaque sense. But the success of Socrates' argument is clearly very limited. To begin with, as an argument against non-Socratic (and non-early-Platonic) explanations of weakness, Socrates' argument is limited *to* 'overcome by pleasure' and *by* its hedonistic premises; what about the other explanations Socrates mentioned at the outset, and what about any of these explanations offered by non-hedonists? In the second place, what happens to Socrates' argument, and, more generally, to the explanations commonly given by the masses, when we interpret 'overcome' in the sense Socrates has ignored — that is, the sense in which 'overcome' refers to the relative *strength* of the desires (feelings, passions) for or against the alternatives before the agent (rather than to the relative values of the alternatives)? Finally, why should Socrates (and Plato) have ignored this important, and indeed more plausible, sense of 'overcome?' In the remaining sections of this chapter I take up each of these questions in turn.

3 *Application of the argument to other cases*

Can Socrates' argument against 'overcome by pleasure,' as reconstructed above, be generalized so as to apply to the other explanations originally mentioned by Socrates — 'overcome by' passion,
love, pain, fear? And can Socrates' argument be 'freed' from its
hedonistic premises, in the sense that some other plausible Platonic
non-question-begging premises can be found which can be successfully substituted for the hedonistic premises? If we can show that
the answers to these questions are affirmative, we thereby show
that the success of Socrates' argument is not so limited after all,
and that his argument is of some general singificance. I shall try to
show in *one move* that the answers to both questions are affirmative by constructing an argument, parallel to Socrates', against
the explanation 'overcome by fear' without relying on hedonistic
premises. The case of weakness and its explanation before us now
is as follows:

> Sometimes a man fails to do something which is good, and
> which he knows to be good, when it is in his power to do it,
> because
> he is overcome by fear.

The main reason I have selected the explanation 'overcome by fear'
is that Socrates later on in the *Protagoras*, when he begins a discussion of courage at 358D, provides us with a definition of fear:

> Well, I said, is there something you call dread or fear? And is it
> — I address myself to you, Prodicus — the same as I have in
> mind — something I describe as an expectation of evil, whether
> you call it fear or dread?

In the argument we are about to construct, this definition of fear
can take the place that ethical hedonism had in Socrates' argument:
that is, if granted as a premise in the new argument, it allows us to
substitute 'expectation of evil' for 'fear' in the explanation:

> Sometimes a man fails to do something which is good, and
> which he knows to be good, when it is in his power to do it,
> because
> he is overcome by the evil he expects.

Socrates can now argue that this explanation is absurd for reasons
similar to the ones we attributed to him for arguing that the
explanation obtained after the first substitution in his own argument is absurd; that was, it may be remembered:

> Sometimes a man does something which is bad, knowing that

it is bad, when it is in his power to avoid it
because
he is overcome by the good.

To see the parallel absurdity of the explanation 'overcome by the evil he expects' we need do only two things: eliminate the ambiguities of the statement, and indicate what principle is to take the place and perform the function of psychological hedonism. Eliminating the ambiguities (that is, eliminating interpretations analogous to E1 and E2 for analogous reasons), we obtain:

Sometimes a man fails to do something which is good on the whole, knowing that it is good on the whole — that is knowing that the good that it contains outweighs the evil (bad) that it contains — when it is in his power to do it
because
he seeks to (chooses, prefers, decides to) avoid the greater good in return for (as the price of) avoiding the lesser evil.

Well, what principle can take the place of psychological hedonism here? A principle that Socrates (and Plato) argues for in many early dialogues,[25] and which can be assumed here without begging any of the questions at issue: that every man desires or seeks (pursues) to get good things and seeks or desires to avoid getting bad or evil things; and the consequent principle that everyone pursues (or desires to do) things that are good on the whole or good in comparison to the alternatives, and seeks to avoid things that are bad in comparison to the alternatives and/or bad on the whole. It is this last part of the principle that contradicts the explanation 'overcome by fear' as reduced above.

4 The strength model

What happens to Socrates' argument against explanations of weakness, and, more important, what happens to these explanations themselves when we take 'overcome by . . .' to refer to the relative *strengths* of the agent's desires for and against the course of action before him?

Let us begin by noticing a point in the argument that we have so far ignored. At 356A, during the second substitution at the last stage of the argument, Socrates briefly raises and answers an objection to his argument:

For if you should say: But, Socrates, the *immediately* pleasant differs widely from the *subsequently* pleasant or painful, I should reply: Do they differ in anything but pleasure and pain?

That is the only distinction. Like a practice weigher, put pleasant things and painful on the scales, and with them the *nearness* and *remoteness*, and tell me which count for more [italics mine].

On the basis of Socrates' answer here, the immediately subsequent passage, and the analogy of size at 356D, we can confidently interpret Socrates' answer as follows. This feature of the case, the pleasure being near in time and the pain remote in the future, does indeed make a difference in the explanation, it is not an irrelevant feature; but the only difference this feature can make is a difference in pain or pleasure or rather in the quantities of pleasure and pain. It is not, however, a difference in the *actual* quantities of pleasure and pain involved in the case (we are not to suppose that the further the pain is in the future the smaller it will be!), but in the *estimated* or *believed* (by the agent) quantities of pleasure and pain. This answer leads Socrates to *his own* explanation of the case, elaborated after the last stage of the argument we have examined: that just as in the case of size and variation of distance, so here also because the pleasure is near the agent in time and the pain far, he mis-estimates the quantities and supposes that the pleasure outweighs the pain; so that he was acting in accordance with, indeed on the basis of, his hedonistic principle, even though he made a mistaken application of it. Socrates' answer to the objection and his own explanation are of course once more predicted on the assumption that 'overcome by pleasure' must refer to the pleasure outweighing the pain (in the agent's estimate).

But it is possible to give quite a different answer to Socrates' question − not an answer that Plato rejects, but one that he seems to ignore. We may suppose, without contradicting anything that Plato says: (a) that the agent, Agathon, knowing or believing what he did, had a desire for the pleasure he expected from eating the pastries and a desire to avoid (or a fear of) the pain he also expected afterward; (b) that these two desires (or the desire and the fear) may be considered as conflicting desires, and conceived as causes; (c) that these desires, considered as causes of behavior, can be supposed to have degrees of causal strength. Making the common additional assumption which is usually treated as a kind of law, that the behavior that issues from conflicting desires is that in accordance with the stronger desire (or the subject always acts in accordance with the stronger desire), we can now construct a causal explanation of our case as follows:

(1) Agathon was faced with the alternatives of eating or not eating Athenian pastries.

(2) Agathon had a desire to eat the pastries and a desire to avoid eating (or a fear of eating) the pastries.

(3) Agathon's desire to eat and desire not to eat the pastries (or the fear of eating) are conflicting desires.

(4) No other (interfering) desires or motives were present that were connected with the two alternatives.

(5) In every case of conflicting desires (and no interfering motives or external forces) the subject satisfies (acts in accordance with) the stronger desire.

(6) Agathon's desire to eat the pastries was stronger than his desire not to eat them.[26]

(7) Agathon ate the pastries.

The phrase 'overcome by pleasure' is now understood as a short-hand for this explanation, and in particular as referring to (6) and (5).

Explanations of this kind — that is, those that use (5) or some version of it as the main explanatory principle — are always logically relevant to cases of weakness (even though we may sometimes prefer other kinds of explanations) since conflicting motivations are characteristic of such cases, whether the conflicting motives be practical beliefs (or knowledge) and desires, as in Plato, or calm and violent passions, as in Hume.[27]

It should be noticed at once that an explanation of this kind can be perfectly respectable provided that we have ways of determining the relative strength of the conflicting desires independently of knowledge or information as to what action ensues from the conflict.[28] This condition (let us call it A) *must* be satisfied: otherwise, if our only way of telling which desire is stronger were to wait and see what action ensues, the main principle of the explanation (5) would be empty of empirical content, and the explanation would be trivial. Applied to our example, condition A requires that we be able to determine whether (6) is true independently of knowledge or information that (7) is true.

Now so far as explanations of weakness are concerned, it is important to realize that condition A may be satisfied in at least two significantly different ways.

(I) One way is to suppose that there is some consistent correlation between the agent's evaluation or ranking of the alternative before him and the strength of the conflicting desires that attach to these alternatives. This supposition would satisfy condition A since it is certainly possible to ascertain the agent's rankings (for example, by asking him) of the alternatives independently of knowing what alternative he actually takes (and, in addition, it is of course possible to rank alternatives without actually acting on the rankings because, say, one is prevented from doing so). Applied to our case, the supposition that would satisfy condition A is that if Agathon believes that the pleasure of eating the pastries outweighs the subsequent pain, then his desire to eat the pastries is stronger than his desire not to eat (or his fear of eating). It is conceivable that some such supposition is true, given some appropriate restriction of its scope; but whether or not this is so, it is certainly plausible, and its plausibility is perhaps enhanced by the difficulty of finding some *other* way to satisfy condition A. We may notice further that, if we satisfy condition A in the way just indicated, the ground or evidence for (6) will usually be a belief statement such as (6'): Agathon believes that the pleasure of eating the pastries outweighs the subsequent pain. The success of such an explanation depends on (6') being true, but not on what Agathon believes being true (Agathon may indeed be mistaken in his ranking and the reason for this may be that the pleasure was near and the pain much later — all this is consistent with the success of the explanation in question).

Before proceeding to the second way of satisfying condition A I wish to point out an important consequence of the first way of satisfying condition A. If one assumed or supposed (whether explicitly or implicitly) that (5) or some version of it is the relevant explanatory principle in cases of conflicting motives or desires or drives, and further that the first way (I) is the *only* way to satisfy condition A, then clearly the occurrence of *akrasia* or weakness will appear an impossibility to him (or, at least, *akrasia* will appear inexplicable). For in cases of *akrasia* the agent is supposed to be acting contrary to his knowledge or belief of which alternative is best (or better) — that is, contrary to *his own* ranking of the alternative; but, given our present supposition, this implies that he acts in accordance with the weaker, not the stronger, of the conflicting motives! At the same time, the present suppositions are quite consistent with the agent's acting against *the correct* ranking (correct even according, for example, to the agent's hedonistic principles); and this will be the case precisely when the belief in (6'), not (6') itself, is false. The explanation will work equally well here; and the inclination will be to say that what occur are cases where the agent acts against the correct (even by his own value principle) ranking, not against his own ranking. There is some evidence in the argument in the *Protagoras*, not that Plato thought of the matter explicitly in this way, but that he was thinking of it in this kind of context. For he begins the whole argument by asking which is stronger or more powerful in directing human conduct, knowledge of good and evil or such things as pleasure, pain, fear, love and so forth; and this language suggests (5) or some version of it as the relevant explanatory principle. And when, as we have seen, he comes to interpreting 'overcome by pleasure,' he does so by referring us to the hedonistic values of the alternatives, and this suggests that the strength of the motive is to be inferred from the value ranking of the alternatives.

(II) A significantly different manner of satisfying condition A would obtain if we had ways of determining the relative strength of the conflicting motives independently of any knowledge (or information) of the agent's evaluations or rankings of the alternatives to which the conflicting motives refer and of course independently of information of what behavior in fact ensues. If condition A can be satisfied in this manner, this allows, at the very least, for the possibility that the stronger (strongest) desire is not always the desire referring to the alternative that has the agent's higher (highest) ranking. Indeed, on the present supposition, there would be no *a priori* reason to expect that 'stronger motive' correlates consistently with 'higher ranking'; we might well find out that under certain conditions (for example, when the agent is in some state of emotional excitement), there is no correlation at all between 'stronger motive' and agent's 'higher ranking.' Now the supposition that sometimes, even quite often, people act against their own rankings or evaluations of the alternatives before them (even though they are not externally forced or compelled to, and have the opportunity to act in accordance with their own evaluations) will not be puzzling at all; for such behavior will no longer appear inexplicable.

Can condition A be satisfied in the second way? It seems that it has been satisfied in cases of explanations of animal behavior resulting from conflicting motives or drives, where the model of explanation used is similar to the one I have outlined, and the explanatory principle (5) or some variant of it is explicitly used.[29] Roughly speaking, it has been possible to show that the strength of two conflicting drives or motives — say, the desire for certain food (approach drive) and the fear of the electric shock that accompanies the obtaining of the food (avoidance drive) — increases as the animal approaches the goal, and that in fact the rate of increase of the avoidance drive is always greater than that of the approach drive (and it has been possible to measure the rate of increase of strength by measuring pull or speed at different points). In addition it has been possible to determine the initial strength (under controlled conditions) of the approach and avoidance drives (by varying such things as the time of deprivation of food

213

or the intensity of the electric shock). In consequence, it has been possible (under controlled conditions) to plot and predict the relative strengths of the approach and avoidance drives or motives at any given distance from the goal, and to predict what behavior will result (reaching the goal or not) in accordance with the principle that the animal's behavior at any given point (and at the end) will be in accordance with the stronger motive. More recently, exactly the same explanatory model has been used, perhaps without enough caution, in cases of human behavior resulting from conflicting motives; but it is not clear to me in this case (of human behavior) that condition A has been satisfied.[30] In any case, the success of the explanatory model in the case of animal behavior seems to point to the possibility that explanations of the same kind, satisfying condition A in the second (II) way, can be given of human behavior in cases of conflicting motives.

5 Weakness and compulsion

We have seen that Plato uses the language of strength[31] and yet overlooks the possibility of interpreting the various explanations of weakness, 'overcome by . . .,' in terms of the strength of the conflicting desires. How can we account for this? One possibility of course is that Plato did not distinguish the concepts of strength and value or value estimate. It is difficult enough to find a way of determining the strengths of conflicting desires (passions, feelings) independently of knowledge of ensuing behavior (condition A) and independently of knowledge of the agent's rankings or value estimates of the objects of his desires — the second way (II) of satisfying A (p. 213 above). The very possibility of doing either or both of these might not occur to one unless he encounters certain difficulties (of which the denial of weakness may be one). William McDougall's discussion is a good illustration of this point.[32] Or the necessity to satisfy condition A may be forced on one but he may not see further any need to satisfy condition A in any way other than (1) (pp. 211–13 above), as Mill's discussion illustrates.[33] I know of no explicit evidence that Plato saw any necessity to satisfy condition A at all, certainly none that condition A is to be satisfied in any other way other than (I). He seems to run together strength and value estimate; when, for instance, he considers an objection that might be understood to imply that strength of desire varies with variation of distance from the object of the desire, he understands it rather to imply that the agent's estimate of the value of the object varies with distance. The whole confusion is made easier to fall into by the fact that strength is not entirely independent of value estimate.[34]

A second possible line of explanation relates to two hitherto unnoticed features of the passage we have examined. One of these is a shift in Plato's language, from the language of strength to the language of value estimates, of which the turning point is at 355D where the passive 'overcome by' is replaced by 'to take' or 'to choose.' A list of the relevant phrases in the order in which they occur is sufficient to confirm this: 'dragged about' (352BC), 'under the control,' 'being overcome by' (repeated five times before 355D), 'being overpowered by,' 'being driven and dazed'; 'take,' 'choose,' 'weigh,' 'choose,' 'choice of odd and even,' 'right choice of pleasure and pain' (357B). This shift from the language of strength (all in the passive voice) to the language of value estimate (all in the active voice) suggests the possibility of another shift during the passage, a shift in the sorts of cases being considered: from cases where the agent is acting in the heat of passion, 'driven out of his sense' (as Wayte says),[35] where he has lost control of himself, to cases of calm and cool choice and action. Indeed, the radical shift in the language cannot but remind one of Austin's charge.[36] The second unnoticed feature of the passage is that Plato repeats three times (up to 355D), as part of the description of cases of weakness, that the agent 'could avoid' what he did or 'did not have to do' what he did.[37] Plato does not say what he means by this; he could be referring to physical ability, lack of physical coercion, or opportunity. It is also possible, I suggest, that he is referring to psychological ability to do or refrain from doing or to lack of psychological compulsion. This concept is of course difficult and in need of analysis; but if for the moment we suppose that this suggestion is near the mark, a new and interesting line of conjecture opens up that makes more intelligible Plato's treatment of weakness in the *Protagoras*, and perhaps even gives new life to his argument. The conjecture is that when a man acts contrary to his knowledge or belief of what is best (for him), *and* the true explanation of his action is in terms of the strength of his conflicting desires (passions, feelings) — an explanation of the sort outlined above (p. 211) — *and* condition A is satisfied in manner (II), then the agent acted under psychological compulsion or was not psychologically able to refrain from doing what he did. Thus, if a man, say, knows or believes that eating another serving of Athenian pastries would give him pleasure but would also harm him, and also believes that the harm outweighs the pleasure (so that he believes the pleasure is not worth the harm), but he eats nevertheless, and the true explanation of his eating is that his desire for the pleasure was stronger than his fear of the harm, and

215

we can determine this independently of knowledge of his action and knowledge of his value estimate, then he was not psychologically able to refrain from eating. The plausibility of connecting this type of explanation with psychological compulsion is enhanced by two considerations. First, when all these conditions are (accepted as) satisfied we have the feeling that our man is no longer an agent; he is not *doing* anything; something is happening to him — the very point suggested by Plato's passive language of strength (overcome, overpowered, dazed, and driven). The second point is that, if we accept the explanation and still say that the man *could* (psychologically) have refrained from eating, it seems that the only thing we can mean is that he *would* have refrained *if* his *fear* had been stronger instead. Now we are faced with the question whether the man had control, in any clear sense, over the *strength* of his feelings (and whether in general one can be said to have any such control). Until a clear affirmative answer can be given to this question, the verdict that the man was not (psychologically) able to refrain will have to stand. Until such an answer is given, we can say, tentatively, that this sort of explanation in terms of strength can be used to give *one* clear sense to the notion of psychological ability or at least psychological compulsion.[38]

Finally, if this conjecture is accepted, it constitutes a defense of Plato's argument. For it follows from it that, if we interpret the explanations of the masses, 'overcome by . . .,' in terms of strength (the interpretation that Plato ignores or overlooks, thus weakening his argument), then one of the conditions included in the description of the case explained is contradicted: namely, the condition that the man could or was able (psychologically) to refrain from acting contrary to his knowledge of what is best (for him). The 'wider' issue in the whole passage in the *Protagoras* was whether it is possible for men to act contrary to their knowledge of what is best when they can refrain. The 'narrower' issue, what the argument was all about, was whether, assuming that this is possible, the explanation can be that men are overcome by their passions, pleasure, pain, fear, love, and so forth. By interpreting 'overcome by' as referring to the value estimates or rankings of the agent, Socrates succeeded in showing that one such explanation leads to contradiction (taking hedonism as a premise). This paved the way to his own explanation (ignorance of what is best), which in effect answers the wider issue negatively, since the explanation cancels out one of the conditions in the description of weakness. It now results that, if we remedy the most serious weakness in Socrates' argument, and construe 'overcome by . . .' on the model of explanations in terms of strength, the wider issue is answered

216

negatively once more, since we now cancel out another condition, namely that the agent could (psychologically) have refrained from acting contrary to his knowledge. That this condition is included in descriptions of weakness is fair enough. For the philosophically puzzling cases of (prudential and moral) weakness, in so far as their occurrence reflects on the notion of having or holding (or 'assenting to') a practical principle, rule, or belief, are the cases where the man was *not* under (psychological as well as physical) compulsion. The cases where he was are after all understandable enough — at least if our concept of compulsion is clear enough.[39]

VIII

Power, Virtue, Pleasure, and Happiness in the *Gorgias*

Introduction

We have seen that the Socratic paradox that virtue is knowledge is logically based on Socrates' view that virtue brings happiness and vice unhappiness (chapter VI). Without the latter view, the prudential paradox, that no man desires things that are bad for him and that no man pursues such things voluntarily, would have only occasional relevance to virtue and vice. If vice occasionally brings unhappiness, then, given the prudential paradox, we would expect men to avoid vice on these occasions if they have the knowledge or true belief that on these occasions vice will bring them unhappiness. And if virtue occasionally brings happiness, we would similarly expect men to pursue virtue on these occasions if they had the relevant knowledge or true belief. But, if vice on other occasions brings happiness, we would equally expect men to pursue vice on these occasions if they had the relevant knowledge or true belief; and if virtue on occasion brings unhappiness, we would expect that men would avoid virtue on these occasions. Clearly enough, knowledge will not *always* be sufficient for virtue unless virtue *always* brings happiness and vice *always* unhappiness. Not unexpectedly, therefore, we find Socrates making strenuous efforts in the *Gorgias* to convince Gorgias, Polus, and Callicles that virtue brings happiness and that it is impossible for a wrongdoer to be happy.

Even aside from the Socratic pardoxes, the relation of virtue to happiness is an important issue for any system of ethics in which happiness is both the final good and also the ultimate motive for all human action. For unless it can be shown that there is some significant connection between virtue and happiness (and vice and unhappiness), it will be difficult if not impossible both to justify the pursuit of virtue and to motivate men for it. To put the matter in modern terms, if happiness is conceived as the final good and also the ultimate motive for all human action, the adoption of any given set of social and ethical norms will depend on the connection between living according to such norms and attaining happiness; unless there is some significant connection between the two it will be difficult to justify the adoption of these norms and equally difficult to motivate men to act in accordance with them. In addition, our notions of moral education and punishment will depend in part on our conception of the relation of virtue to happiness. In part, moral education consists in explaining to younger members of the society why they should acquire and practice certain virtues or adopt certain norms and also in motivating them to do so; and this we will be unable to do satisfactorily unless the practice of these virtues or the adoption of these norms at least tends to bring happiness and their rejection unhappiness. And in considering the justice and rationality of punishment, we cannot fail to consider how to prevent members of society from wrongdoing and how to reform wrongdoers; and these matters also involve moral re-education and our conception of human motivation. It can be seen, therefore, that the relation of virtue to happiness is an issue that cuts wide and deep, whether or not one subscribes strictly to the Socratic paradoxes. And hence it is not surprising that in the *Republic*, where Plato gives up strict adherence to the Socratic paradoxes and where he is considering fundamental questions of ethical and social reform, he is most eager to show that virtue brings happiness and that vice results in unhappiness.

In the *Gorgias* the need to show this is even greater, for the *Gorgias* is essentially Socratic — possibly the last Socratic Dialogue Plato wrote — and Socrates moves entirely within the conceptual framework of the Socratic paradoxes. The moral paradox is reaffirmed and argued for in the round with Gorgias, and the prudential paradox forms part of the logical base of Socrates' arguments against Polus.[1] No examination of Socratic ethics would be complete without a discussion of Socrates' conception of the relation of virtue to happiness, and for this the *Gorgias* is the proper Dialogue to examine, for it is the only Socratic Dialogue before the *Republic* where Socrates argues explicitly that virtue brings happiness and vice unhappiness. In this chapter we shall examine this conception.

In trying to understand Socrates' conception of the relation of virtue to happiness in the *Gorgias* we are faced with a very serious difficulty: in the whole Dialogue Socrates nowhere defines or explicitly explains his conception of virtue, particularly justice and temperance, the two virtues he argues about; nor does he explain very clearly his conception of happiness. This omission seems to be contrary to his own advice (as we saw in chapter V), according to which, in considering such general questions as whether virtue brings happiness, one should proceed by first trying to define virtue or trying to discover what virtue is (and possibly trying to discover what happiness is). This omission occurs once more in the first book of the *Republic*, where Socrates argues against Thrasymachus that justice brings happiness without first securing agreement on a definition of justice. And at the end of that book, Plato has Socrates say quite appropriately (354BC):

> But just as gluttons snatch at every dish that is handed along and taste it before they have properly enjoyed the preceding, so I, methinks, before finding the first object of our inquiry — what justice is — let go of that and set out to consider something about it . . . . For if I don't know what the just is, I shall hardly know whether it is a virtue or not, and whether its possessor is or is not happy.

Aside from the fact that the omission is contrary to the Socratic canons of investigation, the lack of definition of justice or temperance makes it extremely difficult to understand and assess Socrates' arguments to the conclusion that virtue brings happiness and vice unhappiness. This is so because there are many different conceptions of justice, temperance, and happiness, and it may well be the case that, given some of these conceptions, 'virtue' brings 'happiness', and given others it does not. We saw that in the *Charmides* there appear no fewer than seven definitions of temperance — none of which is Socrates' or Plato's; in the first book of the *Republic* there appear at least three different definitions of justice — none of which is Plato's or Socrates'; and in the *Gorgias* itself Polus, Callicles, and Socrates appear to have different conceptions of happiness, and different conceptions of justice. Yet Socrates fails to tell us explicitly what, according to him, justice is, what temperance is, and what happiness is. How then are we to understand his view that justice brings happiness and that it is impossible for the wrongdoer to be happy? And how are we to understand his arguments to that effect? The difficulty is neither slight nor semantic. It is as if someone were trying to convince us that living according to a given set of norms would make us happy, but has failed to specify the set and to explain what happiness he had in mind! But we must not exaggerate the difficulty. Though Socrates does not define or explicitly explain these things, he does say a number of things about them which help us understand his conceptions to some extent. First, his arguments themselves seem to presuppose certain conceptions of virtue and happiness; in addition, he relies on certain illuminating analogies, the most significant of which are the analogies between virtue and τέχνη (science-craft) and between health in the body and virtue in the soul; third, the conceptions of virtue and justice that his opponents have are made fairly clear in the Dialogue; and finally, Socrates himself states at least some of his own code of conduct or his normative ethics. It would be a mistake, then, to focus too narrowly on Socrates' arguments to the conclusion that virtue results in happiness and vice in misery. We must also try to understand in a substantial way the notions of justice and temperance and happiness with which he is working. We shall be concerned, then, with three fundamental questions about Socratic ethics in the *Gorgias*: (1) How does Socrates attempt to show that virtue brings happiness and vice misery? (2) What conceptions does Socrates have of virtue and vice, and specifically of justice and injustice and temperance and intemperance? (3) What conception of happiness does Socrates have? Answering these questions will help us to understand Socrates' conception of how men should live — the most important problem of normative ethics.

We shall begin with an analysis of the discussion between Socrates and Polus, a discussion in which the relation of virtue to happiness is explicitly argued; we shall state and analyze the issues between Socrates and Polus, the arguments Socrates brings against Polus to the general conclusions that justice brings happiness and wrongdoing misery, and the code of conduct that Socrates prescribes on the basis of his conclusions. Second, we shall analyze those portions of the discussion with Callicles that illuminate the Socratic conception of justice, temperance, and happiness, and those portions in which Socrates argues, once more, for his general view that justice and temperance bring happiness and injustice and intemperance misery. Finally, we shall examine in detail Socrates' analogies between virtue and health, and justice and medicine.

1 *The issues of virtue and happiness*

Let us begin with Socrates' statement of the issues between himself and Polus concerning virtue and happiness (472C–473C):

> For indeed the points which we have at issue are by no means of slight importance: rather, one might say, they are matters on which it is most honorable to have knowledge, and most dis-

graceful to lack it; for the main one of these is knowing or not knowing who is happy and who is not. To start at once with the point we are now debating, you consider it possible for a man to be happy [μακάριον] while doing injustice and being unjust, since you regard Archelaus as an unjust man and yet happy [εὐδαίμονα]. We are to conclude, are we not, this is your view?

Polus. Certainly.

Soc. And I say it is impossible [ἀδύνατον]. There we have one point at issue. Very good. But then will a man be happy doing injustice if he comes in for trial and punishment?

Polus. Not at all, since in that case he would be most wretched [ἀθλιώτατος].

Soc. But if he who has done injustice escapes punishment, then according to you he will he happy?

Polus. Yes.

Soc. Whereas according to my opinion, Polus, he who does injustice and is unjust is wretched in every way, but more wretched if he does not pay the penalty and is not punished for his injustice, and less wretched if he pays the penalty and meets with punishment from gods and men.

Polus. What strange things you are trying to maintain, Socrates.

Soc. And I will try to make you too, my friend, maintain them with me; for I count you as a friend. Well now, these are the points on which we differ; examine them yourself. I think I told you at an earlier stage that wrongdoing was worse than being wronged.

Polus. Certainly you did.

Soc. And you thought that being wronged was worse.

Polus. Yes.

Soc. And I said that wrongdoers were wretched, and I was refuted by you.

Polus. Upon my word, yes.

. . . .

Soc. But you say, on the other hand, that wrongdoers are happy, if they pay no penalty.

Polus. Certainly.

Soc. Whereas I say they are more wretched, but those who pay the penalty less so.

Here Socrates asserts and Polus denies the following propositions:

(1)   It is impossible for a man to be happy while doing injustice and being unjust.
(2)   A man who does injustice and is unjust is wretched in every way.
(3)   A man who does injustice and is unjust and who escapes punishment is not happy but rather the most wretched man.
(4)   A man who does injustice and is unjust and receives (just) punishment is less wretched than the man who does similar injustice and is similarly unjust and who does not receive (similar just) punishment.
(5)   Doing injustice is worse (in terms of happiness for the agent) than suffering (similar) injustice (is for the sufferer).

And earlier, at 407E, Socrates repeats a version of (2) and also asserts:

(6)   'The good and honorable man and woman are happy.'

Socrates does not give arguments directly in support of (1), (2), and (6), that is, arguments whose conclusions are these propositions. Rather, he gives arguments for (3), (4), and (5). These arguments we shall examine in the next section. In this section we need to understand more clearly what the issues are between Socrates and Polus, the things they both agree on, and how each conceives resolution of these issues. To do so, we need to look at the context in which Socrates places the dispute between them, particularly the theory of human motivation which both Socrates and Polus accept; and we also need to look at the counter-example by means by which Polus seeks to refute (1), (2), and (3).

The theory of motivation

The theory of motivation which Socrates expounds between 467C and 468E and to which Polus agrees readily without argument is essentially the same as that explained in chapter VI. At 467E Socrates asserts again (as he did in *Lysis* 216D) that all existing things are either good or bad or 'between these' — neither good nor bad. As examples of good things he gives wisdom, health, and wealth ('and the others of the same kind'), and as examples of bad things the opposites of these (ignorance or folly, disease, and poverty). He characterizes things that are neither good nor bad — let us call them intermediates — as 'those things which sometimes partake of the good, sometime of the bad, and sometimes of neither,' and gives as examples 'sitting, waking, running, sailing, and stones and sticks and the others of the same kind.' Socrates and Polus agree that people do intermediate things for the sake of good things, not good things for the sake of intermediate things (468A). They also agree that people want good things, but what is neither good nor bad they do not want, nor do they want what is bad (468C). But apparently, Socrates does not mean that men do not want intermediate things in any sense at all, but rather that they do not want them ἁπλῶς οὕτως — that is, *simpliciter,* for themselves, for their own sake; they want them if they think they will bring benefits or goods, and do not want them if they think they will bring harm or bad things (468C). Earlier, at 467CDE, Socrates and Polus agreed that it is not the case that men want that which they do every time, but rather they want that for the sake of which they do what they do; for example, it is not the case that those who take medicines want to do that, to take the medicine and suffer the pain, but rather they want to become healthy; and those who take sea voyages do not want to sail and suffer the dangers but rather they want to become wealthy, since it is for the sake of wealth that they sail; and later, at 468BC, the same is asserted about putting people to death, expelling them from the city, and confiscating their property — these things are wanted for the sake of such goods as wealth and power. In all these cases it is not necessary for the case that Socrates argues to suppose that he means that these things are not wanted in any sense at all. It is sufficient to suppose that he is saying that all these actions and activities — and possibly all actions and activities — are intermediate; they are wanted if they are thought to lead to the possession of good things and for the sake of such good things; they are not wanted if they are thought to lead to the possession of bad things, and they are not wanted ἁπλῶς οὕτως — for their own sake.

All this theory is explained to Polus and used to show him that it is possible to do something that one thinks is best for himself and yet not do what he wants to do; in particular that it is possible for one to do such things as put men to death or expel them from the city or deprive them unlawfully of their property thinking that it is best for oneself to do these things and yet (in doing these things) not to do what one wants to do. And this would turn out to be the case if in fact these things were to lead to the agent's possession of bad things: for according to the theory just expounded a man would do these things for the sake of possessing good things (in a relativized version, for the sake of what he thought best for himself); and yet these things turn out to lead to the possession of bad things, and so are things which, according to the theory, no one wants to do.

It is in the context of this theory of motivation that the dispute about justice and happiness between Socrates and Polus is set. This can be seen in the following exchange (470B–471A):

Soc. . . . And let us consider another point: is it not the case that we admit that sometimes it is better to do these things that we were mentioning just now – to put people to death or expel them or take their property – and sometimes it is not?

Polus. To be sure.

Soc. And here is a point, it seems, that is admitted both on your side and mine.

Polus. Yes.

Soc. Then when do you say it is better to do these things? Tell me where you draw the line.

Polus. I would rather that you, Socrates, answer that.

Soc. Well then I say, Polus, if you prefer to hear it from me, that when one does these things justly it is better, and when unjustly worse.

Polus. It is so hard to refute you, Socrates! Could not even a child refute you and show that what you say is not true?

Soc. Then I shall be most grateful to the child, and equally to you, if you refute me and rid me of my foolishness. Come now do not tire of benefiting your friend, but refute me.

Polus. Well, to be sure, Socrates, there is no need to refute you with ancient instances: for the things that happened a day or so ago are sufficient to refute you and to prove that many men are happy while they are unjust.

Soc. Which sort of things?

Polus. I suppose you see that Archelaus, son of Perdiccas, is ruler of Macedonia?

Soc. If I do not, I hear it.

Polus. Do you consider him happy or wretched?

Soc. I do not know, Polus, I have never met the man.

Polus. What? Could you find out by meeting him, and cannot otherwise tell, straight off, that he is happy?

Soc. No, by Zeus.

Polus. Then doubtless you will say, Socrates, that you do not know that even the Great King is happy.

Soc. Yes, and I shall be speaking the truth; for I do not know how he stands in point of education and justice.

Polus. Why, does happiness consist entirely in that?

Soc. Yes, by my account, Polus; for a good and honorable man or woman, I say, is happy, and an unjust and wicked one wretched.

Polus. Then this Archelaus, on your statement, is wretched?

Soc. Yes, my friend, if he is unjust.

From this passage it is also clear that when Socrates and Polus disagree as to when it is better to do such things as put people to death, expel them from the city, or take their property (or anything that is intermediate), 'better' is meant in the sense of 'better for the agent' and 'better in terms of the happiness of the agent.' It is not 'morally better' that is meant. This is shown by the form of the counter-examples Polus brings up: many men are happy while being unjust. It is also shown by the fact that to understand the dispute in terms of 'morally better' would trivialize Socrates' position — for what could be more trivial than to say that doing things justly is morally better than doing them unjustly? Throughout the round with Polus the dispute is fought in terms of what is better for the agent in the sense of the goods and evils and happiness that one's actions bring on oneself.

From this passage we also begin to get some idea of the notion of happiness and unhappiness that Socrates and Polus share: both of them think that happiness consists in the possession of good things (and, probably also, in the absence of evils). We find this general characterization of happiness explicitly given in the *Symposium* (204E–205A):

'Come Socrates, he who loves good things, what does he love?'
'That they may be his,' I replied.
'And what will he have who gets good things?'
'I can answer this more easily, I said; he will be happy.'
'Yes,' she said, 'the happy are happy by the acquisition of good things; and there is no longer need to ask further for the sake of

what the man who wants to be happy wants to be happy; the answer seems to be final.

We shall find that Socates' conception of happiness in the *Gorgias* is entirely in accord with this characterization, and Polus has the same view; their disagreements about happiness are about what things are good and evil and how they are to be ranked. We can see that Polus has this view both from the *Gorgias* passage just quoted and from the counter-example he is about to give. Within the theory of goods and evils and the theory of motivation that Socrates has just expounded, the natural answer to the question Socrates asks ('When do you say it is better to do these things?') is the following: a man would be better off doing these intermediate things, rather than not doing them, when by doing these things he would obtain the goods for the sake of which he would do these things; whereas by not doing them he would not obtain these good things, other things being equal between the two alternatives. Socrates' answer to his own question is surprising, since it does not mention any of the goods and evils he previously listed; but later his answer can be seen to conform to the pattern of the natural answer when he argues that justice is the greatest good to the possessor of it and injustice the greatest evil. Polus' objection to Socrates' answer, however, conforms at once to the pattern of the natural answer, on the assumption that happiness consists in the possession of good things. For, within the theory of goods and evils and of motivation that he and Socrates agreed on, his objection to Socrates should take the form: many people who do injustices succeed in obtaining the good things for the sake of which they do the injustices. And this is precisely what he is saying when he says that many men are happy while being unjust, on the assumption that happiness consists in the possession of good things. If there is any doubt of this, it can be laid to rest by considering the counter-example that Polus offers: he presents Archelaus as a man who has done many injustices and has obtained many good things, such as wealth, and power, as a result of his injustices.

The counter-example of Archelaus (471AD)

Polus. Well, but how can he be other than unjust? He had no claim to the throne he now occupies, being the son of a woman who was a slave of Perdiccas' brother Alcetas, and according to what is just he was a slave of Alcetas; and he would be happy according to your argument; but now he has become a prodigy

227

of wretchedness since he has done the most enormous wrongs. First of all, he invited this very master and uncle of his to his court, as if he were going to restore to him the kingdom of which Perdiccas had deprived him; and after entertaining him and his son Alexander — his own cousin, about the same age as himself — and making them drunk, he packed them into a carriage, drove them away by night, and murdered and made away with them both. And having done these injustices he failed to see that he had become most wretched and did not repent but a little later he refused to make himself happy by bringing up, as he was justly bound, his brother, the legitimate son of Perdiccas, a boy about seven years old who had a just title to the throne, and by restoring the kingdom to him; but he cast him into a well and drowned him, and then told his mother Cleopatra that he had fallen in and lost his life while chasing a goose. So now, you see, as the greatest wrongdoer in Macedonia, he is the most wretched of all the Macedonians, not the happiest; and I dare say some Athenians could be found who would join you in preferring to change places with any other Macedonian of them all, rather than with Archelaus!

This passage, full of sarcasm, is worth studying. It contains a list of injustices about which there is no dispute between Socrates and Polus. Indeed, in the whole round between these two there seems to be no disagreement as to what justice and injustice consists in, so far as behavior at least is concerned; stealing, murdering, lying, and generally doing what is contrary to the laws of one's city is behaving unjustly; and living in accordance with the laws is behaving justly. The justice that Polus and Socrates talk about is what Callicles later refers to as 'justice by law,' and it conforms to Socrates' notion of justice in the *Apology* and the *Crito*. (The major possible disagreement between Socrates and Polus on what justice consists in may be the Socratic position that it is not just to harm even one's enemies — but this possible disagreement plays no part in the *Gorgias*.) Nor is there any disagreement between Socrates and Polus as to whether Archelaus was successful in obtaining the goods he sought through these injustices — wealth, power, esteem and admiration from most of the Greeks — and that he was also successful in avoiding punishment. Their disagreement is whether Archelaus is happy; and this disagreement depends on disagreements as to whether other things that Archelaus possessed and avoided as a result of his injustices — the things Polus listed and others — are good or evil and how great these are relative to each other. Finally, Socrates never disputes that Archelaus knew that he was committing injustices; and indeed, the injustices committed are properly presented by Polus as 'the greatest wrongs' (τὰ μέγιστα ἠδίκηκεν, μέγιστα ἠδικηκώς), whose wrongness no man can fail to perceive; what is disputed is whether Archelaus was not mistaken in believing that the things he succeeded in obtaining were goods or at any rate sufficiently great goods to make him happy, and that the things he avoided (e.g., punishment) were evil.

It will be useful to summarize the results of our discussion so far, listing both the major *agreements* between Socrates and Polus concerning goods and evils, motivation, justice, and happiness, and their major disagreements so far.

Agreements between Socrates and Polus (467C—468E, 471AD)

1 All things are good, or bad, or neither good nor bad.
1.1 Wisdom, health, wealth, are good things.
1.2 Ignorance, disease, poverty, are bad things.
1.3 Things that are neither good nor bad sometimes partake of the good, sometimes of the bad, sometimes of neither.
1.4 Sitting, walking running, sailing, taking medicines, putting people to death, expelling people from the city, confiscating people's property, stones and sticks, and other such things are neither good nor bad (intermediates).
2 People want (to possess) good things; they do not want (to possess) bad things, and they do not want (to do or possess) intemediate things for their own sake.
2.1 People do intermediate things for the sake of good things, and do not do or pursue good things for the sake of intermediate things.
3 Unjust behavior consists in stealing, murdering, lying, and doing things contrary to the laws (of one's own city?); just behavior consists in acting according to the laws.
4 Happiness consists in the possession of good things (and the absence of evils), and unhappiness consists in the possession of evils (and the absence of goods).

Disagreements between Socrates and Polus (Socratic theses Polus objects to)

5 The good and honorable man is happy. (470E)
6 The unjust and wicked man is wretched. (460E)
6.1 It is impossible for a man to he happy while doing injustice and being unjust. (472—3)

6.2 A man who does injustice and is unjust is wretched in every way. (472–3)

7 A man who does injustice and is unjust and escapes punishmen is not happy but the most wretched man. (472–3)

7.1 A man who does injustice and is unjust and receives just punishment is less wretched than the man who does similar injustice and is similarly unjust and who does not receive (escapes) similarly just punishment. (472–3)

8 Doing injustice is worse for the agent than suffering it is for the sufferer. (472–3)

9 Injustice in the soul is the greatest evil a man can possess. (477BCDE)

Questions that are open between Socrates and Polus

Q1 What things are good, besides wisdom, health, and wealth?

Q1.1 How are goods ranked relative to each other? (or, which are to be preferred to which in cases of conflict, i.e. cases of competing goods?)

Q2 What things are evil (bad for one to have), besides ignorance or folly, disease, and poverty?

Q2.1 How are evils ranked relative to each other? (or, which evils are more to be avoided in cases of conflicts, i.e. cases of choices among evils?)

2 Socrates' arguments that the unjust man is unhappy

Between 474C and 480 Socrates gives three arguments in support of his general view that doing injustice and being unjust brings unhappiness, and he draws out the consequences of these arguments concerning justice, punishment, and happiness. The first argument is for the conclusion that it is worse for one to do rather than to suffer injustice, the second for the conclusion that *just* punishment is a good to the one who is punished (in that it relieves him from the evil of injustice in his soul), and the third for the conclusion that injustice in the soul is the greatest evil that a man can possess. It is clear from these arguments that Socrates' strategy is *not* to try to show that injustice brings unhappiness by showing that those who do injustice never succeed in obtaining the goods for the sake of which they do injustice. And indeed such a strategy would be hopeless. The proposition that wrongdoers *never* succeed in getting the things for the sake of which they do wrong is obviously false, and the case of Archelaus alone is sufficient to show it. It is clear enough from these three arguments that Socrates

230

in fact holds that doing injustice is an evil to the agent whether or not the agent succeeds in getting the things for the sake of which he does injustice, and, apparently, whether or not the things he does succeed in getting are good. From the first argument it is not clear what evil or harm injustice does to the agent. But from the last two arguments it is clear enough that the evil is the injustice in the soul of the agent. Apparently, Socrates' idea is that if a man does injustice, that shows that he has injustice in his soul; and further the doing of the injustice causes him to continue to have injustice in his soul and possibly to have even greater injustice than before. Thus, if Socrates can show that injustice in the soul is an evil, he will have shown thereby that the man who does injustice harms himself; and if he can show that injustice is the greatest of evils, he will have shown thereby that the man who does injustice does himself the greatest harm (at any rate the greatest harm that can come from a single evil). And, at the very least, who would say that a man who possesses the greatest of evils is happy? On the assumption, then, that doing injustice is caused by injustice in the soul of the agent, and that in turn doing injustice causes continued and greater injustice in the soul of the agent, Socrates' strategy is to prove that injustice in the soul is the greatest evil a man can possess.

The first argument, however, does not try to show directly that injustice in the soul is an evil, but only that doing injustice is an evil to the agent, indeed a greater evil to the agent than suffering the same injustice is to the sufferer. This argument is worth studying carefully for two reasons. First of all, if this argument is successful it establishes a very powerful result and it overthrows in one blow the whole conception that Polus has of how men ought to live — a conception shared by Callicles, Thrasymachus and many others. The argument seeks to establish that doing injustice is worse (a greater evil) to the agent than suffering injustice (presumably the same injustice) is to the sufferer. Now if we consider even briefly the enormous evils that one can suffer unjustly, we can see how extraordinary this proposition is: one can be unjustly deprived of one's property, one can be unjustly expelled from one's city, one can have oneself and one's family unjustly enslaved, and one can be tortured unjustly, and unjustly be put to death — and the Greeks were well acquainted with all these injustices. Socrates is arguing that in all these cases the man who does the injustice does thereby (and aside from what happens to him later!) more harm to himself than the harm done to the sufferers of the injustice: the man who unjustly deprives another of his property does thereby a greater evil to himself than the evil suffered by the man who is so deprived, whether or not the unjust man is punished or enjoys the fruits of his injustice free and unmolested; the man who unjustly expels or enslaves another does thereby a greater evil to himself than the evil suffered by the expelled or enslaved man; and the man who unjustly puts another to death does thereby a greater evil to himself than the evil suffered by the man who is so put to death. The evils just listed, which a man can unjustly suffer, were and are universally admitted to be among the greatest evils that can befall a man. No wonder Socrates says later (477 DE):

> Portentous then must be the extent of the harm, and astonishing the evil, by which the soul's vice exceeds all the other evils . . . .

Since the evil that a man who does injustice brings on himself is the injustice, and generally vice, in his soul, this evil must be greater than any evil the unjust man can unjustly cause another to suffer; indeed, since conceivably by a single act of injustice a man can unjustly deprive another of his property, have his family enslaved and have him put to death, the injustice in the wrongdoer's soul must be a greater evil than all these evils combined! Astonishing indeed must be the evil of injustice in the soul.

The second reason for studying the first argument very carefully is that it contains two crucial premises on which all three arguments depend. These are what appear to be definitions of a pair of opposites, two very general and difficult Greek terms, καλόν, which I shall translate 'beautiful, praiseworthy, or admirable,' and its opposite, αἰσχρόν, which I shall translate 'ugly, blameworthy, or shameful.' These definitions together with two general propositions are the backbone of all three arguments. The two general propositions are that all the virtues, including justice of course, are καλά – beautiful, praiseworthy or admirable, and that all the vices, including injustice, are αἰσχρά – ugly, blameworthy, or shameful. These two general propositions, in a variety of versions, were treated more or less as axiomatic in earlier Socratic Dialogues. In both the Laches and the Charmides it is assumed with certainty and without question that courage and temperance are beautiful, praiseworthy, or admirable, and the opposite vices the opposite. Moreover, in the Charmides it was taken as obvious or axiomatic that if temperance is καλόν then it is beneficial to its possessor and makes him happy – the connections between καλόν and benefit and happiness were taken for granted – and this is understandable, since the relation of virtue to happiness was not in question. And the same is true of Protagoras 358B and 359E, where, again, the relation of virtue to happiness is not in question. But in the *Gorgias*, where this relation is very much in question, Socrates has to *argue* that from these general propositions, which are apparently admitted by all, it follows that justice and virtue are beneficial and injustice harmful. In essence, all three of Socrates' arguments consist of complicated inferences, mediated by the definitions and auxiliary premises, from statements (relativized) that the virtues are καλά to statements that they are good things, and from statements that the vices are αἰσχρά to statements that they are evil or bad things. We shall see that Plato has Callicles find an important ambiguity in the terms αἰσχρόν and καλόν, an ambiguity that appears damaging to Socrates' arguments. And Plato has Adeimantus (*Republic* 364 ff.) give a different account as to why we praise and admire the virtues and condemn the vices, an account that undercuts the inference Socrates wants to make: essentially, he argues that we praise virtue and find it admirable not because it itself is beneficial but because it is beneficial to have the reputation of virtue. Nevertheless, despite these difficulties and others, the line of argument that Socrates pursues in all three arguments is reasonable and cuts deep: for, it seems, our praise and admiration of the virtues could not be well founded or reasonable unless the virtues were of some benefit; and our condemnation of the vices could not be well founded and reasonable unless the vices were in some important sense harmful. Whether the benefits and the harm take the precise form that Socrates argues — namely, that they are benefits and harms *to the agent* (as well as others, presumably), is another matter, and one that we can decide only by a detailed examination of the arguments.

The first argument: it is worse to do rather than to suffer injustice

The argument has two stages. The first stage is an inductive argument whose conclusion is a definition of καλόν; the second stage is a deductive argument to the final conclusion. The most recent and by far the best analysis of this argument, especially the first stage, is that of Professor Gregory Vlastos.[2] I shall follow Vlastos's version of the first stage of the argument, which is as accurate as one could wish (adding only certain premises for the sake of completeness and for the sake of understanding fully the second stage).

P1   Beautiful bodies are called beautiful either on account of their usefulness for some particular purpose, or because of a certain pleasure, if they delight their beholder in beholding them.

P2   Similarly in the case of all such other things as shapes and colors, they are called beautiful either because of a certain pleasure or because of their usefulness or both.

P3 Likewise in the case of sounds and everything else that pertains to music (i.e., these things are called beautiful because of a certain pleasure or usefulness or both).

P4 And further in the case of laws and practices, their beauty falls within the scope of usefulness or pleasure or both (i.e., laws and practices that are called beautiful are called beautiful because of a certain pleasure or usefulness or both).

P5 The beauty of things we learn is the same (i.e., things that we learn are called beautiful because of a certain pleasure or usefulness or both).

C1 Therefore, the beautiful is defined by pleasure or good (useful). (The beautiful is that which is good or pleasant or both.)

P6 (The ugly is the opposite of the beautiful.)

P7 (Evil is the opposite of good, and pain is the opposite of pleasure.)

C2 Therefore, the ugly is defined by their opposites, pain and evil. (The ugly is that which is painful and evil.)

C3 Therefore, when one of two beautiful things is the more beautiful, it must be so by surpassing the other in one or the other or both of these two respects: in pleasure or usefulness (benefit) or both.

C4 Therefore, when one of two ugly things is the uglier, it must be so by surpassing the other in pain or evil or both.

P8 Doing injustice is uglier than suffering it.

C5 Therefore, if doing injustice is uglier than suffering it, it either is more painful and would be uglier by surpassing in pain or (by surpassing) in evil or both.

P9 Doing injustice does not surpass suffering injustice in pain.

C6 Therefore, doing injustice does not surpass injustice in both pain and evil.

C7 Therefore, doing injustice surpasses suffering injustice in evil.

C8 Therefore, doing injustice is worse (= a greater evil) than suffering it.

P10 No one would rather have (= prefer) the greater evil and uglier thing to the lesser.

C9 Therefore, no one would rather have (= prefer) to do injustice rather than to suffer it.[3] (*Gorgias* 474D—475E)

Is this a sound argument? Let us first discuss validity. The deductive argument from C4 to C7 (or C8) is valid: if C4 is stated with the help of variables, C5 follows from it by universal instantiation; C6 follows from P9 by simplification; the consequent of C5 follows from P8 and C5 by *modus ponens*; and C7 (or C8) follows from the consequent of C5, P9, and C6 by disjunctive syllogism. C4 can only be derived from C2, and it can be so derived validly by *modus ponens* provided we grant the following principle which would seem to be true of all concepts or terms admitting of degrees:

$$(F)(G)[(F=G) \supset (x)(y)(x \text{ is more F than } y \supset x \text{ is more G than } y)].$$

C3 follows from C1 in a similar fashion. C2 can be validly derived from C1, P6, and P7, on the assumption that each opposite has only one opposite.[4] Thus, the whole series of deductive arguments from C1 to C7 (or C8) consists of valid arguments. It is in fact a beautiful series of deductive arguments, rigorous and well stated. Only four steps are not spelled out explicitly, C1 to C2, C1 to C3, C2 to C4, and P8 to C5 to the consequent of C5, and of these the last three are very obvious. It is indeed a good-looking deductive argument, as perspicuous as any argument we find in Plato of comparable length.

Are the premises of the deductive argument, C1 to C8, true? Two of the most important premises, P8 and P9, seem to be true. The other two most important premises are C1 and C2. Let us examine the truth of C1 by examining the inductive argument P1 to C1. Is this argument sound; i.e., is it a strong inductive argument, and are its premises true? At first sight this seems like one of Socrates' strongest inductive arguments. The conclusion is inferred from a great variety of kinds of things that can be beautiful, including bodies, colors and shapes, musical sounds, laws and practices, and 'things we learn' which can include all kinds of things including skills, arts, crafts, and sciences. Dodds has compared this list of things that can be called beautiful with similar lists in the *Hippias Major* 298AB and *Symposium* 210AB; the latter passage adds soul ψυχή to this list, and the former adds speeches or arguments and stories (λόγοι and μυθολογίαι). None of these additions seem significant for the purposes of the present argument: we can well imagine Polus giving the same replies. From the premises, then, that in all these cases we call things beautiful with an eye to usefulness (benefit, good) or pleasure and nothing else, or because of usefulness or pleasure and nothing else, the conclusion is reasonably inferred that the beautiful is that which is beneficial (good) or pleasant or both. Indeed, the variety of kinds of things surveyed in the premises is so great that one is tempted to consider the argument as a case of induction by complete enumeration (at any rate if we include the items of the *Symposium*). Moreover, the definition of καλόν in terms of benefit or pleasure or both is very plausible in terms of the uses of that term in the ancient Greek culture. According to Liddell, Scott, Jones, the adjective had three major uses or senses: (1) '*beautiful*, of outward form,' as applied to persons, bodies, dances, parts of the body, clothes, armour, manufactured articles; (2) 'with reference to use, *good, of fine quality*,' applied to harbors, winds, places, times, etc.; and (3) 'in a moral sense, *beautiful, noble, honorable*,' applied to deeds, virtues, etc. In the definition of καλόν Plato would appear to be explicating the first sense in terms of the delight or pleasure that outward beauty causes in the perceiver or spectator, which is plausible enough, and he would appear to be trying to capture senses (2) and (3) together by the concepts of χρήσιμον, ὠφέλιμον and ἀγαθόν — useful, beneficial, good — and the last of the three is certainly wide enough to cover both senses (2) and (3) in Liddell, Scott, Jones (sense (2) is well captured by χρήσιμον and sense (3) by ὠφέλιμον). It would seem, then, that the inductive argument P1 to C1 is very strong, and that the definition C1 is in accord with the Greek use of the term defined.

Despite all these virtues, Socrates' argument, P1 to C7, has universally been judged unsound, until recently entirely on the ground that Plato has Callicles say later on that there is an equivocation in the use of the key term αἰσχρόν (ugly, shameful, blameworthy) during the argument — though I have yet to see a properly detailed analysis of *that* objection and Socrates' reply.[5] This objection we shall consider in due course, when we examine Callicles' attack on Socratic ethics. Here we need to consider an error in the argument that Professor Vlastos has spotted, an error that seems to damage the argument seriously and independently of the dispute between Socrates and Callicles. Vlastos noticed that in P1 the pleasure referred to is explicitly said to be the pleasure that the *viewer* (beholder) of beautiful things derives *in viewing them*; he also observed rightly that this qualification is understood in premises P2, P3, and it is omitted only for stylistic reasons; and further that this qualification is also to be understood in premises P4 and P5. This is clearly correct. But if this is so, Vlastos points out, the conclusion of the induction, C1 (referred to by Vlastos as C), is incorrectly or elliptically stated; the correct conclusion (the conclusion that is faithful to the premises with regard to the qualification explicitly stated in P1 and understood in the other premises) is

C1.1　　The beautiful is that which is useful or else that which delights those who see or hear or contemplate it. (referred to by Vlastos as D)

The difference between C1.1 and C1 makes a big difference to the argument, as Vlastos points out. Given our statement of the argument, we can express the difference as follows. If C1.1 is the correct conclusion of the inductive argument, the definition of the opposite of the beautiful — the ugly — has also to be amended (since this definition is either derived from C1.1 or by a similar induction); thus instead of C2 we shall have:

C2.1　　The ugly is that which is harmful (evil) or else that which gives pain to those who see or hear or contemplate it, or both.

And C4, the immediate operative premises in the deductive argument, will have to be amended accordingly to:

C4.1　　When one of two ugly things is the uglier, it must be so by surpassing the other in harm (evil) or in the pain it gives to those who see or hear or contemplate it.

And now, Vlastos points out, it can be clearly seen that the question that Socrates asks at 475B8—C3 and by which he elicits P9 is illegitimate.

Socrates. First of all then let us consider if to do wrong is more painful than to be wronged, and who are the ones who suffer the greater pain: those who do wrong or those who suffer it?

If C1.1, C2.1, and C4.1 are the correct premises, Socrates is clearly asking the wrong question, and the answer that Polus gives does not help Socrates in the subsequent argument. Given C4.1, the correct question is clearly:[6]

Of the two things, doing wrong and suffering wrong, which is the more painful for those who observe or contemplate the two events?

And of this question Vlastos says:[7]

To that question the answer is, at best, indeterminate. Polus might have argued with some plausibility that most of us would find the former [doing wrong] more painful than the latter [suffering wrong] and, on that ground that it is 'uglier,' just as he had maintained at the start: except in rare, abnormally soft-hearted souls, he might have urged, resentment is more easily aroused than pity, more strongly felt and more disturbing to one who feels it; hence most people would be more pained at the thought or sight of prospering villainy than that of suffering innocence. Whether or not he would be right on this last point is of no consequence in itself. This much at least is clear, and this is all that matters: If Polus had had the sense to opt for D instead of C a moment earlier, a line of argument would have been open to him which would have sufficed to save him from the abject capitulation to which he is forced by Socrates in the text.

I think that Vlastos is certainly right in maintaining that the argument that Socrates in fact gives does not succeed in refuting Polus — Socrates mis-stated the conclusion of his inductive argument and the mistake infects the rest of his argument as indicated above. But suppose now that we correct Socrates' mistake as we did above, following Vlastos, and we have Socrates ask the correct question, the question we quoted above. This is the thing to do if we are interested in the truth of the issue between Socrates and Polus — and in any case when a mistake is found in an argument the question always arises whether it can be corrected. Is then what Vlastos says about the answer to the correct question true? First, is Polus in a position to argue that 'most people would be more pained at the thought or sight of prospering villainy than that of suffering innocence' (and that these would be the people who, like himself, are not 'abnormally soft-hearted souls')? This question admits of a clearly negative answer: for Polus, as we have seen, gave us, just a few pages before this argument, his views and feelings about a paradigmatic case of 'prosperous villainy,' the case of Archelaus. Does Polus express resentment or pain at the thought of Archelaus' wrongdoings, or does he say that most people would? On the contrary, he expresses admiration and envy of Archelaus, and in the latter part of his speech (471CD) he implies that most Athenians feel the same way.[8] To be sure, the envy and admiration that Polus expresses of Archelaus may be envy and admiration not of Archelaus' wrongdoings but of the successes that Archelaus has as a result of his wrongdoings — but is this not fair enough for '*prospering* villainy?' More important, the answer that Polus gives to the wrong question that Socrates asks — namely, that suffering injustice is more painful to the sufferer than doing injustice is to the doer — is not irrelevant to the question of what answer Polus could have given to the *correct* question; nor is it irrelevant to the truth of the matter. For it follows from *that* answer, an answer that seems to be true, that in so far as the pains that witnesses or spectators feel at the witnessing or thought of doing wrong and suffering wrong are the pains felt through sympathy or pity, such spectators and witnesses would feel more pain at the witnessing or thought of suffering of wrong than at the witnessing or thought of doing wrong. Of course the truth of the matter is complicated by the fact that spectators and witnesses may, in addition, feel indignation or resentment at the witnessing or thought of the doing of wrong, and these might be held to be painful feelings. But Polus never brings up such feelings as resentment and indignation: his view of the matter is that doing wrong is not painful, that suffering wrong is painful, that doing wrong is admired and envied if successful, that suffering wrong is pitied, and that doing wrong is pitied only when it results in punishment — which is a different matter, for in his view being punished is suffering an evil. It is clear to me that he is not in a position to make the answer to the correct question that Vlastos has him make. But to find out what the *true* answer is to the *correct* question would take a large and difficult investigation; an investigation that would begin with an analysis of such feelings as pity and sympathy and indignation and resentment, and would include an empirical investigation, which belongs to psychology, into what in fact people feel at the thought or witnessing of doing and suffering wrong. An interesting investigation of how the Greeks felt about these phenomena would be an investigation of how the chorus in Greek tragedies — witnesses and spectators of doing and suffering injustices *par excellence* — is represented as reacting to doing and suffering wrong, by Aeschylus, Sophocles, and Euripides. I would expect such an investigation to support a Socratic answer to the correct question.

Unfortunately, even if we take the liberty to give an answer to the correct question, which is favorable to Socrates, still Socrates' argument is not successful. For besides the error that Vlastos spotted, there is yet another error, somewhat parallel to it. What Socrates is arguing is not simply that doing wrong is more harmful or evil than suffering wrong; rather, he is arguing that doing wrong is more harmful or evil *to the doer* than suffering wrong is *to the sufferer*. But his definitions of beautiful and ugly, and the statements derived from them, are strong enough to support the former statement *but not the latter*. In particular, in the *corrected* versions (as well as the uncorrected ones), C2.1 and C4.1, there is nothing whatsoever as to what or to whom the harm is done. Nothing therefore follows as to the one to whom the greater harm or evil is done; in particular it certainly does not follow that the greater evil or harm of doing wrong is greater evil or harm to the wrongdoer.[9] It may well be that the evil or harm of doing wrong is greater than the harm of suffering wrong; but the definitions allow that this harm may the *total* harm or evil caused by doing wrong — that is, the harm done to the one that suffers the wrong, the harm done possibly to the wrongdoer himself, the harm caused by those who tend to imitate wrongdoers, especially successful ones, and so on. Thus we can allow Socrates the corrected definitions, and we can allow him that doing wrong does not cause greater pain in the witness or spectator of it than suffering wrong does; and we can still account Socratically for the fact that doing wrong is judged to be uglier or more shameful or more blameworthy than suffering wrong by supposing, and supposing truly, that the *total* harm caused by doing wrong is greater than the harm of suffering wrong is to the sufferer. And this is probably the true state of affairs: doing wrong is held to be uglier, or more blameworthy, or more shameful, than suffering wrong because it is more harmful than suffering wrong — but more harmful in its effects on all those affected by it, not more harmful only to the wrongdoer. If so, the line of argument that Socrates has pursued contains some truth in it, but it is not sufficiently strong to prove his conclusion, nor is it clear that his conclusion is true.

The second argument: just punishment benefits the wrongdoer (the wrongdoer is better off receiving just punishment than escaping it)

Socrates now proceeds to the next issue between himself and Polus (476A):

> Now let us leave this matter where is stands, and proceed next to examine the second part on which we found ourselves at issue — whether for a wrongdoer to pay the penalty [= to be justly punished (476A)] is the greatest of evils, as you supposed, or to escape it a greater, as I on my side held.

Let us state and analyze the second argument both in order to understand better the view Socrates is trying to establish, and also in order to see whether this argument is also infected with the difficulties we found in the first argument. The argument may be stated as follows, staying as close to the text as possible.

P1   Paying the just penalty (τό διδόναι δίκην) and being justly punished (τό κολάζεσθαι δικαίως) are the same thing. (476A)

P2   All just things are beautiful or praiseworthy or admirable (καλά) in so far as they are just. (476B)

C1   In all cases of acting and being acted on, the patient (=

what is acted on) receives an effect of the same kind as the agent's action (or, the patient suffers something similar to the way the agent acts — e.g., if one cuts something deeply, the thing cut is cut deeply). (conclusion reached by induction, 476BE)

P3   Paying the just penalty is suffering something by the punisher. (476DE)

P4   Whoever punishes correctly (ὀρθῶς) punishes justly (δικαίως). (476E)

P5   Whoever punishes justly does something just. (476E)

C2   Therefore whoever is punished by paying the just penalty suffers something just. (476E)

C3   Whoever punishes justly does something beautiful or praiseworthy or admirable (καλά); and whoever is punished by paying the just penalty suffers something which is beautiful or praiseworthy or admirable. (476E)

(P6   The beautiful or the praiseworthy or the admirable is the beneficial (good) or the pleasant or both.)

(P7   Suffering the just penalty is not pleasant.) (supplied to explain inference to C4)

C4   Therefore, he who suffers the just penalty suffers something good. (477A)

(P8   Whoever suffers something good is thereby benefited.)

C5   Therefore, whoever suffers the just penalty (for wrongdoing) is thereby benefited. (477A)

It can be seen easily that this argument, whatever its merits, has the two major defects we found in the first argument: the *corrected* definition of the beautiful or praiseworthy or admirable (C1.1), together with the statement that he who suffers just punishment suffers something beautiful or praiseworthy or admirable, imply that he who suffers just punishment suffers something that gives pleasure to the viewer or contemplator of it or that is beneficial; and from this latter and the statement that suffering just punishment is not pleasant (to the sufferer) we cannot validly infer that it is beneficial; and even if this is patched up and we could, we could not validly infer what Socrates needs, that it is beneficial *to the punished wrongdoer.*

Equally important, the argument so far is so abstract that we cannot tell from it just what the benefit is that just punishment confers on the punished. Here, however, Socrates helps us; immediately after C5 we have the following exchange (477A):

Soc. Is then the benefit of just punishment what I understand it to be? That he becomes better in soul if he is justly punished?

241

Polus. Quite likely.

Soc. Therefore, he who pays the just penalty is relieved of bad-ness (κακίας) of soul?

Polus. Yes.

The benefit of just punishment, then according to Socrates is that it relieves the soul of the wrongdoer from 'badness of soul' or, as we see later, from vice in the soul, including injustice, ignorance, cowardice, and the like. From this, and the significant statement that a wrongdoer becomes better in soul if he is justly punished, we can see that Socrates has a rather unusual view of *just* punish-ment: *just* punishment relieves badness (vice) of soul, and punish-ment is not just unless it make a man better in soul. This view of punishment is radically different from that of Polus, who regards punishment, just or not, as 'the greatest of evils' to the punished person; and it is this view of just punishment that makes possible the analogy (which we shall soon discuss) between the art of medicine and the art of justice and between just punishment and correct medical treatment. It should be noted that this view of just punishment and the benefit it confers is not a consequence of the argument we stated above; it is something added to the argument that serves to make clear what evil just punishment relieves. The argument itself is quite abstract, and the most it shows is that in order to account for the fact that we find just punish-ment beautiful or praiseworthy or admirable we must suppose either that it is pleasant or beneficial or both; and that if we find that it is not pleasant either to the punished or to the viewer, then we must conclude that it is beneficial. But nothing validly follows from the premises either as to whom just punishment is beneficial or as to what the benefit is; for all the argument shows, just punishment might be beneficial not only (and not even at all) to the punished but also to others whom it protects from the punished; and the benefit to the punished may be that it scares him out of future wrongdoings and future punishments. Neverthe-less, it is important, as we go along, to try to understand Socrates' conceptions, tacked on or not, as well as the arguments he seeks to support them with. Even if all his arguments were found to fall short of establishing his conclusions, his conclusions may be true and valuable.

The third argument: injustice (and vice) in the soul is the greatest evil a man can possess

Socrates introduces his third argument with his next question

242

(477A):

> And so [he who pays the just penalty is] relieved from the greatest evil?

We can state this argument as follows:

P1 Relative to a man's financial resources, the only evil is poverty. (477B)

P2 Relative to a man's bodily resources, evil consists in weakness and disease and ugliness 'and the like.' (477B)

P3 Relative to a man's soul (ψυχή), there is a certain badness or evil (πονηρία) which consists in injustice and ignorance and cowardice 'and the like' (to these wantonness (ἀκολασία) is added at 477D, so that we have a list here of the opposites of the four cardinal virtues of the *Republic*). (477B)

C1 Therefore, relative to the three kinds of things, poverty (χρημάτων), body, and soul, there are three (kinds of) badness (vice), poverty, disease, and injustice. (477C — from P1, P2, P3, by addition)

P4 Of the three kinds of badness (vice), poverty, disease, and injustice, the badness of the soul, injustice, is the ugliest (or most blameworthy or most shameful). (477C)

P5 The ugliest (or most blameworthy or most shameful) is ugliest by producing (or partaking of) the greatest pain or the greatest harm or both. (477C — derived from the definition of the ugly in the first argument)

C2 Injustice is the ugliest of the three types of badness (poverty, disease, injustice) by surpassing the others (poverty, disease) in pain or harm or both. (477D: if P5 is stated by the help of variables, C2, stated hypothetically, follows from it by instantiation.

P6 Being unjust and wanton and cowardly and ignorant is not more painful than being poor or more painful than being sick. (477D)

C3 Therefore, 'the badness of the soul is ugliest of all, exceeding the others in a monstrous way in terms of great harm and astonishing evil.' (477E — a literal translation of Socrates' hyperbolic statement of the conclusion that follows from C2 and P6 by disjunctive syllogism)

P7 That which exceeds in greatest harm would be the greatest evil of (among?) things (τῶν ὄντων). (477E)

C4 Therefore, injustice and wantonness and the other badness

243

of soul is the greatest evil of existing things. (477E — from C3 and P7 by syllogism in Barbara or hypothetical syllogism if C3 is interpreted as a general (universal) statement)

This argument, parallel to the first two, also seems to contain the two defects we found earlier. In the first place, instead of P5 we should have what follows from the correct definition of the ugly, namely

P5.1 When one of several things is ugliest, it must be so by surpassing each of the others in harm or in the pain it gives to those who see or hear or contemplate it.

Now is it true that injustice and vice in the soul does not give more pain to those who see, hear, or contemplate it than poverty and disease does? Actually, once we raise this question, we may well be inclined to give an affirmative answer: for disease and poverty bring suffering and pain to their possessors in a very evident and familiar way, and the thought or witnessing of them brings pain through sympathy and pity; whereas injustice and the other vices of the soul do not in a similarly evident way bring pain and suffering to their possessors. (Moreover, even if the answer were negative it is far from clear that it would not be a serious mistake to suppose that injustice is or is held to be the ugliest or most shameful or most blameworthy because the thought of it causes more pain than the thought of the others; it is a much more plausible reason to suppose that it is and is held to be the ugliest or most shameful or most blameworthy because it causes more harm.) If so, it may be possible to correct an error in this argument which is equivalent to the error Vlastos spotted in the first argument. Even if this error supposed to be corrected, however, the second error still remains: Socrates means to argue not simply that injustice in the soul is the greatest evil (does the greatest harm), but more specifically that it is the greatest evil to the possessor of it or does the greatest harm to the man who has injustice in his soul. But this does not follow from the argument, since the definition of ugliness does not specify to whom the harm is done. It may well be that injustice and vice in the soul is and is held to be the ugliest or most shameful or most blameworthy because it does the greatest harm; but, for all the argument shows, and in all probability so far as the truth of the matter is concerned, the harm referred to is harm not only to the man who has injustice and vice in his soul but also the harm to others which results from the injustice and vice in the man's soul. Injustice may well be the greatest evil; but it may be so in terms of the harm it does to all those affected by it.

Finally, the argument contains yet another fault. The first three premises refer to three types of evil, and the third premise makes a comparison among these; accordingly, 'all' in C3 is limited in scope to these three evils — 'ugliest of all' has the sense of 'ugliest among all these three evils.' But in P7 and the final conclusion, C4, injustice is said to be the greatest evil of 'existing things'; and this certainly does not follow, even if we set aside all the previous faults; all that follows is that injustice is the greatest evil *among the three evils mentioned*, not that injustice is the greatest thing among all evils. What is the right explanation of this? One possibility is that Socrates has simply made a mistake — but since the mistake is not subtle but rather obvious, this is not perhaps very likely. A second possibility is that Socrates assumes, without explicitly stating it, that the three kinds of evils he enumerated are all the kinds of evils there are. A third possibility is that, though he thinks there are other kinds of evils, he assumes that the three types he mentioned are the three greatest evils, so that if he proves that injustice is the greatest of the three it will follow that it is the greatest of all. And a fourth possibility yet is, that, though he thinks there are other evils, he assumes that all other evils are evil in an instrumental sense; that is, they are evil only in so far as they bring about any one of the three kinds of evils he listed, and that the rankings of things that are evil instrumentally accords with the rankings of things that are evil in themselves, so that no separate proof is needed regarding them. Which of these possibilities represents the truth is not clear. What is clear is, first, that the list Socrates gives is consistent with lists he gives elsewhere in the *Gorgias*; thus at 468E he lists the opposites of wisdom and health and wealth as evils and these correspond well with the three kinds of the present argument; and in 452AD he mentions health, and bodily beauty and strength, and wealth; and the opposites of these are included in his present list. Second, it is clear that there are certain significant omissions in his present list of evils, the most prominent of which is pain; others might be being reduced to slavery, being expelled from one's city, having unhappy children, having a bad mate, having an ill-deserved reputation for injustice, defeat in war, civil strife in one's city, being governed by ignorant men or tyrants or both, and possibly many others. A reading of, say, Euripides' *Medea, Hippolytus, The Trojan Women,* and *Andromache*, will satisfy us that there are more evils than are listed in Socrates' third argument. Unfortunately Socrates does not make certain relevant distinctions in this passage, such as the distinction between intrinsic and instrumental goods and evils, and so it is difficult to know what he would say about all these other

245

evils we listed. Finally, it is clear that in the argument Socrates is not just listing evils; he is *classifying* them into three major categories – those pertaining to a man's pecuniary resources or conditions, those pertaining to bodily conditions, and those pertaining to psychic conditions; and his lists in the last two categories are open-ended as the expression 'and the like' indicates. In the case of bodily conditions we can safely attribute to him the view that health and strength and beauty are goods and their opposites evils; in the case of psychic conditions, that wisdom, temperance, courage, justice, and piety are goods, and their opposites evils; and possibly, in the case of pecuniary conditions, he would list other social evils besides poverty, and other social goods besides wealth, such as honors, offices, reputation and the like.

3 *Goods and evils and happiness and unhappiness: Socrates and Polus*

So far Socrates has tried to refute Polus' view, that a wrongdoer can be happy and is happy if he obtains the goods he seeks and escapes the evils of punishment; and he has also tried to establish his own view that justice and virtue bring happiness and injustice unhappiness. He now (478A–480E) draws the consequences of his arguments as to who is happy and who is not, as to who is happier than whom, and as to what kind of life a man ought to lead. Since his views on these matters are almost diametrically opposed to those of Polus we shall begin with a brief statement of Polus' view on the same matters. It should be remembered that, though they disagree on many things, they agree that happiness depends on the possession of good things, unhappiness on evils, and degrees of happiness and unhappiness on the greatness of the goods and evils possessed.

Polus' view of the happy and unhappy man

To some extent Polus seems to work within Gorgias' previously expressed views as to what is good and evil. Back at 452DE, challenged by Socrates to say what the greatest good is, Gorgias says that it is the power to persuade judges in law courts and statesmen in the council and the Assembly; and (possibly: because) this power, he says, is a cause of freedom to men (who possess it) and of ruling others in one's city. It would appear from this that Gorgias prizes the ability to persuade (or rhetoric) so highly because he who has it has the power to be free from the rule of others and at the same time to rule others. The possession of political power, and at the same time freedom from its restraints, is put forward as a great good — possibly the greatest *intrinsic* good, with rhetoric as the greatest *instrumental* good — and this, as Dodds notes[10] becomes a central theme of the 'second act,' the round with Polus. From 466B—469, and from the example of Archelaus, it is clear that Polus prizes unlimited political power above everything else (though it is not clear whether it is an intrinsic or an instrumental good for him); but possibly he differs from Gorgias in being willing to secure such power not only through rhetoric but also through the greatest of injustices, provided one does not get caught and suffer the evils of punishment. According to Polus, unlimited political power — at once power over others and freedom from the powers of others — is manifested in the ability to 'put someone to death as one thinks fit, or deprive him of his property, or send him to prison,' and in the envy and admiration and homage that others pay to such a man. It is not clear that he thinks that committing great injustices is necessary to securing such power, but given his views on what shows that a man has such power, he probably does think so. His views then of happiness and unhappiness seem to be as follows.

Happiest is the man who secures the greatest good, supreme political power and freedom from the power of others, by doing the greatest injustices, if necessary, provided he escapes the evils of punishment for his injustices. On the other hand, the man who does injustices and suffers the punishments for it (possibly, justly or unjustly) is the most unhappy or most wretched man (472E). It is clear enough here that happiness and unhappiness depends on the possession of 'goods' and 'evils' and that degrees of unhappiness depend on the greatness and smallness of these.

Socrates' view of the happy and unhappy man

After he completed his third argument, that injustice is the greatest evil in the soul, and further concluded that since just punishment relieves us of this evil it is beneficial, Socrates says (478C—479A):

Soc. Is this the happiest state of the body for a man to be in — that of being medically treated — or that of never being ill at all?

Polus. Clearly, never being ill.

Soc. Yes, for what we regard as happiness, it seems, was not this relief from evil, but its non-acquisition at any time.

Polus. That is so.

247

Soc. Well now, which is the more wretched of two persons who have something evil either in body or soul, he who is medically treated and is relieved of the evil, or he who is not treated and keeps it?

Polus. To my thinking, he who is not treated.

Soc. And we found that paying the just penalty is a relief from the greatest evil, badness [of soul]?

Polus. We did.

Soc. Because, I suppose, the justice of the court makes us sound of mind and more just, and becomes medicine for badr.ess?

Polus. Yes.

Soc. Happiest therefore is he who has no vice in his soul, since we found that to be the greatest of evils.

Polus. Clearly so.

Soc. Next after him, I take it, is he who is relieved of it.

Polus. So it seems.

Soc. And that was the man who is reproved, reprimanded, and who pays the just penalty.

Polus. Yes.

Soc. Hence the worst life is led by him who has the vice and is not relieved of it.

Polus. Apparently.

Soc. And this is the man who in committing the greatest wrongs and practicing the greatest injustice has contrived to escape reproof and chastisement and just penalty alike, as you say Archelaus has succeeded in doing, and the rest of the despots and orators and overlords?

Polus. So it seems.

Socrates' ranking of happy and unhappy lives depends, clearly, both on his ranking of goods and evils and also on his view of just punishment as analogous to correct medical treatment. We shall examine the analogy in the last section. Here it is important to note that Socrates' ranking of happy and unhappy lives is very incomplete. First of all, having said that happiness consists in the non-acquisition of evils at any time, he proceeds as if the only evils that matter for happiness and unhappiness are the evils and goods of the soul; as if the evils of the body and the evil of poverty do not matter. But, so far as the goods of the body are concerned at least, this cannot be Socrates' considered and complete view. Aside from the fact that there are numerous passages in which he affirms that health and strength and bodily beauty are goods and their opposites evils, in the *Crito* 47DE (a dialogue very close in philosophy to the *Gorgias*, as we pointed out earlier) he clearly says that life is not worth living (βιωτόν) if one's body is corrupted and ruined. Clearly then, his considered and complete view is that a man who has never had badness of soul and who also has a sound body is happier than one who has never had badness of soul but has a ruined body. (The reason he does not bring up this point is probably that it is not a point in dispute between him and Polus.) Second, though Socrates ranks badness of soul relative to badness of body and of property, he does not rank the last two evils relative to each other, nor does he tell us of any relation of wealth to happiness or poverty to unhappiness. In all probability he does not think wealth and poverty make much difference to happiness and unhappiness, and this is probably the reason he does not bring up the matter; and he would clearly rank disease and ill health as greater evils than poverty, and health and strength and possibly bodily beauty as greater goods than wealth (see e.g., *Apology* 38B). In the third place, in his listing of happy and unhappy men in the passage we just quoted, Socrates leaves out some states of unhappiness which he seems to have admitted back at 469AB:

Polus. I suppose, at any rate, the man who is put to death unjustly is both pitiable and wretched.

Soc. Less so than he who put him to death unjustly, Polus, and less so than he who is put to death justly.

The comparison here is in general between those who do certain deeds unjustly, namely expelling people from their city or depriving them of their property or putting them to death, and those who suffer these things, sometimes justly and sometimes unjustly. Socrates seems to concede clearly that the man who is put to death unjustly is pitiable and wretched, though less so than the man who is put to death justly (who is also conceded to be pitiable and wretched), and less so than the man who puts him to death unjustly. In general then, it seems to be Socrates' view that those who suffer evils (at least great evils) are wretched, and of these those who suffer great evils unjustly are less wretched than those who suffer the same evils justly. In the fourth place, within the class of evils of the soul Socrates does not rank these evils relative to each other; and the same is true of evils and goods of the body. The first omission is perhaps understandable; for since Socrates holds the doctrine of the unity of virtue, that a man either has all the virtues or none of them, ranking the virtues or the vices relative to each other will make no difference for ranking happy and unhappy states. But what of ranking bodily goods and evils? A man may be healthy and strong and also ugly; would he not be happier if he were strong and healthy and beautiful? One would suppose that Socrates would agree, but once more this is not in dispute between himself and Polus, and so it is omitted. Finally, in the passage we quoted (478C–479A), Socrates seems to characterize happiness negatively: 'happiness, it seems, was not this relief from evil, but its non-acquisition at any time,' and 'happiest therefore is he who has no vice in his soul, since we found that to be the greatest of evils.' Either Socrates is taking a very modest view of happiness, for some reason, or he is assuming that if a man does not possess a given evil he possesses the opposite good. But the latter assumption is certainly not true of all the goods and evils listed; a man who is not physically ugly is not necessarily physically beautiful; and a man who is not poor is not necessarily wealthy. Possibly Socrates supposes that the assumption holds for goods of the soul. In any case, it seems true that a man who possesses none of the evils in Socrates' list does not necessarily possess all of the opposite goods; and is not a man who possesses all of the goods and none of the evils happier than a man who possesses none of the evils but not all of the goods?

We see then that when Socrates lists and ranks happy and unhappy men his list of goods and evils is not complete; that his rankings of goods and evils is not complete, both as between classes of goods and evils and within these classes themselves; that some goods and evils are not explicitly related to happiness and unhappiness; and that happiness seems to be characterized negatively. We have also suggested that these are essentially omissions that probably occur because they are not at issue between Socrates and Polus, and that most of these omissions can be made up from other passages in the *Gorgias* and other Socratic Dialogues. In stating below Socrates' views on happiness and unhappiness, goods and evils, and justice (and virtue) and injustice, we shall try to make up these omissions as best we can, and we shall give a much fuller statement of Socrates' views than Socrates himself gives at 478C–479A. Since happiness and unhappiness and degrees of them depend on the possession of goods and evils and on how great these are, we begin with a list of goods and evils ranked as

Socrates does or would rank them; next we state the main assumptions connecting the concepts of good and evil and the concept of happiness and certain assumptions regarding punishment; and finally we list the states of happiness and unhappiness and their degrees.

(I)   *Goods and evils*

   (a)   There are at least the following goods, classified and listed in order from the greater (top) to the lesser:

Goods of the soul	Justice, temperance, wisdom, courage, piety
Goods of the body	Health, strength, beauty
Goods of property	Wealth

   (b)   There are at least the following evils, classified and listed in order from the lesser (top) to the greater:

Evils of property	Poverty
Evils of the body	Disease, weakness, ugliness
Evils of the soul	Injustice, wantonness, ignorance, cowardice, impiety

(II)   *Assumptions*

   (a)   Happiness consists in the possession of good things and the non-possesion of evils; unhappiness consists in the possession of evils and the non-possession of goods.

   (b)   One may come to possess a good or an evil, and one may come to lose a good or an evil one possessed.

   (c)   One can be more or less happy, and more or less unhappy.

   (d)   Just punishment relieves the punished of evils in his soul and makes him better in soul, or else the punishment is not just.

   (e)   The man who does injustice has injustice and the other evils in his soul.

   (f)   The man who suffers evils unjustly possesses the evils he suffers but he has not necessarily had the evils of soul in his soul.

   (g)   The man who suffers evils justly has had the evils of the soul in his soul.

(III)   *Happiness and unhappiness*

   (a)   *Happy men, described, and ranked in order from greater (top) to lesser happiness*

251

The man who has *always* possessed *all* of the goods and has *never* possessed *any* of the evils; the man who is always just, temperate, wise, courageous, pious, healthy, strong, beautiful, and wealthy.

The man who has always possessed all of the goods *except wealth*, and never any of the evils *except poverty*.

The man who has always possessed all the goods except *bodily beauty* and *wealth*, and never possessed any of the evils except *bodily ugliness* and *poverty*.

The man who has always possessed all the goods except *health, strength,* and bodily *beauty* and never possessed any of the evils *except disease, bodily weakness* and bodily *ugliness*.

The man who has always possessed all the goods except *health, strength, beauty* and *wealth*, and never possessed any of the evils except *disease, weakness, ugliness* and *poverty*.

(b) *Unhappy men, described, and ranked in order from lesser (top) to greater unhappiness*

The man who sometimes *suffers evils unjustly* and in consequence comes to possess evils other than the evils of the soul, and who has never had the evils of the soul.

The man who *has done injustice*, and has had injustice and the other evils of the soul, and is relieved of the evils of the soul by *just punishment*.

The man who frequently does injustices and other wrongs, and has injustice and other vices in his soul, who is never relieved of these evils by just punishment, and who is *also poor*.

The man who has *always* possessed *all* of the evils and never any of the goods; the man who is always unjust, ignorant, wanton, cowardly, impious, ill, weak, ugly, and poor.

There are considerable differences between this statement, which is a reconstruction of Socrates' view, and Plato's own statement, at *Gorgias* 478C–479A. To state only one difference, according to Plato's statement Socrates would be the happiest man and Archelaus the most wretched; whereas according to the statement we have reconstructed, Socrates would be the third-happiest (since he did not possess wealth or physical beauty but their opposites), and Archelaus not the most wretched, since he possessed wealth and, so far as we know, health and strength. But whether or not we consider our reconstruction statement or the statement in the text, one thing becomes clear: Socrates places overwhelming importance on the goods and evils of the soul so far as happiness and unhappiness is concerned, and so far as the choice of life is concerned. In our statement, a man who has the goods of the soul can be happy even if he has no other goods; no man can be happy unless he has the goods of the soul; and every man who has the evils of the soul is unhappy no matter what goods he has (other than the opposites of the evils he has). And in Plato's own statement happiness and unhappiness is made to depend *entirely* on the goods and evils of the soul.

But though this is clear enough, what is not clear is just what the harm is that the evils of the soul cause and what the benefit is that the goods of the soul produce. Socrates has argued and has told us in hyperbolic language that injustice in the soul, and the other vices, are the greatest evils that a man can possess, and that happiness and unhappiness depend entirely on these; but just what harm these cause to the soul of the man who has them he has not so far told us. Socrates' arguments against Polus do not help us on these points: Socrates has argued that since injustice is ugly or blameworthy or shameful it must be harmful to the man who has it in his soul; but what the harm is his argument has not revealed. For that matter, it is far from clear just what injustice in the soul is, according to Socrates, or what unhappiness in the soul is. These states of soul and their opposites — Socrates' view of them, at any rate — remain very unclear. Unless Socrates succeeds to some extent in clarifying what these states of soul are, his view will remain at best opaque and at worst shallow. A man who places such overwhelming emphasis on states of soul had better be clear what these are. States of soul are not publicly observable; they are often cloudy and unstable rather than transparent, and our private observations of them are notoriously unreliable. Polus' view of happiness and unhappiness, whatever its demerits, is much easier to understand, and happiness and unhappiness, as he understands them, much easier to judge. To judge whether Archelaus is happy or unhappy, Polus is satisfied to look into Archelaus' court. Socrates needs to look into Archelaus' soul. He better have a clear enough view of happiness and unhappiness, and justice and injustice, to be able to judge what he finds there.

In order to get clear about Socrates' conception of the relevant states of soul, we shall in the next two sections discuss the analogies between virtue and health and between justice and medicine, and some parts of the round between Callicles and Socrates. The analogies help us to understand how Socrates conceives the goods and evils of the soul; and the round with Callicles helps us to understand in a deeper way the opposition Socrates was fighting, and also Socrates' understanding of the virtue of temperance.

4 Callicles' view of virtue, pleasure, and happiness

Socrates and Polus seemed to have similar conceptions of justice, at least so far as just and unjust behavior is concerned. They seemed to have different conceptions of happiness, since they disagreed violently as to whether Archelaus was happy without disagreeing about the basic facts of his case. Further, they disagreed as to whether justice as they both conceive it brings happiness. When Callicles enters the discussion he introduces at once a new concept of justice (and virtue) which he calls 'justice by nature,' whereas the concept of justice that Socrates and Polus shared he calls 'justice by convention [law] .' He shares apparently the concept of happiness that Polus had, and reveals its foundations to be hedonism — the view that what is good and what is pleasant are always the same. He agrees with Polus, and disagrees with Socrates, on the relation of justice by convention to happiness (as he and Polus understand happiness). And he argues that justice by nature brings happiness! But this apparent, superficial, and perhaps ironic agreement with Socrates is no agreement at all: for his justice by nature is the opposite of Socratic justice, and the happiness *it* brings is not a state Socrates would call happy.

Callicles' views are valuable to consider because they represent a version of the opposition that Socrates and Plato had to contend with all their lives, an opposition that is again taken up by Thrasymachus in the *Republic*, an opposition that is inextricably bound up with some version of hedonism and the concept of a happy life as a life of pleasure. Callicles' view is also valuable to consider because we can better understand, by contrast, Socrates' own concepts of virtue and happiness. But it should be remembered that, though Socrates' and Callicles' views of how men should live are opposed and cannot be reconciled, they do not exhaust the alternatives. Hence, even if Socrates succeeds in refuting Callicles, which is far from clear, he does not thereby succeed in establishing his own view (and at 509A Socrates seems to be aware of this).

Callicles' view is best revealed in the long speech at 482C—486D (of which 482E—483B appear below), the first round of questioning by Socrates at 488B—491E, and the smaller speech Callicles makes at 491E—492D.

For my own part, where I am not satisfied with Polus is just that concession he made to you — that doing wrong is uglier

254

[more shameful, more blameworthy] , than suffering it; for owing to this admission he too [in addition to Gorgias earlier] in his turn got entangled in your argument and had his mouth stopped, being ashamed to say what he thought. For you, Socrates, really turn the talk into such low, popular clap-trap, while you give out that you are pursuing the truth — into stuff that is beautiful [admirable, praiseworthy] , not by nature but by convention [law; νόμῳ] . Yet for the most part these two — nature and convention — are opposed to each other; accordingly if a man is ashamed and does not dare say what he thinks he is forced to say the opposite [of what he thinks] . And this, look you, is the clever trick you have devised for our undoing in your discussions: when a man states anything according to convention you ask artfully according to nature, and when according to nature you ask according to convention. In the present case, for instance, of doing and suffering wrong, when Polus was speaking of what is uglier by convention, you followed it up in the sense of uglier according to nature. For by nature everything is uglier which is more evil, such as suffering wrong, while doing wrong is uglier by convention. Indeed this endurance of wrong done is not a man's part at all, but a poor slave's . . . .

Having attacked Socrates' refutation of Polus by drawing the distinction between what is uglier by nature and what is uglier by convention, Callicles now explains justice by nature (483B—E):

But I suppose the makers of laws are the weaker sort of men, and the more numerous. So it is with a view to themselves and their own interest (τὸ αὐτοῖς συμφέρον) that they make their laws and distribute their praises and censures; and to terrorize the stronger of men who are able to get an advantage (πλέον ἔχειν) so that they have no advantage over *them*, they tell them that such aggrandizement (τὸ πλεονεκτεῖν) is ugly and unjust, and that injustice is precisely this — to seek to have more than others. For, I think, being inferior they themselves love to have equality. So this is why by convention it is said to be unjust and ugly to seek to have more than the many, and why they call this doing injustice. But I think that nature itself shows that it is just for the better (ἀμείνω) to have more than the worse and the abler to have more than the weaker. It is obvious in many cases that this is so, not only in the animal world, but in the states and races of men, that the just has been judged to be the stronger (κρείττω) ruling over and having more than the weaker.

After an interchange in which Socrates asks Callicles whether he means the same by the 'better' and the 'stronger,' Callicles makes another speech in which he reveals the basis of his conception of justice by nature (491E—492D):

> the beautiful [admirable, praiseworthy] and the just by nature, I tell you quite frankly is this — that he who would live rightly (τὸν ὀρθῶς βιωσόμενον) should let his desires be as strong as possible and not chasten them, and should be able to minister to them when they are at their height through his manliness and intelligence, and satisfy each appetite in turn with what it desires. But this, I suppose, is not possible for the many; whence it comes that they decry such persons out of shame, to disguise their own impotence, and are so good as to tell us that wantonness is shameful, thus enslaving — as I remarked before — the better type of mankind; and being unable themselves to procure achievement of their pleasures they praise temperance and justice because of their own unmanliness. For to those who started with the advantage of being either kings' sons or able by their own parts to procure some authority or monarchy or absolute power, what in truth would be uglier and worse to such men than justice and temperance? Finding themselves free [able] to enjoy good things with no obstacle in the way, they would be merely imposing on themselves a master in the form of the law, the speech, and the censure of the many. Or how could they fail to be sunk in wretchedness by that 'beauty' of justice and temperance, if they had no larger portion to give to their own friends than to their enemies, and that too when they were rulers in their own cities? No, in truth, Socrates, which you claim to pursue, — the fact is this: luxury and wantonness and liberty, if they have the support of force, that is what virtue and happiness is. As for these other embellishments — the unnatural covenants of them — these are all nonsense and worth nothing.

Socrates praises Callicles for his candor, saying that he put forth a view that others hold but are reluctant to voice; and he exhorts Callicles to continue being frank, for if he does they will discover how man should live (πῶς βιωτέον). Let us first sort out the various elements in Callicles' view and then briefly consider Socrates' attack on it.

Callicles' view of happiness

Callicles would, I think, agree with the general characterization of happiness, which Polus and Socrates also share; happiness consists in the possession of good things and the absence of evils, and the more good things and the fewer evils a man possesses, and the longer he possesses them, the happier he is. But he differs fundamentally from Socrates as to what things are good. Though he does not make all the necessary distinctions, he appears to think that pleasures are the only things that are good in themselves, and that things that cause pleasures or enable one to obtain pleasures (or avoid pains) are the only things that are good as means. Pain, as the opposite of pleasure, would be the only intrinsic evil. Callicles appears to make no distinction among pleasures except in quantity and intensity. Further, he appears to think that pleasure is produced by the satisfaction of desires or appetites such as hunger, thirst, sex, and the like; and that, the stronger or more intense the desires or appetites, which themselves tend to be painful, the greater the pleasure that ensues from their satisfaction. Consequently, his conception of happiness is that the happy man is he who experiences pleasures and no pains, and that the more pleasures a man experiences and the more intensely and frequently he experiences them (and the fewer pains), the happier he is. Further, since Callicles appears to think that the satisfaction of desires or appetites is either the chief or the only source of pleasure, he probably also holds that the more desires a man has, and the more intense they are, and the more frequently they arise, the happier he will be, provided that he has the means to satisfy them when they are at their very peak of intensity and as frequently as they arise. A man such as Socrates, who has few or moderate desires, whether constitutionally or by conditioning, will have correspondingly few and moderate pleasures, and consequently little or no happiness. And a man such as Alcibiades, who has many and intense and frequently arising desires, will also have little or no happiness if he does not have the means to satisfy his desires at the peak of their intensity and as frequently as they arise.

This view of happiness, of what is good, and of the sources of happiness, dominates the rest of Callicles' view: his attitude towards justice by convention, his concept of justice and virtue by nature, and his contempt for temperance as Socrates and most Greeks understood it.

Callicles' view of justice

On Callicles' view, to enjoy great happiness a man would need at least two things: (1) a physical constitution full of many and intense desires which arise with great frequency, and (2) the means to satisfy all these desires constantly and at the peak of their intensity. Though Callicles seems to think mainly of physical desires and appetites, he does not confine himself to them: a man may desire not only the pleasures of food, drink, and sex, but also the pleasures of power, the pleasures of friendship, admiration and esteem, and so on. When we consider the range of desires that may be included, and the extent and frequency of their demands, the means required for their satisfaction may be enormous. And this makes Callicles' espousal of unlimited political power as the best means to (his type of) happiness understandable. To rule over others and to have more than others (τὸ ἄρχειν καὶ πλέον ἔχειν) may be the best means to Callicles' happiness. But how can he call this virtue and justice? After all, to rule over others without limit and to have more than others and what belongs to others seem to be the very opposite of equality and fairness. Callicles explicitly contrasts his justice by nature with τὸ ἴσον, equality (484A). In democratic Athens this equality probably included equality of political rights and political power (the right of all citizens to participate in the Assembly and the courts, and rotation in office), and if not equality of property at least equal protection before the law of one's person and the property that belongs to one.[11] How then can Callicles call a condition that is the very opposite of equality and fairness, whether political or economic, virtue and particularly justice? Perhaps part of the answer is that Callicles and Socrates agree that there must be some essential connection between virtue and happiness; perhaps so strong a connection that it may be best expressed by saying that virtue is not virtue unless it brings or at least contributes importantly to happiness. This proposition, together with Callicles' conception of happiness, explains why he calls the ability to rule over others and to have more than others and to have what belongs to others 'virtue' and particularly 'justice,' and why he downgrades the justice whose essential element is the equality explained above. He is probably right in thinking that this ability can bring *Calliclean* happiness, and this is the main reason he would possibly offer for calling it a virtue; and this is also the main reason he would offer for calling it justice, for *if* it is a virtue it could only be justice, since justice is the only social virtue, among the Greek virtues (justice, wisdom, temperance, courage, and piety), which is concerned with the distribution of rights, power, and property.[12] Correspondingly, Callicles' downgrading of justice by convention can only be based on the probably true proposition that the practice of *such* justice is not likely, to say the least, to bring

Calliclean happiness to the agent. Such justice, in his view, is a virtue of the weak and for the weak; it barely qualifies as a virtue, for it does not bring Calliclean happiness, but only a lesser good — namely, protection of the weak from suffering evils at the hands of stronger men. This interpretation is confirmed by the fact that Socrates does not attack Callicles' view that justice by nature brings Calliclean happiness whereas justice by convention does not; nor does he attack the implied proposition that if justice by nature brings happiness and justice by convention does not, then the former is to be preferred to the latter and men should live according to justice by nature. The simplest explanation of this is that these are propositions on which they all agree. What Socrates does attack is Callicles' conception of happiness, as we shall presently see.

Callicles' view of temperance

Callicles' attitude toward temperance, as Socrates understands it, is explained by similar considerations: temperance, as Socrates understands it, prevents a person from attaining Calliclean happiness; hence, Callicles says that it is the virtue of 'simpletons' or 'fools' (τοὺς ἠλιθίους 491 E). The following exchange reveals some of Socrates' conception of temperance, and also Callicles' attitude towards it along the lines just explained (491 DE):

> *Callicles.* But I have told you already [what I mean by the 'better'] : men of wisdom and manliness [φρονίμους καὶ ἀνδρείους] in the affairs of the city. For these are the persons who should rule cities, and justice means this — that these should have more than other people, the rulers than the ruled.
>
> *Soc.* How so? More than themselves, my friend?
>
> *Cal.* How do you mean?
>
> *Soc.* I mean that every man is his own ruler; or is there no need of one's ruling oneself, but only of ruling others?
>
> *Cal.* What do you mean by one who rules oneself?
>
> *Soc.* Nothing recondite, but what most people mean; he who, being temperate and in control of himself [σώφρονα ὄντα καὶ ἐγκρατῆ αὐτὸν ἑαυτοῦ], is ruler of desires and pleasures in himself.
>
> *Cal.* You will have your pleasantry. By the temperate you mean the simpletons [or fools] .

259

Soc. How so? Nobody can fail to see that I do not mean that.

Cal. Oh, you most certainly do, Socrates. For how can a man be happy if he is slave to anyone at all?

Being temperate, as Socrates understands this notion (and, as he claims, as most of his compatriots would understand it), entails restraining (not satisfying) certain desires, or certain desires on certain occasions, and this is certainly depriving oneself of the pleasures that would ensue from the satisfaction of these desires, and therefore depriving oneself to some extent of Calliclean happiness. Socratic temperance deprives one of Calliclean happiness by definition, it seems! That is, by the definitions of these two concepts. And this is plainly the reason why Callicles says that these people are not temperate but foolish; though he does not put forth a concept of Calliclean temperance, he clearly implies that Socratic temperance is not a virtue at all (not καλόν) since it does the very opposite of bringing happiness. And once more, Socrates does not attack Callicles' notion that temperance does not bring Calliclean happiness; nor does he dispute the implied proposition that if temperance did not bring happiness and intemperance did, then the latter is to be preferred to the former. Once more, what he attacks is Callicles' conception of happiness, and, on the positive side, he argues that temperance brings happiness as *he* understands happiness.

5 Socrates' attack on Callicles' view: the arguments against justice by nature, and against hedonism

The first round: who are the better?

In his initial statement Callicles has used two sets of terms in expounding his view, one set of terms that refer to strength or power, and one set of terms that refer to what is good or bad and better or worse. At 483D he uses terms of both sets:

> it is just (by nature) that the better [ἀμείνω] have more than the worse and the more powerful [δυνατώτερον] than the less powerful.

A few lines later he uses terms that refer to strength:

> the just (by nature) is judged to be this, that the stronger [κρείττω] rule over and have more than the weaker.

And again he uses both types of terms at 483E. The first question that Socrates asks Callicles is whether in his view 'the better' and 'the stronger' have the same definition, or, as he rephrases the question, whether 'the better' and 'the stronger' are the same or different. Callicles answers in the affirmative and the next interchange is:

> Now are the many stronger by nature to the one? I mean those who make the laws to keep a check on the one, as you yourself were saying just now.
> Of course.

From these two replies and other subsequent replies Socrates constructs his first argument against Callicles: it is an argument that is supposed to show Callicles' view to be incoherent (on the assumption that by 'the better' Callicles means 'the stronger') and at the same time to vindicate Socrates' arguments against Polus from the charge of equivocation. The argument may be reconstructed as follows:

P1 Justice by nature consists in the better or the stronger ruling over and having more than the worse and the weaker. (Callicles' definition: 483D)

P2 The better are the same as the stronger. (488D)

P3 The many are stronger by nature to the one (the many = the majority who make laws in a democracy). (488D)

C1 The laws of the many are the laws of the stronger. (488D; from P3)

C2 The laws of the many are the laws of the better. (488E; from P2 and C1)

C3 The laws of the many are beautiful (admirable, praiseworthy) by nature. (488E, apparently from P3 and C1, on the assumption that what is just by nature is beautiful by nature).

P4 According to the many (their opinion or their laws or both) (a) it is just to have the equal (rather than to have more), and (b) it is uglier (more shameful, more blameworthy) to do injustice rather than to suffer it. (488E–489A)

C4 It is not only according to law that it is uglier to do, rather than suffer, injustice and that it is just to have the equal, but also according to nature. (489AB; apparently from P1, C1, C2, C3 and P4)

Right after the conclusion Socrates says to Callicles (489B):

> And therefore you are in danger of not saying the truth and also not criticizing me correctly when, in your previous statement,

you said that nature and law are opposite and that I knowingly
made a bad argument by taking something that was said according to nature to mean according to law, and according to law
to mean according to nature.

But the argument, in addition to showing these two things, if it is
sound, also shows that Callicles' definition of justice by nature is
incorrect. For part of the conclusion, C4, is that it is just by
nature to have the equal (at least sometimes — namely in a
democracy). But 'to have the equal' and 'to have more' are certainly
contraries (even contradictories): whether the equality in question
is equality of political rights or equality of property or equal treatment before the laws among all the citizens, it cannot be the case
that any of these equalities obtains and also that the corresponding
inequality or 'having more' obtains. So it cannot always be just
by nature for the stronger to have more than the weaker (Callicles'
definition or part thereof) and also sometimes be just by nature
that all have the equal (which is part of C4). So, if the argument is
sound, not only does it destroy at least in part the opposition
between nature and law, and not only does it destroy Callicles'
criticism of Socrates' arguments against Polus, but it also destroys
Callicles' definition of justice by nature. These are powerful
results for such a little argument. Is it sound?

Now the first question that Socrates raises about Callicles'
definition of justice by nature, namely what is meant by 'the
stronger' and 'the better', is an extremely important one. We can
see that from two considerations alone. First, if, say, Callicles were
to mean by 'the better' the more wise or knowledgeable in what is
good or bad for a city, Socrates might well agree that *they* should
rule over the less wise ones and that this is just; though he probably
would not agree that they should have more property or political
rights or equality of treatment before the law. Indeed, Socrates'
chief political belief may well be described as the belief that the
wiser should rule but that all citizens should have equal treatment
before the laws and equal legal protection of person and property
(cf. *Apology* and *Crito*). So what Callicles means by 'the better'
will make a great difference to what his definition of justice means.
In the second place, Callicles must be able to characterize 'the
stronger' and 'the better' independently of the notions of ruling
over and having more: that is, to the question, 'Who are the better
and the stronger?' he cannot simply answer, 'Those who rule over
and have more.' For if that were his only answer his definition
would turn out to be uninformative, to say the least: 'Justice by
nature consists in those who rule over and have more ruling over

and having more.' And, further, injustice by nature would consist in 'those who rule over and have more not ruling over and having more,' so that injustice by nature would be impossible! So it is clear enough that Callicles must be able to give some characterization of 'the stronger' and 'the better,' which gives definite content to his definition and which is independent of the notions of ruling over and having more.

But, granting all this, it is difficult to see how Socrates' argument is valid. Let us grant the first interpretation of 'the better,' namely, the physically stronger. And let us grant further that in a democracy the many are physically stronger than 'the one' (any one person, let us say, Alcibiades); and let us grant further that in such a democracy the many make the laws, and that their laws say that justice consists in the equal, and further that their laws or the many themselves say that it is uglier to do rather than to suffer injustice. This is granting Socrates all that he asks for (P2, P3, C1, C2, C3, and P4). It still does not follow that it is just by nature to have the equal. For Callicles' definition does not say or directly entail that justice by nature consists in what the stronger *says* it consists in or in what the stronger *legislates*; it only says that justice by nature consists in the stronger ruling over and having more than the weaker — and Socrates needs the *former* to make his inferences valid. So, if the many are stronger than the one, justice by nature according to Callicles' definition consists in their ruling over the one and their having more than the one.

The problems that Callicles has gotten in so far arise because, unfortunately, Plato has allowed Callicles already to slip up twice. One slip-up occurs when Callicles admits in the present argument that the many are stronger by nature to the one and that they are also the makers of laws. This is a slip-up because it contradicts what Callicles said in his first speech at 483B: that the makers of laws are the weaker sort of men and the more numerous,[13] and that they make laws to their own advantage, which in this case (since they are the weaker sort of men) consists in having the equal. The second slip-up consists in Callicles' making this sort of unqualified statement in his speech to begin with. The makers of laws may be the weaker sort of men and the more numerous in a democracy; not so in a Homeric kingdom or an oligarchy or a tyranny or a monarchy such as the regime of Archelaus. In the latter cases it would be more accurate to say that the makers of laws are the stronger and the less numerous and that they make laws to *their* advantage, which in *this* case may well be not having the equal but the rulers having more. Further, in his original speech, back at 482E, Callicles has said that law and nature are opposed to each other in many cases or possibly in most cases; he has not said that they are opposed to each other in all cases. Now let us ask ourselves, in which cases are they likely to be opposed and in which not? The answer clearly is that they are likely to be opposed in democratic constitutions where the laws are egalitarian and justice consists in equal rights and equality before the law. But in such regimes as Homeric kingdoms, oligarchies, monarchies, and tyrannies Calliclean justice by nature and justice by law are not likely to be opposed; for in such regimes it is likely that the laws, made by the few or by one, are made to favor the few or the one both in political rights and power and in property and wealth. And in such cases justice by nature and justice by convention may well coincide. Now in the present argument Socrates has tried to show that justice by law is also justice by nature in the very case where, according to Callicles' view, we expect the two to be opposed, namely the case of a democracy. But this argument, as we have seen, fails. It is not part of Callicles' definition, nor is it entailed by it, that the stronger and the better legislate what is in accord with justice by nature. He may indeed assume, and he most probably does, that the stronger and the better legislate to their advantage, and he assumes that their advantage is ruling over and having more. But even from these assumptions and the definition it does not follow that, even in genuine cases of the Calliclean stronger and better legislating (Homeric kingdoms, oligarchies, tyrannies), justice by nature and justice by law would coincide; for the stronger may well make mistakes and legislate the equal instead of having more, or they may be benevolent. In the case of democracies the argument is even more fallacious: for in addition to the above gaps, we have also the fact that the many who legislate are collectively stronger but individually weaker, and they legislate what they consider their advantage relative to their individual weakness, not relative to their collective strength; therefore, even if they make no mistakes, what they are likely to legislate will be opposite to having more, namely the equal; their legislation is made with a view to their individual weakness, and their laws are therefore laws of the weaker, not the stronger. We conclude, then, that when Callicles' position is clearly stated, Socrates' first argument against it fails. And similar considerations apply to Socrates' reply to Callicles' criticism of Socrates' arguments against Polus.

Callicles now retreats from the interpretation of 'the better' as 'the stronger,' and Socrates suggests that by 'the better' perhaps Callicles means the wiser (τοὺς φρονιμωτέρους) (489E); Callicles accepts this interpretation and his definition or principle of justice by nature becomes accordingly:

P1.1 Justice by nature consists in the wiser ruling over and having more than the less wise.

Socrates immediately raises the right questions about this definition: wiser *in what*? And, having more *of what*? Socrates proposes answers to these questions by applying the principle to technical skills and the goods they produce or use. Perhaps Callicles means that it is just by nature that a physician, who is wiser than non-physicians in matters of food, should rule over the distribution of food and should distribute more food to himself than to others! Or perhaps it is just by nature that 'the ablest weaver should have the largest coat, and go about arrayed in the greatest variety of the finest clothes' (490D)! Callicles is made to evade the questions (whether, e.g., it is just by nature for the clothes-maker — the wiser in making clothes — to have more clothes than others), and is made to protest that he is not talking about doctors and cobblers and food and clothes, but rather that he was referring to wisdom concerning public affairs; he says that by 'the better' he means (491CD)

> men of wisdom and courage in public affairs. These are the persons who ought to rule the cities, and justice means this — that these should have more than other people, the rulers than the ruled.

The line of questioning with which this round has begun (Who are the better? Wiser in what? Have more of what?) is now abruptly dropped. Though it is not clear why this line of argument is not pursued, it is clear enough how it could be effectively developed. If it is not just by nature (nor perhaps unjust by nature, for that matter) that those who are wise in making shoes (or those who know how to cure the body, or those who know how to make houses) should have more shoes (more or better cures for their own bodies, more or larger houses) than those who are not, why should it be just by nature that those who are wise in public affairs should have more political power and political rights and property?[14] Perhaps Socrates would agree that those who are wise, say, in making ships should be the ones who should be consulted on how to make ships and the ones who should be in charge of making ships; and similarly the ones who are wise in the affairs of the city should be in charge of the affairs of the city. Even this agreement with Callicles, though, is more apparent than real, because by 'wisdom in the affairs of the city' Socrates means wisdom as to what is good or bad for the city, whereas Callicles probably means wisdom in how to obtain and hold political power; the former may be considered as a reasonable ground for entitling one to ruling since if one has such wisdom one is likely to rule well, that is, to rule so that the city fares well. But how is Calliclean wisdom about public affairs a ground for ruling? Further, how can it be a ground that it is just to have more, when either kind of wisdom in other areas does not entitle one to have more in these areas?

It would seem that the only way that Callicles can try to justify his view, that it is just by nature that the wiser and braver rule over and have more than the less wise and courageous, is that ruling over and having more is the way, perhaps the only way, to Calliclean happiness, and that being wiser and braver in public affairs is the way, perhaps the only way, to ruling over and having more. Whether or not Socrates would agree with the general assumption implicit in this — that if something is the only means to happiness then it is just and virtuous — is not clear; nor is it clear whether he would agree that ruling over and having more is a means to Calliclean happiness. In any case, he does not attack these propositions. Rather he focuses his big arguments on Callicles' conception of happiness, and tries to destroy it.

The second round: is pleasant and good the same?

We have seen that Callicles' view of happiness contains three main elements: (1) happiness consists in the possession of good things and the absence of evils; (2) pleasant and good are the same; and (3) pleasures arise in the fulfillment or satisfaction of desires. Socrates agrees with (1) and (3), and very much disagrees with (2). His whole attack on Callicles' view of happiness consists in trying to show that (2) is false. Between 495A and 499B he presents us with a battery of arguments against (2). In the Socratic Dialogues these are the chief arguments against hedonism. Let us state and analyze them.

At 495 the issue is introduced by Socrates as follows:

> What, is it I who am leading it [the discussion] there [the life of catamites], noble sir, or the person who says outright that those who enjoy themselves, with whatever kind of enjoyment, are happy, and draws no distinction between the kinds of pleasures which are good and the kind which are bad? But come, try and tell me, which do you say is the case, that pleasant and good are the same, or that there are some pleasant things which are not good?

Callicles chooses the first alternative, and we may notice that the

266

statement affirmed is ambiguous: 'plesant and good are the same' may mean that the terms 'pleasant' and 'good' are extentionally equivalent (the set of pleasant things and the set of good things have exactly the same members), or it may mean the stronger statement, that the two terms are intentionally equivalent (signify one and the same property). The weaker interpretation appears sufficient for Callicles' view, but we should remain aware of the ambiguity.

The first argument (495E—497A): the logic of the pairs, good, bad, pleasant, painful

P1   Those who fare well feel a feeling (possibly: are in a condition) opposite to that of those who fare badly.

P2   If these (faring well and faring badly?) are opposite to each other, the same must hold of them as of health and disease: (a) a man is not sick and well at the same time; (b) nor does one get rid of health and disease at the same time. For example, one does not have health and disease of the eyes at the same time, nor does he get rid of them at the same time, for that would be an astonishing and irrational thing; rather, one gets and loses either in turn.

P3   The same holds of strength and weakness and speed and slowness: one does not have both (of each pair) at the same time, nor does one lose (or acquire) both at the same time, but rather in turn.

P4   The same holds of good things and happiness and their opposites (bad things and wretchedness); (a) one does not have both at the same time, (b) nor does one acquire or lose both at the same time, but (c) one acquires or loses each in turn.

C1   Then if we find any two things such that (a) a man loses them at the same time, or (b) a man has them at the same time, these things could not be the good and the bad. (from P4)

P5   (a) Being hungry is painful, eating while (when) being hungry is pleasant. (b) Similarly, being thirsty is painful, and drinking while being thirsty is pleasant. (c) All want and desire is painful (and all satisfaction of want pleasant).

C2   Then, when one drinks while thirsty, while one is in pain he enjoys himself at the same time (feeling pleasure?). This (the enjoying and the pain) occurs together, at the same place and time, whether in the body or soul. (from P5)

C3   It is not possible for one to fare well and fare ill at the

267

same time. (from P1 and P2)

C4 Then enjoying oneself is not (the same as) faring well, and being in pain is not (the same as) faring ill. Therefore, the pleasant is different from the good. (from P4 (a) and C2 and C3)

The second argument. This is a continuation of the first, and uses principles P4(b)(c) instead of P4(a) which the first argument uses; so we shall state the second argument right away, and as a continuation of the first (497B–E):

P6 Each of us ceases at the same time to be thirsty and to have the pleasure he gets from drinking. And the same is true of hunger and the other desires and pleasures.

C5 Then one ceases at the same time to have the pain (of being thirsty, or other desires) and to have the pleasure (of drinking, or other satisfactions). (from P5(b) and P6)

C6 Then good things are not (the same as) pleasant things, nor are bad things (the same as) painful things. (from P4(b) and C5)

Are these arguments sound? I have stayed very close to the text in order to obtain maximum accuracy in stating the argument. Some rewriting would be required to bridge several gaps and give rigor to the argument. This, however, is perhaps not necessary to do, for the logic of the argument is clear enough, and Socrates summarizes it at 497D: the two pairs, pleasant and painful, and good and bad, are presumably shown not to be identical by showing that pleasant and painful can occur at the same time and can cease at the same time, whereas good and bad cannot either occur at the same time or cease at the same time. Several objections have been raised to these arguments.[15] Some of these, such as the dispute between Dodds and Robinson, as to whether the argument assumes that pleasure and pain are not contraries, seem to arise from gross inaccuracy in their statements of the argument. Others, such as the objection that the pleasure and pain of drinking while thirsty are not strictly simultaneous, would require psychological experiments to determine whether they are true. We can actually bypass all these objections, for it can be shown that the argument contains a fault of logic which disables it even if everything else is patched up. The objection is that even if it is entirely conceded that, say, the pain of being thirsty and the pleasure of drinking occur at the same time in the same subject, and that they leave at the same time, still *what* is painful and *what* is pleasant are different: Callicles and Socrates agree that being thirsty is painful and that drinking while thirsty is pleasant (496CD); this is said several times clearly enough. But the state of being thirsty and the state of drinking while thirsty are clearly not identical since one can be in the first state without also being in the second. Now if this is so, Callicles can correctly point out that we can have an exactly parallel situation with good and bad: we can say truly that sometimes (this is all that is required) being thirsty is bad and drinking while thirsty is good. Here, good and bad occur at the same time and in the same subject, and in a parallel manner to the manner in which pleasant and painful occurred together; but there is no more problem in this case than there was in the case of the painful and the pleasant, for, as in that case, *what* is good and *what* is bad are not identical. Thus Callicles can admit P4(a)(b)(c) and also all that is said about desires and their satisfaction, and still deny the conclusion and maintain his own position. During the argument Socrates makes some moves that might suggest an answer to this objection: at 496BC he makes sure that the pair being talked about, pleasure–pain, good–bad, is a pair that occurs in the same subject; at 496E he makes sure that the pleasure and pain talked about is the pleasure and pain that obtain from the arising and the satisfaction of one and the same desire — and he says that 'these occur together at the same place and time, whether in the body or the soul.' (So he is not pairing, say, the pleasure of one man and the pain of another, or the pleasure of drinking and the pain of being hungry, or the pain of one thirst and the pleasure of quenching another thirst.) These qualifications and restrictions are all going in the right direction, but they are not sufficient to overcome the objection. In 496CE the predicate ἀνιαρόν (painful) is applied to τὸ πεινῆν (being hungry), and the predicate ἡδύ (pleasant) is applied to τὸ πεινῶντα ἐσθίειν (eating while hungry). These being different states, there is no problem applying the predicates good and bad to them in a similar way. So the objection stands.

It may be replied that, even though Socrates' actual examples do not work out, it may be possible to find cases where one and the same thing is both pleasant and painful at the same time. Perhaps. But a lot of argument would be required to show that we cannot have parallel cases with good and bad (witness Heraclitus!): after all, one and the same thing may be both good and bad at the same time in a variety of cases: good and bad in different aspects or parts (as a poem can be good and bad in such ways), good and bad in different effects (as drugs can be), good and bad at different things, as men can be, and so on. In any case, though this direction might prove eventually effective, our objection is to the argument

269

Socrates gives, not to one — and a very vague one at that — that he might have given.

It may also be replied that, though our objection holds against the first argument, it does not hold against the second. Let us suppose that being thirsty is painful and also bad, and drinking while thirsty is pleasant and also good, all at the same time in the same subject and with respect to the same thirst. Now it makes sense to suppose that the pleasure and the pain cease at the same time or that the subject ceases to feel pain and pleasure at the same time. But what sense does it make to say that good and bad leave the subject at the same time, or that the bad of being thirsty and the good of drinking while thirsty leave the subject at the same time? The answer perhaps is not clear. In the case of pleasure and pain, Socrates probably supposes that the pleasure of drinking depends on being thirsty, so that when being thirsty ceases, and therefore being in the pain of thirst ceases, the pleasure of drinking also ceases. But what are we to suppose in the case of good and bad? Well, P4 clearly shows that Socrates thinks that good and evils can be acquired and lost. Thus health and disease, say, can be acquired and lost; and they can also be acquired or lost at the same time and in the same subject provided they are not health and disease of the same part of the body (see P2). If we suppose that being thirsty is a bad state for the organism and drinking while thirsty is a good state (sometimes, anyway), perhaps 'the good and the bad leave the subject at the same time' can mean in this case that the two states cease at the same time; though drinking can continue after being thirsty ceases, it can also cease at the same time. This is sufficient to defeat the second argument unless Socrates means to argue that the pain of being thirsty and the pleasure of drinking while thirsty *always* leave the subject at the same time.

The third argument: hedonism and the goodness of good men (497E–499B)

Staying close to the text we can reconstruct the last argument against hedonism as follows:

P1 Good and pleasant are the same; bad and painful are the same (or, good things and pleasant things are the same; bad things and painful things are the same). (495A, 497B, 499B)

P2 Good men are good by reason of the presence of good things. (497DE, 498D)

P3 Courageous and wise men are good men; foolish men and cowards are bad men. (497E, 498C)

270

P4 Foolish men and wise men feel enjoyment (χαίρουσι) or
pain (λυποῦνται) in about the same measure (or, foolish
men do not feel enjoyment or pain much more or much
less than wise men). (497E—498A)

P5 When the enemy withdraws the courageous and the
cowards feel enjoyment about the same, or if not the same
the cowards more. (498AB) When the enemy advances the
courageous and the cowards both feel pain about the same,
or perhaps the cowards more. (498B)

C1 So the foolish and the wise and the courageous and the
cowardly feel enjoyment and pain about the same, the
cowards perhaps more than the courageous. (498BC;
inference from P4 and P5 by conjunction)

C2 So good men and bad men feel enjoyment and pain about
the same. (498C; inference apparently from P3 and C1,
possibly on the assumption that in Callicles' view wisdom
and courage are the only virtues, and all and only courageous and wise men are good men)

C3 So the good and the bad men are (each) good and bad
about the same, or the bad men are good and bad more
than the good men are good and bad. (498C; inference
apparently from P1, P2 and C2)

Callicles says he does not understand what Socates is saying;
apparently he means that he does not see how Socrates reached
his conclusion, and Socrates proceeds to enlighten him, by repeat-
ing premises to make clear what he is inferring from what, and by
making some steps more explicit:

P2 (repeated)   P1 (repeated)

C4 So those who feel enjoyment have good things, namely
pleasures, present to them, when they feel enjoyment.
(489D; inference apparently from the assumption that
those who feel enjoyment have pleasure present to them
and from P1, by substitution)

C5 So those who feel enjoyment, having good things present
to them, are good men. (498D; inference apparently from
C4 and P2)

C6 Those who feel pain have bad things, namely pains, present
to them. (498D, inference parallel to C4)

C7 Those who feel pain, having bad things present to them,
are bad men. (498E; inference parallel to C5)

C8 Those who feel enjoyment are good men; those who feel
pain are bad men. (498E; inference from C5 and C7 by
conjunction)

271

P6   Those who feel these (enjoyments) more are more so
      (better men); those less less, and those about the same
      about the same. (498E; this may be held plausibly on the
      basis of C8)
C1   repeated

At this point, Socrates says to Callicles:

> Syllogise then in common with me, to see the results of our
> admissions; for you know they say it is a fine thing to tell and
> examine fine things two and three times.

Then, appropriately, he repeats himself as follows:

P3   (repeated)
C5   (repeated)
C6   (repeated)
C1.1 The good and the bad man feel enjoyment and pain
      similarly, but perhaps the bad man more. (499A; a
      version of C1)
C3.1 Then the bad man becomes good and bad similarly to the
      good man, or the bad man (becomes) more (good and
      bad) than the good man. (499AB; the grand conclusion,
      but really only a variant of C3; presumably the inference
      is from C1, P3, C5, C6, C1 and P6)

The last repetitions do not really help much. C4 through C8,
though, is helpful, since it shows the use made in the argument of
the hypothesis P1 and the principle P2. The argument has the
form of a *reductio ad absurdum*, the first premise, P1, being the
hypothesis to be refuted. C3 is supposed to be a logically false or
contradictory statement; so if the argument is valid, and the
premises other than P1 are all true, it follows that P1 is false.

Is the argument sound? It is a complex argument subject to a
variety of interpretations and criticisms. The criticisms that have
been leveled against it are sometimes more puzzling than the
argument itself, and they all suffer from the fact that they do not
begin with a statement of the argument that even roughly approxi-
mates our text.[16]

The most recent critic of the argument has concentrated on the
principle that good men are good by the presence of good things
(P2):[17]

> Now Socrates suggests that a good man is good because goods
> are present to him, just as men are beautiful because beauty is
> present to them (497E1—3). He seems to be equivocating in his
> most unscrupulous way. For surely we would not agree that a

man is good because he happens to acquire goods. Nor need
Callicles agree that a man is good if he happens to acquire many
pleasures. The goods that make a good man are the restricted
subsets of goods called virtues. Callicles agrees that courage is a
virtue. On the view of virtue that will suit his remarks on justice,
a man will have a virtue if and only if he has the power to acquire what is good for him (cf. M. 77b). He need not agree that
a man will be good if goods come to him any way at all; but this
is what Socrates' argument demands.

Now in connection with the principle P2 that men are good by
reason of (because of) the presence of good things, there are two
distinct points to be considered, both of which are touched on by
Crombie and Irwin. (1) Is 'presence' ($\pi\alpha\rho\sigma\nu\sigma\iota\alpha$) ambiguous, and
does this ambiguity affect the argument? and (2) is there restriction
on the set of good things implied or presupposed in the principle?
As to (1), both Crombie and Irwin appeal to two kinds of $\pi\alpha\rho\sigma\nu\sigma\iota\alpha$
distinguished in *Lysis* 217, but this is fruitless: in that passage one
kind of presence is indeed distinguished from another by means of
an example (lead being present in one's hair makes the hair appear
white but does not make the hair white, whereas when old age
turns hair white this is a case where white is present and the hair is
white), but no characterization of the distinction is given, beyond
saying that in one case presence of a thing of a given kind renders
the thing to which it is present of that kind and in another case it
does not. Nor is principle P2 an instance of the formula 'x is f by
the presence of the F'; it is not a matter of Socrates having 'no
right' to apply this formula to the present case to draw the required
conclusion because 'presence' is ambiguous, as Irwin suggests:[18]
the formula cannot apply to the present case, for in principle P2
we have the plural 'good things' ($\dot\alpha\gamma\alpha\vartheta\dot\alpha$) — and this is true
throughout the argument (497DE, 498D, 498E) — and by no
strength of the imagination can $\dot\alpha\gamma\alpha\vartheta\dot\alpha$ or 'good things' be thought
of as substituends for 'the F.' For the same reason, Crombie's
suggestion, that possibly 'the relation of a universal to its instances
is identified with the relation of a man to his pleasures,' is simply
wild.

In the present argument the most natural way to take the
notion of presence in principle P2 is the way in which 'F thing(s)
are present to x' is equivalent, at least in truth value, to 'x has F
things' and 'x is F.' This suits many examples very well: a man to
whom the virtues are present is a man who has the virtues and a
man who is virtuous; a man to whom courage is present is a man
who has courage and is a courageous man; a man to whom wealth

273

is present is a man who has wealth and is a wealthy man; a man to whom health is present has health and is a healthy man. Of course these equivalences will not hold in all cases, in particular they will not hold in the case of good things and good men, as critics have pointed out, and, we may add, they will not hold in the case of pleasures and pleasant men either: 'good things are present to x' may be equivalent to 'x had good things,' but neither seems to be equivalent to 'x is a good man;' and 'pleasures are present to x' may be equivalent to 'x has pleasures' but neither seems equivalent to 'x is a pleasant man.' Nevertheless, this is the natural sense in which to take the notion of presence, and once a restriction is placed on the notion of 'good things' in P2, it renders that principle very plausible.

Concerning (2), clearly P2 is ambiguous concerning the scope of 'good things:' It may be taken in the sense of

P2.1   Good men are good by reason of the presence of *any* good things

or

P2.2   There are some good things such that good men are good by reason of *their* presence.

Now Irwin's objection to P2 — 'for surely we would not agree that a man is good because he happens to acquire good things' — seems to put the burden of the objection on the notion of happening to acquire. But these notions do not seem to be involved in the principle, nor do they seem to be the cause of the trouble. We would not say that a man is good because of the presence of health or wealth, no matter how he happened to acquire these; and, I think, we would say that a man is good because justice is present to him no matter how he acquired the virtue of justice. Clearly, the trouble is rather the scope of 'good things'; as Irwin subsequently suggests, we would agree that the goods that make a man good are the restricted subset of good things, namely the virtues; and Callicles himself agrees that the virtues of courage and wisdom at least make a man good if they are present to a man. Clearly, then, the objections to P2 are neutralized if we do not take P2 in the sense of P2.1, and we take the notion of presence in the way I suggested above. But aside from Crombie and Irwin's intuitive objections to P2, or rather to P2.1, and aside from the fact that P2.1 is indeed an absurd principle (i.e. has absurd consequences), we have no reason to suppose that Plato or Socrates held it and plenty of reason to suppose that they did not. In general, goodness in Plato is goodness relative to kinds.[19] In the *Gorgias* itself Socrates makes statements which are inconsistent with P2.1 (506D):

And is that thing pleasant by whose advent we feel pleasure,
and that thing good by whose presence we are good? Certainly.
But further, both we and everything else that is good, are good
by the advent of some virtue? In my view that must be so,
Callicles.

Now the first statement affirmed is not that if something is good
then by its presence we become good (men), but rather that if something is such that by its presence we become good it is a good
thing. And the second statement is clearly inconsistent with P2.1
on the assumption that different kinds of things have different
virtues. Though the virtue of a given kind of thing may have things
in common with the virtue of another kind, especially if the two
kinds are species of the same genus, the presence of the virtue of
one kind of thing in another kind, if possible, would not make the
latter a good thing of *that* kind; the virtue of chariots whatever it
may be will not render knives good if it could be present in knives;
nor will the virtue of knives render horses good; nor will the virtue
of pigs make men good. It is clear enough, then, that P2.1 has
absurd consequences, and equally clear that Socrates and Plato
rejected it.

This being the case, only two serious possibilities remain concerning the meaning of P2 and its use in the argument: (1) Socrates
means P2 not in the unrestricted sense of P2.1 but in some
restricted version such as P2.2; or (2) Socrates means P2 in the
sense of P2.1, but though he himself does not hold it he thinks
that Callicles holds it or is committed to it. Let us explore each in
turn.

(1) If we substitute P2.2 for P2 in the argument, it becomes
clear at once that the argument becomes invalid at step C5, or
that C5 does not follow from C4 and P2.2. From the statement,
say, that foolish men feel enjoyment or have pleasure present to
them (equally with the wise men), it will validly follow by substitution warranted by P1 that foolish men have good things
present to them (equally with wise men); but it will not follow
from this latter statement and P2.2 that foolish men are good
men, whereas *it does* follow from the same statement and P1.1.
At any rate, it follows if we allow substitution into modal contexts, assuming that 'by reason of the presence of —' introduces a
modal context. So clearly P2.2 is too weak to support the inferences Socrates makes. Let us try to strengthen it a bit, taking our
cue from the general remarks of Socrates just quoted and from the
fact that in the argument Socrates and Callicles agree that courage
and intelligence (or wisdom) are good things the presence of which
in men makes men good men:

P2.3 Good men are good by the presence of some good things such as courage and wisdom; and bad men are bad by the presence of some bad things such as cowardice and foolishness.

This principle is so stated as to accommodate the fact that Socrates and Callicles agree that these are virtues and their presence makes men good men, the fact that they seem to disagree as to whether other virtues make men good (e.g. temperance), and the possibility that they disagree on their definitions of courage and wisdom. Now P2.3 is still not strong enough to support inference to C5; even so we are better off with P2.3 (than we were with P2.2) since the rest of the argument is concerned with the pleasures and pains of wise men and fools and the pleasures and pains of courageous men and cowards, so that we can begin to see how we might apply P2.3 to the argument. To do so, however, we need to overcome yet another obstacle, aside from considerations of scope, namely this. At C5 (and C7) and possibly before, Socrates seems to proceed as if Callicles, given his hedonism (P1), is obliged to say that it is the presence of pleasures that make men good men; but, though there is a grain of truth in this, we shall see later, this is not so. In Callicles' view the presence of pleasures will make men happy, but not necessarily good men, even though happy men may also be good men. Given his hedonistic view, that 'pleasant' and 'good' are at least coextensive (denote the same set of things), Callicles is obliged to say that any good thing is also pleasant, and hence that if courage and wisdom are good things they are also pleasant; but he is not obliged to say that all pleasant things are pleasures! Just as we make the distinction between things that are good in themselves and things that are good in the sense of having good effects or the sense of enabling us to obtain things that are good in themselves, so an intelligent hedonist can distinguish between things that are pleasant in the sense of being pleasures (pleasant feelings or sensations), things that are pleasant in the sense that they cause or tend to cause pleasure (such as sweet strawberries, Corinthian girls, and Lydian music), and things that are pleasant in the sense that they enable us to obtain pleasures and avoid pains (such as skills, powers, and abilities). Callicles can and should, consistently with his hedonism, say that if courage and wisdom are good things they are good in the sense that they enable us to obtain good things and avoid evils, and they are pleasant in the sense that they enable us to obtain pleasure and avoid pains. So, if Callicles holds that courage and wisdom are good things, and that the presence of these goods makes men good men, he is committed to saying, given his hedonism, that the presence of the power to obtain pleasures and avoid pains makes men good men; he is not committed to the view that the presence of the pleasures themselves makes men good men, as Socrates has him admit at step C5. Irwin and Crombie have noticed most of this, but they do not systematically follow up with the next step. The next stp is clearly to make the required corrections in Socrates' argument. For, clearly, the adjustments we have made in Callicles' view do not destroy Socrates' argument entirely: for, giving Callicles all the benefits of all the doubts, as we have done, it is still the case that on his view the courageous and wise men should enjoy more pleasures and fewer pains than the cowardly and the foolish. But he says that they do not! He says at one and the same time that the courageous and the wise have the powers (or abilities or skills) to maximize their pleasures, and that the cowardly and foolish do not have these powers, and also that the wise and the courageous enjoy pleasures and pains about as much as and no more than the foolish and the cowards! So, if we make the now obvious corrections in Socrates' argument, using no more than P2.3 and P1 as the main principles, the psychological propositions (P4, P5, C1), and Calliclean definitions of wisdom and courage (as qualities that enable us to maximize pleasures and minimize pains), Callicles' view is indeed validly shown to be inconsistent. The corrected version of Socrates' argument might run as follows:

P1   Good and pleasant are the same, bad and painful are the same (or, the class of good things and the class of pleasant things are identical in membership, and the class of bad things and the class of painful things are identical in membership). (hypothesis)

P2.3 Good men are good by reason of the presence of some good things, such as courage and wisdom; bad men are bad by reason of the presence of the opposites. (the corrected version of P2)

P2.4 The presence of courage and wisdom makes a man a good man if and only if it enables him to choose and sustain courses of action that maximize his (the agent's) pleasures and minimize his pains; the presence of foolishness and cowardice make a man a bad man if and only if it prevents him from choosing and sustaining courses of action that maximize his pleasures and minimize his pains. (from what presumably would be Calliclean definitions of courage and wisdom, derived from P1 and P2.3)

277

C1.1 Courageous men and wise men feel pleasures and pains in about the same quantities (about the same) as the cowards and the fools. (C1)

C1.2 Then the presence of wisdom and courage does not enable a man to maximize his pleasure and minimize his pains more than the presence of foolishness and cowardice enables a man to maximize his pleasures and minimize his pains; and the presence of foolishness and cowardice does not prevent a man from maximizing his pleasures and minimizing his pains more than the presence of wisdom and courage prevents a man from maximizing his pleasure and minimizing his pains. (from C1.1)

C3.1 Then if the presence of wisdom and courage makes men good it does not make them good any more than the presence of cowardice and foolishness makes them good; and if the presence of foolishness and cowardice makes men bad it does not make them bad any more than the presence of wisdom and courage makes them bad. (from P2.4 and C1.2; a version of C3)

But is Callicles' hedonism refuted? An affirmative answer to this question does not follow from what we have just argued, for Callicles has admitted many propositions besides hedonism and the inconsistency may lie in these admissions. In particular, he has claimed and admitted that courage and wisdom are good qualities and qualities that make men good, and that wise and courageous men enjoy pleasures and pains about the same as fools and cowards. It would seem that a hedonist need not admit any of these propositions, and it is not clear that the last of these propositions is true. Has Socrates then failed entirely in his attack on P1?

To appreciate Socrates' attack and make a worthy estimate of its effectiveness, we need to be more systematic about hedonism, about Callicles' hedonism, and about the other elements in his view and their connection with his hedonism. To begin with, hedonism is a view about the good, not a view about the right. Second, there are several species of hedonism, the most important of which are psychological hedonism,[20] and ethical hedonism; and the two most important varieties of the latter are analytic[21] and non-analytic ethical hedonism. Callicles' view is of this very last variety; it is a view as to what things are good and what bad and it is properly expressed by proposition P1. Now Callicles, in addition to his hedonism, which is a view about the good, has also views about the right, namely his view on justice. Views about what actions are right and wrong may be roughly divided into two kinds: teleological views according to which the rightness of actions depends on the balance of good over evil in the consequences of the actions; and non-teleological views, according to which the rightness of actions is independent of the goodness and badness of the consequences, and depends rather on the agreement or disagreement of the actions to certain moral principles or rules.[22] It is clear that in teleological theories rightness depends on goodness, whereas in non-teleological theories it does not; consequently the theory of goodness that a teleologist holds will affect in some way his theory of rightness. Now Callicles is a hedonist concerning the good, and appears to be a teleologist concerning the right, that is, what is just by nature (as well perhaps as what is just by law — but this need not concern us). For he tells us that it is just by nature that the better or stronger rule over and have more than the worse and weaker; and he clearly regards ruling and having more wealth as goods, at least goods in the sense that they are instrumental in obtaining pleasures and avoiding pains. So it would appear that whether an action is just or right would depend, in Callicles' view of what is right, on whether it promotes or tends to promote — whether it has consequences of — the better or the stronger ruling over and having more than the worse and weaker. Clearly then Callicles is a teleologist of some kind concerning the right. But what kind of teleologist is he? The two most important varieties of teleologist are the egoist and the universalist (or as is more commonly known, the utilitarian). The universalist or utilitarian teleologist says that rightness of actions depends on goodness and badness of the consequences of the actions and counts the goodness and badness *to all persons affected by the actions* and to the society at large; whereas the egoistic teleologist claims that only the good and the bad *to the agent* is to be counted in determining the rightness of actions. Now is Callicles an egoistic teleologist or a utilitarian (universalist) teleologist? If we combine his teleologism and his hedonism, he is a hedonist concerning the good and an egoistic teleologist concerning the right if he claims the following:

HET: An action is right (just) if and only if it has the consequence of bringing *to the agent* a balance of pleasure over pain which is at least as great as that of any other alternative action that was open to the agent.

On the other hand, he is a hedonist and a utilitarian (universalist) teleologist if he claims the following:

279

HUT: An action is right (just) if and only if it has the consequence of bringing *to all those affected by the action*
collectively (rather than individually) a balance of
pleasure over pain which is at least as great as that of
any other alternative action open to the agent.

Callicles does not appear to state either of these positions, but he
certainly does not appear to be a universalist. I think we have to
suppose that he is an egoist, and that his definition or principle of
justice is something he arrives at from his hedonistic position concerning the good and his teleological egoism concerning the right
and certain other judgments that he makes: among these is probably the judgment that political power (ruling over) and having
more than others (having more property and wealth) are *the*
instrumental goods necessary and sufficient for a life of great
happiness, a life of great and many and continuous pleasures and
none or few pains. In addition he evidently makes the judgment
that not every one can have these goods: clearly in any group not
everyone can rule over others and have more than others in the
group. And further, he makes the judgment that it takes great
natural endowments, such as great intelligence and great courage,
to go after and acquire the vital instrumental goods — and the
people who have these endowments he calls the better and the
stronger. So, we might say, as an egoistic teleological hedonist
he might be willing to say that, theoretically, it is just by nature
that everyone rules over and has more than others but since this is
not possible, and in all probability only those with great natural
endowments can obtain these goods, his main principle or right or
justice turns out to be that it is just by nature that the stronger
and better rule over and have more than the worse and the weaker.
    Seen against this combination of teleological, egoistic, and
hedonistic views, Socrates' argument, in its easily corrected
version, is in fact very formidable and as good an attack as one
can make on that position. For it attacks the complex Calliclean
view at one of its weakest points: its account of goodness in men.
The notion of goodness is a very general and abstract one and
applies to countless sorts of things: artifacts, organs, animals,
natural objects, abstract objects, theories, men as holders of
offices or in roles or as possessors of skills, and also to men as men
or as human beings. We speak of good houses, good eyes, good
horses, good plane trees, good numbers, good theories, good
presidents, good actors, good philosophers, good runners. We also
speak of good (and bad or evil) men, men who are honest, or just,
courageous, benevolent, humane, considerate. What account can

an egoistic teleologist who is also a hedonist, such as Callicles, give of the good man? This is the question Socrates is pressing with his argument, and it is as philosophically embarrassing a question as one could ask of such a position. Goodness as applied to men cannot probably be explained or understood by relying on hedonism alone; since hedonism is a theory as to what things are good (it by itself says nothing as to what things are right), and the goodness of persons cannot probably be explained or understood without reference to a theory as to what is right (this is true it seems both of teleological theories such as Plato's and John Stuart Mill's and of deontological theories such as Kant's and Rawls's). Still, if one is a hedonist, his notion of a good man will retain some connection with his hedonism since the notion of a good man falls under the notion of goodness (unless at any rate one holds that 'good' is systematically and completely equivocal when applied to different sorts of things). A good man is clearly not *the same thing* as a pleasant man (even though of course being pleasant may be held to be a desirable characteristic in persons), but being a good man will in all cases have something to do with pleasures and pains (on the theory of hedonism). It can be seen already that being an ethical hedonist places some limitations in explaining the notion of a good man. But now let us suppose that one is a teleologist about the right as well as a hedonist concerning the good. Assuming that in general a good man is one who has the disposition and ability to choose and do what is right and avoid what is wrong (however right and wrong may be defined within teleological theories), a teleologist and hedonist will have to say that in general a good man is a man who has the disposition to choose and act so as to maximize pleasures and minimize pains and avoid courses of action that maximize pains and minimize pleasures. If he is a universalist or utilitarian teleologist he will count the pleasures and pains of all those affected by a given action. The combination of universal teleologism about the right and hedonism about the good imposes further limitations in explaining goodness as applied to men. If a hedonistic universal teleologist (hedonistic utilitarian, for short) says that conformity to justice makes an act right, other things equal, and that consequently justice is a quality the presence of which makes a man a good man, then he will also have to agree that just men when acting *qua* just men maximize pleasures and minimize pains more than unjust men do; that, say, a judge when he metes out just punishment for a given offense is maximizing pleasures and minimizing pains (for all affected by the action) more than an unjust judge who metes out unjust punishment for the same offense under the same circumstances. Again, if courage is a quality that makes men good, the hedonistic utilitarian will have to say that courageous men when acting *qua* courageous men maximize pleasures and minimize pains more than do cowardly men; that, say, the 300 Spartans, if they were acting courageously in being willing to face the Persians at Thermopylae and fight them and die fighting, were maximizing pleasures and minimizing pains more than they would have had they behaved as cowards; indeed, that in choosing to be courageous they believed that they were maximizing pleasures and minimizing pains more than they would have had they behaved in a cowardly fashion. Though there is no doubt that they were courageous, it is doubtful, to say the least, that they maximized pleasures and minimized pains of all those affected by their action or, more importantly, that their choice *qua* courageous turned on their belief.

Let us next suppose that our man is an *egoistic* teleologist and a hedonist. How would he understand the notion of goodness as applied to men? In general he will have to say that a good man is a man who has the disposition and ability to choose actions that will maximize *his* pleasures and minimize *his* pains and avoid actions that do not do this, no matter what pleasures and pains his actions cause to other people. Consequently, if he says that practical wisdom, courage, justice, honesty, consideration of others, and other such qualities make men good men, he will have also to say that all these qualities have to do with the disposition or ability to choose courses of action that will maximize *one's own* (agent's) pleasures and minimize *one's own* pains. Thus he will have to say that practical wisdom is the knowledge or ability to make correct judgments more often than not as to what will so maximize and minimize one's own pleasures and pains; that courage is the ability to take risks and face dangers and conquer fears for the sake of maximizing one's pleasures and minimizing one's pains, and that if one is being courageous in, say, going to war and facing the enemy he would have to believe that going to war is pleasanter than not going (precisely what Socrates says about courageous men going to war in the *Protagoras*, when he is expounding the virtue of courage on hedonistic assumptions!). So if the Spartans at Thermopylae were courageous they faced the Persians in the belief that it would be pleasanter to do so than to flee or surrender! And if the hedonistic and egoistic teleologist says that justice is a quality that makes men good men, he will also have to say that a man is being just when, in matters of rights and property and contracts, he so acts as to maximize his pleasures and minimize his pains no matter what other effects his actions have!

And if he says that altruism or consideration of others is a quality that makes men good, he will also have to say that a man can be altruistic or considerate of others when he acts for the sake of maximizing his pleasures and minimizing his pains no matter what other effects his actions have. Here we have clearly reached an absurdity. Clearly, Callicles would avoid this absurdity (namely a Calliclean definition of altruism or consideration of others) by saying that altruism and consideration of others are not qualities that make men good men; they are not good qualities at all. We saw that he rejects temperance as a virtue for somewhat similar reasons: temperance at times dictates restraint of desires and denial of pleasures, and thus prevents one from maximizing one's pleasures and minimizing one's pains to the fullest possible extent. For similar reasons he rejects what he calls justice by law as a virtue, i.e. as a quality that makes men good men. That is, Callicles cannot possibly explain, on his view, the fact that, in his own culture as well as in many others, consideration of others, justice in the sense of fairness and equality, and temperance are held to be qualities that make men good men. So he has to reject them entirely as good qualities. And this itself is an objection to his theory. Socrates (or Plato) has Callicles retain, as qualities that make men good men, the two qualities that he has any chance to explain at all on his theory: practical wisdom and courage. Both of these have a chance to retain their role as qualities that make men good in Callicles' theory because they can both be instrumental in enabling men to choose courses of action that will maximize their pleasures and minimize their pains. These two qualities would appear to be just about the only qualities left for Callicles to claim as qualities that make men good — if these go also, it will be difficult to see how Callicles can have a notion of a good man at all. It is precisely this last stronghold that Socrates' argument attacks. The argument shows that, if we assume Calliclean definitions of practical wisdom and courage, it follows that men who are good in the sense of being wise and courageous will have more enjoyments and fewer pains than men who are foolish and cowardly. And this seems to be generally false. Callicles might be allowed to protest that this seems to be false only if we mean men who are wise and courageous according to the ordinary conceptions of these virtues; if we think of those who have Calliclean wisdom and courage we will see that it is true that these people enjoy more pleasures and fewer pains than Calliclean fools and cowards. But the answer to this is that he is now distorting radically the notions of practical wisdom and courage — that is, distorting them to the point where *their* presence no longer makes men good men. Calliclean wisdom is knowledge or ability to judge truly what will maximize one's own pleasures and minimize one's own pains; and Calliclean courage is the ability to act, in the face of risk and danger and fear, so as to maximize one's pleasures and minimize one's pains. Now perhaps Calliclean wise and courageous men do enjoy more pleasures in life and fewer pains than Calliclean fools and cowards. But are these now qualities whose presence makes men good men? The Calliclean notion of a good man has been reduced to a man who has no sense of fairness or equality, who has no consideration for others, and whose wisdom and courage consist *entirely* in the ability to maximize his pleasures and minimize his pains. This notion of a good man is entirely at variance with our moral intuitions, and with those of the Greeks as well. More important than that, if men are to live with each other in any kind of social unit with any degree of co-operation and a chance for development and happiness, then the notion of a good man must include at least some qualities that involve some recognition of others as human beings on an equal footing with oneself. Even this bare minimum seems to be missing from Callicles' notion of a good man. It would be hard to think of a weaker point in Callicles' theory, or of a stronger argument than the one Socrates delivers against it.

But Socrates' argument has its limitations. It does not show Callicles' view to be internally contradictory: his hedonism is not shown to be self-contradictory, nor of course is his hedonism shown to contradict the rest of his view, his egoistic teleologism about what is right. The position remains logically consistent. But a theory, in ethics or elsewhere, has to be more than logically consistent to be adequate: it has to explain adequately a range of facts and concepts. It is fair enough to expect of a theory as to what is good to give an adequate account of the good man; and it is an absolute requirement of a theory as to what is good and what is right that it give an adequate account of the notion of a good man. Callicles' theory excludes entirely some qualities that are commonly held to be qualities that make men good men, and distorts the remaining ones radically. And these exclusions and distortions are faulty not only in the sense of being contrary to our moral intuitions; they are faulty and are to be rejected also because the notion of a good man that they allow has no connection whatsoever with the notion of a man being good as a social being.

At the end of the argument we have been discussing, Plato has Callicles say (499B):

Let me tell you, Socrates, all the time that I have been listening to you and yielding you agreement, I have been remarking the puerile delight with which you cling to any concession one may make to you, even in jest. So you suppose that I or anybody else in the world does not regard some pleasures as better, and others worse!

Callicles is not represented at making this concession *as a result of* the argument, only *at the end of* the argument. And quite rightly so: Callicles needs to give up something out of all the propositions he has admitted — Socrates' argument is successful to that extent — but he need not give up the view that all pleasures are good and all pains bad. But further, what he has just said is in fact consistent with hedonism if 'better' and 'worse' are interpreted hedonistically, as they can be (and the Socrates of the *Protagoras* does interpret them so in 358—60): a pleasure is better than another if, other things equal, it is of greater intensity or duration; or if obtaining it brings with it other pleasures whereas obtaining the other does not, again other things being equal between the two. But Socrates proceeds to introduce the notions of good and bad pleasures and to give them non-hedonistic interpretations:

Well then, what you now state, it seems, is that some particular pleasures are good, and some bad; is that not so?
Yes.
And are the beneficial ones good and the harmful ones bad?
Certainly.
And those are beneficial that do some good, and those bad that do some bad?
I agree.
Now are these the sort you mean — for instance, in the body, the pleasures of eating and drinking that we mentioned a moment ago? Then the pleasures of this sort which produce health in the body, or strength, or any other bodily excellence, are these good, and those which have the opposite effects, bad?
Certainly.

This is obviously a Socratic, not a Calliclean, interpretation of good and bad pleasures — it is doubtful that Callicles was drinking for his health! Callicles has ceased giving candid answers, and Socrates picks up where he left off with Polus, expounding once more his conception of the good life. And it is time for us to take up two keys to understanding that conception: the analogy between goodness in the body — health — and goodness in the soul — virtue; and the related analogy between the sciences that

tend the body — gymnastics and medicine — and the sciences that
tend the soul — legislation and justice. In this way we might be
able to understand the overwhelming emphasis Socrates places on
goods and evils of the soul, and the good and harm these are
supposed to cause. Without some progress in these matters we are
left not only with an extreme view of happiness and unhappiness
but with an opaque one as well: extreme because it either does not
include or downgrades radically the goods of the body and social
goods — it does not even *include* pleasure in the things that are
good in themselves! — and opaque because the benefit and harm
that these goods and evils are supposed to bring have not been
explained.

6 *Virtue as health of the soul and justice as medicine*

Analogies or similarities between bodily states and states of the
soul are a constant feature of Socratic ethics. We have already
examined the use of one such analogy in the *Crito* 46—8. Burnet
has noticed that a similar use is made of the same analogy in the
Gorgias 512A and in the *Republic* 445A.[23] Clearly, Socrates
thought that there are some instructive and illuminating similarities between good bodily states, such as health and strength, and
good soul states, such as virtue and happiness; or at least, that
good soul states should be thought of on the model of good
bodily states. It is also clear, from all three passages and others,
that Socrates used the analogies as a powerful argument in support
of his view that virtue brings happiness and vice misery. These
analogies are therefore central both in trying to understand the
states of soul that Socrates called virtue and happiness and in
trying to assess his view that virtue brings happiness and vice
misery.

Let us begin with what is perhaps the most systematic statement of the analogies, *Gorgias* 463E—466A:

Soc. There are things that you call body and soul?

Gorg. Of course.

Soc. And of each of these you think there is a good condition
[εὐεξία]?

Gorg. I do.

Soc. And again, a condition that may seem so but is not? For
example many people seem to be in good bodily condition when
it would not be easy for anyone but a doctor or an athletic
trainer to perceive that they are not.

Gor. You speak truly.

Soc. Something similar there is, I say, in body and soul, which makes the body or soul seem to be in a good condition, though it is not so in fact.

Gorg. Quite so.

Soc. Now let me see if I can explain my meaning to you more clearly. There are two different arts [τέχναι] : the one which has to do with the soul I call politics [πολιτική] ; the other which concerns the body I cannot give a name to off hand, but being one concerning the care of the body it has two elements [branches] , gymnastic and medicine. Under politics, I set legislation in the place of [in a place similar to that of] gymnastic, and justice in the place of medicine. In each of these pairs, medicine and gymnastic, justice and legislation, there is some intercommunication, as both deal with the same thing, but they are also different from each other in some things. Now these four, which tend the body and the soul always with a view to what is best for each, are noticed by flattery which without knowledge but with speculation divides itself into four parts, and then, insinuating itself into each of these branches, pretends to be that into which she has crept, and cares nothing for what is best, but dangles what is most pleasant for the moment as a bait for folly, and deceives into thinking that she is of the highest value. . . . Flattery, however, is what I call it, and I say that this sort of thing is a disgrace . . . because it thinks of the pleasant without [thinking] of the best; and I say it is not an art but a habitude, and so cannot tell the cause of any of them. . . . Well, to avoid a long speech, I am willing to put it to you like a geometer . . .; as self-adornment is to gymnastic, so is sophistry to legislation; and as cookery is to medicine, so is rhetoric to justice.

Relying on this and related passages, let us try to give a systematic exposition of the analogies. First, the analogy we are interested in is not that between the four art-sciences, gymnastic, medicine, legislation, and justice, on the one hand, and the four corresponding pseudo-sciences, self-adornment, cookery, sophistry, and legislation, on the other. The distinctions Socrates draws between the first four and the second four, however, are of interest. The first four according to him aim at what is best in body and soul (or work with a view to what is the best condition in body and soul); the last four aim at what is pleasant; and we know that his view also is that what is best and what is (most)

287

pleasant not only are not identical but are even opposed frequently. In addition, the four art-sciences have knowledge of the nature of their subject (body and soul) and the causes of its various conditions, whereas the pseudo-sciences do not. This probably means that, say, medicine knows at least what health and diseases are (the good and bad conditions of the body) and what their causes are, whereas cookery does not.[24]

Second, the analogy we are interested in is between gymnastic and medicine on the one hand and legislature and justice on the other. All four are practical rather than theoretical art-sciences. And all four are beneficial rather than productive: they do not make good objects, they 'make objects good,' as Young puts it.[25] The object of gymnastic and medicine — that on which they work — is the body; the object of legislature and justice is the soul. But though the object (that on which they work) is the same for gymnastic and medicine, their functions are different. In the above passage Socrates does not say what the good condition of the body is but later when he resumes discussion of this topic he says that it is health and strength (*Gorgias* 504AE). And earlier, when he was again talking about the doctor and the physcial trainer, he said that the ἔργον or function of the first is to bring about health and that of the second to bring about strength and beauty (*Gorgias* 452AB). In addition, gymnastic may have been conceived as primarily regulative and medicine as primarily corrective; that is, gymnastic may have been conceived as a body of principles and rules and practices such that if one followed them one would develop and maintain physical fitness (physical strength and physical beauty — these possibly presupposing health); whereas medicine was conceived as a body of principles and rules and practices such that if one followed them one would recover his health. The regulative–corrective distinction, however, may have been a matter of degree and emphasis.[26] Parallel to gymnastic and medicine, we have legislation and justice. Unlike the first two, the second pair have as their object — that on which they work — the human soul; and like the first pair, they aim at bringing about the best condition of the human soul. In *Gorgias* 504AE Socrates tells us that this condition is temperance and justice. So presumably the function of the art of legislature and justice, both of which work on the human soul, is to bring about the good condition of the soul, which is temperance and justice. But it is not clear how Socrates would distinguish between the art of legislature and the art of justice: since they have the same object (that on which they work), apparently they must have different functions; the difference in functions may be that the art of legislature aims at bringing about temperance in the soul and the art of justice aims at bringing about justice in the soul (*Gorgias* 504D), but this is not clear. In addition, at *Gorgias* 478AB Socrates says that medicine relieves us from disease and justice from wantonness and injustice. Apparently, Socrates' thought is that the art of legislature, which contains knowledge of the best condition of the human soul and aims at bringing it about, consists of a body of principles and laws such that if a man follows them his soul will be in the best condition — temperance and justice; and the art of justice, which also knows what the best condition of the soul is and aims at bringing it back, consists of a body of principles and rules such that if an unjust man follows them he will become just again.

This much we can get out of the texts we quoted and cited. In order to make further progress in understanding Socrates' analogy, its problems, and the uses Socrates makes of it, we shall first exhibit the structure of each of the four crafts, according to the pattern that Young has developed, and then we shall state the analogy, and consider its problems and uses.

According to Young:[27]

A *practical* craft art-science may be thought of as exemplifying the structure depicted by the following chart:

craftsman	object or material
his *ergon* (= function)	its *ergon* (= function)
his *techne* (= craft)	its *arete* (= virtue or excellence)

I shall use the example of a trainer of racing horses to explain this chart. The trainer has a function, the training of racing horses, and a craft, which consists of the theory and techniques, whatever they may be, that enables him (if he knows them) to perform that function well. He does his work on racing horses, whose function is to run races. If the trainer does his work well, he will achieve the end or goal of his craft, which is to give the racing horses he trains their specific *arete*: those qualities (say speed and endurance) the possession of which will enable them to perform their function (running races) well.

Let us now fill in this chart for each of the four art-crafts of the analogy, using the information from the texts and putting question marks where Socrates does not supply the required information.

Gymnastic

Physical trainer (gymnast)	human body
To develop strength and beauty in the human body	?

Gymnastic	strength and beauty

Medicine

Physician	human body
To bring back health or relieve the human body of disease	?
Medicine	health

Legislature

Legislator	human soul
To produce temperance (and justice?) in the human soul	?
Legislature (art of legislator)	temperance and justice (states of soul)

Justice (art of judge)

Judge (?)	human soul
To bring back justice in the soul or relieve the human soul of injustice and wantonness	?
Justice (art of judge)	justice and temperance (states of soul)

The analogy that Socrates draws among the four art-crafts is simply this: as gymnastic is to the human body, so is legislature to the human soul, and as medicine is to the human body, so is justice to the human soul. Or,

$$\frac{\text{gymnastic}}{\text{body}} = \frac{\text{legislature}}{\text{soul}} \text{ and } \frac{\text{medicine}}{\text{body}} = \frac{\text{justice}}{\text{soul}}$$

Let us first consider each filled-in chart and then take up the analogy. An educated look at the filled-in charts reveals some omissions and some surprises. The omissions are obviously the question marks: Socrates does not tell us what the function of the human body is, or what the function of the human soul is. Assuming some version of the theory of function in *Republic* I, we can try to infer what Socrates thinks the function of the body is from what he thinks the virtues of the body are: if the virtues of the body are health and strength and beauty, the functions of the body will be all the bodily activities that these virtues enable the body to perform well; these will obviously include all the functions of the various bodily organs, such as respiration, digestion, reproduction, and so on, and all the activities that the body as a whole performs, including walking, sitting, running, physical labor, athletic exercises, and so on. As for the function of the soul, Socrates tells us explicitly in *Republic* I, (353D), that it is to manage, to rule, to deliberate, and in general to live. And the virtues, justice, temperance, wisdom, piety, and courage, enable the soul to perform these functions well, i.e. to deliberate well, to rule (oneself) well, to live well. The omissions then are not too difficult to fill in. Moreover, the conceptions of gymnastic and medicine that Socrates seems to have seem to be the normal Greek conceptions of these arts. When we come to legislature and justice, however, the Socratic conception seems to be very much at variance with the ordinary Greek conception of these arts (as well as our own). According to the chart we filled in for legislature, the object of legislature, that on which legislature works with a view to bringing about its best condition, is the human soul. As a description of what, say, Solon as a legislator was concerned with, this seems to be false. The principal objects of Solon as a legislator were the practices of securing debts by one's person (a practice that resulted in slavery), the practice of confining participation in government to those of noble birth, and the fact that these practices resulted in civil strife; and Solon's reforms were concerned with changing these practices which he thought were unjust and destructive of the city.[28] The same seems to be true of Socrates' view that the object of the art of justice is the human soul: the art of retributive justice or the justice of punishment, which is the branch of justice that Socrates seems to be referring to in this analogy, seems to be concerned largely with the harmful consequences (to individuals and communities) of criminal acts, such as homicide and theft, and with ways of preventing and deterring such acts through appropriate punishments. The jurors in Socrates' trial, for instance, seem to be concerned with what they conceived was the harm that Socrates was doing to the city and with ways of putting an end to that harm; they did not seem very concerned about Socrates' soul. Then as a descriptive statement, the view that the object of the art of retributive justice is the human soul seems to be false. We must not suppose, however, that legislation and justice, as conceived by the Greeks (or by us, for that matter) had nothing to do with the human soul. On the contrary, nothing was more common in the fifth century than the belief that bad social practices had their roots in evil in the human soul, and that in turn they made human souls worse. This belief is shared for different reasons by such diverse thinkers as Solon, Democritus, and Socrates.[29] The practices that Solon abolished made men resentful, rebellious, unhappy, and unjust; and the main cause of these practices, according to Solon, was greed or excessive love of money. Moreover, education was a matter of social legislation, and education was certainly conceived as developing the human soul as well as the human body. So, what is surprising in Socrates' concept of the objects of legislation and justice is not that there is no connection between the human soul and legislation and justice: what is surprising is that we would expect the subject of legislation and justice to be the conduct of human beings rather than their souls, and the conduct of human beings in so far as they are members of a community, not their conduct considered as individuals. Even if the legislator has to consider the effects of the laws he enacts on each individual soul, his laws will regulate the behavior, not the soul, of each citizen (behavior that may issue from desires or beliefs, not desires or beliefs); and he clearly must also consider the effects on sections of the community and on the community as a whole. We could say with more accuracy that the subject of the legislator is the welfare of the community as a whole and that what he legislates about is the conduct of individuals as members of the community. It is clear enough, I think, that Socrates' statements of the object and function of legislature and justice, considered as descriptive statements, cannot be brought entirely into line, to say the least, with Greek practices, or for that matter with modern practices.

It is also clear, however, that Socrates' statements on the subjects and functions of legislature and justice are at least in part meant as recommendations or proposals: the analogy is meant to tell us what legislature and justice *should* be. To put it differently, the analogy is in part normative: legislation and justice are best conceived on the models of the art of gymnastic (physical fitness) and medicine. Nowhere is this clearer than in the statement Socrates makes about just punishment in the middle of an argument we already considered (*Gorgias* 477A):

> *Soc.* Is then the benefit what I understand it to be? That he becomes better in soul if he is justly punished?

The statement that a man becomes better in soul if he is justly punished is not meant as a statement that describes what happens to the souls of people who were 'justly' punished by Athenian courts. The statement clearly sets up a standard for just punishment, since it follows from it that a man who has been punished and whose soul has not become better by that punishment has not received just punishment — and this would be so no matter what other conditions have been satisfied. Thus a man may have been found guilty of a criminal offense, a violation of a known criminal law, by a duly constituted court, and may have been given a punishment as prescribed by law for that offense, the judges having taken into account extenuating circumstances. Even if all these conditions are satisfied, which are the normal conditions for judging a particular punishment just, Socrates' statement entails that the man's punishment would not be just if it did not improve his soul. And the improvement that Socrates has in mind, we know, is the removing of the injustice or other vice in the soul that caused the man to act unjustly in the first place. Clearly Socrates is setting up a new and additional condition for just punishment. Moreover, this condition is a strict logical consequence of his analogy between the art of (retributive) justice and the art of medicine. In this analogy punishment of a wrongdoer is the analogue of medical treatment of a sick man: as medical treatment would (and should) normally be pronounced incorrect if the patient did not improve in body as a result of it (this would be a truism in Greek medicine), so punishment should be pronounced unjust if it does not improve the wrongdoer's soul. Moreover, just as correct medical treatment removes the causes of disease, which manifests itself in symptoms and malfunctions, and restores health, so just punishment should remove the causes of injustice, which manifests itself in unjust behavior, and restore justice in the soul. Though analogies between bodily disease and corrupt souls were common enough in Greek thought, the remedy that Socrates is proposing — a new conception of the objects and functions of legislation and justice, and a new standard of just punishment — was entirely new and revolutionary. Moreover, the standard he is proposing, and the whole conception that goes with it, is admirable and rational — the only question is whether we would ever have enough knowledge to put it into effect in a good way. It is admirable and rational because it offers a substantial solution to the main problems that any theory of punishment has to face. A theory of punishment must discover and propose institutions and practices of punishment that solve at least three problems: (1) how to protect communities from criminal acts; (2) how to safeguard at the same time the rights of the criminal as a human being and as a citizen; and (3) how to relate punishments to the causes of the criminal acts for which the punishments are punishments. From ancient times to the present, institutions and practices of punishment have tried to solve (1) by depriving the criminal of his liberty (which protects the community from him during the time of his confinement) and by making his confinement unpleasant (which is supposed to deter him and others from further criminal acts); they have tried to solve (2), at least in constitutional regimes, by due process of law; and they have failed miserably to solve (3). Socrates' proposal, that just punishment be thought of on the model of sound medical treatment, may require some modifications to the usual solutions of (1); it is perfectly compatible with (2), and we know from the *Apology* and the *Crito* that Socrates was a strict adherent of due process of law (cf. chapter II above); and it offers an admirable solution to (3), on the assumption that the causes of criminal conduct are to be found in 'malfunctions' in the human soul — an example of such malfunctions being Calliclean beliefs about the good life and the consequent non-restraint of any desire whatsoever. What could be a more rational and admirable solution to (3) than punishment being the removal of the causes of criminal acts? If we are to eradicate diseases we must tackle their causes; and if we are to eradicate criminal acts we must similarly tackle their causes. The notion that the punishment must fit the crime, in the sense that the criminal must get what he deserves, is far less rational, if it is rational at all, than the notion that the punishment must fit the crime in the sense in which a medical treatment must fit the disease (the sense in which the treatment is designed to remove the causes of disease). Modern penology is gradually moving toward the Socratic position, as is shown by the assigning of psychiatrists and similar experts to courts for advice and consultation as to what punishment would bear some relation to the causes of the criminal act. The main modification that has to be made to Socrates' proposal is in his assumption that the causes of unjust behavior are to be found in the human soul; often all or some of these causes are to be found in social practices and circumstances — the *Republic* shows that Plato appreciated this point much more than Socrates did. Needless to say, any solutions to the problems of punishment along the lines Socrates proposes would have to pay strict adherence to due process of law, to the rights of individuals as citizens and as human beings — for one can easily imagine abuses of rights in the name of 'curing' the patient. But there is not an *a priori* reason to suppose that adequate safeguards could not be devised; similar safeguards in the practice of medicine could provide the model, though additional safeguards may be necessary because of important differences.

So far we have considered the Socratic analogies between the arts of gymnastic and medicine on the one hand and legislation and justice on the other. It remains to consider a related analogy, that between health in the body and justice (and virtue) in the soul. The latter analogy is the basis for the arts analogy. In the *Gorgias* 463E—466A the arts analogy begins with a statement of the parallel between the good bodily condition and the good soul condition, and the four arts are defined in terms of aiming at engendering these good bodily and soul states. It is therefore important to consider how Socrates conceived the parallel between the good bodily condition (health) and the good soul conditions (justice and virtue).

Now the best statement of the parallel between health and justice occurs in *Republic* 444BE — there the analogy is stated systematically and Socrates uses it as an argument to convince Glaucon that justice brings happiness and injustice misery. Though the *Republic* is of course not a Socratic Dialogue, the analogy is Socratic; as Burnet has pointed out,[30] the argument is essentially the same as those in the *Crito* 47 and the *Gorgias* 512. The main difference between these passages and the *Republic* is that in the latter the analogy is drawn explicitly between health and justice as given by what Vlastos calls the psychological definition, not between health and justice as given by the social definition. The distinction between psychological and social justice does not occur in the *Gorgias* and the *Crito*, but of course Socrates does distinguish between justice in the soul and just behavior.

The analogy and the argument based on it may be stated as follows:

(I) *Elements in the analogy* (*Rep.* 444BE)

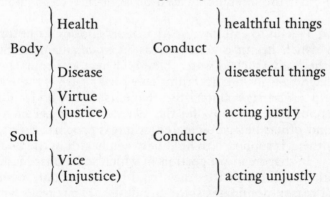

Body		Conduct	
}	Health	}	healthful things
}	Disease	}	diseaseful things

Soul		Conduct	
}	Virtue (justice)	}	acting justly
}	Vice (Injustice)	}	acting unjustly

(II) *The analogy*

1 As healthful and diseaseful things are in the body, so just and unjust actions are in the soul; i.e.,

2 as healthful things engender health and diseaseful things engender disease, so acting justly engenders justice and acting unjustly engenders injustice; and

3 to engender health is to establish the elements in the body

in a relation of dominating and being dominated in accordance with nature; disease contrary to nature; and to engender justice is to establish the elements of the soul in relation of dominating and being dominated according to nature, injustice contrary to nature.

(III)   *The use of the analogy to show that justice brings happiness, and injustice unhappiness*

4   Hence, virtue is a sort of health and beauty and good condition of soul, vice a disease and ugliness and weakness.
5   Hence, as doing healthful things is profitable, and diseaseful things, unprofitable (more so, if one escapes treatment), so acting justly is profitable, and acting unjustly unprofitable (more so if one escapes punishment).
6   If one's life is not worth living when one's body is ruined, even if one has all the food and drink and wealth and power in the world, then (so) life is not worth living when one's soul is similarly ruined and disordered, even if one can do whatever he pleases except what can restore his soul.

Let us not analyze the main parallel between justice and health, as stated in propositions 1, 2 and 3, to see how far the analogy holds and whether the inferences based on it, namely, 4, 5 and 6, are sound.

Proposition 3 seems to employ not Alcmaeon's notion of health, according to which health is conceived as an *equality* among the elements of the body (such as water, blood, or heat and cold), but rather a Pythagorean notion, according to which health is thought to consist in a *proportion* among the elements of the body. For equality does not seem to allow for the relation of some elements dominating and others being dominated, whereas proportion does. The parallel, then, is supposed to hold between health in the body conceived as a Pythagorean proportion in which some unspecified elements in the body dominate others, and justice, a state of the soul in which reason dominates spirit and desire. The reasons why Plato thinks that this 'proportion' in the soul is 'according to nature' we need not enter into in great detail. The main idea appears to be that reason is the only instrument or the best instrument (among the elements of the soul) for guiding or piloting a person's life, because reason is the only instrument or the best instrument for determining what actions and activities are good or bad for the person as a whole. This idea also is basically Socratic. For, though Socrates does not distinguish explicitly among all the elements of the soul, as Plato does in the *Republic*, he distinguishes reasoning from desiring, and in both the *Gorgias* and the *Crito* he makes it clear, as we have seen, that it is by reasoning and argument that we should decide what we ought to do, not by following our desires.

Does the analogy between health and justice hold, as specified in propositions 1, 2 and 3? When we are asking this question we are asking whether any similarities between the two concepts are such that noting them will enhance our understanding of the concept of justice in its various applications and uses; and whether, at the same time, the differences between the two concepts are not strong enough to make health a misleading model for the concept of justice.

We may note, first off, that the analogy between justice and health, as stated in 3, is remarkable. For we think of health as primarily a biological and medical concept that applies to organisms not in virtue of their relation to each other but in virtue of such things as the physiological structure, condition, and function of each organism and its organs; whereas, as Aristotle makes it clear (*Nicomachean Ethics*, Bk V), we think of justice as a social and legal concept that applies to persons or citizens by virtue of their relations and conduct toward each other. To be sure, the analogy in the *Republic* is drawn between justice as a state of the soul (justice as specified by the psychological definition) and health, not between justice as specified by the social definition and health. But of course, as Vlastos again has pointed out, there must be some essential connection between the two definitions: a man whose state of soul satisfies the psychological definition must be such that his behavior satisfies the social definition, and possibly the reverse. Were this not so, we would have two unrelated notions of justice; and, further, the analogy specified by 1, 2, and 3 would be useless in trying to show that acting justly brings happiness and acting unjustly misery. In the *Gorgias* we do not have two distinct definitions of justice; indeed, we have no definitions of justice at all. But the distinction between justice in the soul and just acts is presupposed, and an essential connection between the two is affirmed. Thus at 460BC Socrates affirms that the just man will do what is just and of necessity will desire what is just. Socrates is not here affirming a tautology — by the just man he does not mean merely a man who does what is just; in the context, he means that a man whose soul is in a certain condition, namely has knowledge of what is just and what is beneficial, will do and desire what is just. Further, in 504D, in a context where the virtue-health analogy is again discussed, Socrates says that 'the regular and orderly states of the soul are called lawfulness and law, whereby men are similarly (to the case orderliness in the body and health) made law-abiding and orderly; and these are justice and temperance.' Clearly, then, in both the *Republic* and the *Gorgias*, justice in the soul is distinguished from just conduct, and it is held that justice in the soul of necessity leads to just conduct. Therefore, equally clearly, even though the analogy we are examining is drawn between health and justice as a state of soul, any dis-analogies between health and *social* justice will be relevant to this analogy, because of the connection between justice in the soul and social justice (the justice of conduct toward others).

In addition to the connection we just discussed between justice in the soul and social justice (a man whose soul is just will be just in his conduct toward others), the analogy states another connection yet, namely the one specified by proposition 2:

2   Healthful things engender health and diseaseful things
    disease, and acting justly engenders justice, and acting un-
    justly injustice.

This proposition, taken in conjunction with 1, states not merely a parallel, but a proportion: as healthful things are to health and diseaseful to disease in the body, so just actions are to justice and unjust to injustice in the soul. Proposition 2 is an amplification of 1 and states the relation that is identical in the two parts of the proposition, namely engendering. Once more, because of this connection between acting justly and justice in the soul, dis-analogies between social justice and health will be relevant to the analogy between justice in the soul and health.

Are there any dis-analogies, then, between social justice and health, which either make health a misleading model for justice or seriously affect the argument (inferences 4, 5 and 6) that Socrates bases on this analogy, the argument designed to convince us that acting justly makes us happy and acting unjustly, unhappy?

There seem in fact to be fundamental dis-analogies between the relations that hold among justice in the soul and just acts, on the one hand, and the relations that hold among health in the body and healthful things, on the other.

The two relations we have found asserted between justice in the soul and just acts are:

J_1 Justice in the soul in person A of necessity leads to just acts
      by person A

and

J_2 Just acts by person A engender justice in the soul of person A, and unjust injustice.

The two analogous propositions in the case of health and healthful things are:

H_1 Health in the body of person A of necessity leads to healthful things by person A

and

H_2 Healthful things by person A engender health in the body of person A, and diseaseful disease.

Socrates seems to take J_1 for granted in the *Gorgias*; in the *Republic* Plato gives an argument for J_1, an argument recently analyzed by Vlastos.[31] Whatever the merits of this argument, the analogous proposition for health, H_1, does not seem to hold even generally or for the most part, leaving aside universality or necessity. A man who is in perfectly good bodily health may, for example, begin to smoke, go on an inadequate diet, or stop exercising, all of which are not healthful things but rather are diseaseful. In such a case, we would not say that the man is no longer healthy, but rather than he is endangering his health. Whereas, of a man who begins to do unjust acts, we would say that he is no longer just, unless he did unjust acts in ignorance or under compulsion. The analogy, therefore, between J_1 and H_1 does not hold, either in the form 'as H_1 so J_1,' or in the form 'as J_1 so H_1.' Even if we were to find that in most or all cases people in bodily health do not begin to do diseaseful things (which I clearly think is not true), we would not say that their bodily health was the cause of their refraining from diseaseful things; rather we would say that the cause was their desires and fears and beliefs about health and disease. One might reply that the case is similar for justice. It is not justice in the soul that causes men to do just things, but their desires and fears and beliefs about justice and injustice and their benefits. But, if I'm not mistaken, this reply is of no avail, because for Plato these desires and beliefs are part of the state of justice in the soul, whereas, clearly, beliefs and desires and fears about bodily health and disease are not parts of bodily health.

But the analogy between H_2 and J_2 also seems to fail, and this is the analogy explicitly drawn, and it is the analogy used to support crucial inferences 4, 5, and 6. Let us ask, first, in what sense H_2 seems to be true. By healthful and diseaseful things such things are probably meant as physical exercise and training, intake of foods and drugs, and medical procedures such as surgery. It

299

would seem to be a necessary and sufficient condition of a thing being healthful that it engenders or causes the development or maintenance of health in an organism, where health is judged by the structure of such things as bones and joints, physiological conditions such as temperature, and well functioning of the whole organism and its organs. For example, if a given exercise by person A results in strengthening of muscles or joints or in better functioning of limbs or organs, it would be judged healthful to A; if it results in weakening of muscles or joints or in malfunctioning of such organs as heart or liver, it would be judged diseaseful. And similarly with intakes of food or drugs or surgical procedures. The judgment that an activity or intake or treatment by or to person A is healthful for A seems to depend entirely on the effects of such activity or intake or treatment on A's body. But J_2 does not seem true in a similar sense. It does not seem to be the case that it is a necessary and sufficient condition of an act by A being just that the act causes A's soul to become just or to continue to be just, whether or not justice in the soul be defined in a Platonic way (*Republic* IV) or conceived in a Socratic way (*Gorgias, Crito*). Here it would seem that the effects that A's action has on other persons would *have* to be considered before the action can be pronounced just. This seems to hold even within Socratic ethics. It would seem, for example, that both in the *Crito* and the *Gorgias* Socrates believes that an action is just in so far as it is lawful, at any rate when the laws in question are those of democratic Athens. And he certainly holds, both in the *Crito* and in *Republic* I, that an action by A cannot be just if it harms another person. Whether or not harm to another person is construed in the narrow Socratic sense, in which it is confined to making another person unjust or less just, this is a very different necessary condition for an act being just from conditions that relate solely to the effects of the action *on the agent's* soul. And so is the condition of an act being lawful. At best, one would need an additional argument or evidence to show that the condition of an action being lawful and/or not harming another person coincide with the condition of causing or maintaining justice in the agent's soul. Proposition H_2 by itself would not support J_2. No such argument exists in the Socratic Dialogues, and Socrates does not even seem to see the need for one.

In sum, J_2 does not seem to be true in the sense in which H_2 is true; it is a necessary and sufficient condition of an activity by A or treatment for A being healthful that the activity or treatment produce or maintain health in A's body; but it is not the case that it is a necessary and sufficient condition for an act by A being just that the act produce or maintain justice in A's soul. Hence the inference 'As H_2 holds so J_2 holds' seems unsound.

It should be noted that there is a sense in which J_2 is true; but it is a sense that is not helpful to Socrates' argument, though it might have misled Plato or Socrates into the parallel with H_2. As Aristotle has noted (*Nicomachean Ethics*, II, i), we acquire the virtues by first actually practicing them, as we acquire the arts: we become virtuous by doing virtuous deeds, 'we become just [men] by doing just acts' (1103b 1—2). Isn't it true then, as Socrates has argued, that just acts engender justice in the soul, as healthful acts engender health in the body? Contrary to appearances, however, this is of no help to Socrates' argument. In Aristotle, justice in a man is defined, in turn, by reference to just acts, and there is no vicious circle because just acts are defined independently of justice in the soul: 'everybody means by justice that disposition by which men become just in practice and which causes men to do and wish to do what is just' (Bk V 1129a 3—6). Thus, the proposition 'we become just by doing just things' is analyzed into 'we acquire the disposition to do just things by doing just things.' Hence, within Aristotle's view, if one were to argue that the disposition to act justly is beneficial to the agent, one would have to argue it on the ground that acting justly is beneficial to the agent. But within the Socratic health–justice analogy, the inference is made the other way around: it is argued that just acts are beneficial to the agent on the ground that they produce justice in the soul of the agent, and *that* (justice in the soul) is beneficial to the agent, as health in the body is. And such an argument requires a definition of justice in the soul that is independent of reference to just acts, as health is defined independently of healthful acts.

If we next examine the inferences that Socrates draws on the basis of the health–virtue analogy, that is, conclusions 4, 5, and 6, we can see that these inferences are at best problematic even if we pass over all the problems we have discussed about proposition 2. Let us look at inferences 4 and 5, as inferences from 2 and 3. 4 can only be an inference from 3, and 5 from 2, 3, and 4. An implicit premise in the whole argument is clearly the proposition that health in the body is a good to the man who has health; this proposition is no doubt taken for granted, quite rightly. It is from this implicit premise, in conjunction with 3, that inference 4 is drawn. The argument from 3 to 4, thus reconstructed is:

3a   Health in the body is . . . . (3)
3b   Health is a good (to the person who has it).
3c   Justice in the soul is a similar condition to health in the body . . . . (3)

4   Hence, justice in the soul is a good to the man who has it.

Then from 4 and 2 inference 5 is drawn: since healthful things produce health in the body and health is a good to the man who has it, healthful things are a good to the man who does them; similarly, since just acts produce justice in the soul, and justice is a good to the man who has it, just acts are a good to the man who does them. Clearly, then, inference 4 is crucial to the whole argument.

Is inference to 4, from 3a, 3b, and 3c, sound? First of all, the definition of health given by 3a is dubious; it is dubious because it seems to be a definition in purely structural terms, and vague ones at that, without any reference to functioning of the body, its limbs, and its organs. Such a definition seems faulty, apart from its vagueness: for it is likely that a man whose body as a whole, whose limbs, and whose bodily organs, are functioning well would be judged healthy no matter what the structure of his bodily elements is. In the case of judging bodily health, it would seem that well functioning would, at any rate, take priority over structure. Even if we forgo this fault, the inference to 4 seems dubious because it seems to be supported too weakly by 3c: granted that y is a good, can we safely infer that x is a good on the ground that x is structurally similar to y, even though x and y are as widely different as body and soul? Even in the case of two things of the same kind the inference would be risky: if we found that a body of a certain structure is in a good condition, we could not infer safely that another similar body of the same structure is in a good condition; we would need the additional premise that it is the structure of the first body that is responsible for its good condition. In the case of entirely different sorts of things, such as bodies and souls, the inference is very weak, to say the least. If, for example, we found that a certain proportion in the elements of a painting account for its goodness or beauty, it would be a very risky inference that the same proportion of the somehow corresponding elements in a symphony would render the symphony good or beautiful. It looks as if Socrates' inference to 4, from 3, relies on some very strong, hidden, principle, something like 'goodness is purely a matter of form or structure.' Even if we grant such a principle, its application is faulty because the elements in the body are not specified, and we are not told how 'corresponding' elements are to be determined.

In sum, the analogy of justice to health seems to fail because of the dis-analogies we have found in proposition 2, and the argument based on the analogy — one of the chief arguments to the conclusion that justice benefits the agent and makes him happy — fails because inference 4 fails.

Is the Socratic analogy of virtue and justice to health, then, totally useless and totally unenlightening? I think not. In the discussion of punishment, where just punishment is likened to correct medical treatment, we saw that this part of the analogy is enlightening and provides a more rational model of punishment than other models of punishment that ignore entirely the causes in the soul of unjust conduct. The total analogy is limited by the fact that justice is a social and legal concept, whereas health is a biological and medical concept. Nevertheless, the analogy is useful in correcting partial conceptions of justice and law. For, as the punishment part of the analogy shows us, the concepts of justice and law must be enlightened not only by sociology and economics, and not only by the concept of the rights of citizens, but also by psychology and ethics, by the concepts of mental health and the emotional well-being of individuals.

Appendix

Copi's rules of inference

1 *Modus ponens* (MP)
$$p \supset q$$
$$p$$
$$\therefore q$$

2 *Modus tollens* (MT)
$$p \supset q$$
$$\sim q$$
$$\therefore \sim q$$

3 *Hypothetical syllogism* (HS)
$$p \supset q$$
$$q \supset r$$
$$\therefore p \supset r$$

4 *Disjunctive syllogism* (DS)
$$p \vee q$$
$$\sim p$$
$$\therefore q$$

5 *Constructive dilemma* (CD)
$$(p \supset q) \cdot (r \supset s)$$
$$p \vee r$$
$$\therefore q \vee s$$

6 *Absorption* (abs.)
$$p \supset q$$
$$\therefore p \supset (p \cdot q)$$

7 *Simplification* (simp.)
$$p \cdot r$$
$$\therefore p$$

8 *Conjunction* (conj.)
$$p$$
$$q$$
$$\therefore p \cdot q$$

9 *Addition* (add.)
$$p$$
$$\therefore p \vee q$$

Replacement

Any of the following logically equivalent expressions can replace each other wherever they occur:

10 De Morgan's theorems $\sim(p \cdot q) \equiv (\sim p \vee \sim q)$
    (De M.): $\sim(p \vee q) \equiv (\sim p \cdot \sim q)$

11 Commutation (com.): $(p \lor q) \equiv (q \lor p)$
$(p \cdot q) \equiv (q \cdot p)$

12 Association (assoc.): $[p \lor (q \lor r)] \equiv [(p \lor q) \lor r]$
$[p \cdot (q \cdot r)] \equiv [(p \cdot q) \cdot r]$

13 Distribution (dist.): $[p \cdot (q \lor r)] \equiv [(p \cdot q) \lor (p \cdot r)]$
$[p \lor (q \cdot r)] \equiv [(p \lor q) \cdot (p \lor r)]$

14 Double negation (DN): $p \equiv \sim \sim p$

15 Transposition (trans.): $(p \supset q) \equiv (\sim q \supset \sim p)$

16 Material implication
(impl.): $(p \supset q) \equiv (\sim p \lor q)$

17 Material equivalence $(p \equiv q) \equiv [(p \supset q) \cdot (q \supset p)]$
(equiv.): $(p \equiv q) \equiv [(p \cdot q) \lor (\sim p \cdot \sim q)]$

18 Exportation (exp.): $[(p \cdot q) \supset r] \equiv (p \supset (q \supset r))$

19 Tautology (taut.): $p \equiv (p \lor p)$
$p \equiv (p \cdot p)$

Copi's quantification rules

UI: $\dfrac{(x)\phi x}{\therefore \phi v}$ (where v is any individual symbol)

UG: $\dfrac{\phi y}{\therefore (x)\phi x}$ (where y denotes 'any arbitrarily selected individual')

EI: $\dfrac{(\exists x)\phi x}{\therefore \phi v}$ (where v is any individual constant (other than y) having no previous occurrence in the context)

EG: $\dfrac{\phi v}{\therefore (\exists x)\phi x}$ (where v is any individual symbol)

     UI = Universal Instantiation
     UG = Universal Generalization
     EI = Existential Instantiation
     EG = Existential Generalization

Notes

I INTRODUCTION TO PLATO'S SOCRATES

1 See Kenneth Dover's contention that Aristophanes was caricaturing a type, in 'Socrates in the Clouds' (Dover, 1971).

2 For some recent judicious comparisons of Plato's and Xenophon's Socrates, see T. Irwin's review (Irwin, 1974, pp. 409–13).

3 Vlastos (1956, p. xxiv).

4 Russell (1945, p. 89).

II SOCRATES AND THE LAWS OF ATHENS

1 See also Burnet (1924), p. 201.

2 See *ibid*., pp. 203–4.

3 This coheres well with his position in the *Crito* if we suppose that under the government of Thirty there was no agreement from the citizens to obey the law, nor were their laws designed to benefit the citizens through marriage, nurture, and education. If so, the reasons Socrates gave that one must obey the laws would not hold true of the laws of the government of the Thirty. And these reasons might hold true only of democratic constitutions.

4 In the *Crito* 51B, as we saw, Socrates says that one's country (and possibly its laws and courts under a democratic regime) is more to be revered and is holier and is held in higher esteem than one's parents in the eyes of gods and men of understanding. Thus, it is not far-fetched to suppose that Socrates held that the court is better than he.

5 There is difficulty in the argument as it stands: principle A3 says that it is bad and disgraceful *to do injustice to and disobey the better* . . . . But nowhere in the passage does Socrates say that ceasing to philosophize would be doing injustice to god, nor can we tell whether this can be plausibly attributed to him; and yet this is what we would need to supply for the argument to be valid if the principle is left to read as we have it now. A solution would be to take the *kai* that joins the two underlined

phrases to mean *or* rather than *and*; this is possible, but it is difficult to say beyond that. Another solution is to take A3 to read, 'It is bad and disgraceful to do injustice and it is bad and disgraceful to disobey the better . . . .' This is also possible, but again difficult to say beyond that.

6 Grote (1888, vol. I) and Woozley (1971). Grote maintained that the contradiction was real and deliberate on the part of Plato, who was trying to repair Socrates' image in the *Crito* by presenting him as an all-out defender of the laws. This interpretation we need not take very seriously, both for the reasons Woozley gives, and for others. A fairly conclusive reason is the fact that Plato has Socrates say several times in the *Crito* (46B—48B) that he is not going to give up the principles and arguments he used before but he is going to make his decision by the same principles and arguments he used all his life.

7 Woozley (1971, pp. 300—1).

8 *Ibid.*, pp. 302—3.

9 I find Woozley's solution contradictory and also textually inaccurate. The main elements of his solution are as follows. On p. 306, Woozley notes that in *Crito* 51C Socrates agrees to the view put forward by the laws that 'a man must either do whatever his city orders him to do or must persuade her where the rightness of the matter lies.' He then begins his solution as follows. 'Nevertheless, the permitted alternative to obedience, viz., persuading the laws that their order is wrong suggests a solution to the difficulty.' He then points correctly to certain differences between disobeying by escaping in the *Crito* and his disobedience in the hypothetical case of the *Apology* (the former is secretive and harmful, the latter is not), and continues (Woozley, 1971, pp. 307—8):

> But this permitted exception to the rule of obedience is precisely what he had proposed to follow in the *Apology*. There, while insisting that he must obey God rather than the court, he made it clear that obedience to God not merely coincided with trying to convince Athens he was right, it actually consisted in that . . . . [Here Woozley quotes 29D] This is civil disobedience indeed, but of the kind that stays and attempts to change minds by reason . . . . The one course other than obedience to the law and its commands which Socrates' argument in the *Crito* (51—52) permits is the one course which he had said in the *Apology* (29—30) he would, if banned from philosophy, take. Once we see that it is not the doctrine of the *Crito* that a man must always, and no matter what, obey the laws of his state, the supposed conflict between that dialogue and the *Apology* disappears.

To begin with, it is difficult to see how Woozley can say *both* that what Socrates proposes to do in the hypothetical case of the *Apology* is 'the permitted alternative to obedience' or 'the permitted exception to the rule of obedience' *and also* that it is disobedience, civil or otherwise. Surely if what Socrates is doing, or rather proposing to do, is a *permitted* alternative or exception, then it is not disobedience? Perhaps Woozley means 'permitted by Socrates' argument in the *Crito*' and not also 'permitted by the laws.' This is not very accurate, since Socrates has the laws speak and say that they do not order a man roughly to do what they command but rather allow him a choice of two things, convince the city where the right lies or do what the laws command (−1E, 52A); but it allows a way out of the apparent inconsistency in Woozley's solution.

Aside and independently of all this, however, it is completely false that what Socrates proposes to do in the hypothetical case of the *Apology* is to take the permitted alternative of persuading the laws where the right lies. Consider: The hypothesis in the *Apology* 29CD is:

(1)   The court acquits Socrates and orders him to cease philosophizing, with the penalty of death for disobedience of that order.

And Socrates says:

(2)   I shall obey god rather than you [the court].

And further, Socrates clearly takes the order of god to conflict with the order of the court, so that (2) clearly implies:

(3)   I shall obey god and disobey you [the court].

Further, the two alternatives in the *Crito* are:

(4)   One must (a) persuade the laws (including the courts) where justice lies or (b) obey the laws (or the orders of the courts).

Is Socrates then, in declaring what he will do in (3), satisfying what is required by (4)? He clearly would not be satisfying (4)(b); and we note that in the *Crito* the laws say that if he were to escape he would be satisfying neither (4)(a) nor (4)(b). In doing what he proposed to do then in the hypothetical case of the *Apology*, would he be satisfying (4)(a)? It is true that right after he declares (2) Socrates proceeds to say that he will continue philosophizing in his accustomed way and will be trying to convince his fellow citizens that this philosophizing is the most important thing they can do, for it is caring for their souls and for truth and wisdom, rather than for wealth and reputation and honor. This is apparently what Woozley construes as Socrates taking alternative (4)(a). In declaring that he would continue to philosophize in the face of their order Socrates is surely not satisfying (4)(b). But perhaps he could be construed as satisfying alternative (4)(a). Is not then Woozley correct? I think not. For Socrates never makes his disobeying the court contingent on his success or failure in persuading the court their order is wrong. It is axiomatic that one may succeed or fail in attempting to persuade someone of something; and also that one has persuaded or convinced someone of something only if he has attempted to persuade or convince him and has succeeded. Now clearly, in (4) 'persuade' must be taken in the sense of 'succeed in persuading' not in the sense of 'attempt to persuade'; if we take the latter sense, (4) would become almost a trivial requirement since anyone could get out of having to obey any law or order simply by attempting to persuade. In order to satisfy (4), then, one who is faced with an order or law requiring or forbidding him to do something must either succeed in persuading the appropriate authority that the law (or order) is wrong, or obey; clearly, if one attempts to persuade but fails then, to satisfy (4), one must obey. It is perfectly clear that what Socrates describes can be at best characterized as attempting to persuade; there is nothing about succeeding, and, if anything, Socrates does not expect to succeed. More importantly, there is absolutely nothing in the text to the effect that Socrates will obey if he fails to persuade. On the contrary, his declaration that he will not obey the court order is completely unconditional. If he were taking himself to be acting within the requirements of (4) by attempting to satisfy (4)(a), he should not have declared that he would obey god rather than the court order: for if he were taking himself to be acting within the requirements of (4) and trying to satisfy (4)(a), he would not be disobeying whether he succeeded or failed; if he failed in attempting to persuade, he would have to obey; if he succeeded he *need* not obey, rather than disobey, and further he would have no need to appeal to god.

10 Rawls (1972, p. 341).

11 They are characteristics that mark the actions of some of the great civil disobedients such as Antigone, Thoreau, Gandhi, and Martin Luther King; for the last three the reader may consult the relevant essays in Bedau (1969).

III SOCRATIC QUESTIONS AND ASSUMPTIONS

1 The reader should consult Burnet (1924; 1961, chapter IX), Zeller (1962), Vlastos (1956), Taylor (1937).

2 Cf. Belnap (1963).

3 Robinson (1953, pp. 8, 9).

4 See also Vlastos (1971, pp. 7—8, 10).

5 *Ibid.*, p. 10.

6 Burnet (1961, p. 132).

7 Belnap (1963, p. 13).

8 It should also be noted that in this analysis of the presented alternatives of a question Belnap is taking as his model the multiple-choice examination question, not the true–false examination question. A question is not conceived as presenting a single proposition to which a respondent can assent or dissent (affirm or deny), but as presenting two or more propositions from which the respondent is invited to select and construct an answer. Belnap gives convincing reasons why this is a more fruitful approach (Belnap, 1963, p. 15).

9 E.g. Robinson (1953, chapter V).

10 Aristotle, *De Interpretatione*, 20B20—30; Prior (1955, pp. 44—5).

11 Belnap (1963, pp. 37—8).

12 *Ibid.*, p. 40.

13 *Ibid.*, p. 42.

14 Robinson (1953, p. 49).

15 In *Euthyphro* 7A Socrates praises Euthyphro for having answered as Socrates wanted him to answer, but remarks that it remains to be seen whether the answer is true. Cf. also Belnap's useful notion of 'direct answer' (1963, pp. 18—20).

16 Belnap (1963, 1969).

17 Leonard (1967, part 1, unit 4).

18 Belnap (1963, p. 127); for the fundamental notion of 'direct answer' see Belnap (1963, pp. 18—21).

19 It must not be supposed that SP2 is contradicted by what Socrates allows in *Phaedo* 105C; that a collection may be odd-numbered because it has three members and another odd-numbered because it has five members; for here neither reason is that by virtue of which *all* odd numbered collections are odd numbered.

20 See for example Smyth (1966, p. 46, 199C): 'Feminine are most abstract words, that is, words denoting a quality or condition.'

IV SOCRATIC DEFINITIONS

1 Aristotle, *Metaphysics*, 1078b18–30.

2 The main answers in the *Lysis* about friendship are not included in this list since it is not entirely clear that they are given as definitions. With respect to the form of Socratic primary questions and the typical form of Socratic definitions, the *Lysis* does not seem to conform to the other Socratic dialogues. Whether this would justify modifying the results of this chapter will have to wait till there is a detailed study of this fascinating little dialogue. For a related discussion of the *Lysis* see also chapter V, where a beginning in such a detailed study is made.

3 Smyth (1966) introduces the notion of 'abstract word' in what appears to be a semantic fashion, that is, by what the words denote: 'Feminine are most abstract words, that is, words denoting a quality or condition' (p. 46, 199C).

4 Pap (1964). I follow Pap's formal classification of definitions. Under general definition he includes explicit, contextual, recursive, and axiomatic definitions; under contextual he includes operational and non-operational; and under explicit he includes disjunctive (enumeration of species), definition by genus and difference, and by simple synonym, and quantitive definition. The reader should consult this useful paper for the criteria of this classification and for examples.

5 Nakhnikian (1971, p. 138).

6 The way to introduce this new category, which is not included in Pap's classification, is to introduce conjunctive definitions as a coordinate class with the classes of disjunctive definitions, definitions by simple synonym, and quantitive definitions. Conjunctive definitions are then divided into two groups: definitions by genus and difference and definitions by conjunctive enumeration.

7 For the concept of nominal definition the reader should consult Ajdukiewicz (1958). Pap (1964), following Copi, used the related concept of lexical definition.

8 This has been pointed out by A. Wedberg in his excellent paper, 'The Theory of Ideas' (Wedberg, 1970, pp. 38–43). It has also been pointed out by P. Geach in 'The Third Man Again,' (Geach, 1956).

9 *Meno*, 72C.

10 *Laches*, 191E, 192AB.

11 *Protagoras*, 358D.

12 *Hippias Major*, 287C–D.

13 We use 'the F' and 'F-ness' as variables whose substituends are the expressions in the last section: singular feminine abstract nouns and singular

neuter adjectives preceded by the definite article, all substantive, in ancient Greek; and their syntactic and semantic equivalents in any other language. For what we mean by 'attribute' and the distinction between 'attribute' and 'class', the reader is referred to Wedberg's brief discussion (1970, pp. 38–41).

14 Nakhnikian (1971), p. 131.
15 *Ibid.* (Nakhnikian's italics.)
16 Vlastos (1973a and 1973b).
17 Sharvy (1972, p. 134).
18 *Ibid.*, pp. 127–8.
19 Cohen (1971).
20 *Ibid.*, p. 160.
21 Vlastos (1970).
22 This is perhaps the case with definitions that are essentially introduced for abbreviation purposes.
23 Robinson (1953, p. 53); Geach (1966).
24 For a recent discussion of αἰτία in Plato, see Vlastos (1970).
25 For these reasons see Hintikka (1967; 1973) and Santas (1973).
26 In 'The Socratic Fallacy' (Santas, 1972) I argued against Geach's view (1966) that Socrates assumes that (1) knowledge of the definition of, say, courage is a necessary condition for knowing that a given action is courageous. I am now allowing that Socrates possibly held (1). At the time I wrote 'The Socratic Fallacy' I did not distinguish sharply enough between (1) and quite a different proposition, namely that (2) knowledge of the definition of, say, courage, is a necessary condition for judging or believing that a given act is courageous. Socrates certainly does not hold (2). But the evidence from the *Hippias Major* and the *Lysis*, though not in the least conclusive — for (1) is neither stated nor clearly implied — suggests that Socrates possibly held (1). And the study of the uses of definition in this chapter certainly makes it plausible that Socrates held (1). But though he may sometimes have taken (1) for granted, I doubt that he ever had it in clear sight or that he reflected on it. For one thing, it is not clear that Socrates holds that we can have knowledge that any physical object or event is of a given character. Aside from this, making assumption (1) would lead to some of the difficulties of holding assumption (2), p. 116 above. A specific difficulty can be illustrated as follows. Suppose Socrates claimed to know that a certain action, a, was courageous; challenged to defend his claim, he produces a definition of courage, say, Courage = df. KE (where 'K' and 'E' are names of properties or kinds), and argues as follows. Courage = df. KE; a is an instance of KE; therefore a is an instance of courage. Now if he holds (1), without challenging his claim to know the definition of courage, we can point out that he cannot know that a is an instance of KE unless he also knows the definition of KE. If he produces a definition of KE and argues similarly, our question will arise over again, and so on. Clearly, we shall have an infinite regress, or circular definitions, and assumption (1) will have to be given up. Of course, this and similar difficulties do not show that Socrates did not hold (1). But these difficulties are reason enough

311

for us to be cautious about burdening Socrates with (1) unless we have clear evidence that he held it.

27 Robinson (1953, p. 53), and Ross (1951, p. 16).

28 For recent discussion of some of these difficulties, see Nakhnikian (1971, pp. 147—54); Geach (1966) and Santas (1972).

29 One interpretation of the definition Socrates puts in Meno's mouth is: Virtue = df. the ability to produce goods justly *or* piously *or* temperately *or* wisely *or* courageously. Socrates correctly criticizes this definition as implying that justice, e.g., is the whole and not part of virtue, since the definition implies that if one acquires goods justly he acquires them virtuously, even though impiously, intemperately, etc. I am not concerned here with *this* criticism.

30 The phrase 'does not know —' in this argument is ambiguous of course: it may mean 'does not know the definition of —' 'does not know or is not able to give examples of —' or possibly something else. But these ambiguities do not affect the point I am making.

31 It is not at all clear that the definition is circular. If it is, why are not definitions 39 and 40 also circular? Aren't the pleasant and the beneficial non-exclusive parts of the fair, just as the various virtues are non-exclusive parts of virtue? Again, isn't the generality that seems to be implied by premise 1, namely that one who does not know a whole cannot know a part of that whole, too strong? Wouldn't it exclude all definitions by analysis? These questions and these unclarities, present as they may be, again do not affect the points I am making, though they would very much affect a complete analysis of the argument.

V SOCRATIC ARGUMENTS

1 Copi (1972). See the appendix for a list of Copi's nineteen rules of inference and four quantification rules.

2 For a recent useful discussion of inductive arguments see Barker (1974, ch. 6).

3 In evaluating inductive arguments we use the notion of strength, rather than the notions of soundness and validity which are appropriate for deductive arguments. The strength of an inductive argument depends on several factors, such as the number of instances from which the conclusion is drawn, the similarities and dissimilarities among these instances, the known similarities between these instances and the instance in the conclusion, the known relations, if any, among the properties S and P. For an elementary discussion the reader can consult Copi (1972, chs 11 and 12) and Barker (1974, ch. 6).

4 This issue is an instance of the so-called 'voluntary incompetence issue': whether those who are able to practice voluntary incompetence in a given science-craft are the same as those who are competent in that science-craft. See Young (1974, pp. 175—83).

5 See, for example, Barker (1974, ch. 6).

6 We give P4 through C3 only because it makes clear what Socrates takes 'just man' to imply.

7   In Greek the root for the word here translated 'love' is the same as the root of the word which is translated 'friend': φιλεῖν, φίλος.

8   Vlastos (1973b, p. 7).

9   On the usual interpretation of 'because' C1R would not imply C2.1R; however, since the hypothesis is probably offered as a definition, we can plausibly take the 'because' in C1R to mean 'because and only because.' This allows us to reconstruct the argument in a way that is extremely faithful to the text. C1R is simply the relativized version of C1, that is:

(x)(y)(x is a friend to y because x is a good F and y is a good F).

10 For the most recent interpretation of Socrates' theses and his arguments — though not the argument we are examining, which so far as I know has never been analyzed in detail — see Vlastos (1973c).

11 This argument and the agreement that emerge from it are analyzed below in chapter VII and also in Vlastos (1969, pp. 71—88).

12 Where UI = Universal Instantiation, equiv. = material equivalence, HS = hypothetical syllogism, simp. = simplification and UG = Universal Generalization (see appendix, pp. 304—5 above).

13 The negation of P5.1 is inconsistent with P1.2 and the assumption that 'x thinks y is fearful' implies 'x thinks y is evil.' Further, 'x thinks y is fearful' is taken in the sense of 'x thinks y is more fearful than the alternatives open to him.'

14 Apparently Socrates takes 'x thinks not y fearful' or 'x does not think y is fearful' to imply 'x thinks y is dared;' at least his inference from C2 to C2.1 requires that he do this.

15 Vlastos (1969).

16 For the statement 'war is pleasant' in an earlier writer see Pindar fr. 110 (76):

γλυκὺ δ' ἀπείρῳ πόλεμος πεπειραμένων δέ τις ταρβεῖ προσίοντα νιν
καρδίᾳ περισσῶς.
(War is pleasant (sweet) to the inexperienced, but someone who has experienced it greatly fears its approach in his heart.)

It is doubtful that it was a universal or even a very popular belief that going to war is more honorable and better and pleasanter than not going, especially during the Peloponnesian Wars (cf. e.g., Euripides, *Helen*, 1151ff; *Suppliants*, 481—85). The anti-war attitude in some of Euripides' plays, such as *Trojan Women, Hecuba, Andromache,* is well traced in McDonald (1975).

17 Vlastos (1973c, p. 244). By the statement we quoted at 332CD Socrates probably means that each opposite has exactly one opposite — that is, at least one and at most one. We have stated in P16 only that part of this principle that is needed in the argument. The stronger version justifies Vlastos's interpretation.

18 This notion of σοφία would contradict the results John Lyons has reached, that there is no significant difference between σοφία and ἐπιστήμη in Plato (Lyons, 1963, pp. 227—8).

19 As Professor Benson Mates has pointed out to me, one must be cautious in using the apparatus of symbolic logic to represent the structure of Socrates' arguments. As he points out, the use of the horseshoe for 'if . . . then . . .' sometimes changes the strength of the assertions, and quantification into oblique contexts following 'thinks that . . .' can give rise to paradoxes. I have tried to be cautious in these matters, though I am far from confident that I have avoided mistakes.

VI VIRTUE AND KNOWLEDGE I: THE SOCRATIC PARADOXES

1 Reprinted from the *Philosophical Review,* 1964, with minor revisions.
2 *Meno* 77B–78B, *Prot.* 358C, *Gorg.* 468C5–7. Numbers and letters refer to the Stephanus pages and page sections, except for the numbers that follow the letters, which refer to the lines in the edition of John Burnet (1903–7). The translations are those of the Loeb Classical Library unless otherwise indicated.
3 *Gorg.* 460B–D, 509E5–7; *Prot.* 345C, 360D3; indirect statements of the doctrine occur in *Meno* 87, 98; *Laches* 198; *Charm.* 173.
4 Gomperz (1905, II, p. 67).
5 *Nic. Ethics* 1145B22–29; St Thomas Aquinas (1960 edn, p. 312); Jaeger (1943, II, pp. 64–5); Cornford (1932, p. 51).
6 To my knowledge, only A. E. Taylor denies that Socrates meant to contradict the fact of moral weakness; in *Socrates* (1932, p. 133).
7 Gomperz (1905, II, pp. 66–7).
8 Gould (1955, p. 6).
9 *Ibid.,* ch. i. Very briefly, Gould argues that the knowledge which Socrates thought sufficient for virtuous behavior is a form of 'knowing how,' a kind of moral ability comparable to the creative ability of the craftsmen. Professor Gregory Vlastos has shown, I believe, that this is not what Plato meant by 'knowledge' in crucial cases such as 'Courage is knowledge' (Vlastos, 1957, pp. 227–32). Some considerations to the same effect are also produced by Allen (1960).
10 *In Platonis Gorgiam Commentaria*, ed. W. Korvin (1936, p. 55).
11 Generally, the neuters *agathon* and *kakon* have a prudential sense, though the story is quite different with the masculine and feminine forms; see, e.g., Adkins (1960), pp. 30–1, 249–56. The neuter form is of course involved in every case of the prudential paradox. R. S. Bluck concurs that *kaka* is used in a prudential sense in the *Meno* 77–8 where the chief argument for the prudential paradox is given (Bluck, 1961, p. 257). But he claims that by a fallacious argument 'Plato is virtually making an assertion – that κακά must be harmful (in *some* way) to *all* concerned, *including the person who does the harm*' (Bluck's italics). In that argument, however, Plato neither assumes, nor does he need to, that *kaka* must be harmful to all concerned, but only that they are harmful to anyone who has (possesses, gets) them; moreover, that argument is not at all concerned with people who do harm, but only with people who, according to Meno, desire (to possess, get, have) *kaka*, knowing or not that they are *kaka*. In the *Meno* and the *Gorgias* it is fairly easy to distinguish

between versions of the moral and prudential paradoxes, but unfortunately the situation in the *Protagoras* is not so clear cut. At 345D8--9, for instance, we seem to have a version of the prudential paradox, but two lines later we get a restatement of it in which *kaka* is coupled with *aischra*, a term that often, and probably here also, has moral connotations. More important, it is not entirely clear which paradox is involved in the well-known and difficult argument at 352B—358D4, and this is reflected in Professor Vlastos's treatment where both prudential and moral cases are given as counter examples (Vlastos, 1956, pp. xlii, xliv). I think this argument makes far better sense if we suppose that it is concerned chiefly, if not entirely, with prudential situations; the language of the passage is heavily in favor of this, the only possible exception being 353C7 where *ponera* is used instead of *kaka*.

12 Cornford (1932, p. 51).

13 Unfortunately, Socrates' statement of the two hypotheses is faulty since they are exclusive but not exhaustive of the class of people who, according to Meno, desire bad things, unless we also suppose that the class of people who, according to Meno, desire bad things *thinking that they are good things* is the same as the class of people who desire bad things *not knowing that they are bad*. But it is not clear that Socrates could suppose this without begging the question.

14 Τί ἐπιθυμεῖν λέγεις; ἢ γενέσθαι αὐτῷ; Γενέσθαι· τί γὰρ ἄλλο. We have exactly the same answers to similar questions at *Symp.* 204D5--7 and 204E2—4. For what may perhaps be regarded as grounds for this doctrine, see *Lysis* 221D—222, *Symp.* 200A2.

15 This conclusion is not drawn in the text, but clearly it must be understood to follow from Meno's admissions so far, if his next admission — that no one wants to be miserable and ill-starred — is to be relevant to the argument. Unfortunately, it is doubtful that this conclusion really follows: the argument has the form 'If S desires X and knows that X brings about Y, then S desires Y'; it seems doubtful that an argument of this form is valid since people may have conflicting desires.

16 Up to this point in the argument Plato has used ἐπιθυμεῖν (to desire); now he introduces βούλεσθαι (to want, wish) and uses it for the rest of the argument. Scholars disagree as to whether the change is significant here, and generally whether in the Dialogues different concepts correspond to the two words; cf., e.g., Croiset and Bodin (1948, III, p. 245), Bluck (1961, p. 259) and Vlastos (1969). In point of fact, in addition to the definitions of βούλησις in *Definitions* 413C8--9, we have two pieces of explicit evidence that Plato has some important distinction between the two words: *Charmides* 167E1--6 clearly implies, it seems to me, that the object of every desire (ἐπιθυμία) is a pleasure, and the object of every wish (βούλησις) is a good, and of course Plato holds that some pleasures are bad for one; and in *Lysis* 221A7—B3 we are told that the satisfaction of desires sometimes will benefit one and other times will harm, and two lines later it is implied that there are such things as bad desires (κακαὶ ἐπιθυμίαι), whereas Plato never speaks, to my knowledge, of bad or harmful βούλησις. Using the terminology that I introduce

below (p. 187), the distinction suggested by these two passages, can be stated as follows: In no case can the *intended* object of a desire (ἐπιθυμια) be a bad thing, but the *actual* object can be, and often is, a bad thing; whereas in the case of wish (βούλησις), neither the intended nor the actual object of wish can ever be a bad thing. This distinction is consistent with Plato's uses in the present argument, where he uses βούλεσθαι to deny Meno's claim that there are people who desire bad things knowing that they are bad, and ἐπιθυμεῖν to deny the claim that there are people who desire what are in fact bad things not knowing that they are bad; his using ἐπιθυμεῖν in the latter case allows us to interpret the denial as not including a denial that the actual objects of these people's desires are bad things. Interpreted in this way, Socrates' denial to the second hypothesis is consistent with the view in the *Lysis* and elsewhere that some desires are bad or harmful.

17 Where Lamb has 'evil' and 'good,' I have 'bad things' and 'good things;' we have the neuter plural in the text throughout this passage. The expressions in brackets have been supplied by me. Croiset and Bodin go as far as to transfer Socrates' last sentence as '*de sorte qu'*en desirant ce mal *qu'ils ne connaissent pas*'; I think this is correct *as an interpretation*, but there is certainly nothing in the text that corresponds to the phrase I have emphasized.

18 Frege lists several other cases where words are used indirectly or have their indirect reference (Frege, 1952, pp. 66 ff.). For more recent discussions, see, e.g., Kneale and Kneale (1962, pp. 601—18) and Quine (1960, pp. 151—6).

19 Frege (1952, p. 67).

20 I have taken this phrase from Anscombe (1958, p. 65). It may be asked, how can we tell when a description is the description under which something is desired (wanted)? One way is to ask the man what he wants or to see how he asks for what he wants; if a man says (to the grocer) 'I want a loaf of wheat bread,' it is under the description 'loaf of wheat bread' that he wants to buy what the grocer brings him. It is worth noting that if a man wants something that is in fact F, and the man knows that it is F, this is necessary but not sufficient for concluding that it is under the description F that the man wants it. For it may not be the case that he wants it *qua* F; he may be indifferent to its being F.

21 That we have reasonable evidence for saying so is compatible with changing our minds on the basis of subsequent behavior (e.g., his showing surprise when salt pours out of the object he got).

22 I have already switched from 'description of intended object' to 'intended object.' It may be asked what the intended object of desire is. Suppose, e.g., (1) Jones wants a loaf of wheat bread (in the sense that 'loaf of wheat bread' is the description of the intended object of his desire). What is the intended object of Jones's desire? It is not of course the description 'loaf of wheat bread' — that would be absurd. Now why can't we give the obvious answer: the intended object of his desire is a loaf of wheat bread? It is sometimes held that this obvious answer is mistaken on the ground that it is possible for (1) to be true even though it is also true that

(2) there are not in fact any loaves of wheat bread. This objection is very puzzling; I can understand it only on the supposition that the objector assumes that (3) if someone desires something, then there is something which is desired. But this seems to me a complete mistake. I do not know of what logical form (1) is, but the fact that both (1) and (2) can be true at once shows conclusively, it seems to me, that (1) is not of the form ($\exists x$) (x is a loaf of bread. Jones desires x). And if (3) says anything at all, it says that (1) has this form. The fact that (1) and (2) can both be true, far from being an objection to the obvious answer, shows that the above objection is mistaken. I do not see, therefore, that, in order to say correctly 'The intended object of Jones's desire is such and such,' the such and such must exist.

23 ἐν ἀνθρώπου φύσει, *Protagoras* 358D1—2. If I am right in thinking that the argument here is confined to prudential situations (see n. 9), it should not be supposed that Plato is saying here that it is not in human nature to wish to do wrong — an extraordinary proposition indeed.

24 The whole argument with Polus, *Gorgias* 466B—470C, presupposes this doctrine, which is stated explicitly at 467C—468E. See also *Symposium*, 181A—B, 182E—183B; Ritter (1933, pp. 41, 53); Shorey (1933, p. 139); Dodds (1959, p. 235).

25 Cf. e.g. Aristotle, *Eudemian Ethics*, 1216B. There is of course no universal agreement on this. Some writers seem to suppose that it is knowledge of one's own good: see, e.g., Adam (1913, p. 15). This is as much of a mistake as the interpretation I am criticizing. Even if virtuous behavior is always to one's own good and wrong behavior always harmful to the agent, it does not follow that knowledge of one's own good presupposes knowledge of this proposition or knowledge of what is virtuous or wrong behavior. Knowledge of one's own good can be sufficient, at most, for behavior that is to one's own good.

26 μηδένα βουλόμενον ἀδικεῖν, ἀλλ᾿ἄκοντας τοὺς ἀδικοῦντας πάντας ἀδικεῖν. 'Willingly' and 'involuntarily' may be bad translations. If we place this proposition in its proper context (the discussion with Polus), it is clear that Plato does not mean that these people act reluctantly or with reservations or that they are forced to do injustice; he means that they act in ignorance that what they do is unjust or harmful to them or both. And if the corresponding knowledge, together with the universal desire for things that are good for one, is sufficient for acting justly, this implies that the people in question would not have acted unjustly, and would not have wanted to, if they had this knowledge. This gives some plausibility to saying that these people act unwillingly or involuntarily, though of course it remains doubtful at best that acting involuntarily in this sense can exempt one from blame (see *Nicomachean Ethics* 1110B).

27 *Protagoras* 360B—C, 360D1—2. The argument here provides ample evidence also that the wisdom that is sufficient for being courageous includes knowledge of what is better for one.

VII VIRTUE AND KNOWLEDGE II: AN ARGUMENT
AGAINST EXPLANATIONS OF WEAKNESS

1 Reprinted from the *Philosophical Review*, 1966.

2 For recent discussions of explanations of weakness, see Hare (1963, pp. 67–85); and Steven Lukes's criticism of Hare (Lukes, 1965). Lukes's criticism is perceptive, but neither he nor Hare goes much further than discussing phrases that suggest explanations, whereas what is needed most is an elucidation of the models of explanations that can be offered.

3 The first and last of these characteristics are explicitly stated by Plato and Aristotle: *Protagoras* 352–6, *Nicomachean Ethics*, 1152A. Occasion and opportunity may be associated with circumstances that give rise to temptation and circumstances that make the object of the temptation available, respectively: one may be tempted by the sight or smell of food but the food may not be available, or it may be available but one has no desire for it. Both must be present to have a case of weakness (or strength), and both conditions are usually implicit in Plato's and Aristotle's discussions. Donald Davidson rightly makes two corrections to the account I have given: 'First, weakness of the will does not require that the alternative action actually be available, only that the agent think it is': and second it is essential to incontinence that the agent act intentionally (Davidson, 1969, p. 94).

4 Cf., e.g., Sullivan 6 (1961), pp. 18–20; Sesonske (1963); Vlastos (1956); Gallop 9 (1964). The first two papers try to account for the fact that Socrates (and Plato) makes his argument against weakness depend on hedonism which he elsewhere consistently attacks. Too much of the discussion has been centered on this at the expense of more important philosophical questions about the passages that have been raised by Professor Vlastos: the reconstruction, validity, and philosophical significance of Plato's argument against weakness. Although I disagree with Vlastos's interpretation I have learned more from his essay than I can begin to acknowledge. More recently, Gallop has also discussed the issues raised by Vlastos, but his interpretation seems to me wide of the mark. I am in substantial agreement, however, with Vlastos's most recent paper on this topic, 'Socrates on Akrasia' (Vlastos, 1969).

5 At 352E and again at 354E Socrates says explicitly that the argument is about (b).

6 Vlastos (1956, p. xxxix). The italicized words referred to are: 'To pursue what one believes to be evil rather than what is good *is not in human nature.*' *K* is the proposition that knowledge is virtue.

7 Here it is worth noting that Aristotle (*Nicomachean Ethics*, Bk. VII, chs ii and iii) in a passage that refers us to the present argument in the *Protagoras*, dismisses the question whether *akrasia* occurs, and concentrates on providing explanations that make its occurrence possible. For a detailed account of Aristotle's treatment of *akrasia* see Santas (1969).

8 This seems to me to settle the question whether 'the hedonism of the *Protagoras*' is compatible with the antihedonism of the *Gorgias* and other

Dialogues. As for the question why did Socrates use hedonistic premises in his argument, I see no mystery here at all, for the argument is in fact a perfect example of Socrates' favorite mode of argument; it attempts to show that one belief of the many, that in certain cases men are 'overcome by pleasure,' is incompatible with another belief of theirs, the belief in hedonism. For a disagreement on this point, see Vlastos (1969).

9 Cf. 352B for the explanations, and 352D, 353C, 355B for the descriptions.

10 One of the alternative phrases to 'overcome' that Socrates uses. For a discussion of these, cf. final section of this chapter.

11 The pleasures of food, drink, and sex are the proper objects of weakness according to Aristotle (*Nicomachean Ethics*, Bk III, ch. x, and Bk VII, ch. iv).

12 Within the second sort of case, if what a man does is bad on the whole, then it is also bad in comparison to the alternatives since the latter are thought of as nothing lost and nothing gained.

13 Sullivan (1961) makes out a good case that both ethical and psychological hedonism are involved. We can add the following linguistic evidence for Sullivan's view. In eliciting hedonism from the many (353D–354E) Socrates introduces his questions with two sorts of verbs: (a) 'call,' 'say,' 'assert,' in questions such as 'Why do you . . . such and such good (bad)?'; (b) 'pursue' and 'avoid' in 'Do you . . . pleasure (pain)?' The answers he gives to the questions introduced by verbs in (a) clearly suggest ethical hedonism, those in (b) psychological.

14 It looks as if we must suppose that the agent, as well as the *hoi polloi*, is a hedonist since some of Socrates' substitutions are within intensional or referentially opaque contexts; thus at 355E, in the sentence 'He knows it to be bad' he substitutes 'painful' for 'bad.'

15 Gallop (1964, pp. 119–21) suggests that in order to see the absurdity that Socrates has in mind, we must go all the way to 357D–E, but this does not account for what Socrates does and what he says he does in 355B–356C. The two entailments that Gallop gives (p. 121) are not in the text, and do not hold unless we add psychological hedonism in the premises; but once we do that we obtain the absurdity and need not bother to go beyond 356C.

16 Without realizing it Gallop slips from the first to the second statement (Gallop, 1964, pp. 118, 120) and argues that there is nothing absurd about the second; this of course does not show that there is nothing absurd about the first.

17 Cf. also Sauppe and Towle (1892, p. 152).

18 δῆλον, ἄρα, φήσει, ὅτι τὸ ἡττᾶσθαι τοῦτο λέγετε, ἀντὶ ἐλαττόνων ἀγεθῶν μείζω κακὰ λαμβάνειν.

19 *Lambanein* can also mean 'to receive,' 'to accept,' and possibly even 'to prefer.'

20 At 356D *lambanein* is coupled with *prattein* (καὶ πράττειν καὶ λαμβάνειν); unless we take this to be mere repetition, the addition of *lambanein* suggests an intensional aspect. E. G. Sihler (1881, p. 127) has noticed that this pair is parallel to another pair five lines later: *kai en tais πράξεσι*

kai ἐν ταῖς αἰρέσι, the last term corresponding to *lambanein*, again suggesting that *lambanein* is to be taken in an intensional sense.

21 A second reason against the interpretation of E3 with *lambanein* in sense (1) is that the preposition *anti* cannot with good sense be taken with a verb that refers only to the execution of an action (behavior divorced from any intensional element).

22 Ληπτέα and πρακτέα 'are to (or must) be preferred' and 'are to (or must) be done' – need not be taken in a sense in which they entail '*will* be preferred' and 'will be done.' They should be taken in the sense of 'will be preferred *if* psychological hedonism is true (all men desire or seek to maximize [their] pleasures and/or minimize [their] pains),' and in the sense of 'will be done *if* psychological hedonism is true and the agent knows, has the opportunity and ability, and is not prevented.' Gallop's supposition that Socrates needs (for his argument) the first sense of ληπτέα and πρακτέα is quite unfounded (Gallop, 1964, pp. 128–9). People have failed to appreciate that Socrates takes (quite correctly once we grant his sense of 'overcome') the explanation 'overcome by pleasure' to be an explanation of behavior in terms of what men seek or desire to do, not in terms of what they actually do (cf. n. 24); and consequently, in order to obtain contradictions, all that he needs is a principle only as to what men seek or desire to do, not what they in fact do.

23 At 356 φεύγειν (*pheugein*) is coupled with μὴ πράττειν and contrasted with *lambanein* (not πράττειν) of the pair in the previous line, thus suggesting that *pheugein* introduces an intensional element. Cf. also n. 20.

24 A model explanation along the lines suggested by the hedonism that Socrates attributes to the masses:

Why did S do A at t_1?
(1) S did A at t_1.
because
(2) All men seek to maximize their pleasures and/or minimize their pains.
and
(3) S knew (believed) at t_1 that A would maximize his pleasures and not-A (avoiding A) would not (or A is pleasant on the whole and not-A is not).

This model (Model I) may be the model that Plato has in mind and it may properly be called a teleological model. It is to be noticed that (2) and (3) do *not* logically entail (1); this model does not satisfy Hempel's requirements for a scientific explanation.

Now this may happen: one may argue that only a limited number of factors can account for the possibility of (2) and (3) being true and (1) being false – say, lack of physical ability to carry out the action (e.g., the man does not swim or ride a bike or is blind), lack of opportunity, or, finally, external, physical coercion. Now on the basis of *this* one might argue that (2) implies a stronger generalization: (2′) Whenever a man is faced with two or more alternatives and he has the physical ability and the opportunity to do either and is not physically coerced to do any, he will do the one which he knows or believes at the time will maximize his pleasures and/or minimize his pains.

(2′) together with appropriate factual premises entails (1), and makes it possible to have, in logical form, a deductive type explanation of a certain sort (II). Whether Socrates would go on to attribute (2′) as well as (2) to hedonists is not clear; what is clear from the text is, first, that he does not in fact do so, and second that he does not need to for his argument. For his argument all that he needs to suppose is that hedonists hold (2) and that their model of explanation of behavior is (I). For once 'overcome by . . .' is interpreted in Socrates' way, the explanation contradicts (2), and that is enough. For a recent discussion of attempts to reduce teleological explanation (I) to those of type II, cf. Scheffler (1963, pp. 88—110). Several variants of teleological explanations are implicit in the patterns of practical inference that G. H. von Wright discusses in 'Practical Inference' (1963, pp. 159—79).

25 Cf., e.g., *Meno* 77B—78B, *Gorgias* 468C, and Santas (1964, pp. 147—64).

26 This premise could be inferred from the fact that the pleasure of eating is near and the pain far, if it could be established that, in general, strength of desire varies (in some consistent way) with distance (space and/or time) of the object of the desire from the agent.

27 What appears as a violent disagreement between Plato (*Republic* IV) and Hume (*Treatise*, Bk. II, Pt. III, sec. iii) as to whether 'reason' and the 'passions' can conflict may not be so violent. Plato holds that if a man believes that something is good (for him) then he wants (to have, to get, to possess) it (cf. chapter VI for the evidence). If it happens, say, that the man also fears the object, then the conflict between the belief and the fear can be 'reduced' to the conflict between the want and the fear.

28 With minor modifications this kind of explanation can satisfy the Hempel—Oppenheim (1948, pp. 135—46) requirements of a scientific explanation provided that condition A is satisfied. The similar type of explanation that I cite below, employed by Neal Miller, does satisfy these requirements.

29 Miller (1951—2, pp. 82—100). This is a careful and philosophically sophisticated account of experiments in verification of a theory that could be used to explain behavior in cases of conflicting 'tendencies,' 'responses,' or 'drives,' or 'motives.' One of the hypotheses verified by the experiments is: 'when two incompatible responses are in conflict, the stronger one will occur.' This article, and the related literature cited below, is worth reading by all those who talk of human beings being 'overcome,' 'seduced,' etc., by their passions, feelings, etc.

30 Gordon (1963, pp. 389—426). Gordon applies the Miller models to human behavior, but Miller's care and clarity are nowhere to be found, and Gordon leaves us in the dark as to how strength is to be measured in the case of humans. Gordon does not display the caution and safeguards that are necessary when models, successful in the case of lower animals, are applied to humans. General applications of the Miller models are summarized in Berelson and Steiner (1964, pp. 271—6). Cf. especially C6 and C6.1.

31 E.g., ἰσχυρὸν, κράτιστον, ἡττᾶσθαι, νικᾶν. In the *Phaedrus* (237D–238A) we have the following passage: 'We must observe that in each one of us there are two ruling and leading principles, which we follow whithersoever they lead; one is the innate desire for pleasures, the other an acquired opinion which strives for the best. These two sometimes agree within us and are sometimes in strife [στασιάζετον]; and sometimes one, and sometimes the other has the greater power.' Aside from the fact that the language of strength is also used here, it is illuminating to compare the doctrine of this passage with the hedonism assumed in the *Protagoras* and the explanation 'overcome by pleasure.'

32 McDougall (1960, ch. ix). In ch. ix McDougall quotes with approval William James's conception of the problem in case of 'moral conflict': '*I* (ideal impulse) in itself weaker than *P* (the native propensity). *I* + *E* (effort of the will) stronger than *P*.' McDougall thinks that the occurrence of weakness exemplifies the first proposition, which he treats as a law of psychology, and thus can easily be accounted for; it is the occurrence of the opposite of weakness that is difficult to account for, and here the problem is the analysis of *E*. He uses the language of strength constantly but he does not seem to see that there is a problem about giving a sense to the notion of 'stronger than.'

33 Mill (1867, ch. xxvi).

34 Berelson and Steiner (1964, p. 271, C5).

35 'harried along and driven out of his senses' (Wayte, 1871, p. 147).

36 'Or we collapse succumbing to temptation into losing control of ourselves — a bad patch, this, for telescoping . . . Plato, I suppose, and after him Aristotle, fastened this confusion upon us, as bad in its day and way as the later, grotesque, confusion of moral weakness and weakness of will. I am very partial to ice cream, and a bombe is served divided into segments corresponding one to one with the persons at High Table: I am tempted to help myself to two segments and do so, thus succumbing to temptation and even conceivably (but why necessarily?) going against my principles. But do I lose control of myself? Do I rave, do I snatch the morsels from the dish and wolf them down, inpervious to the consternation of my colleagues? Not a bit of it. We often succumb to temptation with calm and even with finesse' (Austin, 1961, p. 146).

37 ἐξὸν αὐτοῖς, ἐξὸν μὴ πράττειν, οὐ δέον αὐτὸν πράττειν (352D, 355A, 355D).

38 It is worth noticing that what I have said here does not necessarily hold of explanations in terms of strength where condition A is satisfied in the first way (I). Socrates' remark at 357C, when he reverts to the language of strength, is no objection to what I am saying here.

39 I now doubt that Socrates could or would have accepted this line of defence. As Professor G. Vlastos pointed out in correspondence, Socrates could not admit cases of psychological compulsion and also maintain that 'whoever learns what is good and what is bad will *never* be swayed by anything to act otherwise than as knowledge bids . . . .' And, in any case, he probably did not have the notion of psychological compulsion at all. Intuitively, one feels that extreme and clear cases of psychological

compulsion should not count as cases of weakness, but the criteria for such cases, unlike those for physical compulsion, are complex, unclear, and quite subtle. It is, therefore, difficult for anyone who holds the Socratic position to exclude psychological compulsion with trivializing or giving up the substance of his position.

VIII POWER, VIRTUE, PLEASURE, AND HAPPINESS IN THE *GORGIAS*

1 Most of the ethical beliefs that Socrates argues for in this Dialogue, beliefs about doing wrong and suffering wrong, about justice and happiness, and about punishment, are to be found in the certainly Socratic Dialogues, the *Apology* and the *Crito* (cf. Irwin, 1973, p. 731).

2 Vlastos (1969, pp. 454–60).

3 I have included P10 and C9, which are in the text, to show that the conclusions C7 and C8 are meant by Socrates to be taken in the sense of 'worse for the doer of injustice than the sufferer' or 'a greater evil to the doer of injustice than the sufferer.' Any doubts on this point can be laid to rest by consulting *Gorgias* 508E–509B, where Socrates is quite explicit on these points. If the argument as I have stated seems unnecessarily long and complex, I can only reply that it is all in the text, except for P6 and P7. Dodds's statement of the argument is so abbreviated as to be grossly inaccurate – when so much is left out neither the virtues nor the faults of the argument can be appreciated (Dodds, 1959, p. 248).

4 We have a similar derivation in *Protagoras* 360CD, which I have reconstructed in chapter V, p. 177, and another such derivation in *Lysis* 231AB. We can validly derive C2 from C1, P6 and P7, if we assume that (a) each opposite has exactly one opposite, and (b) that the relation of an opposite to its opposite is the relation of a class to its complement. The derivation is as follows:

1 The beautiful is the pleasant or the good or both. (C1)
2 The opposite of the pleasant or good is the not (pleasant or good). (by (b))
3 Therefore, the opposite of the beautiful is the not (pleasant or good). (from 1 and 2 by substitution)
4 The opposite of the beautiful is the ugly.
5 The ugly is the not (pleasant or good). (from 3 and 4 by (a))
6 The not (pleasant or good) ≡ the not-pleasant and the non-good. (by DeMorgan)
7 The ugly is the non-pleasant and the not-good. (from 5 and 6 by substitution)
8 Painful is the opposite of pleasant, and evil the opposite of good. (P7)
9 The not-pleasant ≡ the painful, and the not-good ≡ the evil. (from 8 by (b))
10 Therefore, the ugly is the painful and the evil. (from 7 and 9 by substitution)

Several comments are in order. First, assumptions (a) and (b) are very strong assumptions, especially (b). It is doubtful that Plato held (b) since he holds, e.g. that good and evil are opposites and also (in the *Lysis* and the *Gorgias*) that something may be neither good nor evil. Yet he also seems to hold that, if an opposite is defined, the opposite of the definiendum is to be defined by the opposite(s) of the definiens. How this view can be defended without assumption (b) is not clear. Second, it should be noticed that the ugly is defined in terms of a conjunction of evil and painful, not in terms of a disjunction of the two. I had originally supposed that Plato's definition of the ugly was 'The ugly is the evil *or* painful.' But as Professor Burnyeat pointed out, this cannot be correct, since *this* definition, together with the definition of the beautiful, would allow that something could be both beautiful and ugly (in the cases whether something were both good and painful or both evil and pleasant). In addition we could not derive a disjunctive definition of the ugly, even on the assumption (a) and (b), without fallacy resulting from violation of DeMorgan's rules.

5 See Vlastos (1969, p. 454, n. 2) for the relevant literature.

6 *Ibid.*, p. 458.

7 *Ibid.*

8 See also Dodds's comments and evidence (Dodds, 1959, pp. 471–2).

9 This error is easy to miss because Socrates does not state in his conclusion explicitly what he is actually arguing: C8 should read, not 'Doing injustice is worse [= a greater evil] than suffering it,' but rather 'Doing injustice is worse [= a greater evil] to the doer than suffering it is to the sufferer.' Once we compare the latter statement with the definitions and statements derived from the definitions, the gap becomes perspicuous.

10 Dodds (1959, p. 202).

11 See Vlastos's fine discussion of the political and economic aspects of equality under the democracies in '*Isonomia*' (Vlastos, 1953 especially pp. 347 ff.).

12 Another reason Callicles might give for calling this ability virtue and justice is that the *better deserve* to have more than the worse; and perhaps that it is better that the better rule over the worse. But once we understand what Callicles means by 'the better,' namely either those who are stronger or those who have more ability in terms of intelligence and courage to satisfy their desires, these reasons become very implausible.

13 The contradiction may be avoided if we suppose that Callicles meant that the makers of laws are weaker individually; this allows that collectively, since they are more numerous, they are stronger. But when they consider their advantage to be having the equal, rather than having more, and legislate accordingly, clearly — Callicles' thought is — they consider the equal to be their advantage relative to their individual weakness (each, being weak, considers that having more is beyond his grasp and settles for the equal to avoid suffering at the hands of the stronger). So their case of legislating is not a case of the stronger legislating to his advantage, which would be having more.

14 These are the most obvious means to Calliclean happiness, and so these

are probably the things that the wiser are to have more of.

15 See Dodds (1959, pp. 309–10).

16 According to Dodds, for example, 'the initial premise' of the argument is, 'The "good" man is both brave and wise [admitted at 491bc]'; he then claims that 'A consistent hedonist would of course refuse to admit the initial premise' (Dodds, 1959, p. 314). Just what the inconsistency is supposed to be Dodds does not tell us (he only says that Callicles is 'not a consistent hedonist' and that 'the argument serves to expose his inconsistency'). I see no inconsistency whatsoever between P1 and P3. A hedonist will indeed give a particular interpretation to goodness as applied to men, but the interpretation that Socrates gives is actually, as we shall see, very close if not identical to the interpretation a hedonist should give. Another recent critic gives a mysterious rendering of the argument and then, not surprisingly, finds its workings mysterious. Crombie writes (1969, pp. 230–1):

> There is another interesting argument in the *Gorgias* 497–9. Callicles (who is depicted as a ferocious cynic) has claimed that all pleasures are good. To refute this Socrates stipulates that good men are good by virtue of the presence of good things to them, just as beautiful men are beautiful by virtue of the presence of beauty. He then argues that it is such properties as intelligence and courage that make good men good, and that brave and intelligent men are just as capable of feeling pleasure and pain as fools and cowards. But if (a) good men are good by virtue of the presence of good things, and (b) all pleasures are good things and all pains are bad things, then fools and cowards, who are ordinarily thought bad men, will be just as good and also just as bad as intelligent and brave men; for just as many good and just as many bad things (pleasures and pains) will happen to each.
>
> The moral of this argument is obvious enough (that you cannot classify people as good or bad according to what happens to them), but its workings are mysterious.

One thing that is certainly mysterious is why Crombie states the weaker statement (b) rather than the stronger hypothesis that he recognizes Callicles holds, namely that 'good' and 'pleasant' are coextensive; (b) is too weak to allow for the required substitutions, so that the argument as stated by Crombie is obviously invalid as well as unfaithful to the text. It is also mysterious where Crombie gets the notion of good that '*happen* to each'; the 'moral' he draws from the argument, another mystery in itself, apparently is partly due to this notion, for which I can find nothing in the text. All these woes are directly attributable to a grossly inaccurate statement of the argument. Next Crombie casts about for presuppositions to the argument (which 'is not at all plausible to us') that make the argument plausible to us. He concentrates on P2, which other critics have also found ambiguous, and says (p. 231):

> The word 'presence' (*parousia*) is one of Plato's regular words for the relation of a universal to its instances (though it is observed in the

325

Lysis (217) that the word is ambiguous); and of course in the parallel example of beautiful men it is the universal (*kallos*) whose presence is said to make them beautiful. It follows from this parallel either that (by a blunder of Plato's or by malice of Socrates') there is a gross equivocation on *parousia*, and the relation of a universal to its instances is identified with the relation of a man to his pleasures or his property, or that having good things is thought to be the same as being good. Anybody therefore who felt that the argument was convincing would so feel because he interpreted it in the latter way, because he took for granted that the good man is the man 'to whom good things are present', or the man who has accomplished what is worth accomplishing. On this presupposition it is easy to show that you cannot simply say that 'X is pleasant' implies 'X is good' without thereby overturning all normal judgments of moral goodness. It is of course possible that few readers would have been convinced by the argument, and that Plato is deceived (or Callicles supposed to be deceived) by its apparent conclusiveness. I am inclined to think, however, that to one who does not make the required presupposition, the argument is so obviously bogus that it is more likely that we are expected to presuppose that it is his possession of genuinely good things which entitles a man to be called good.

We shall come back to the ambiguity Crombie talks about later. For the moment it is worth noting that the way to make the argument plausible suggested by Crombie in the last statement will not work: if by 'we are expected to presuppose' Crombie means that 'we are expected to take as a presupposition of the argument, i.e., an implicit premise,' and if by 'genuinely good things' he means things other than those that a hedonist would admit as good, then clearly the argument so interpreted would beg the question. If the question is whether 'good' and 'pleasant' are coextensive, in an argument for a negative answer to this question we cannot presuppose that there are good things other than pleasant things. Perhaps Crombie means something else.

17 Irwin (1973, p. 297).
18 *Ibid.*, pp. 741–2.
19 See Young's beautiful discussions on this point of ἀρετή and ἀγαθός (Young, 1974, pp. 24–7); what it means, among other things, to say that goodness is relative to kinds is that in defining the notion we would not be defining 'x is good' but rather 'x is a good K'; see e.g., Rawls's definition (1972, p. 399).
20 Psychological hedonism is a theory as to what men pursue and what they avoid; it says that men pursue pleasure as the only thing good in itself, and avoid pain as the only thing evil in itself.
21 Analytic ethical hedonism is a view as to what 'good' means (rather than a theory as to which things are good); it holds that 'good' and 'pleasant' mean the same thing or have the same sense or connotation.
22 For an elementary account of these distinctions see Frankena (1963, ch. 2). Cf. also Brandt (1959, chs 14 and 15); and Broad (1959, ch. VII).

23 Burnet (1924, p. 139). Burnet says that the arguments in *Gorgias* and *Republic* are 'exactly the same' as that of the *Crito*.

24 The passages where Socrates explains this point is somewhat problematic; see Dodds's note (1959, pp. 229–30); the references throughout, however, are to the subject of medicine, the body, not the individual patient.

25 Young (1974, p. 31).

26 Dodds (1959, pp. 226–7).

27 Young (1974, pp. 30–1).

28 See Vlastos (1946, pp. 65–83). This is by far the best paper known to me on this subject. See also Aristotle, *Athenian Constitution*, V–VII.

29 See Vlastos (1945).

30 Burnet (1924, p. 193).

31 Vlastos (1973c, pp. 126–9).

Bibliography

Adam, A. M. (1913), *Plato*, Cambridge.

Adkins, A. W. H. (1960), *Merit and Responsibility*, Oxford.

Ajdukiewicz, K. (1958), 'Three Concepts of Definition,' *Logique et Analyse*, 3, reprinted in T. Olshewsky, *Problems in the Philosophy of Language*, New York, 1969.

Allen, R. E. (1960), 'The Socratic Paradox,' *Journal of the History of Ideas*, 21, pp. 256–65.

Allen, R. E. (1970), *The Euthyphro and Plato's Earlier Theory of Forms*, London.

Anderson, A. (1969), 'Socratic Reasoning in the *Euthyphro*,' *Review of Metaphysics*, 22, pp. 461–81.

Anscombe, E. (1958), *Intention*, Oxford.

Aquinas, T. (1960), *Philosophical Texts*, trans. T. Gilby, ed., New York.

Aristotle, *Metaphysics*, trans. W. D. Ross, Oxford, 1908–52.

Aristotle, *Nicomachean Ethics*, trans. W. D. Ross, Oxford 1908–52.

Aristotle, *Athenian Constitution*, Cambridge, Mass., 1956.

Austin, John (1961), 'A Plea for Excuses,' *Philosophical Papers*, Oxford.

Bambrough, J. (1960), 'The Socratic Paradox,' *Philosophical Quarterly*, 10, pp. 229–30.

Barker, S. F. (1974), *The Elements of Logic*, 2nd ed., New York.

Bedau, A. H., ed. (1969), *Civil Disobedience*, New York.

Belnap, N., Jr (1963), *An Analysis of Questions: Preliminary Report*, Santa Monica, Calif.

Belnap, N. (1969), 'Questions', in K. Lambert, ed., *The Logical Way of Doing Things*, New Haven, Conn.

Berelson, B. and Steiner, G. A. (1964), *Human Behavior: An Inventory of Scientific Findings*, New York.

Bluck, R. S. (1961), *Plato's Meno*, Cambridge.

Brandt, R. (1959), *Ethical Theory*, 13. Englewood Cliffs, NJ.

Broad, D. C. (1959), *Five Types of Ethical Theory*, Patterson, NJ.

Burnet, John (1903–7), *Platonis Opera*, Oxford.

BIBLIOGRAPHY

Burnet, John (1934; 1961), *Plato's Euthyphro, Apology of Socrates and Crito*, edited with notes, Oxford.

Burnet, John (1961), *Greek Philosophy*, New York.

Burnyeat, M. F. (1971), 'Virtues in Action' in G. Vlastos, ed., *The Philosophy of Socrates*, New York.

Burton, R. W. B. (1962), *Pindar's Pythian Odes*, Oxford.

The Cambridge Ancient History, 5.

Chisholm, R. (1966), *Theory of Knowledge*, Englewood Cliffs, N.J.

Chroust, A. H. (1957), *Socrates, Man and Myth*, London.

Cohen, S. Mark (1971), 'Socrates on the Definition of Piety: *Euthyphro* 10A−11B', in G. Vlastos, ed., *The Philosophy of Socrates*, New York.

Copi, I. M. (1972), *Introduction to Logic*, 3rd ed., London.

Cornford, F. M. (1932), *Before and after Socrates*, Cambridge.

Croiset, A. and Bodin, L. (1948), *Platon, Oeuvres Complètes*, Paris.

Crombie, I. M. (1969), *An Examination of Plato's Doctrines*, I, London.

Davidson, Donald (1969), 'How is Moral Weakness Possible?', in J. Feinberg, ed., *Moral Concepts*, Oxford.

Dodds, E. R. (1959), *Plato, Gorgias*, Oxford.

Dover, Kenneth J. (1971), 'Socrates in the Clouds,' in G. Vlastos, ed., *The Philosophy of Socrates*, New York.

Frankena, W. (1963), *Ethics*, Englewood Cliffs, NJ.

Frege, G. (1952), 'On Sense and Reference,' in P. Geach and M. Black, eds, *Translations from the Writings of Gottlob Frege*, Oxford.

Friedlander, P. (1958), *Plato*, vol. 2, New York.

Gallop, D. (1964), 'The Socratic Paradox in the *Protagoras*,' *Phronesis*, 9, pp. 117−29.

Gauthier, D. P., (1968), 'The Unity of Wisdom and Temperance,' *Journal of the History of Philosophy*, vol. 6, pp. 157−9.

Geach, P. (1956), 'The Third Man Again,' *The Philosophical Review*, 65, pp. 72−82.

Geach, P. (1966), 'Plato's *Euthyphro*: Analysis and Commentary,' *The Monist*, vol. 50, pp. 369−82.

Gomperz, T. (1905), *Greek Thinkers*, trans. G. G. Berry, London.

Gordon, J. E. (1963), *Personality and Behavior*, New York.

Gould, J. (1955), *The Development of Plato's Ethics*, Cambridge.

Grote, George (1888), *Plato and the Other Companions of Socrates*, 3 vols, London.

Gulley, N. (1968), *The Philosophy of Socrates*, London.

Guthrie, W. K. C. (1971), *Socrates*, Cambridge.

Hare, R. M. (1963), *Freedom and Reason*, Oxford.

Hempel, C. G. and Oppenheim, P. (1948), 'Studies in the Logic of Explanation,' *Philosophy of Science*, vol. 15, no. 2.

Hintikka, J. (1962), *Knowledge and Belief*, Ithaca, NY.

Hintikka, J. (1967), 'Time, Truth and Knowledge in Ancient Greek Philosophy,' *American Philosophical Quarterly*, vol. 4, pp. 1−14.

Hintikka, J. (1973), 'Knowledge and its Objects in Plato,' in J. Moravcsik and D. Reidel, eds, *Patterns in Plato's Thought*, Boston.

Hume, D., *Treatise*.

Irwin, T. (1973), 'Theories of Virtue and Knowledge in Plato's Early and Middle Dialogues,' unpublished PhD dissertation, Princeton University.

Irwin, T. (1974), 'Review of Leo Stauss's *Xenophon's Socrates,' Philosophical Review*, vol. 83, pp. 409—13, July.

Jaeger, W. (1943), *Paedeia*, trans. A Highet, New York.

Kneale, W. and Kneale, M. (1962), *The Development of Logic*, Oxford.

Korvin, W., ed. (1936), *In Platonis Gorgiam Commentaria*, Leipzig.

Lamb, W. R. M. (1952), *Plato*, vol. 4, Cambridge, Mass.

Leonard, Henry (1967), *Principles of Reasoning*, New York.

Lukes, Steven (1965), 'Moral Weakness,' *Philosophical Quarterly*, vol. 15.

Lyons, John (1963), *Structural Semantics*, Oxford.

McDonald, Marianne (1975), 'Terms of Happiness in Euripides,' unpublished PhD dissertation, Irvine, Calif.

McDougall, W. (1960), *Social Psychology*, 23rd ed., New York.

Marchant, E. C. (1959), *Xenophon, Memorabilia and Oeconomicus*, London.

Mill, J. S. (1867), *An Examination of Sir William Hamilton's Philosophy*, London.

Miller, N. E. (1951—2), 'Comments on Theoretical Models Illustrated by the Development of a Theory of Conflict,' *Journal of Personality*, vol. 20, pp. 82—100.

Mortimer, G. W., ed. (1971), *Weakness of Will*, London.

Nakhnikian, G. (1971), 'Elenctic Definitions,' in Gregory Vlastos, ed., *The Philosophy of Socrates*, New York.

North, Helen (1966), *Sophrosyne*, Ithaca, New York.

O'Brien, M. J. (1967), *The Socratic Paradoxes and the Greek Mind*, Chapel Hill, NC.

Pap, Arthur (1964), 'Theory of Definition,' *Philosophy of Science*, vol. 31 reprinted in T. Olshewsky, *Problems in the Philosophy of Language*, New York, 1969.

Phillipson, Coleman (1928), *The Trial of Socrates*, London.

Prior, A. (1955), 'Erotetic Logic,' *Philosophical Review*, January, vol. 64, pp. 43—59.

Quine, W. V. O. (1960), *Word and Object*, New York.

Rawls, John (1972), *A Theory of Justice*, Cambridge, Mass.

Ritter, C. (1933), *The Essence of Plato's Thought*, New York.

Robinson, R. (1953), *Plato's Earlier Dialectic*, 2nd ed., Oxford.

Ross, W. D. (1951), *Plato's Theory of Ideas*, Oxford.

Russell, Bertrand (1945), *A History of Western Philosophy*, New York.

Ryle, Gilbert (1966), *Plato's Progress*, Cambridge.

Santas, Gerasimos (1964), 'The Socratic Paradoxes,' *Philosophical Review*, 73.

Santas, Gerasimos (1969), 'Aristotle on Practical Inference, the Explanation of Action and Akrasia,' *Phronesis*.

Santas, Gerasimos (1971), 'Socrates at Work on Virtue and Knowledge in Plato's *Laches*,' in G. Vlastos, ed., *The Philosophy of Socrates*, New York.

Santas, Gerasimos (1972), 'The Socratic Fallacy,' *Journal of the History of Philosophy*, April, vol. 10, pp. 127—41.

Santas, Gerasimos (1973), 'Hintikka on Knowledge and its Objects in Plato,' in J. Moravcsik and D. Reidel, eds, *Patterns in Plato's Thought*, Boston.

Santas, Gerasimos (1973), 'Socrates at Work on Virtue and Knowledge in Plato's *Charmides*,' in E. N. Lee *et al.*, eds, *Exegesis and Argument*, Assen.

Sauppe, H. and Towle, J. A. (1892), *Plato's Protagoras*, Boston.

Savan, D. (1965), 'Socrates' Logic and the Unity of Wisdom and Temperance,' in R. B. J. Butler, ed., *Analytical Philosophy*, vol. II, Oxford.

Scheffler, I. (1963), *The Anatomy of Inquiry*, New York.

Sesonske, A. (1963), 'Hedonism in the *Protagoras*,' *Journal of the History of Philosophy*, 1.

Sesonske, A. and Fleming, I. (1965), eds, *Plato's Meno*, Wadsworth, Belmont, Calif.

Sharvy, Richard (1972), 'Euthyphro 9d—11b: Analysis and Definition in Plato and Others,' *Nous*, vol. 6, pp. 119—37.

Shorey, P. (1933), *What Plato Said*, Chicago.

Sihler, E. G. (1881), *The Protagoras of Plato*, New York.

Smyth, H. W. (1966), *Greek Grammar*, Cambridge, Mass.

Speigelberg, H. (1964), *The Socratic Enigma*, New York.

Stenzel, Julius (1964), *Plato's Method of Dialectic*, New York.

Stocks, J. L. (1913), 'The Argument of Plato, Prot. 351A—356C,' *Classical Quarterly*, vol. 7.

Sullivan, J. P. (1961), 'The Hedonism in Plato's *Protagoras*,' *Phronesis*, vol. 6, pp. 9—28.

Taylor, A. E. (1911), *Varia Socratica*, Oxford.

Taylor, A. E. (1932), *Socrates*, New York.

Taylor, A. E. (1937), *Plato, the Man and his Work*, 4th ed., London.

Thucydides, *History of the Peloponnesian War*, Cambridge, Mass., 1956.

Tuckey, T. G. (1951), *Plato's Charmides*, Cambridge.

Versenyi, Lazzlo (1963), *Socratic Humanism*, New Haven, Conn.

Vlastos, Gregory (1945), 'Ethics and Physics in Democritus,' *Philosophical Review*, 54, pp. 578—92.

Vlastos, Gregory (1946), 'Solonian Justice,' *Classical Philology*, 41, pp. 65—83.

Vlastos, Gregory (1953), 'Isonomia,' *American Journal of Philology*, 74, pp. 337—66.

Vlastos, Gregory (1956), *Plato's Protagoras*, edited (in translation) with introduction, New York.

Vlastos, Gregory (1957), 'Socratic Knowledge and Platonic Pessimism,' *Philosophical Review*, 66, pp. 226—38.

Vlastos, Gregory (1967), 'Was Polus Refuted?,' *American Journal of Philology*, 88, pp. 454—60.

Vlastos, Gregory (1969), 'Socrates on Akrasia,' *Phoenix*, 23, pp. 71—88.

Vlastos, Gregory (1970), 'Reasons and Causes in the *Phaedo*,' in G. Vlastos, ed., *Plato I*, New York.

Vlastos, Gregory (1971), 'The Paradox of Socrates,' in G. Vlastos, ed., *The Philosophy of Socrates*, New York.

Vlastos, Gregory (1973a), 'An Ambiguity in the *Sophist*,' in *Platonic Studies*, Princeton, NJ.

Vlastos, Gregory (1973b), 'The Individual as Object of Love in Plato,' in *Platonic Studies*, Princeton, NJ, p. 7.

Vlastos, Gregory (1973c), 'The Unity of Virtues in the *Protagoras*,' in *Platonic Studies*, Princeton, NJ.

Von Wright, G. H. (1963), 'Practical Inference,' *Philosophical Review*, 72, pp. 159–79.

Walsh, J. (1963), *Aristotle's Conception of Moral Weakness*, New York.

Wayte, W. (1871), *The Protagoras of Plato*, Cambridge.

Wedberg, A. (1970), 'The Theory of Ideas,' in G. Vlastos, ed., *Plato* I, New York.

Woozley, A. D. (1971), 'Socrates on Disobeying the Law,' in G. Vlastos, ed., *The Philosophy of Socrates*, New York.

Xenophon, *Hellenica* II, Cambridge, Mass., 1956.

Young, Charles (1974), 'Justice and Techne in Plato's *Republic*,' unpublished PhD dissertation, Johns Hopkins University.

Zeller, E. (1962), *Socrates and the Socratic Schools*, New York.

Relevant Works published too late for Consideration

Burnyeat, M. F. (1977), 'Examples in Epistemology: Socrates, Theaetetus and G. E. Moore,' *Philosophy*, vol. 52, pp. 381–98.

Irwin, T. (1977), *Plato's Moral Theory*, New York.

Taylor, C. C. W. (1977), *Plato: Protagoras*, Oxford.

General Index

absorption, 304
abstract expressions, 101–2, 107
Adam, A. M., 317, 328
Adkins, A. W., 314, 328
agatha, 184–5, 314
aischra, 314, 232–3
Ajdukiewicz, K., 310, 328
akrasia, 195, 318
ambiguity, 92
analogies, 138–47, 286–303
analysis, of arguments, 137–8
Anscombe, E., 316, 328
Apology: on citizenship, 29–42; and *Crito*, 43–56, 113; on injustice, 32–42; on laws, 29; questions in, 60, 75–6; Socrates in, 8–9; summary, 10
Aquinas, St Thomas, 184, 314
arete, 289
arguments, Socratic: analysis, 137–8; deductive, 155–80; definitions in, 126; inductive, 138–55; and paradoxes, 183–94
Aristophanes, 4, 29, 117, 306
Aristotle: on *akrasia*, 318; on definitions, 97, 102–3, 113, 124, 310; on ethics, 317; on justice, 297; on paradoxes, 184; on questions, 309; on temptation, 318–19; *see also Nicomachean Ethics*
art-sciences, 138–55, 287–90
arts and health, 294–5
astronomy, 148
Athenian Constitution, 18

athletics, 60, 143–4
attribute, *see* property
Austin, J., 215, 322, 328

bad: and friendship, 155–6, 163–5; and good, 64, 144–5, 208–9, 251; *see also* evil; vice
Barker, S. F., 312, 328
baseness, 174–6
beauty: 100, 118–20, 134; and good, 233–7, 251; and happiness, 241–4, 249–50; and justice, 233–7, 241–4, 249, 253–7
Bedau, A. H., 309, 328
belief, 64, 178, 192–3
Belnap, Noel, 72–86, 309–10, 328
benefit, 158, 184–5, 190–4
Berelson, B., 321–2, 328
Bluck, R. S., 314–15, 328
Bodin, L., 315–16, 329
body: evils of, 251–3; function of, 290; goods of, 251–3; punishment of, 293; and soul, 64, 145–7, 249, 286, 303
Brandt, R., 326, 328
Broad, D. C., 326, 328
Burnet, John, 72, 306, 309, 314, 327–8
Burnyeat, M. F., 324, 329, 332

Callicles: the man, 66; his views, 228, 230–3, 236, 253–86, 324
Charmides: definitions in, 99, 103, 110, 113, 127–8, 220, 232; ques-

333

Index to Passages

D'Youville College Library
320 Porter Avenue
Buffalo, New York 14201